Ghost Hunting in Montana

Ghost Hunting in Montana

A Search for Roots
in the Old West

BARNABY CONRAD III

HarperCollins*West*

A Division of HarperCollins*Publishers*

HarperCollins West and the author, in association with the Rainforest Action Network, will facilitate the planting of two trees for every one tree used in the manufacture of this book.

GHOST HUNTING IN MONTANA: *A Search for Roots in the Old West.* Copyright © 1994 by Barnaby Conrad III. All rights reserved. Printed in the United States of America. No part of this book may be used or reproduced in any manner whatsoever without written permission except in the case of brief quotations embodied in critical articles and reviews. For information address HarperCollins Publishers, 10 East 53rd Street, New York, NY 10022.

FIRST EDITION

Library of Congress Cataloging-in-Publication Data
Conrad, Barnaby, 1952–
    Ghost hunting in Montana : a search for roots in the Old West / Barnaby Conrad III. — 1st ed.
        p.   cm.
    ISBN 0–06–258551–7 (alk. paper)
    1. Montana—Description and travel. 2. Montana—History, local. 3. Conrad, Barnaby, 1953– —Journeys—Montana. I. Title
F735.C66   1994
978.6—dc20   94–1353
                                                                                                        CIP

94 95 96 97 98 ❖ RRD(H) 10 9 8 7 6 5 4 3 2 1

This edition is printed on acid-free paper that meets the American National Standards Institute Z39.48 Standard.

For my father
with love

"You're a long way off of your range. What you
aiming to do in Montana?"
"I want to be woolly."
I looked at him and laughed. He didn't seem to
like my laughing at him.

> Patrick Tucker to greenhorn
> Charlie Russell, in *Riding
> the High Country,* 1933

You are lost
in miles of land without people, without
one fear of being found, in the dash
of rabbits, soar of antelope, swirl
merge and clatter of streams.

> Richard Hugo, "Driving Montana,"
> 1973

Contents

Acknowledgments

My gratitude to Anthony Weller, Mark Miller, Frederick Turner, Charles Corn, Shirley Christine, and Becky Draper for their editorial skills; my thanks to Michael Congdon for his faith, to Bill and Pam Bryan for their guidance, and to Jean Baucus, the Van Cleve family, Tom and Laurie McGuane, the Vick family, Len and Sandy Sargent, Herb and Betty Conrad, and Jackie Low for their true Montana hospitality.

My great-grandfather, John
H. Conrad, ran for governor
of Montana in 1889.

Gold miner panning at Alder Gulch in
the 1860s.
(Courtesy Montana Historical Society)

Chapter 1
Ghost Hunting in Montana

I am in love with Montana. For other states I
have admiration, respect, recognition, even some
affection, but with Montana it is love, and it's
difficult to analyze love when you're in it.
    John Steinbeck, *Travels with Charley*, 1961

An hour after crossing the Idaho border I pulled into Dillon, the first town in southwest Montana. Once considered part of the vast unknown boondocks, Montana has risen in the nation's consciousness as the Last Best Place, a mythic hinterland of buffalo days and coyote nights. The media tell us that Big Sky country is undergoing a modern land rush spurred by reclusive movie stars, yuppie fly-fishermen, and paranoid survivalists burned out on urban life. Yet in Dillon, little had changed, and I didn't mind.

Rivaling California in size, dramatic landscape, and mineral wealth, Montana runs 559 miles along the Canadian border and over 250 miles deep, making it the fourth largest state in the Union. It is really two distinct regions: the western third is alpine, dominated by the Rocky Mountains (which cradle Glacier and Yellowstone Parks), while the eastern part flattens into hundreds of miles of prairie, badlands, and gumbo. With a nearly static population of around eight hundred thousand (in comparison to California's 30 million), there are only five people per square mile. While the rest of America becomes more urban, Montana sends just one congressman to Washington—to represent a populace that is still creating ghost towns.

Fifty years ago Dillon was an important rail link from both coasts. Now it is a hangdog hamlet on Blacktail Deer Creek. I followed the railroad tracks past grain elevators, C&C Farm and Ranch Supply, and the *Dillon Tribune's* 1888 iron-front building, then parked and walked into the Moose Bar. It was a Sunday evening, and the saloon had a comfortably depressed feeling to it. Four men played poker in the corner. Two sun-wizened old cowhands sat on stools at the bar, smoking and staring into their drinks as if the ice cubes might offer them an explanation about man's fate.

My hands still vibrated from the thousand-mile drive up from San Francisco, and my face was gritty with the dust of five states. I was a long ways off my range, as they say in Montana, but no one paid much attention, except the bartender, who slid me whiskey and ice in a plastic cup.

In the corner sat a blind accordionist who wore dark glasses held together with duct tape. His fingers were white and tapered like an old woman's, but he played well, squeezing out a lugubrious "That's What It's Like to Be Lonesome" and "Tumbling Tumbleweeds," followed by a few shit-kicking polkas. Nobody danced. There wasn't a woman in the place. All was peaceful until a grimy man stumbled through the door with gray stubble on his jaw and the wasted, unsteady look of someone near the end of a hellacious bender.

"Sam, what're you doing here?" asked a cowboy in a battered, sweat-stained Stetson.

"I'm lookin' fer you," said Sam. His eyes were glazed and bloodshot.

"Oh, yeah? Sit down, have a drink."

Sam looked balefully at the libation the bartender poured. "Call that a drink?"

"Brandy and ditch. Usual, ain't it?"

Still rocking, his eyes drifting out of focus, Sam swiveled to face the cowboy. "You been messin' with my wife."

The cowboy let out a soft, whiskey-hoarse chuckle. "Aw, cut it out."

Sam steadied himself on the edge of the bar and pointed at the cowboy. "Somebody messing with—I'm gonna—" As the sentence died, he grimaced and unleashed a surrealistically slow roundhouse right that clipped the cowboy on the shoulder. He followed it with a left that missed entirely.

A breeze of smothered laughter waffled across the barroom. "Send him back to Warm Springs for shock treatment," said a voice.

The cowboy appealed to the others at the bar. "See that? He's out of his mind!"

"Take it outside, fellas," said the bartender.

"Look, I don't *want* to fight him," drawled the cowboy.

With a growl, Sam wrapped his arms around the cowboy in a bear hug and the two of them spun once, twice around the barroom, then banged through the door. Outside, there was a thud as they keeled over on the sidewalk. Several of us moved to the doorway to watch them rolling in the gutter, fists flailing, unable to connect. "Don't want to hurt you, Sam, but you're makin' me angry," panted the cowboy, his boots scrambling for leverage on the concrete. A solid punch to Sam's stubbled jaw ended the fight. The bartender moved past me and poured a bucket of ice water over the groggy man. A small gasp issued from Sam's lips, but he lay still. "What do we do with him now?" asked the cowboy.

"Don't ask me," said the bartender. "He's your friend, not mine."

The blind man took up another polka on the accordion. As I walked away I saw them loading the half-conscious Sam into the back of a pickup truck.

Across the railroad tracks from the old Union Pacific depot—now the Beaverhead County museum—stood the seedily grand Hotel Metlen Bar and Lounge. It was a three-story white brick building with impressive columns and an elegant cupola topped by the American flag. Senators and tycoons once bunked here. Now the Metlen was the kind of place whose clients consider a Slim Jim and a shot of Old Grand Dad a square meal. For fifteen dollars I got a dingy cubicle near the back, with a sink that dripped loudly through the night.

The next morning I was headed west toward Badger Pass and Bloody Dick Peak when I spotted a dozen pronghorn antelope sprinting across an irrigated field and into the sagebrush flats. Unlike deer, which bound and hop, antelope gallop like horses and are the fastest animals in North America. The great expanse of the landscape made me wonder what I was doing here, made me question the logic of my journey. As Wallace Stegner observed, the open lands of the West "not only expose your little identity, but they tempt and threaten it." A mirage turned the antelope into tan and white ghosts floating above the sagebrush; then they disappeared into the heat-warped horizon.

Westward ho! Opportunity beckons! Fortunes to be made! Forsake the smoke-shrouded cities of the East for the glories of the Rockies! Trap beaver! Kill buffalo! Fight Indians! Pan gold! Mine silver! Smelt copper! Drive cattle! Tame the Great Plains! Farm sugar beets and wheat! Roam free! Dominate the wilderness and grow rich and powerful!

All this was possible in nineteenth-century Montana. Now the land was spotted with abandoned bank buildings, alcohol-ravaged Indian reservations, arsenic-filled copper mines, naked clear-cuts of timber, plowed-under prairie with eroded topsoil—a legacy of enterprises gone bust, dreams turned to nightmare—making you think not of how the West was won, but of how it was lost. And how, at least in the mind, it might be saved.

I had been in love with the *idea* of Montana since 1960, when I visited the state as a buck-toothed eight-year-old. On that trip a black bear climbed in the back of our station wagon at Yellowstone Park ("Dad, he wants my sandwich. Should I give it to him?") and a wild trout succumbed to a dry fly dangled over Otter Creek. After branding a calf at the Lazy K Bar Ranch near Big Timber, I was allowed to ride the bawling creature until it bucked me off and stomped my ribs in—the perfect finale to a kid's vacation. For the next three decades I kept a print of Charlie Russell's painting *Bronc to Breakfast* on my dresser. Whenever a big city got me down, I would make week-long trips to that wild, cinch-busting country, to fish the salmon-fly hatch on the Madison River or to ride at the Lazy K Bar Ranch with my father and siblings. Yet these were contained trips, pleasantly packaged vacations rather than adventure. Each time we drove the rented car back to the Billings airport, I looked up from the road map to the distant mountains, wishing I could veer off, explore, maybe get lost in this country.

My father took us to Montana instead of Wyoming or Idaho because my family was part of this state's pioneer history. My father's grandfather, John Howard Conrad, came to the territory in 1870 as a fourteen-year-old boy. He began by trading whiskey to Indians and in two decades became a renegade cattle baron, mining tycoon, and gubernatorial candidate. His son, my grandfather Barnaby, spent his youth on ranches and railroad gangs, and married a Montana woman, Helen Hunt, who was born in Helena in 1889, the year of statehood.

Ghosts were the reason for my trip: I was ghost hunting in Montana. For five months in 1989, the year of Montana's centennial of statehood, I journeyed nine thousand miles over Montana's dusty roads, through her snow-capped mountains, down her big rivers, up her box canyons, into her vast forests, and across her sagebrush flats, traveling wherever possible by horse or canoe. I was in search of firsthand adventure, family roots, and history still breathing in the carcass of myth.

During my journey, I consulted a dog-eared manuscript, the memoir of my grandmother Helen's father, William Henry Hunt, who disembarked from a Missouri River steamboat at Fort Benton in 1879. In that little river town on the prairie, Hunt began his rise from a frontier lawyer and district attorney to a supreme court justice of the state. Judge Hunt was the beloved patriarch of my father's maternal side of the family.

My two ancestors couldn't have been more different. Conrad was a rough-cut southerner and Democrat; Hunt was a Yankee aristocrat and Republican. Conrad was an alcoholic womanizer, high-stakes gambler, and millionaire entrepreneur, while Hunt was a solid family man, a gentleman, and a trusted confidant of Teddy Roosevelt and President Taft. Where Judge Hunt's exemplary life remains cherished by our family, John Conrad's story—an ambitious journey tainted with alcoholism, adultery, and even murder—was rarely mentioned by his son, my late grandfather. When my father asked why he never spoke of John, my grandfather only replied, "I didn't like the man."

Why, I wondered. And why had our family left the state—even when there was a town called Conrad, Montana? I decided to track these two ancestors across Montana, to measure their losses and triumphs against the historical backdrop of the West, and to find out how a vast Indian country had been transformed into a state rich in mining, cattle, and agriculture—and then gone into decline.

At least that's what I told anyone who asked me. The real reason for the trip was more personal. I'd lived a privileged youth in San Francisco, far from the dust storms and blizzards of Montana. After Yale, I spent six years in New York as a magazine editor, and five more in Paris as an art historian and travel writer, but Montana was always in the back of my mind. I was in Paris when my mother suddenly died. Grieving, I returned to America to assume dreary responsibilities and seek life among ashes. At thirty-seven, I was still unmarried and suddenly not feeling young anymore. I was also not feeling very American. Between New York, Paris, Zermatt, and Calcutta, I had become a chameleon, a citizen of the world, but also a man without a country. I mean a *real* country—not the America concocted by *USA Today.* I needed to find the American inside me.

That summer, as the tourists jammed the foggy streets of San Francisco, I bought a used Jeep, packed my tent, pistol, and fly rod, and hit the trail for Montana.

Ahead of me rumbled a gunmetal gray pickup with a black and tan shepherd perched in the truck bed. The dog's black gums were pulled back in a toothy smile as his nostrils sucked in an aromatic smorgasbord: green hay, dead skunk, hot asphalt, cow manure, and musky coyotes that had passed in the night. Almost every pickup in Montana has a dog riding in the truck bed. Animal-rights groups have tried to forbid this, because occasionally a dog will fall out on a bumpy turn, but Montanans believe this kind of restriction would be unfair to the dogs. There's also a rifle suspended in the back window of every pickup, and the NRA sticker is ubiquitous. This is a land where firearms are not only a hunting tool but an unapologetic symbol of ornery self-reliance. In the West, there's nothing more American than firing a bullet.

On the radio came the voices of Montana: "Sooner or later you have to come down and face reality. Are you scared? Too *dumb* to be scared? Or would you like to know Jesus Christ as your personal savior? This is Pastor John Short of the Gateway Bible Church in Gallatin Gateway hoping you'll cast off the—"

Then a little news out of the northwest: "A Glacier Park spokesman reported that a one-year-old grizzly bear was struck by a Burlington Northern train at Windy Point. The bear was feeding on fermented corn that had been spilled by a derailed train last winter—"

Then the livestock and agricultural report: "Steers were dollarin' up really good at the Chicago market until corn futures came in lower. Winter wheat moved up—"

Then on came news for a guy like me: "Hi, this is Dave Comeling from Montana's Troutfitters Orvis shop in Bozeman. Bob Jacklin's Fly Shop of West Yellowstone reports some good fishing on the Madison with the number-fourteen Irresistible and Royal Humpie. John Bailey at Dan Bailey's Fly Shop in Livingston says the Hoppers are not as effective on the Yellowstone as they have been. He suggests smaller fly patterns on the open river above Yankee Jim Canyon."

Dave Comeling caught his breath and shuffled his notes near the microphone. "Talked to Ray Coney at the Tackle Shop in Innis—reports some great days from his guides on the Madison. The bigger patterns are working well. Parachute Hopper, Goddard Caddis, also some Flying Ants because the ants are starting to show at Varney in a big way—"

A flying-ant hatch! I would have liked to see that, but right then I was looking for my first big piece of Montana history. Over breakfast in Dillon, a trucker had given me directions to Bannack, a gold-mining camp that became the first territorial capital of Montana in 1864. Bannack was now a ghost town, but I wanted to see where Montana's political history began.

Ahead of me on the road was a lone figure with his thumb out. I pulled the Jeep over with a crunch of gravel and popped open the passenger door.

"Howdy," said the dusty hitchhiker as he slipped into the front seat with a strange clanking of gear. David from Oklahoma was in his twenties, but he already had the vacant eye of a career vagabond. I asked what he did on the road. "Little bit of everything," he said wearily. "Pickin' fruit. Buckin' bales. You know, here and there."

"Where's that?"

"Oh, thirty-nine of the fifty states. I just travel and pan for gold."

He wore a broad-brimmed black hat, wire-rim glasses, and a scraggly beard. From his backpack hung a prospector's pan two feet in diameter. He smelled, not unpleasantly, like a bag of oats.

"You going to camp at Bannack?"

"Yup."

"What do you use for cooking equipment?"

"Got my gold pan." He cocked a thumb over his shoulder. "Makes a pretty good coffeepot and cookware. Eat beans. Fish."

"Where's your rod?"

"Just cut me a stick, tie on line and a hook. I got corn in a can. They love corn."

"You just eat beans and fish?"

"Sometimes rabbit, maybe."

"How do you catch the rabbits?"

"Rock."

"You find much gold?"

"Some."

"Where?"

"Creeks."

"Is it hard to pan?"

"Nope."

We rode the last five miles of dirt road in silence. Just before we reached the main gate at Bannack, the prospector asked me to stop. He got out, barely remembered to thank me for the ride, and slunk off through the sagebrush. A minute later I figured out why: they charge admission to get into Bannack, now a state park.

Surrounded by miles of sagebrush flats, Bannack was a ghostly testament to that strange nineteenth-century virus, gold fever. In midsummer 1862, gold was discovered in Grasshopper Creek; by the following spring there were a thousand men in log cabins and tents along the creek bed. An estimated $5 million in gold came out of the gulch at Bannack in the first year alone, and with hotter discoveries the following year, five thousand miners moved to nearby Virginia City and Alder Gulch. The land that constitutes Montana today was then still part of the giant Territory of Idaho and full of Indians.

Bleached silver from blizzard and sun, Bannack's old wooden buildings were remarkably intact and had not been retouched by the Park Service. I wandered through the abandoned rooms of the Hotel Meade and the old saloons, houses, and livery stables. I trudged up to a gallows silhouetted against the sagebrush hills. This was Hangman's Gulch, where crooked men were made straight. Between the winters of 1862 and 1864, a band of road agents known as the Innocents murdered over a hundred known victims—and probably dozens more. As the robberies and murders intensified, local citizens organized the Vigilantes, a group sworn to secrecy who pledged to rid the countryside of criminals.

The citizens of Bannack began to wonder about their handsome, soft-spoken sheriff, Henry Plummer, who had done time in California for second-degree murder. In his first months in Bannack he killed his traveling companion in a bar, but this was overlooked because the man had been a scoundrel. Plummer then married a respectable woman and, as the elected sheriff of Bannack, was on the verge of being made a U.S. marshal when astute citizens noted that Plummer's deputies went off on business or hunting trips at the same time the holdups occurred.

The Vigilantes arrested Sheriff Plummer and marched him across the snow to Hangman's Gulch, to the gallows Plummer himself had built. A crowd gathered. Plummer demanded a trial, but the request was ignored. His crooked deputies were hanged first, and their feet had barely finished twitching when the men grabbed Plummer. The condemned sheriff went out like a gent. As they tied his hands and slipped the noose over his head, he said, "Give me a high drop, boys."

Frontier justice cleaned up Bannack, but thieves appeared in other boomtowns. New mining camps were born every month, and from 1862 to 1876, Montana produced over $90 million in gold. In the summer of 1864, Bannack was named the capital of newly designated Montana Territory. Although gold mining continued here for fifty years, most of Bannack's fickle population moved en masse to nearby Virginia City, which became the territorial capital in 1865. More mineral strikes brought more miners, and the population grew on a heady mixture of greed, backbreaking work, and optimism.

I saw the log jail that Sheriff Plummer had built by private subscription—two dollars and fifty cents from each citizen. (Many refused, feeling it was cheaper and more satisfying to hang criminals than to house them.) Leaving the jail, I exchanged greetings with a stooped man in his eighties, an old-timer who had lived in Bannack until the fifties. He had just come back to visit the house he was born in. "You can still see the blue linoleum on the old kitchen floor," he said.

"Ever see any ghosts here?"

"Ghosts?" He frowned. "That's why I left, by God!"

A mile outside of Bannack I pulled the Jeep off the road, took out my fishing rod, and walked through the pungent sagebrush to Grasshopper Creek. The sagebrush and pink-flowered cacti petered out at the grassy stream bank, a ribbon of rust-colored water. A storm on the horizon hammered distant thunder.

No visible insects were hatching, so I selected a number-fourteen yellow-bodied Goofus Bug from my fly box and tied it to my leader tippet. After casting five times to a promising pool, I was about to move on when a fish struck. I raised my rod tip, but managed only to turn him and he was gone.

Upstream lay a pool where the water had carved out a ledge under an overhanging bush. From the stream bank protruded fragments of wood and corroded metal, remnants of an electric dredge abandoned when the gold gave out. A muskrat slithered into an eddy and disappeared. I cast once and missed a strike from a small fish. On the fourth cast, I watched the fly ride the riffles and nearly disappear in the shadows of the bank.

Like a prospector's dream, a dark bar of gold loomed up from the depths of Grasshopper Creek and lunged for the fly. I lifted my tip and the rod bent into a vibrating arc. A large brown trout swooped back and forth in the pool, breaking water twice. It was a good fish in any stream, but in this slender creek it seemed a leviathan. When the big fish gave up, I slid it to the shallows. It was a German brown, a species imported to America at the end of the last century, a competitive immigrant that has driven the native cutthroat trout into scarcity. The big-jawed head told me it was a male. Cadmium red dots dappled his glistening amber belly; the olive green back was tattooed with black spots. The dorsal fin was half chewed away, an old scar of survival. Before Scarfin could flop, I lay my fly rod next to him. His nose just hit the eighteen-inch mark. I began to think that I had known this brown trout from somewhere else. It is often this way with a big fish in a small stream—an illusion of intimacy that seems predestined and wholly undeserved.

I gripped him gently, removed the fly from his mouth, and held him in the current as he flexed his gills and gathered his wits. When he wiggled his tail, I let him go free to the darkness of the pool. A few minutes later the storm broke, dropping rain that made the sagebrush more pungent than ever. I had found something better than gold in Grasshopper Creek.

Bareback bronco rider at the Livingston rodeo.
(Courtesy Steve Matlow)

Chapter 2
The Livingston Roundup

Between the bellering of that horse, the ringing
of the spur-rowels, the sound of that pony's hoofs
hitting the earth—a-popping, and keeping time—it
sure made a sound worth sticking around for by
itself; and even if a man couldn't of seen the
goings-on, he could of told by them sounds that
here was a hard horse to ride, and on top of him
was a hard man to throw.

Will James, *Cow Country,* 1931

The place to be on July Fourth is Livingston, a fading railroad town on the banks of the Yellowstone River. July Fourth is the cowboy's Christmas, and there are at least thirty-five professional rodeos held on that holiday. Without being the biggest, the Livingston wingding is one of the best. Two cowboys in black hats were riding horses down Park Street when I pulled up near the grubby old Murray Hotel. It was a hot day, and when I slid out of my Jeep my shirt stuck to my back.

The Murray's tiled lobby was unremarkable except for a thin man smoking in a battered armchair. With his white shirt, gray trousers, and ashen face he resembled a giant crumpled cigarette butt. This was Ralph White. The wall clock ticked audibly. Ralph looked as if he had been sitting in that lobby smoking since the bad news from the Little Bighorn; later I learned he had only been there since 1934. The one thing about Ralph that implied a life outside this smoky lobby was the missing index finger on his left hand, the result of a doubtful career in a butcher shop.

"Have any rooms?"

"What?"

"A room," I said rather loudly. "Do you have a room?"

Ralph gave me a look, but with a sigh, he got up out of the chair, went behind the office partition, and handed me a key. "Twelve dollars. Bath down the hall."

"How about with a bath?"

"What?" That same incredulous look on the ashtray face.

"How about," I repeated cautiously, "a room with a bath?"

"Fifteen."

"I'll take it."

"Suit yourself." He shrugged and went back to his armchair.

I got my stuff out of the car, and lugged it upstairs to a room that was simple, and almost clean. The Murray Hotel—"the historic Murray Hotel," as a brochure insisted—was built in 1900 and had seen a wagonload of famous visitors, from Theodore Roosevelt and Charlie Russell to Richard Brautigan and Peter Fonda. Supposedly Chief Plenty Coups of the Crows and the queen of Denmark also bunked here, though not at the same time. Walter Hill, son of the railroad tycoon James J. Hill, once rode his horse into the lobby of the Murray, but couldn't squeeze the horse into the elevator. The film director Sam Peckinpah lived for five years in a dingy suite toward the back that is still proudly called Peck's Place. During the sixties the hotel acquired a bad reputation as a flophouse and drug depot, but the present owners have cleaned it up—all except for Ralph. "Ralph is over eighty years old," said the owner. "He's just part of the place. He was a billiards expert. His true love died about ten years ago, and it affected him deeply. He's seen it all."

I still wondered about that index finger.

Down the street is Dan Bailey's Fly Shop, a mecca for fly-fishermen and one of the largest mail-order tackle shops in the world. My father took me here in 1960, and for an eight-year-old trout nut it was piscatorial nirvana. The store had lost little of its magic. The walls were covered with silhouettes of trophy or near-trophy trout painted on wood with army green paint. There were wading boots, reels sculpted from single pieces of metal, fly-tying kits, and insect guides. You could get any fly here, from Woolly Buggers and Yuck Bugs to finely tied size-eighteen Pale Morning Duns or even Rat-Faced MacDougalls.

I bought a few Joe's Hoppers, a couple of Haystacks and Humpies, a half dozen Royal Wulffs, and some bigger Muddler Minnows for the Yellowstone. What I liked about Dan Bailey's was the way the flies are tied—

not by gray-whiskered, pipe-smoking old anglers but by a dozen middle-aged housewives sitting in a big room that looks like a sweatshop. Whipping bobbins of thread around pinched deer hair or peacock plumes, the women tied dozens of flies an hour. Most of the women have never cast a fly or caught a trout, and never intend to, but their nimble fingers earned them enough to pay off the car, get a perm, or take a trip to Missoula with the kids.

It is almost eight o'clock—rodeo time—and the bright sun has softened on the Crazy Mountains. The heat no longer makes your hatband wet. The Jeeps, trucks, and cars swarm to the fairgrounds down by the Yellowstone River. There are two kinds of tickets: regular bleachers for five, and grandstand for eight. You can also get tickets for beer and hamburgers, while the Jaycees offer corn on the cob dripping with butter, pepper, and salt at a dollar apiece. I eat two of these and take a frosty Coors to the stands.

Everyone, from kids to grandmothers, is wearing a cowboy hat. There are a number of Indians and a handful of Hispanics, but only one Asian couple and three black people are to be found in the whole crowd; Montana's population is still 93 percent white, with 5 per cent Indians. Around the arena are placards of businesses sponsoring the roundup: John's IGA, the Breakfast Nook, Mint Bar & Casino, Corralwest Ranchwear, and High Country Bakery Pizza. Beyond the bleachers tall cottonwoods line the Yellowstone River, and above all rise the snow-covered peaks of the Absaroka Range—pronounced *ab-SOR-ka*—the mountains of the Crow.

The music strikes up and into the arena gallops last year's Livingston Roundup queen, then three smiling contestants for this year's title, and a host of rodeo dignitaries. Over the loudspeaker: "Ladies and gentlemen, we will now stand for our national anthem." Hundreds of cowboy hats come off, revealing pale brows above tan lines. An old cowboy brings an absentminded boy to his feet with a slap on his butt. Montanans take patriotism seriously. (Ten percent of the population enlisted in World War I, the highest turnout in America.)

Bareback bronc riding is the first event, and the announcer croons, "Comin' out of box number three is . . . *Midnight!*" (There is a Midnight in nearly every rodeo.) The black gelding catapults into the ring. As Midnight crow-hops across the dirt, the cowboy lies back as if on a runaway luge, raking his spurs across the horse's shoulders to score points. His gloved hand is heavily coated in rosin, nearly mortared into the handgrip of the bronc rigging. The torque on his wrist and forearm is excruciating.

His other hand flails high above his head in an effort to maintain balance; by rule, this hand cannot touch any part of the horse or even of his own body. This hand must do nothing but beat the air like one of those vibrating rods scientists use to calibrate patterns of chaos. Each leap of the horse looks as if it will snap the cowboy in half at the waist, and by the end of the ride he begins to flop.

Eight seconds—an eternity in the cowboy's universe—have passed when the horn sounds. Like a pilot in a burning aircraft, the cowboy is ready to bail out, but Midnight continues to buck furiously even as the pickup men swoop in with their all-knowing horses. These pickup men, in identical red and white leather bat-wing chaps, are great horsemen, usually former rodeo stars, with a sort of Chuck Yeager–*The Right Stuff* cool. The cowboy grabs the closest pickup man by the waist, is pulled free of the chugging bronc, and drops to the ground. The other pickup man yanks the flank strap on the bronc and Midnight immediately becomes docile, trotting to the exit gate.

The cowboy limps in a bowlegged strut across the arena, flexing a hand that throbs painfully in the stiff leather bronc glove. With the other he reaches behind and unsnaps his bat-wing chaps so they flop open. This is something all cowboys do after their ride.

The announcer speaks: "The judges score the cowboy's ride at sixty-eight. Ladies and gentlemen, let's give this cowboy from Twodot a big hand for an excellent ride." (The score, based on a zero-to-one-hundred rating, comes from averaging the difficulty of the horse with the performance of the cowboy.) This cowboy doesn't acknowledge the applause—rodeo cowboys never do—and he dips his head in an aw-shucks pose of modesty. The applause ends just as he reaches the fence.

Back at his trailer, this cowboy may find his young wife and their jam-smeared two-year-old staring at him, once again wondering when he'll stop this crazy life with the romantic aura, slim pay, and no future. Why not get a job timbering with Plum Creek or selling grain with Cargill? Even if, as the rodeo announcer keeps grandiosely telling us, "rodeo is America's number-one spectator sport," it's tough on a family man. And on his family.

On the next ride, the horse sits down in the chute and refuses to come out. "Must be a conscientious objector, folks," says the announcer. The cowboy jumps off, the horse is led away, and the announcer continues his easy banter. "This cowboy will get a re-ride in just a few minutes. While you're waiting, why not try some of that fine roasted corn the Jaycees are offering?"

Next come the calf ropers. This is where a smart cowboy ends up if he can get the bucking disease out of his system. The key to calf roping is to have a good horse and be a good cowboy—and to practice. It's that simple, and that hard. You have to try it yourself to appreciate the eye-hand coordination a cowboy needs to rope a running calf from a galloping horse, jump off, run down the taut rope to the bucking calf, flip it to the ground, and bind three of its four legs with a cord in, say, twelve seconds.

The bull-riding event draws the biggest applause, because bulls are both comical and dangerous. The rodeo announcer croons, "Two things a Montana mother fears most to hear: that her son wants to become a bull rider—or that he's going to study ballet in San Francisco!" The line gets a big laugh in homophobic Montana.

The gates open on Satan, a hornless bull known as a *muley*, and he's full of fire. He spins round and round until the cowboy is flung to earth. He charges the dazed cowboy but Dwayne, the rodeo clown—often called "the bullfighter"—diverts his attention by flashing a makeshift red cape in the bull's face. An exit gate is pulled open and Satan is gone. No score for the cowboy.

Bulls have names like Grand Coulee, Rain Dance, and Roughneck. "Now here's one of the roughest, rankest bulls in the West coming out of chute number four—*Steamroller!*" The bull lives up to his name and sends the rider into orbit. There's a little problem getting bull number three out of the gate, so the announcer picks up the slack again. "Here's a little cowboy humor for you folks: Did you know that when all the cowboys of North Dakota moved to Iowa it raised the IQ of both states?"

North Dakota jokes are told without meanness because a great number of Montanans came from there, fleeing a hostile climate that tends to reduce humor and imagination. "And a little history for you," says the announcer. "Did you know in 1887 there was a fierce battle between Montana and North Dakota? The North Dakotans kept throwing sticks of dynamite over the state line. The Montanans lit them and threw them back." Laughter from the crowd.

The rodeo clown plays a peculiar role in the rodeo drama. He is usually an ex-cowboy himself, and his main job is to protect tossed riders from being attacked by the bulls. When a bull tosses a cowboy, then charges him, the rodeo clown intervenes. Announcer: "That cowboy almost got an ivory enema, didn't he folks? Man, that's fifteen hundred pounds of suppository!" As the cowboy heads to the fence with dejection in his bent shoulders, the announcer croons, "Ladies and gentlemen, this cowboy gets no score for the ride, so the only pay he'll take home is your appreciation. Let's give this Oklahoma cowboy a big hand so he'll remember this good-hearted crowd until next year's Livingston Roundup!"

The bulls provide enough bloodthirsty action to keep everyone happy. A cowboy from Kalispell named Leatherberry comes out on a big gray bull, rides until the horn sounds, then lets the bull throw him to freedom. He lands on his feet but his hand, tightly wrapped in the chest strap, becomes trapped. The bull lunges ahead, dragging Leatherberry with him. The crowd sucks in its breath, bewitched by the vision of a man struggling to free his hand before the wrist bone breaks. The rigging slips, the cowboy begins to go under the hooves, and the crowd groans in agony. Finally the strap pulls loose, the clown distracts the bull, and two cowboys help the barely conscious Leatherberry to his feet. The announcer croons, "Folks, how about giving that cowboy from Kalispell a good hand? He'll feel a whole lot better if he hears your applause."

Though there are occasionally all-women rodeos (and California has sponsored a gay men's rodeo), in Montana rodeo is still largely a man's game. The only women's event is barrel racing. Wearing bright satin shirts and the tightest jeans possible, the barrel racers goad their big-rumped quarter horses to explosive sprints and whipsaw turns around a triangular course marked by three tipsy barrels. As they make a mad dash to the finish line, it is normal for the male spectators to fall in love with one or two of them. With the women, I mean, although the horses, too, call up something, and it is possible that you are really in love with the woman and horse united, a vision heightened by a patriotic beer buzz on the Fourth of July.

Once a pastime with its origins in work on the open range, rodeo has become professional, a money sport. Some rodeos offer purses of five thousand dollars per event; the best cowboys earn over fifty thousand dollars a year. Not much compared with what baseball stars make in a week, but you can buy a little house in Livingston for just sixty thousand dollars, and it beats riding the range for grub, a bunk, and eight hundred dollars a month. Some western colleges treat the sport as seriously as football, and provide rodeo scholarships. Yet if the Society for the Prevention of Cruelty to Animals has its way, all rodeos will be outlawed by the turn of the century.

While handlers prod the next bull into his box, the announcer kills time with the rodeo clown the way a news anchor might banter with an overseas correspondent reporting live from Beirut. "What's that you say, Dwayne?"

The clown shouts something and the announcer chuckles: "Folks, Dwayne says we have a celebrity in the crowd, the country-and-western star

Dolly Parton! Would you stand up please, Miss Dolly? Wait a minute, made a mistake, folks, it's just two bald-headed men sitting next to each other!"

The clown does a front flip, then speaks to the announcer again.

"Dwayne says the Louisiana swamp cowboys are really upset because all the alligators are dying down there. What's killing those gators, Dwayne?"

Dwayne babbles at the announcer.

"Now, Dwayne—say what?" The announcer chuckles softly into the microphone, then shares the news with us. "Dwayne says they're all dying of gator-AIDS." Guffaws from the crowd.

In a halftime show, out comes Dwayne in a small white car with red light and siren, a miniature ambulance on whose door is written "Dr. Ben Crazy," a reference to a 1960s television character, Dr. Ben Casey. The clown-doctor orders four assistants to seek a volunteer from the audience. They climb the fence and capture a local girl who protests, but it is obviously a prenegotiated abduction. The Sabine woman is carried over the fence and placed in a six-foot-long box so that only her head and feet protrude. Never mind that the boots that extend are a lighter shade of brown than those actually on her feet; they wiggle.

Dwayne, as Dr. Ben Crazy, pulls out a three-foot-tall Styrofoam bottle labeled "Whiskey," and the announcer croons, "There's the anesthetic!" The good doctor gives some of the "whiskey" to the patient and takes a big swig himself. "Now he's sterilizing the instruments!" says the announcer as the clown rubs the carpenter's saw in the arena dirt. Then the clown begins to saw through the box. "The doctor isn't satisfied with the slow progress of the blade!" Dwayne casts the prop aside and jerks the cord on a small chain saw—a real one. In seconds he has cut through the box. Small children scream with pleasure at this gory demonstration. The announcer croons, "Dr. Ben Crazy finds the operation is successful!"

Suddenly the lower half of the box springs open. Out leap the legs and hips of the "patient," running for the arena exit. This is someone's pint-size kid stuffed into oversize jeans topped with a "bloody" stump made of red silk. The crowd shrieks with laughter, more so when Dr. Ben Crazy whips out a rifle and shoots the stump as it flees. The orderlies pick up the legs and cart them away. By golly, the crowd chuckles, what will that clown think up next—and ain't it just like the medical profession?

The rodeo clown's antics brought back a terrible family memory. In July 1933, my father's older brother Hunt, just fifteen, was spending the summer at the Lazy K Bar Ranch in Big Timber. An excellent roper and polo player, Hunt drove up to Livingston with several cowboys a few days early to practice for the horse-racing event at the July Fourth roundup. Hunt was galloping full speed around the arena when a horse tied to a gate suddenly swung its rump out, and they collided. Hunt's leg was crushed between the two beasts, and it snapped just above the knee. He slid from his mount and crumpled to the ground. He was taken, barely conscious, to the hospital.

One of the participants in the Livingston rodeo parade that year was Will James, author of the classic tales *Lone Cowboy* and *Smoky, the Cowhorse*. James was a legendary drinker and a mysterious character. Will James wasn't even his real name. Born in 1892 in Quebec, Ernest Dufault left Canada under strange circumstances—possibly wanted for murder—and reinvented himself in Montana. James became a top hand and bronc buster, but fell in with the wrong crowd and was arrested in 1915 for cattle rustling. During a year in a Nevada prison he began drawing cowboys. Over the next twenty years, Scribner's published two dozen books written and illustrated by James. But with the bottle and a divorce, James's personal life fell apart, and he was dead at fifty. The last line of his final book proclaimed, in capital letters: "THE COWBOY WILL NEVER DIE!"

During the 1933 July Fourth parade some friends loaded James, stinking of whiskey, into a wheelbarrow and rolled him half conscious through the streets, much to everyone's amusement. But when he sobered up and somebody told him that a kid had been badly injured, Will James went to the hospital. Hunt lifted his head from the pillow and smiled, thrilled to meet his favorite author. James sat down and charmed him with stories about mustangs in the badlands. Then he gave him a copy of *Lone Cowboy* and wrote in it: "For Hunt—Sun's comin' up—Will James." For a sick boy who loved rodeo and was far from his family, this meant a lot.

The local doctor was unskilled, possibly a drunk, and the break had been badly set. These were pre-penicillin days, and infection moved up the leg, swelling it like a pink balloon. Hunt's leg was punctured to drain the fluids. He was feverish for a month, and barely conscious when they took him to the Livingston railroad station. Two cowboys helped the orderlies awkwardly hoist the stretcher through the window of the private railroad car bound for San Francisco.

A year and a half later, after many complications, a surgeon amputated the leg just below the knee. Hunt was almost eighteen and had spent over two years in the hospital. No one ever heard him complain. He got a prosthesis, and for the rest of his life my uncle, in his own jaunty words, held his socks up with "a garter and a thumbtack." People noticed the stiff-kneed limp but rarely knew the extent of his handicap. He married and had three

pated members of that early group of writers and artists who moved to Montana.

"What a lush," said Scott. "I remember seeing Brautigan in a bar once—drunk and upset because no one wanted to hear him recite his poetry through his sodden mustache. He had this big wet mustache he was always rubbing on my girlfriends. I never really got along with him. If he'd been anyone else, I might have beat him up. He used to sneak into high school keg parties and try to recite poetry to the girls. But I'm glad he was here. I'm real glad. I read *Trout Fishing in America* and liked it a lot."

More recently ranches have been bought by newsman Tom Brokaw, beef-cake photographer Bruce Weber, and actors Tom Selleck and Mel Gibson. The recent influx of Hollywood people to the Livingston area, Scott felt, hasn't really changed the economy much, but it has boosted the price of recreational property. "These people like to have ranches, but they're not really into ranching. The Big Hat, No Cattle syndrome. Still, they've done some good things environmentally, like putting in conservation easements which block development."

Their presence also made Livingston a lot more interesting, but some residents resented newcomers trying to broaden the aesthetic and political scope. "It's part of the anti-intellectual mentality that's so strong in Montana. The worst thing you can be around here is *smart*. We had a city planner here who did a lot of great things for Livingston, but they basically ran him out of town. You can be somewhat smart if you're a local, but not if you're from out of town. You see it in the newspaper's Letters to the Editor department: 'Who do these smart guys think they are, telling us how to live?' That kind of thing. Montana is basically anti-intellectual."

Scott and I moseyed down to the Long Branch Saloon, pushed through the swinging doors, and were swallowed by a sea of high-crowned Stetsons. One young cowboy wore a T-shirt that said, "I came, I drank, I offended." Scott fought his way to the bar and grabbed four bottles of beer for us.

Livingston was a small town, and Scott knew almost everyone's story. "See that chick near the pool table? Looks pretty normal, doesn't she? Used to be she had every guy in town. Went up to Bozeman and was charging for it from truckers. Now she's straightened out and working as a waitress. Don't know what it was that made her do that. Boredom or drugs." Our conversation grew hoarse competing with the country-and-western band twanging in the back.

The saloon doors swung open and a long-haired young man came in with a troublesome-looking woman on his arm. She was almost six feet tall, with an urban slatternly look. He was taller and dressed in a sloppy tan suit and Hawaiian shirt. His pallor, heavy-lidded eyes, and crooked smile indicated a private joke that only a pharmacist would understand. Long-haired types and short-haired cowboys are still nitro and glycerine in Montana bars; I felt something about to happen.

The cowboy was young, with short-cropped dark hair, a caterpillar mustache, and dissatisfied blue eyes. He stood near the jukebox brooding. When the longhair and the woman lurched by and bumped him slightly, he became as tense as a sparrow hawk on a barbed-wire fence.

"You faggot," he growled.

The longhair whipped around. "What'd you say?"

"Faggot," said the cowboy in measured tones. "I said you're a goddamn faggot!"

I don't know who threw the first punch, but in two seconds the longhair and the cowboy had grappled and exchanged a flurry of choppy, ineffectual blows. They bounced off the jukebox, then off the bar, and again off the jukebox. The longhair's woman pummeled the cowboy's shoulders with her fists. The longhair put two deep punches into the cowboy's belly. The bartender came around the bar with a billy club, but the longhair and cowboy caromed like Siamese twins down the bar and smashed through the swinging saloon doors.

They fell to the sidewalk and rolled into the gutter. The longhair straddled the cowboy and began to systematically pound his neatly trimmed mustache back into his face. The hippie woman shrieked for blood and kicked the cowboy's legs. In less than a minute a siren sounded, and the Livingston police arrived. As they shoved the bleeding longhair and cowboy into separate squad cars, the woman screamed, "You cowboy cocksucker!" One of the Livingston police said curtly, "Ma'am, if you don't clean up that mouth of yours you'll join them in jail." We watched the squad cars leave and went back inside for a beer.

"My third day in Montana and I've already seen two bar fights," I said.

"Doesn't take much for things to get western around here," said Scott with a grin. We shouldered up to the bar again.

"You going to file a story for the *Bozeman Chronicle?*"

"Hell no, this stuff happens all the time. Somebody's got to *die* before it becomes a story. Anyway, glad to see a longhair take out a cowboy for once."

Livingston has always been a wild town. In 1873, when the settlement was just a trading post, the superintendent for Indian affairs in Montana wrote to his superiors: "Men pass by this shop and obtain whiskey, get drunk, come here on business and annoy us very much." In the 1880s, most of the action was in the Bucket of Blood Saloon, which is now the Livingston Bar and Grill. There were fights every night between cowboys, railroaders, and drifters. One night, two sheepherders clashed outside, and one came back in with the other's severed head, which he dumped on the bar, saying, "Can you set my friend up for a drink?"

The Bucket of Blood was run by Kitty Leary, known as Madame Bulldog, who at six feet and two hundred pounds often did her own bouncing when customers misbehaved. One person she threw out many times was Martha Jane Cannary Burk, better known as Calamity Jane. More false legend festoons this braggadocious dame than any other character in the West. It was partly her own doing, but mostly thanks to the dime novelists who fantasized about a woman who wore buckskins, handled a rifle like a trooper, and lived like a man on the frontier. It is true that she supported herself as a "bullwhacker," and was a master at cracking a sixteen-foot whip over the ears of ox teams. She also participated in army and survey expeditions, but she was not a scout with General Custer as she boasted, and was probably never an army scout of any kind.

Little is known about her early life. Once Calamity became indignant over reports that she was "a horse thief, a highway woman, a three-card monte sharp, and a minister's daughter." All the claims were false, she said, "especially the latter." Most historians agree that she was born in the Midwest and was taken to Virginia City, Montana, with her family in 1865. Her parents died when she was a teenager, and one biographer described her earliest occupation as "a camp follower" of railroad construction crews, "with none seeming to doubt her calling."

One thing was sure: Calamity Jane drank whiskey and was a nuisance at bars around the West. She lived in a cabin in Livingston and supported herself by conning drunks and telling tall tales. She had many lovers, but claimed that the great romance of her life was Wild Bill Hickok. Though Calamity was with him when he was killed in Deadwood, South Dakota, one of her detractors said Wild Bill "was much too fastidious a man to be involved with the likes of her." She cried over his grave and said she wanted to be buried with him. When she died of cirrhosis in 1903, she got her wish. Yet before she was buried, the womenfolk of Deadwood clipped off so many souvenir locks that a friend had to put a wire screen over the coffin to preserve what was left of her hair.

Hung over from the Long Branch, the following day Scott and I canoed ten miles of the Yellowstone. "I'll tell you one thing," said Scott, uttering an incontrovertible truth, "fishing and beer will cure most ailments." We took only four fish—about one per beer—but the biggest was a three-pound brown trout. Afterward both of us were sunburned from the canoe trip, so we picked up more beer—Scott considered beer a balm for sunburn—and drove out to his house on North Yellowstone Street.

Scott deftly grilled the big brown trout over a hibachi, serving it with salad and a cold sauvignon blanc. From his back porch, we watched the sun set on the nine-thousand-foot peaks of the Absaroka Mountains. "Drink up," said Scott. "I want to take you back into town to the Owl Club."

Only Livingston locals frequent the Owl Club. We approached it from the back alley, and I remarked on the five Harley Davidsons parked near the garbage cans. "Yeah, nice scooters. Belong to the Livingston Brothers, local biker gang," said Scott. "I just did a story for the *Chronicle* on them. We rode down to Wyoming for a little bikers' rendezvous."

"Did you take a cycle yourself or ride on the back?"

Scott looked at me as if I had blasphemed. "Ride on the *back?* Shit, I ain't *never* gonna ride *bitch* on *nobody's* scooter." He shook his head and guffawed at the thought of it. "Hell no, I took my car."

It was dark inside, and the dark red booths made you think of clotting blood. "Looks mainly like scooter trash," said Scott under his breath. "And the women's bowling team." Four husky women in black T-shirts were sitting in a booth, chuckling like chicken-fed badgers. The bikers were quietly drinking beer and talking with the bartender. One of them greeted Scott in a friendly manner. Since Scott's biker article hadn't been printed yet, I assumed we were safe.

Also at the bar was Tim Cahill, part of the local literary fauna. Cahill was a hefty, brindle-bearded fellow in a Hawaiian shirt and a green farmer's cap. His arm was bandaged from a recent exploit—sail-gliding off nearby cliffs—and his mouth was deep in his beer. Cahill's reputation stems from his writing in *Esquire* and *Outside* (which he cofounded), mainly nonfiction adventure tales in which he puts himself on the line meeting gorillas in Rwanda, climbing the Andes, and swimming with sharks and poisonous sea snakes in the Pacific. His book titles have a jaunty, masochistic tone: *Jaguars Ripped My Flesh* and *A Wolverine Is Eating My Leg*. His next book project, he said, would be to drive from the tip of Argentina to Point Barrow, Alaska, in less than a month: *Road Fever.*

Cahill explained why Livingston was different from other parts of Montana. "Those places attracted farmers who wanted schools for their children, a good police force, churches, and hard work. The people who settled Livingston were mountain men, railroaders, and cowboys. They wanted a place where they could hunt, fish, get drunk, gamble, and fuck whores. There's still a big difference today. The people here are still very liberal, while all the people in the surrounding area are conservative to a fault."

Standing near Cahill at the bar was a woman called Bonnie. She was perhaps thirty, dressed in a black turtleneck, black leather jacket, and Indian moccasins. With long straight brown hair parted in the middle above serious dark brown eyes, she might have been pretty if she'd been happier.

"So you're writing a book about Montana? Huh! That's so typically Californian to think you can come up here for a few months and write a book. You have to spend years here. Actually, I'm glad you're *not* spending years here," she said with a bitter smile.

"Why?"

"Too many out-of-staters as it is."

When I told her that my family had lived in Montana a century ago, she reconsidered.

"Okay, okay, you're a little different. But I'll tell you, the problem with Montana is all these out-of-staters. They just mess everything up."

"Are you a native Montanan?" I asked.

"What difference does it make?"

"You just said there was a difference."

An evasive look came into her eyes. "It's not an issue."

"So where were you born?"

"Okay, *okay.* Michigan—but that doesn't mean anything. I came out here for college ten years ago, but it's like I've really lived in Montana all my life."

"What do you mean?"

"See, in *spirit*—even when I was a baby—I've *always* been a Montanan."

"So now you want to pull up the drawbridge behind you?"

"Look, you're from California, you wouldn't understand. You're from a land of parking lots and malls."

When I said she was right, she seemed to warm up, and said, "You know, you really should write about the environmental issues. Write about the bears." She herself was a member of the Great Bear Society, a group dedicated to saving the grizzlies. It sounded nearly like a religion.

"Well, I thought I'd talk to the Craigheads," I said. The Craighead family were famous for their pioneering studies of grizzlies in which they used radio collars; they had created numerous programs in Montana and Alaska.

"The Craigheads?" she said. "You mean *meatheads!* We don't talk about the Craigheads at the Great Bear Society."

"Why not?"

"Why not? Because they've killed more bears in their studies than all the hunters put together!" She laughed cynically, turned, and called over to the table of bikers. "Hey, Bobby, this guy wants to know about the Craigheads."

Bobby immediately got up and darted over to us. He was a small man in black leather. His large, tragic, angry eyes peered from a gaunt face framed by a graying mane and beard. I was glad he was several inches shorter than I was, because he had a twitchy, hair-trigger look. "What's he want to know about those bastards?"

"Why are they bastards?" I asked.

"Why? I'll tell you why. Because they killed one bear while they were airlifting him out—'for his own benefit.' Hah! Dropped him accidentally from about five hundred feet up!" snapped Bobby.

Now Bonnie jumped in. "Don't you *understand?* They used to shoot those bears with so many tranquilizers that they rattled their brains! I mean that stuff is *angel dust!* No wonder the bears were going around attacking campers! Then they have to be destroyed. Thank the Craigheads for turning the grizzlies into a bunch of whacked-out *drug addicts!* " Bonnie sucked down the rest of her scotch.

"Man, one of them Craigheads walked in the door right now, I'd kill him no sweat," said Bobby, poking a finger in my chest. *"Fuckin' Craigheads!"* He smacked the bar with his fist.

"Easy, honey," said Bonnie, massaging his neck muscles.

Having vented his spleen, the biker whispered, "I just love that animal. The grizzly means everything to me. I would *kill* anyone that messes with a grizzly bear." Bonnie gazed at Bobby in a zonked-out, beatific trance, her eyes glowing with the overwhelming vision of the grizzly bear as a symbol of untamable wilderness. Suddenly, they put their arms around each other and embraced, their black leather jackets creaking with passion. As they began to gnaw on each other's tongues, I backed down the bar to find Tim Cahill chortling to Scott about a loony fashion model he'd met in New York who wanted to get a wolverine as a pet. Too much whiskey and too much sun had done me in. I said good night and ambled outside to the empty street.

As I lay in my darkened room in the Murray Hotel, the same hotel where my grandmother had stayed when she wondered if her son Hunt would live or die after the Livingston rodeo, a train rumbled through the yard on its way to Billings. Its horn gave a full-throated cry, like a man playing the harmonica after too much whiskey.

The people of Big Sky country still judge a man on how he chooses to live his daily life, not on his fame or his bank account. At fifty, Russell Chatham was an unusual painter with a growing reputation that had nimbly bypassed the New York star system. His big oils now sell for the price of a small Mercedes-Benz, yet he still drove a fleet of rusting American sedans that wouldn't fetch much even as spare parts. Montanans like that attitude.

One morning I stopped by his huge studio above the Sax and Fryer stationery store. Born in Stanford, California, Chatham grew up in the Bay Area. His Swiss Italian grandfather, Gottardo Piazzoni, was a respected plein-air landscape painter who did a series of majestic, Postimpressionist murals in the San Francisco Public Library. Chatham cites his grandfather and Albert Pinkham Ryder as the two major influences in his life. Russ still remembered boyhood summers spent roaming the Piazzoni ranch in Carmel Valley with his paint box as a golden time in his life. The whole family—aunts, uncles, and cousins—painted for fun. A lackluster student, Russ dropped out of college and turned to painting as a profession. When Marin County became overly gentrified, Chatham grew restless. On the suggestion of his friend Thomas McGuane, Russ and his second wife settled in at Deep Creek near Livingston.

It was good country for a sportsman and artist, but debts plagued him. Instead of falling back on odd jobs as he had in California, Russ became an inveterate trader of art for services. He swapped paintings for carpentry, beef, cases of California wine, and even car tune-ups. A few of the women in town (Chatham was divorced again) also ended up owning paintings. As things improved, Tom McGuane found that trading a riverboat and its trailer would get him only a small Chatham oil painting.

With the help of the novelist Jim Harrison, Chatham's work was bought by writers like Hunter S. Thompson, George Plimpton, and William Styron. Then came the Hollywood tidal wave of Warren Beatty, Jeff Bridges, Peter Fonda, Margot Kidder, Jack Nicholson, Robert Redford, and Harrison Ford; the collectors' names read like the guest list for the Academy Awards. But

Chatham still prefers to sell or trade paintings to local ranchers or friends. "I think it keeps things in perspective," he said.

Russell Chatham was respected at the Livingston Bar and Grill and in Dan Bailey's Fly Shop not because he was a successful artist, but because he is great company in a bar or in a fishing boat. For instance, in 1966 near San Francisco, Russ caught the world-record striped bass on a fly rod, but he never talked about fishing for records.

In addition to painting, Chatham also had a reputation as an outdoor writer, a career encouraged by his late friend Richard Brautigan. Russ wrote two books on fishing and a recent collection of sporting essays, *Dark Waters*. In the preface to a recent book he wrote: "With the exception of painting, nothing in this life has held my interest as much as fishing. Fishing with a fly, a bait, a handline; I don't much care. Fishing, in my estimation, is not a challenge, or an escape. Like painting, it is a necessary passion . . . to be anything less than passionate about these very personal enterprises is unacceptable."

Chatham's paintings capture the mountains, valleys, and rivers that make up the great land that dwarfs the railroad town of Livingston. And it is still *land,* not real estate. "I couldn't tell you what the poetic feeling is that I get with a landscape, but I just know it's there," he said. "A painting should be a poem, a thing which cannot be translated out of its original state; it is what it is. The origin of a true painting is the spirit, the soul of the painter."

For that very reason, it made sense to Chatham to be far away from the Manhattan hype factory. The spirit of the country, as Chatham says, "affirms there is something bigger out there than we are. I believe in some force around us. We call it God. Who knows what it is? But I guess that wouldn't be taken too seriously on West Fifty-seventh Street in New York."

Chatham spoke of the landscape painters Monet and Cézanne as if they were special neighbors. "They loved to paint; they loved what they saw, and they said it in their work. They said something positive and life giving." His own landscapes were nearly abstract, with a pronounced sense of modernist surface. Against the wall stood a large unfinished picture of a canyon in winter that, at this stage, looked like a smokier version of a Franz Kline. I asked if he was interested in abstract painting.

"Yes and no," said Russ. "To me, the failure of abstract expressionism was that the paint and the action were the *point* of the pictures. The picture may be more important to the artist himself than the viewer. I did some real abstract paintings myself when I was younger, but it seemed like writing a book without a story, typing words without actually saying anything. Now I know that's not exactly true, because painting isn't really narrative, but I think a picture has to have a *voice* rather than just sound."

Russ worked hard, but didn't question the passion that made him leave his studio, fly rod in hand, on a summer day when the stone-fly hatch overtook the Yellowstone. Between casts, he could look across the river at the Crazy Mountains and think of a canvas sitting on his easel. Then, painting a river scene back in the studio, he could think about trout rising on the Yellowstone, and the whole picture would change. By casting and painting and hunting and writing he could hold it all.

Left: The Conrads' steamer *Red Cloud* sank in 1882 along with the fortunes of Fort Benton.

Above: The port of Fort Benton was the supply hub for Montana Territory in the 1870s. Right: William Henry Hunt, my great-grandfather, became district attorney of Montana at age twenty-seven. (All courtesy Montana Historical Society)

Chapter 3

Fort Benton: The World's Innermost Port

It is said that one of the leading saloonkeepers of
Benton is negotiating for an invoice of hurdy-gurdys, to
be shipped from Bismarck via the river. We are not sure
that this enterprise will be any detriment to Benton.
Dancing damsels of questionable repute may not improve
the morals of a community, but they are several shades
better than negro prostitutes, and it is thought they
will have the effect of driving out the latter. If
social evils are an indispensable feature of Benton,
by all means let us have the hurdys.

Benton Record, 1879

Driving two hundred miles north, I still had plenty of Montana between
me and the Canadian border when the sign for Fort Benton rose up out of
the prairie. From the bluffs above the Missouri River I looked down on a
town cradled in an oasis of cottonwoods.

The members of the Lewis and Clark Expedition were the first white
Americans to visit this bend in the river, and Lewis was forced to kill a
Blackfeet here in 1806. The American Fur Company arrived in 1843, and
made peace with the tribe to encourage trade; but with the discovery of gold
at Bannack and Virginia City, gold seekers, entrepreneurs, and veterans of
the Civil War rushed in—a few to kill off the buffalo and Indians, some to
homestead and freeze to death, some to raise cattle, cut timber, farm wheat,
and make babies in little wind-sheared shacks on the prairie. As late as

1869, Indian skirmishes in the Fort Benton area accounted for fifty-six white deaths and thousands of stolen horses. Civilization meant contamination: only after a smallpox epidemic massacred the Blackfeet in 1869 did the tribe settle down.

Fort Benton became the doorway to Montana Territory, the last stop for steamboats from St. Louis, and it was here that my two great-grandfathers Conrad and Hunt became westerners. A century later the town was nearly unchanged from the faded prints in my family's photographic albums. The only major change seemed to be the absence of riverboats on the Missouri and a single blinking traffic light at the busiest intersection. Today, Fort Benton's population is exactly the same as it was in 1880—about seventeen hundred—and Chouteau County, inhabited mainly by farmers, produces more wheat than any other county in Montana.

Early Montanans faithfully read the *Fort Benton River Press*. I found its current editor, Joel Overholser, in the office on Front Street. He was seated by an ancient printing press that noisily churned out the latest edition of the daily-turned-weekly. A short stocky man with ears like mud flaps, Joel had a pixie face with a grayish pallor, but his eyes were lively. At nearly eighty, Joel talked about frontier life as if it were his childhood, which it nearly was. I'd read his life's work, *Fort Benton, World's Innermost Port*, and had corresponded with him.

"Your great-granddad, John Howard, was the mystery man of the Conrad family," said Joel. "I had a hell of a time figuring out when he got here. Finally pinpointed his arrival in Benton in the summer of 1870."

At fourteen John Conrad left his home in Virginia, boarded a steamboat in St. Louis, and traveled two thousand miles alone up the Missouri River. The voyage took over two months. With the crew he went ashore to shoot his first buffalo and ate the liver uncooked and steaming, a ritual meal of the Great Plains. He met the proud Indians who rode up to trade with the boatmen. At Fort Benton, my ancestor was greeted by a pair of tall mustached men—his older brothers, William and Charles, who'd arrived two years earlier. When their native Shenandoah Valley had been invaded by Union soldiers, the two brothers, then aged sixteen and fourteen, had fought beside their father, Colonel James Conrad, in the guerrilla cavalry known as Mosby's Raiders. The end of slavery shut down the Conrads' Front Royal plantation, and the colonel sent his sons west in 1868.

The bustling river port of Fort Benton was a shipping hub for the entire Northwest. Hundreds of tons of food and hardware were loaded onto wagons pulled by oxen and mules bound for all points of the compass, even up to

Canada. The Conrad brothers became clerks for Isaac G. Baker, the most powerful merchant in town and one of the masters of the Missouri River. One of Baker's employees was a fellow Virginian who'd started Fort Ashby on the Marias River near Willow Rounds. Ashby was doing good business trading for buffalo robes, but he was having trouble with pilfering Indians and dishonest interpreters. Baker sent twenty-year-old William Conrad to help out.

Fort Ashby was less grand than it sounds, just a rough stockade and storehouse manned by a dozen men. When the Indians came to trade, however, they came by the thousands—North Blackfeet, North Piegans, and Bloods from Canada. When illegal whiskey traders showed up, things quickly got out of hand. The drunken braves rode around the stockade, firing their guns and shouting, "You miserable dirty white dogs! You are here with your cattle eating our grass, drinking our water, and cutting our wood! Get out of here or we will wipe you out!"

Isaac Baker gave the young Conrads full rein in his business. William planned the shipping network of ox teams, Charles built trading forts with stockades, and young John became a stock clerk, handling the sacks of gold dust that pioneers deposited in the company safe. Big for his age—John was six foot three—my great-grandfather worked as a link between his older brothers, often accompanying wagon trains that shipped to Helena, to newly constructed Fort Conrad on the Marias, and to Fort Whoop-Up, the most infamous of the Canadian whiskey forts. Baker and the Conrads traded guns, food, clothing, and whiskey to the Indians for buffalo robes and wolf pelts.

"It was against the law to sell alcohol to an Indian in the United States, but nothing stopped them from selling to the Bloods in Canada," said Joel, puffing on his pipe. "The border didn't mean a damn thing in those days."

As Joel spouted facts and anecdotes in a steady stream, his conversation resembled his pipe smoke, swirling back and forth in history, fading away in the light. "Benton was one of the roughest towns in the West. About a hundred and fifty saloons. Nick Welch's place, the Occident, was the toughest in the West." Joel pointed his pipe at an early map hanging on the wall. "Now, on this corner, they had squaw hurdy-gurdies every Saturday night. You'd have two hundred teamsters here ready to spend their money and have some fun. And this whole block was occupied by bundles of joy: the Cosmopolitan, the Jungle, and the Extradition Saloon."

Fort Benton was not a pretty town in the early days. Few trees were planted among the rough log cabins and shanties. Careless citizens tossed garbage and slop into the street or along the levee. Fires were frequent. During dry spells, dust swirled in the roads. In the rainy season, the streets became a sea of mud; in winter, they froze solid. In the spring, ice jams on the Missouri brought floods. Indians as well as the Chinese and Negro laborers suffered from violence and racism. The crude pleasures of the frontier reigned, from card games and shoot-outs in saloons to flesh exchanges in the hurdy-gurdies. In 1876, the editor of the *Benton Record* (an early rival to the *River Press)* urged bachelors to go farther upstream to bathe since "they don't look well with their clothes off and might be mistaken for catfish." He also warned that "making love to a squaw across a hotel fence, in broad daylight, is something that even the good-natured proprietors of the Overland [Hotel] must condemn."

Furs and gold brought Fort Benton its first boom, but by 1871, the Union Pacific Railway was siphoning off travelers and only six steamboats came up the river. The town underwent a slump, worsened by the national depression of 1873; the next year the three Conrads acquired a controlling interest in the Baker Company and Isaac Baker returned to St. Louis. By 1878, the Baker firm was operating eight trading posts in Montana Territory and as far north as the Arctic Circle in Canada. Thanks to a whole new crop of settlers, Fort Benton bounced back. "In the next boom, all the Conrads became rich," said Joel. "They never changed the business's name, and for that reason historians mistakenly credit Baker the *man* with the company's success under the Conrads."

That was nice to hear, but it also made me wonder how our family fortune—and the general prosperity of Montana—had disappeared in just two generations.

The Fort Benton Museum was a cinder-block building the size of a bungalow, filled with photographs and dioramas of steamboats and wagon trains. Photographs of William and Charles Conrad (bushy eyebrows, beady eyes, and huge mustaches) were displayed next to their main competition—the dapper, well-trimmed Power brothers, who also sold whiskey to the Canadian Indians and ran steamboats.

I was especially struck by an enlarged photograph of several men in front of the Baker store circa 1875. In the center stood a tall mustached man in shirtsleeves. The picture was grainy, and his features remained obscure under the shadow of his hat, yet I felt a nervous charge. It was the first photograph of my great-grandfather I had ever seen. John would have been just twenty-one, yet he already looked tough, seasoned by the frontier.

The museum also displayed a beautiful scale model of the house William Conrad built in 1878, shortly before he became the first mayor of

Fort Benton. It was Second Empire style, of brick, with a turret, elegant grillwork, and a mansard roof. "It was the finest house in town," said Joel Overholser. "The Catholic church owned the property and about ten years ago decided they needed a parking lot. The old priest didn't care about history. He let the Fort Benton Fire Department set the house afire and practice putting it out."

"The fire department *practiced* on it?"

"Afraid so. Then it was razed."

"Wasn't the house a national historic site?"

"That doesn't mean it's automatically protected. Private owners can do anything they want if they don't touch government funds. We lost a lot of good buildings that way."

Today Fort Benton is a farming community, and farmers tend to be pragmatic, not sentimental, and not history buffs. They have been leaving their farms, moving into town, and replacing the old houses with "ranch-style" homes sheathed in all-weather aluminum siding. Their migration, I reasoned, would eventually silence all echoes of Fort Benton's rowdy past.

Joel bolstered my spirits by leading me to the town's architectural jewel, the Grand Union Hotel. An orange brick structure by the river, it was built at a cost of two hundred thousand dollars. Its opening in 1882 as one of the handsomest hostelries west of the Mississippi was the greatest social event in Fort Benton's history. When the railroads to Great Falls bypassed the port, the hotel went broke. A succession of local citizens ran it at a loss for a century until it closed its doors two years ago. "The last owner, a farmer, just went bust. You could probably buy it for a song," said Joel. "Feel lucky?"

With the Grand Union closed, I drove down Front Street to the Pioneer Hotel, which had once been the old Power store. Unfortunately, the Pioneer Hotel's middle-aged owners, Marvin and Winnie Appleby, had shoehorned a sterile modern motel into the old mercantile building. The architectural conversion was disappointing, but I shelved that gripe when the Applebys invited me to their quarters for a drink.

"Wine or whiskey?" asked Marvin.

The first sip of Marvin's sickly sweet wine told me I had made a mistake. Fort Benton was still a whiskey town.

Marvin didn't care much for history, but he was full of gossip about Fort Benton today—the stuff that would one day be history. The biggest thing to happen here recently was an $11-million marijuana bust. "A family called Kurtz found they couldn't make ends meet and were about to lose their farm," said Marvin. "They decided to go for a good cash crop. They grew four thousand marijuana plants in Quonset huts with false ceilings and artificial lighting. Now the state is demanding seven hundred thousand dollars in taxes."

"It was on TV," Winnie offered. "Right there on *Sixty Minutes.*"

That evening I hooked up with Brian Morger, a twenty-seven-year-old artist descended from another pioneer family of Fort Benton. I'd seen his paintings in a tourist gallery on Front Street, and telephoned. All his paintings depict yesteryear Montana, with steamboats and wagon trains and steam locomotives. Brian owns buckskins and a black-powder rifle, and often sells his art at mountain-man rendezvous around the state. He also does Elvis Presley imitations on a professional basis and uses television to sell his limited-edition prints. Obsessed with Fort Benton's history, Brian readily volunteered to show me the town's night life.

After a medium-rare dinner at June's Steakhouse, we walked down to the Chouteau House, which was built by Power and Baker as a hotel in 1868; the downstairs still functions as a bar, but there were only two customers that night. "Imagine the stuff that went on in this place," said Brian. "The shoot-outs, the dance-hall girls, the gamblers fleecing greenhorns. I mean, just *imagine!*"

He led me out a back door into the so-called Paradise Alley. "There's a room up there that was only reachable from the outside." He pointed to the second floor. "For the hookers. The *soiled doves*—don't you love that expression? Indians, blacks, and whites. The most famous hooker was known as Madame Moustache. Of course, they're long gone," said Brian wistfully. "There hasn't been a hooker in Fort Benton for seventy or eighty years. Wouldn't it be great to turn the clock back a century—just for one night?"

When we stepped into the Pastime Bar, it seemed that Brian had been granted his wish. Strutting along the bar in high heels, their pale skin glowing in the overhead lights, two half-naked white women were stripping to music. Instead of buckskinned frontiersmen gone bleary with firewater, their audience was twenty all-American refugees from a golf tournament, guys in lime green, azure, and fuchsia golf shirts, whistling, clapping, and sucking down Bud Lite.

The women had been hired from the Playground in Great Falls—a runty blonde, and a long-legged brunette with a bright smile whom the men clearly preferred. Her name was Renée from Neenah, Wisconsin; she had a marvelous figure and a coquettish personality. She cleverly yanked the elastic G-string every which way in time to the music so that all the prying men's eyes saw was a flash of fur.

"Want to model for me sometime, gorgeous? I'll paint you as a moonbeam," said Brian, inserting his dollar bill into Renée's G-string. Another man lay down on the bar with a rolled-up dollar bill gripped between his teeth. Renée danced over him and crouched gracefully. His eyeballs nearly crossed as her creamy buttocks eclipsed his face and removed the dollar bill. The crowd went wild.

One of the golfers, a straight-arrow type in his early forties, slapped Brian on his back. "Great party, huh, Brian?"

Brian turned to me, and said, "I'd like you to meet the mayor of Fort Benton."

Then he introduced me and the mayor's smile faded into a ghastly grimace.

"A *journalist?* Oh, hey—" His eyes flickered to the girls stuffing dollar bills into their G-strings. "Listen, I just stopped in for a beer on my way home. I mean, you wouldn't want to *write* about something as silly as this, would you?" He tried to laugh it off, but at that moment, Renée came up behind him on the bar and pressed her breasts down over his head like earmuffs.

As we left, I noticed a sign tacked up on the wall behind the bar:

> The longer I know women, the more
> I understand the guy who shot Bambi's mother.

So it goes in the West: stirring tales of buffalo hunts replaced by misogynist bar jokes.

Fort Benton was at the peak of its frontier wildness in 1879, when a tall, bespectacled gentleman with a neat mustache and a dusty bowler hat arrived. William Henry Hunt was just twenty-two, and his only assets were a suitcase of dirty clothes, a good mind, and a certificate allowing him to practice law. Unlike the rough-and-ready Conrads, my other great-grandfather looked more like an anemic poet than a frontiersman.

Hunt was from a family of American statesmen, being a direct descendant of Robert Livingston, who was coauthor of the Declaration of Independence, ambassador to France, and the chief negotiator of the Louisiana Purchase. Raised on one of the Livingston estates in the Hudson River valley, Hunt was sent to Yale but became so ill with peritonitis that he was obliged to drop out. Tutored at home, he then worked as a customs clerk in New Orleans, studied law at Tulane, and wrote for local newspapers.

When his father took a judgeship in Washington, D.C., William followed his older brother to the boomtown of Fargo, Dakota Territory. There he worked as a surveyor, a newspaper reporter, and a law clerk until he passed the "absurdly easy examinations." A freight train brought him to Bismarck, where he saw steamboats on the Missouri pointing north. Nearly penniless, he charmed the steamboat agent into granting him free passage to Fort Benton in exchange for writing a newspaper article about the journey.

The Missouri River was so low that year that passengers were obliged to disembark at Cow Island, 125 miles east of Fort Benton. The night before, a band of Indians had stolen the army's horses, so the soldiers showed only cursory concern for the passengers. Hunt spent one night huddled under a blanket, then luckily met an old frontiersman, Redstone Congdon, who carried freight for the army on his four-horse team. Redstone allowed Hunt to ride with him for a dollar a day if he'd keep watch at night for Indians and horse thieves.

The wide expanse of the plains and the great herds of buffalo astonished the young easterner. "We met several Indian hunting parties," he wrote. "Redstone knew their language and how to greet them in a friendly tone, using the few words that Indians employ and by making the signs with his hands by which they interchanged thoughts." Redstone also taught Hunt how to sneak up on a herd of buffalo from downwind. "We did kill and left carcasses for the Indians."

Hunt arrived in Fort Benton late one night in early October. The town was in full swing, with saloons and hurdy-gurdy halls serving rotgut whiskey to prospectors, bullwhackers, prostitutes, squaws, and squaw men. When he registered at the Overland Hotel, he noted that the clerk had lost both ears—frozen off in a blizzard. Over buffalo steaks in the dining room, he pumped the veterans for stories of Indian fights and gold strikes.

Word soon got around that he was a lawyer. That winter a schoolmate from Yale, Horace Buck—a Mississippian with a genteel drawl—arrived and they immediately set up the firm of Buck and Hunt in a two-room log cabin. The eight-by-ten-foot office was sparsely furnished, and the living quarters in the back were just as primitive. Their beds were buffalo robes spread in the corner, the washstand was a packing box with one side open to hold dirty laundry, and "for a mirror we used the dim reflection which came from the panes of the little window."

Their first client was a saloonkeeper who had advertised in an eastern paper for a wife to come west. The woman sent a pleasing photograph of herself in profile, and the man mailed her money for passage from St. Louis to Fort Benton. But when she stepped off the boat and the eager bride-groom discovered that the unseen side of the woman's face was disfigured from some accident or illness, the man refused her. "The situation was fur-ther confused by the lady's impecuniousness," wrote Hunt. As the ratio of men to women—not counting prostitutes—was about a hundred to one in Fort Benton, Horace Buck soon located a freighter who said he would be happy to marry her and promptly paid off the disillusioned saloonkeeper to everyone's satisfaction.

For a time, the practice thrived. "We defended men charged with mur-der, horse stealing, assault, selling liquor to Indians, robbery, forgery and other offenses." In the winter of 1880–81, the mercury dropped to fifty below. "At night the ink froze," wrote Hunt. "So did the water in the pitcher in the bedroom. Even the kerosene in the lamps thickened." Their fortunes soon followed the thermometer. "The wolf gnawed at the seats of our trousers in February. There was no business, no fuel, no money, no amuse-ment, no comfort, no happiness, no work, no mails, no telegrams, no news, no travelling, no improvement, no dissipation, no food, no enterprise, no prospect, no hope, *no law.* Taken all in all it was the darkest period of our legal and journalistic existence. Horace Buck took sick in February to make things more cheerful."

In the spring of 1881, Hunt's father was named secretary of the navy by President Garfield. It so happened that the office of U.S. collector of cus-toms for Montana and Idaho Territories was located in Fort Benton, just seventy-five miles from the Canadian border. When the job became avail-able, Hunt, aged twenty-four, was given a political plum worth eighteen hundred dollars a year.

To be sure, Hunt's social connections helped him succeed, but his mem-oirs are not those of a snob. He wrote admiringly of the rough frontiersmen and their self-reliant character and distinctive humor. One favorite was a cattleman named Bowles, who still dressed in the frontiersman's moccasins and buckskins. Bowles had a quiet unobtrusive manner until he drank; then he liked to fight. "One time the man he was abusing left him and went out of the saloon. Bowles, much enraged at what he called an 'act of cowardice,' went into the probate judge's office and asked the judge to lend him a pair of heavy boots. 'I just want to kick a cur over here on Front Street and then

I'll return the boots.' The judge was agreeable; so Bowles thanked the judge, took off his moccasins, put on the boots, and left the courthouse. He found his man in a saloon, engaged him in a hand to hand fight, gave him a terrific kicking, and after knocking him down, returned to the judge's office where he took off the boots, resumed his moccasins, and after courteously thanking the judge, left the court house."

Gunfights and hangings were standard fare, but Fort Benton grew more gentrified as white women arrived and churches were built. The white women resented Indian squaws living openly with frontiersmen and began a campaign against adultery. "Finally a grand jury met and hailed into court many prominent citizens who were obliged to plead guilty to the charge of adultery. Some, particularly where there were children, married their squaws, while others sent them into the Indian reservations to rejoin the Indian tribes from which they had been taken."

Just before Christmas, Hunt visited his family in Washington and attended a string of dinners, balls, and cotillions. One evening he was invited to the home of Admiral John Upshur and his wife, who had several lovely daughters, "and before many weeks I was betrothed to Gertrude, then twenty-one years old, the youngest of the three girls. Light hair, bright blue eyes, petite figure, and a vivacious nature, with a ready interest in my tales of the West—the combination overwhelmed me." After a romance by mail, William and Gertrude were married in August 1882 in Brooklyn, where Admiral Upshur commanded the navy yard. It was a big wedding, and the newspapers proudly reported that the bride was a great-great-granddaughter of Martha Washington, and that the the bridegroom's father, who had just been named minister to Russia, was, alas, away in Saint Petersburg.

For Gertrude to go west—"she who had known nothing but the life of Washington society, with Newport or Europe in the summers," as Hunt wrote—was like a heroine from an Edith Wharton novel being transplanted into the Wild West. Crossing the prairie by train and stagecoach, Gertrude had her first sight of Indians, drunken cavalry soldiers, and buffalo wolves.

Fort Benton was a shock to her. "Our bungalow was in the bottom, back toward the hills," wrote Hunt. "Fort Benton was primitive. There were no paved streets, no running water, no sewers, no gas, no electricity, no telephones. We drank river water which we hauled in a cart and delivered in barrels back of our house . . . ." They did, however, have servants, thanks to an abundance of "Chinamen who were faithful and efficient."

Indians were very much a presence in Fort Benton. One evening while Gertrude was soaping herself in a bathtub, she looked up at the window to find an Indian in buckskins mesmerized by her nakedness. She froze in terror, and the brave watched her for a good five minutes before moving away. When the Hunts' first daughter, Elizabeth, was born in 1883, her nanny was a ten-year-old Indian girl named Ida, daughter of a squaw and a frontiersman. "She was very near savage when she came to us direct from a tepee," wrote Hunt, but with Gertrude's guidance, young Ida quickly learned English and "the ways of a more civilized life."

Hunt's career took on new stature when in November 1884 the Republican Party, á minority, submitted Hunt as a "sacrifice" candidate for attorney general of the territory. He was told his chances of victory were slim. "I did not like that attitude and was self-confident enough to believe that with a vigorous campaign the Democratic majority could be overcome." Hunt rode hundreds of miles by stagecoach to greet crowds of miners and ranchmen, and won by a narrow margin. At twenty-seven, he became the highest-ranking law officer in Montana Territory.

Driving down Fort Benton's elm-shaded streets, I stopped in front of a red brick house on the corner of Washington and Sixteenth Streets. It was small but elegant, with white gingerbread trim on the veranda. My great-great-uncle Charles Conrad built this house in 1881 for his second wife, a woman from Nova Scotia named Alicia Stanford, who was known as Lettie.

A petite, busty blonde, Lettie was eighteen when she arrived by steamboat in Fort Benton in June 1879, accompanied by her widowed mother and her younger brother Harry. That fall, Lettie and a colleague, Miss Kitty Tonge, opened the Select School for Ladies and Children, offering instruction ranging from ancient and modern history to chemistry, French, and music. To Fort Benton, these women were the embodiment of civilization; when they passed on the muddy streets, even the roughest frontiersman removed his hat.

At thirty-six, Charles Conrad was now a successful Missouri River trader and banker. Although exactly twice Lettie's age, he began to court her discreetly. The polite invitations grew into love letters. When Charles proposed marriage by letter he felt compelled to reveal his past: "I feel that there is a great barrier between us, and that is my former character. Previous to the advent of ladies into the Northwest, I like many others, led a somewhat reckless life (undoubtedly of which you have heard) but meeting you and my love for you have made a new man of me. If you will consent to share your life with me, I will be to you a kind and true husband leaving nothing undone to make you happy. "

During the 1870s, while working at a Canadian whiskey fort, Charles had had a love affair with Sings-in-the-Middle Woman, a maiden from the Blood tribe. Sometime prior to 1876, she bore him a son whom they called Charles Edward Conrad Jr. Unlike most "squaw men," Charles Conrad formally married her, but Sings-in-the-Middle Woman never lived in Fort Benton, and soon returned to her tribe in Canada. Here she remarried, to an Indian, and died in 1881 during childbirth. The Conrads built the first Episcopal church in Fort Benton, but Sings-in-the-Middle Woman had been previously converted by Catholic missionaries; her last wish was that her son be educated by the "black robes." After her death Charles sent the boy to a Catholic boarding school in Montreal.

Lettie wasn't deterred by Charles's murky past, and they married in January 1881 with the temperature outside at thirty degrees below zero. The following year she bore a son whom they called Charles Davenport Conrad. The half-Indian son, Charles Jr., was now called by his middle name, Edward, and was never allowed to visit the Fort Benton house.

That night I crossed over the Missouri and pitched my tent in a campground bowered by cottonwoods. I made no fire but sat by the shore until it got dark, watching the bats and nighthawks swoop for insects in the twilight. In midcurrent small fish jumped, but they weren't trout; the water was too warm. Probably golden-eye. A wind out of the south brought mild smoke from a distant forest or prairie fire. It reminded me that the Plains Indians often set fire to the prairie to chase game or frighten their enemies.

As darkness fell, I suspended a flashlight from the center of my tent with a piece of green dental floss. My tent quivered in the light breeze, and the electric beam sent circles of light whirling around the tent fabric. I got into my sleeping bag to read about the Conrad brothers and the last days of the Missouri River traffic. I thought of steamboats like *Red Cloud,* which John Conrad purchased in 1876 for twenty-five thousand dollars cash. Originally built for the Tennessee River Fleet, *Red Cloud* was 228 feet long, with powerful engines and a shallow draft. A year later *Red Cloud* ran from Bismarck, North Dakota, to Fort Benton in eight days and seventeen hours, a record that was never matched. She could carry three hundred tons of goods and up to 330 passengers, and soon became the most popular boat on the river and the Conrads' flagship.

The coming of the railways in the 1880s—the Canadian Pacific to the north and the Northern Pacific to the south—doomed the isolated port of Fort Benton. In 1882, *Red Cloud* struck a submerged snag near Fort Peck and sank in three minutes flat. No lives were lost, but the great ship lay derelict through the winter and broke apart with the spring flood, a death knell to Fort Benton's life as a shipping center.

The wind in the cottonwoods and the river's rippling music took me back a century, to when my ancestors had traveled this same water by steamboat. What I would have given to experience Montana as they had—to hear and smell a mile-long buffalo herd or to watch painted Blackfeet warriors brandishing Crow scalps as they galloped across the prairie. In a fit of nostalgia, I christened my burgundy-colored Jeep *Red Cloud* after the sunken steamboat. The coyotes began to sing from across the Missouri, and it was another hour before I could sleep.

Top: Blackfeet chiefs, 1892, sold the ancestral lands that became Glacier Park. (Courtesy Montana Historical Society)

Inset: A closed-up hamburger stand at Browning, Blackfeet Reservation.

Joe Bear Medicine at his home on the Blackfeet Reservation in 1989.

Chapter 4

Browning: From Concentration Camp to Homeland

Chiefs White Calf, Big Nose, and Tearing Lodge
constitute a police tribunal to try misdemeanors
committed on the reservation. Thirty days on the
wood pile is the fate of the Indians caught drunk
or having liquor. Despite all precautions, some
Indians get whiskey. When caught the liquor is
spilt by one of the police breaking the bottle on
the Agency flag staff. Shortly after one of these
breakings an old squaw picked up a glass fragment
and sorrowfully licked it."

Fort Benton River Press, November 11, 1889

From Cut Bank west to Browning, a route once taken by Lewis and
Clark, the road now crosses the Blackfeet Indian Reservation, a million and
a half acres of tribal land. No Blackfeet are alive today who remember hunting the buffalo.

Of all the Conrad brothers, Charles best understood the Indians and
their problems after the whites dominated the plains. The Blackfeet knew
him from his trading days at Fort Conrad in Montana and Fort Whoop-Up
in Canada. I wanted to see if any Blackfeet still remembered him, but I kept
in mind that Charles had been a whiskey trader, and I wondered, uneasily, if
this would be held against me. Firewater has remained the Indians' greatest
enemy, with alcoholism running as high as 70 percent on some reservations.

Passing four white metal crosses marking road deaths, perhaps a family, I
imagined a beat-up gas guzzler filled with liquor breath as it swerved into

oncoming headlights. Then, through my bug-splattered windshield, I saw the eastern slope of the Rockies rising gloriously from the plains. No wonder the Blackfeet lived here.

Browning looks like any American town on the skids, but the boarded-up stores and unpainted houses indicate that the inhabitants still aren't taken with Euro-American civilization. I passed the War Bonnet Motel, a Tastee-Freez, then a closed-up hamburger stand made of poured concrete in the shape of a giant tepee. This is a war zone for a tribe still mourning its past, a people tormented by cultural schizophrenia. To be an Indian, or not to be an Indian: that is the question.

The arrival of Europeans in the eighteenth century brought horses, metal knives, and guns that jerked the Plains Indians out of the Stone Age, revolutionized their hunting skills, and turned them into a warrior society. The Indian brave no longer had to struggle for food; his goals were to make a vision quest, count coup on his enemies, and steal other tribes' horses and women. They had greater leisure time to develop weapons, clothing, and artwork with beads acquired from a white man's trading post. And more time to drink whiskey. The Crows, Blackfeet, and Assiniboines fought among themselves. Then came the slaughter of the buffalo and the making and breaking of treaties; by 1890, all the Indians were corralled on reservations. The West was "won." Celebrants of a highly ritualized culture were now a living curiosity, fallen descendants of the Noble Savage. Under unsympathetic and even corrupt government agents, the harsher aspects of Christian schools battered their language and religion.

Just off Browning's main strip I found my destination: a fishing-tackle store. Northern High Plains Outfitters was a dimly lit cinder-block building, more of a storage shed than a shop. In the middle of the bare cement floor stood a glass counter sparsely filled with fishing flies and a few reels. There were two fishing vests for sale, a float tube, and a handful of rods. The capital for this enterprise had been frugally invested: one summer of bad fishing and the store might go under.

The proprietor, Ed Anderson, was about thirty, with light brown hair and blue-gray eyes. He looked more white than Indian due to his mixed ancestry, but he had high, broad cheekbones, and his body was nearly hairless—another Indian trait. He had an Indian way about him, too—a polite, soft-spoken manner. I told him I wanted to fish and to meet people of the tribe.

We parked my Jeep in a cow pasture near Cut Bank Creek, tied on some light caddis flies, and split up. The stream ran in a great curve under a fifty-foot cliff. I cast against the cliff wall, bouncing my fly off it, and a rainbow struck the moment it hit the surface. I pulled it into the shallows and released it. We caught a few more fish, quit for lunch, and headed back to town.

"I think you should meet Bob Scriver," Ed said.

"He's an Indian?"

"Might be. Been here forever."

Might be? This was a peculiar way of describing someone. We pulled up in front of the Bob Scriver Studio and Wildlife Museum and went inside. It was a big operation. To the left was a wildlife museum of stuffed animals: bears, cougars, moose. To the right were two rooms of Scriver's magnificent bronze sculptures of animals and Indians. There was piped-in tom-tom music.

We found Bob Scriver in his studio, putting the finishing touches on a life-size group sculpture of explorers Lewis, Clark, and their black manservant York. Three Indian lads were making rubber molds of the sculpture. In his seventies, Scriver was a short, powerful man with a graying Vandyke beard and a slightly crazed look in his blue eyes. He was dressed in khaki shirt and pants and wore a four-inch-wide leather belt around his ample girth. He'd been born in Browning in 1914, son of a man who owned a trading post on the reservation.

Scriver had been a taxidermist before turning to sculpture. He put his carving tools aside to give us a tour of the taxidermy studio. We stood under a grizzly bear that reared on his hind legs, jaws bared, forepaws extended. "Shot thirteen times before they brought it down," said Scriver. "Eight hundred and fifty pounds of fury. I remember carrying that bear's arms—each of them weighed ninety pounds. You have to learn the anatomy of the animals from the bones and the muscles, not to mention their habits. While I was stuffing that bear, I made a little scale model of it in clay. That's when I decided to take up sculpting professionally. I did animals, then cowboys. I began doing the Blackfeet, because I knew their culture and I knew it was disappearing. That was 1952." He now gets high prices for his bronzes, which are sold from Texas to New York.

When Ed stepped out for a Coke, Scriver invited me into his house behind the studio. It was a treasure trove of western art: a classic moose painting by Carl Rungius, a watercolor by Charlie Russell, drawings by Frederick Remington, a landscape by Thomas Moran, and a magnificent portrait of an Indian chief by Winold Reiss, the German artist who lived with the Blackfeet in the 1920s and 1930s. Sitting on his cluttered desk was one of

Scriver's own works in progress, a nearly finished sculpture of Theodore Roosevelt on horseback.

"So you're interested in Indians, huh? Aren't many left. Real Indians, that is. Hell, I'm more Indian than that kid out there"—Scriver's thumb indicated the absent Ed Anderson—"and I don't have a drop of Indian blood in me. It's a matter of spirit. And knowledge. I speak Blackfeet and can put up a tepee the right way. Not many can do that anymore. No sir, not many at all. All being forgotten." He tapped his head.

"Look, over there." He pointed to a strange leather bundle about the size of a woman's purse. It sat on a tripod of sticks. "That's my medicine bundle. And here's the medicine pipe. Only three of us on the reservation that even have them, much less understand them. I was given that by one of the old men of the tribe."

The pipe was three feet long, ornately wrapped with eagle feathers and dyed porcupine quills, with a green duck head lashed to the end of it. "It's purely ceremonial, never smoked. Just look at the colors in that pipe! That green against that yellow quillwork. Look at that! They didn't have to go to art school—they just knew it. That's art! That's *high* art."

He turned the pipe in his hands, lost for a moment in its beauty. "How do Indians today know about their culture? They get it by reading books written in English by white men. You're not born knowing how to put up a tepee—nosirree."

Scriver was dead set against the current arrangement between the Blackfeet and the Bureau of Indian Affairs. "The government is doing an injustice to the Indians in the long haul. They're treating them like invalids or children. Coddling them. Anything they want, they get. No good. No good," he said, shaking his bearded jowls. "Don't know if the Indians even know what the truth is anymore. They call themselves a 'sovereign nation.' What does that mean? To me, a sovereign nation is one that stands on its own two feet without help from anyone. You have your own currency and economy. You pay your own way. That certainly isn't the case here. This ain't no Liechtenstein or Monaco.

"The old ways were great—don't get me wrong. It was a beautiful culture. Just look at the craftsmanship in this." He pointed to porcupine quillwork stitched into a hundred-year-old buckskin shirt. "That's as fine work as the cut edges on the stones of the Great Pyramids! It's beautiful. But that's not today's culture, is it? It's all gone. And it's not coming back. . . . What's your ancestry?"

"English."

"Well, do you want to go back to the days of King Arthur and Sir Lancelot? You want to become a Druid? Or clank around in armor and sport a codpiece? How about some bloodletting with leeches? Huh? No, you couldn't. Can't turn back the clock. But that's what some of these Indians are trying to do." He winced theatrically, grimaced, shook his head in grave mystification.

"After all, this reservation was a military concentration camp. The Blackfeet were placed here as prisoners of war with the U.S. Army as their guards. A sad history, but they were a conquered people. Now they call it a homeland for the Blackfeet Nation. And they're beginning to *believe* that! How can a concentration camp become a nation? I'd rather look ahead than backwards. Railing against the injustices caused by whites isn't going to help the Blackfeet survive or grow.

"Still, the whites hold the Indians in awe. The minute they put on the war bonnet and speak a few words in their language, the whites fall down on their knees as if they were gods. The Indians want to take back the Sweetgrass Hills because they say it was sacred land. But if you understand the Indian culture, all land was sacred, filled with the Great Spirit. Every rock, bush, and stream. What are they going to do? Take back the whole state of Montana? Why not the whole country? It's too late! Too damned late."

This seventy-five-year-old artist, with his strong worn arms and sad blue eyes, had spent his best years recording the life of the Blackfeet in bronze. Fifty years from now, when he is long dead, his sculptures of dancing warriors and women tanning buffalo hide will remind us—and the Blackfeet of the future—of what they once were.

To the Blackfeet and Bloods, the fur trader Charles Conrad was known as Spotted Cap. Fluent in their dialects, he liked as well as understood Indians, but he also had a resolute side when it came to dealing with hostiles. In his obituary in the *Anaconda Standard,* an old-timer remembered an incident from 1882:

> It reminds me that he [Conrad] was one of the coolest men in the face of danger and one of the best Indian traders this country ever saw. He had a certain power over the red man that seemed to compel him to do as he wished. I remember one time when he and a number of us were up on the Blackfoot reserve when the Indians had become peaceable, but they were not to be trusted at all when they thought they had the advantage of the white man. Nothing but the cool-headed

bravery of Mr. Conrad saved us from annihilation. We had a warrant for an Indian boy who was charged with killing a calf that belonged to the Conrad Company and we wanted to arrest him.

There were at least 5000 warriors camped in that place and they were packed in very closely. Johnnie Healy was then sheriff and he was and is, as everyone knows, so brave that he is simply reckless, and he held the warrant that was to enable us to take the boy into custody. We had no interpreter along as Conrad was an expert and we located the boy by information from the same Indian that had told us about his killing the calf and we were sure we had the right boy. In fact they—that is, the boy and his parents—did not attempt to deny it. We had explained the arrest and I was assisting in putting the boy on a horse and tying him to the saddle when the father slowly pulled out his rifle and leveling it at my head said something to me in Indian that I knew meant "stop that."

I hardly knew what to do, and I suppose did not realize my danger when Johnnie Healy whipped out his revolver and was about to shoot the Indian.

At the same instant another Indian gave a war whoop and in the time it takes to tell it we were surrounded by 1000 warriors and most of them were armed. Things looked pretty serious for us and if Healy had shot we would have been wiped off the face of the earth, but luckily for us, Mr. Conrad grabbed Healy's gun and forced him to put it up. Then Mr. Conrad told the Indians that we did not want to hurt the boy, that we would take him to Benton and have him tried before the court for killing the calf. "He will come back to you safe and sound whether he is guilty or not," said Mr. Conrad. "And even if you kill all of us, the soldiers will come and kill you. You cannot escape. Make the father of the boy put down his rifle and we promise you that we will not hurt the boy."

The Indians then took the rifle away from the angry father, who under the circumstances was not to be blamed very much. He stood around in a sullen attitude as if uncertain what to do. Mr. Conrad asked them to make an opening for us so we could go home but they seemed determined not to do so. Mr. Conrad, after parlaying with them for quite a while told us to draw our guns but not shoot 'til we had to. Then he told the Indians that the first one who touched the horse's reins he would kill instantly and if they gave him any trouble, we would kill the boy, even if all the white men were killed. After a moment's hesitation they began to give way as we advanced. . . .

To finish the story, we took the boy to Fort Benton where we placed him in jail until the next term of court. His mother followed us on foot all the way, slept on the jail floor until her boy left for the penitentiary when she returned to her home. The sentence in the state prison for two years was a good thing for the young man, whom the Indians called White Calf on account of his misdemeanor for it taught him a trade and he is now a respected Indian carpenter up on the reservation.

Charles's relationship with the Indians was an enduring but ambiguous one. In 1895, the Blackfeet were approached by the United States government to sell a strip of land running north and south along the western border of the Blackfeet reservation—land that would eventually become the eastern half of present-day Glacier Park. Several years earlier, white prospectors following rumors of mineral riches had explored the mountains around St. Mary's Lake, twenty miles from the Canadian border. Both the tribe and the whites were uneasy, because just one arrow in the back of a prospector would unleash the wrath of the U.S. Army. The government favored the land sale to give free rein to Manifest Destiny and to avoid conflict. Without the buffalo, the Indians were barely eking out an existence, and saw the sale as a way to get cash.

The Blackfeet chiefs went to Charles and asked him to represent them in negotiations with the government. In mid-August 1895, he traveled from Kalispell to St. Mary's to have a look at the mineral sites with Indian agent George Steell, several Blackfeet chiefs, and twelve Indian police. In a letter to his wife, Conrad wrote: "The Indians have asked me to serve as their Attorney. I presume I shall be here all of next week. It commenced snowing here this morning and there is now four inches of snow and quite cold . . . ." Charles spent September consulting with the Indians at Browning. By this time three government-appointed commissioners, including the naturalist George Bird Grinnell, had arrived, ready to negotiate.

The government offered $1,250,000 for a piece of land extending from the Canadian border down to Birch Creek. The Indians didn't want to give up the prairie, only the mountainous land north of the Great Northern tracks (near present-day East Glacier). Charles urged the Indians to counter with a higher price, and Little Dog told the commissioners: "There are many things in which the Great Father has cheated us. Therefore we ask $3,000,000 for that land. Those mountains will never disappear. We will see them as long as we live; our children will see them all their lives, and when we are all dead they will still be there."

Representing the government, William Pollock replied, "It is true that the money you may get will be gone after a time, but in the meantime you will be getting clothing, blankets, cattle, wagons, food, etc. That money offers you all those things, while the mountains offer you nothing but snow and ice and rock."

For some of the Indians, this "useless" land of snow, ice, and rock held more than material significance. It was a place for summer retreats and vision quests. As White Calf eloquently put it a few days later, "Chief Mountain is my head. Now my head is cut off. The mountains have been my last refuge. We have been driven here and now we are settled."

A compromise was reached at $1.5 million. Even as the Indians were applauding the verbal agreement, Charles spoke up on their behalf, telling the interpreter, "You might say to the Indians that it is nothing more than right that they should get interest on their money from the time the treaty goes into effect until the money is paid." Pollock countered by saying that the extra $250,000 reached in the compromise would take the place of accrued interest. Charles disagreed. "I should not, as a businessman, make this treaty without asking interest, unless it was considered in the price asked. No businessman would do so." He then turned to the Indians: "I want you to consider well before signing this treaty."

The Indians listened to Conrad, and the government agreed to pay a total of $1.5 million, with a down payment of $300,000; half the latter sum would go into an interesting-bearing U.S. Treasury account at 4 percent, and half would be payable directly to the tribe. The remaining $1.2 million would be paid in eight annual installments of $150,000.

The treaty was signed by 306 Indians out of a total enrollment of 381 male adults, including mixed bloods. Their names have a poetical ring: White Calf, Eagle Ribs, Curly Bear, Calf Standing in Middle, Tail Feathers Coming over Hill, Takes Gun at Night, Took Gun at Morning, Yellow Wolf, Yellow Kidney, Joe Skunk Cap, and Chewing Black Bones.

The total land area sold was eight hundred thousand acres—at less than two dollars per acre. Article 2 of the treaty provided that the sums be expended "in the purchase of cows, bulls, and other live stock, goods, clothing, subsistence, agricultural implements, in providing employees in the education of Indian children, in procuring medicine and medical attendance, in the care and the support of the aged, sick, and infirm, . . . and in such other ways as may best promote their civilization and improvement."

The Indians had little say in these expenditures. They were immediately launched into the cattle business, and by 1900 the Blackfeet Agency owned nine thousand head. The Indians were forced to fence their entire reservation at their own expense to keep out trespassing cattle from—I am embarrassed to say—the nearby ranch of William Conrad. Many Indians lost their cattle by gambling and paying off debts to traders and bartenders. Predictably, their cattle industry failed.

The government allowed the Indians the right to hunt, to fish, and to chop wood for sustenance on the Ceded Strip as long as the land remained in public hands. In return, the government had the right-of-way to install railroads and highways and canals through any part of the Blackfeet reservation.

Was the sale a good deal for the Blackfeet? A lot of Indians today don't think so. As real estate, the Blackfeet's Ceded Strip land might be worth $100 million to $200 million today. But money invested at a 5 percent return doubles roughly every fourteen years. If the original $1.5 million had been properly invested and not spent by the government on ludicrous "social benefits," it would be worth about $180 million today. Of course, it is not a simple question of money. In 1910 the Ceded Strip became part of Glacier National Park, one of the great natural preserves of the world. In the long run, the ghosts of the old chiefs might approve. Might.

At the Blackfeet government offices I interviewed Vickie Santana, a tribal lawyer. Fortyish, elegant in a blue skirt and white blouse, she wore glasses that gave her a bookish mien. She looked more Latin than Indian, and, in fact, her father was Puerto Rican, her mother Blackfeet. Raised in Puerto Rico and at St. Mary's (near Glacier), she'd attended law school in New Mexico. Vickie was aloof until I mentioned Charles Conrad; then her eyebrows rose.

"That's an interesting family connection to have—particularly around here. You know about his role in the Ceded Strip, don't you? He had beautiful handwriting. We just wish he had written down more of what happened during the government negotiations."

Vickie was pessimistic about the Blackfeet and the current state of reservation affairs. "The fraud and corruption have to be cleaned up before anything constructive can begin. The trouble is, this place is a quagmire of lies. We lie tremendously. We lie for federal programs. Consistently. It's very bad for the soul. And very bad for the government. When you lie then you don't have a reality anymore."

Vickie's outspoken criticism of the tribe made her unpopular in certain sectors, but earned her respect. "My great interest is the ethical tradition. Which we haven't followed at all. Or rather, the classical ethic. I don't even like to use the word *traditional*—because to many Indians it means horses and guns and eight wives and nineteenth-century stuff and the beginning of unnaturalness. We lost the ethics when the lying came in."

"What kind of lying?"

"Indians misreport their income. Even for their own tribal programs. We have a program to help families stay in Great Falls if a sick family member has to go to the hospital. It gives them money to stay in a motel for three nights. But people misuse that privilege tremendously. One family took thirteen thousand dollars about four years ago. They just cheated and lied."

"Do tribal members pay community dues or taxes?"

"None," she answered forlornly. "There's no sense of owing anything."

One of Vickie's main concerns was fish and game on the reservation. "For the first time we're going to have written tribal laws to control this resource. Before the white people came, there were unwritten Indian laws regarding hunting. When our culture fell apart, we lost those laws and many Indians simply thought we *had* no laws. It's going to take time for people to adjust to regulating fish and game. Right now, Glacier Park is producing most of the animals that come onto this reservation. I'm not so interested in bringing back the elk for the meat; it's to bring back an element of *naturalness*. So that people can look around and feel a connection to nature and have a sense of being an Indian.

"We want a hunting season so that we will produce more elk in the areas bordering the park. Tribal members come to us and say, 'We have to hunt. We are starving.' You cannot make me believe that there are people here who are honest-to-God starving. We have a welfare state with food stamps and child care and general assistance. A lot of this is junk hunting—people who go out and slaughter and just leave animals. And then there's the myth of, 'Oh, no, we're Indians, we use every scrap of meat.' What's reality in hunting? Only game control will bring back the animals."

"How many other people feel like you do?"

"A few. Not many. We have a lot of talent in this tribe, but most of the energetic people are living outside the reservation. They've also developed more skills. Vice president of Del Monte Company. Vice president of the Bon Marché stores. Guys who are in charge of multimillion-dollar aerospace companies in California. Tremendous organizational and technical skills. And they come back here wanting a job. And they're rejected. Because of tribal politics and corruption."

"Why don't *you* run for the tribal council?" I suggested.

She shook her head and smiled. "I don't ever want to be a politician. But I have a lot of ideas. I'd like to take time to organize the tribal archives. I was an undergraduate history major. I don't speak Blackfeet myself, but I'm going to be tutored. I want to go out and study all the historical sites on the reservation and develop a program to protect them. We took one of the last sun-dance sites of the forties—a time when people still spoke Blackfeet and did everything the old way—and destroyed this historic site. We've done terrible things to our own culture—and we have to recognize this."

According to Vickie, the Blackfeet (known as Piegan in their native tongue) currently had only 243 full-bloods enrolled out of 13,800 tribal members. "At one time it was a social issue. It was cooler to be mixed blood. It was lower class to be full-blood. Now it doesn't mean anything except to a few people. We're having a discussion right now over whether we should change our enrollment policies. You have to be one-quarter Blackfeet to be a member. But that one-quarter is based on these fraudulent entries that were done in 1908—a legal fiction we're relying on four generations later. People come up to you and say, 'Hey, I'm twelve sixty-fourths Blackfeet, and I'm more Indian than that guy who's only eleven sixty-fourths.' What I like is what my grand-father said: 'It's how you *act* that makes you an Indian.' *Manners.*"

She sat back in her chair, and by simply moving a pen on her blotter she graciously ended our meeting. As she walked me to the door she said, "If in your research you should see any reference to the earlier, 1872 treaty, let me know. There's still so much we don't know about the past."

Ed Anderson took me to meet his grandparents, the Browns, who lived in a clean little house off the main street. Vincent Brown was sitting in a worn armchair. A half-breed, he looked more white than Indian, a toothless old fellow with mirthful eyes. His wife, who steadfastly watched *Jeopardy* on television in the alcove, was almost pure-blood, and she wore her graying hair in long braids. Ed coaxed a story from his grandfather about his life as a cowboy:

"I was up in Cardston, Alberta, in the thirties when a Texas desperado caught a Chinaman spitting on the grill and he took his six-gun and shot him. No one blinked an eye. The man's name was Charlie Gannan. He was dodging the cops when he came north working on ranches. There was a cop named Hayward that had tracked Gannan from Seattle, then over to us. We were all sitting in the bunkhouse one winter when Hayward came in. Charlie Gannan had one of them pearl-handled six-shooters called a pearly. It was a forty-five on a thirty-eight frame with a hair trigger. Always kept it with him. When Hayward tried to grab him, Gannan shot him four times right in the goddamn heart before he hit the floor. He was that quick.

"When Hayward fell on his face, Gannan shot him once more in the neck to be sure. The other fellas came in and wanted to pick Hayward up and put him on a bunk. 'No,' said Charlie Gannan, 'leave the son of a bitch lie on the floor.' The cook got scared and tried to drive into town in an old car, but he went off the road into a drift. The boys brought him back. The law would get there soon enough, and they all liked Charlie Gannan. They wanted to give him time to get away.

"Gannan fixed his bedroll and had something to eat, real relaxed. Said he'd killed a few men before and it didn't spoil his appetite. But he got depressed and said, 'I can't go no place. Can't stand the running no more. I'm tired of running.' He told the boys he was going to kill himself. They didn't like to hear this because, shit, he was a good-hearted bastard. He had a high-class bedroll, too—Hudson's Bay blankets and all. When he got ready to kill himself, he put the good blankets on the bottom and the old blankets on top. He told them to share his blankets among themselves after he died.

"While they were all in the other room drinking coffee, he spread newspapers on the floor neat-like. Then he took that pearl-handled pistol and shot himself above the ear. Exploded his brains out right onto the wall. There was a hole in the wall, with bloody brains around it, and we tried to wash it off. Shit, you couldn't get it off. It was driven into the wood grain. We nailed a flattened tin can over the stain."

Ed's grandfather had worked as a carpenter, but his greatest talent was finding underground water with a forked willow branch. He knew how to witch wells. "Learned it from an old prospector. Used to do it for a six-pack of beer. Now I get a hundred bucks to witch a well." The old man got up and pulled a forked willow branch off the shelf. It was about two feet long. He grasped the forked ends in his hands lightly and began to walk around the room. Suddenly the willow branch twitched and went straight down, quivering. "Must be a water pipe under the floor," he said. Then he handed the willow branch to me. I tried it over the same spot, but I couldn't get it to twitch. He laughed a long toothless laugh and settled back in his chair. His wife, still watching television, never said a word.

Ed took me an hour's drive west to the edge of Glacier Park, to meet Darrell Kipp, a teacher at the Piegan Institute, at his house on St. Mary's River. We stopped by a house in the woods, and I heard the river flowing and saw the dark green mountains beyond. A large canvas tepee had been pitched among the aspens. Darrell Kipp was sitting on a sofa in his house, listening to an old Grateful Dead album. He was a large, dark Indian in his forties with long hair in braids, a sociology degree from Harvard, and a renegade spirit. He was married to a white woman, Roberta, who had worked as a flight attendant. He offered us beer, then settled back on the couch, urging us to relax and listen to the music. But I wanted to talk about Indians.

"Are you related to the Joe Kipp who ran Fort Conrad?" I asked.

"Yes and no," said Darrell. "My true ancestors were killed at the Baker Massacre in 1870, and one of the Kipps adopted the orphans, giving them the Kipp name. Frankly, I often suspected that Kipp played some horrible part in the Baker Massacre and adopted my ancestors out of guilt."

The Baker Massacre was one of the saddest chapters in Blackfeet (Piegan) history. From 1867 to 1869, the Blackfeet stole thousands of horses between Chouteau, Lewis and Clark, and Meagher Counties. Dozens of settlers were killed, and the Thirteenth Infantry had its hands full. On August 23, 1869, Piegans killed a white man named Malcolm Clarke at his ranch home near the mouth of Prickly Pear Creek and made off with his horses. Clarke was a former Blackfeet trader, and his wife was a Piegan.

A grand jury identified five Indians by name and indicted them for the murder. Copies of the indictment were sent to Washington. The surrender of the five Indians was demanded. The chiefs of the Piegans agreed to deliver the culprits, but the killers fled to Canada. General Phil Sheridan selected Major Eugene Baker to handle the situation and ordered, "If you have to fight the Indians, hit them hard."

Midwinter was the best time for striking Indian encampments. In subzero weather in January 1870, Baker left Fort Ellis with four troops of cavalry. On January 22, a Piegan camp was spotted on the Marias River. The next morning, the troops struck the camp, killing 173 Indians, among them about fifty women and children. The eastern press shrieked about the deaths of women and children. Sheridan was forced to make an inquiry. Then it came out that Baker had struck the wrong camp. The real culprits had been sheltered by Mountain Chief and were camped up on the Belly River in Canada.

The Baker Massacre broke the fighting spirit of the Blackfeet, who were now convinced that the government had the power and the desire to eliminate them entirely. Treaties continued to be broken as more and more whites came to the territory, taking more and more land. The slaughter of the buffalo doomed the Blackfeet to accepting meager handouts from the whites. With cattle contracts from the government, the Conrads profited from their misfortune.

Darrell Kipp knew who Charles Conrad was, and he didn't necessarily approve of him. "Your ancestors—or *colleagues* of your ancestors—contributed to the Indians' problems by selling whiskey and other items of white culture across the counter to them. They created whiskey addicts! Is that something to be proud of?" He snickered. "Is that 'American'?"

I was dismayed by the attack, and he must have seen this in my face.

"Okay, okay, I'll be nice," said Darrell. He took a slug of beer and cleared his throat. "Let's talk about history first. If the buffalo herds had remained stable, there would've been no problem with the Blackfeet. But they were introduced to a dependent culture. Read K. Ross Toole's books on Montana, and you'll see that the history of Montana is a story of exploitation by a cadre of individuals—the entrepreneurs.

"Your family, the Conrads, didn't come here because they liked the scenery. They came here because of the tremendous profits to be made! Look at it from an Indian point of view: in the winter of 1884, when the Blackfeet were starving on the reservation, less than a hundred miles away in Helena white men like the Conrads would get a gourmet meal of oysters and steak and go to the opera and think nothing of it."

I asked what he thought about the idea of dividing the reservation up, giving each tribal member a portion of land. His face darkened with annoyance.

"Oh, look. All this is an ugly repeat of the Dawes Allotment Act, which was one of the greatest land steals in American history. In 1906 they wanted to give each person 160 acres and then take what's left over. Why shouldn't the Blackfeet hang on to a million and a half acres? Even if there are only three Blackfeet Indians left on earth? The only cohesiveness that remains is when things are held in trust—in communal trust.

"The Dawes Act set the stage for a lot of rip-offs. The Indians were hoodwinked out of their allotments. For food bills! They'd go into the stores of entrepreneurs—your ancestors' colleagues—and buy groceries. When they couldn't pay their food bills, they would lose their forty acres of land to these people. That was an exploitative situation. Let's say this scenario did happen today and we sold out for fifty thousand each. Do you think the Indians would pack up and go to Hawaii or Toledo? No, they'd still be here in Montana. People here want this reservation to survive. So the idea is outlandish. And it's a poorly disguised eradication plan."

I could tell Darrell was warming up. He turned off the music and resumed his position on the couch. "If you deculturate a people, they have to start at the bottom of this culture and work their way up. But they can't even appreciate the aesthetics of their original culture."

Ed Anderson suddenly spoke up. "It's like myself. I went through a lot of hard times with drugs and booze. I couldn't understand if I was a really an Indian or a white guy, because I can pass as a white."

Darrell Kipp nodded. "These days I don't recommend that Indian people study the Blackfeet language out of some kind of psychological militancy that we're going to return to the past; I see it as a step *ahead*. Studying your own language will give you information about yourself. Everybody says, 'I don't speak the language but my grandma does and my older aunt does.' We take it for granted that someone will always be around who speaks it. Well, grandma is going to die. Then we'll ask, 'Who are we?' Without the language we become a different people."

Darrell predicted that of the 250 or so American Indian languages currently spoken, only five will survive by the year 2050. "These languages are endangered species. We should be trying to save them just like we try to save the California condor. And we'll lose some beautiful stuff if they die out. The language! The words! The Indians really did call trains 'the iron horse.' And they called the automobile 'it moves by itself'—also 'skunk wagon,' which I think was appropriate. For motion pictures they say, 'They walked in front of me.' That's the thing: if you don't keep a language alive, then it becomes archaic, without vibrancy. We *should* keep it alive!"

"Do they teach Blackfeet in school?" I asked.

"Browning has a huge remedial reading program. They use flash cards, computers—you name it; they use all the modern methods. Yet I don't think anyone has tried to use two languages—a comparative approach. You've got this language that has a huge attraction to the person. If he's Norwegian, give him Norwegian. If he's Blackfeet, give him Blackfeet. See? You can do amazing things with comparative grammar. Even at its most mediocre it couldn't be any worse than some of the expensive curriculums on the market right now. Yet there's still reluctance to go back."

How did Kipp explain the Blackfeet's attachment to the reservation, even with all its faults?

"There's a human phenomenon recognized by just about everyone: that people want to return to their homeland. The state of Israel is an example. Indian people look to the reservation as a homeland. In the 1950s the Bureau of Indian Affairs relocation program had a goal of dispersing the American Indian from the reservation—'to integrate him into society.' They sent Indian families to cities, urban ghettos. They marooned thousands of Indian people in the ugliest form of city life. Some survived and raised happy, wholesome families. But the majority of them died of violence and alcoholism or wandered home with wrecked lives.

"There's less pressure now to leave the reservation. We have new businesses here, like the pencil factory, but that industry doesn't mesh with our culture. The people who are brought in to fix the latest so-called Indian problem invariably give bad advice, because we're always trying to go in an assimilationist direction. It was done with excellent intentions: to turn Indians into good Americans. And we *have* been good Americans. Many of us served honorably in the military service from the Battle of the Bulge to Vietnam. And we're good citizens of Montana. Indians participate fully in Montana society. Look at the championship high school basketball teams and the rodeo stars. We know the Pledge of Allegiance and the history of Montana. *But we don't even know our own culture!*"

"How will the Indians celebrate the Montana centennial?" I asked.

"Oh, yeah, big Montana state centennial this year," grumbled Darrell. "Everyone's in a joyful mood. Lot of Indians have centennial plates on their cars. Good Montana citizens. But take a careful look at this place a hundred years ago: all in all, the Blackfeet lost 17 million acres of land. So why would we Indians want to celebrate the Montana centennial? I'd think it would be a day of mourning."

One of the major issues facing the tribe today is the question of enrollment. "You have to be at least one-fourth Indian to be a member of the tribe. That was a government directive, but now people don't really know what an Indian is—even themselves. I don't think blood should be the issue. It's not a question of what you *look* like. It's not about *passing* as an Indian. It's about *passing on the heritage.* It's finding out whether you're responsible enough to act the way the older Indians did, who said, 'We can't sell you this land because our grandparents are buried here.' It's just as valid today. They fought to keep this land so that I could sit on this porch next to this beautiful lake. They fought a long hard battle.

"In spite of the assimilation process—forced education, forced Christianization, even architectural and dietetic change—the ethos of these people remains. And we remain Blackfeet Indians. We're not leftovers of, extensions of, or faded memories of this tribe. *We are the dynamic front end of a culture.* Whatever we're doing—whether we're fighting for water rights or sitting in wrecked cars and getting boozed out of our heads—*we are still Blackfeet.*"

There was a moment of silence in the room. Ed Anderson cupped his hands over his mouth and let out a deep breath. The evening sun played through the cottonwood trees, casting a shimmering pattern of light and shadow on the walls of the house. What did all this add up to? Then Darrell spoke. "Hey, guys, this is turning a nice afternoon into a heavy-duty evening. Now, will you shut that goddamn tape recorder off and let's relax and have a drink, okay?" He was smiling now.

Darrell's wife, Roberta, cooked an excellent meal of buffalo steaks, salad, and potatoes. We drank beer and talked into the night. There were many jokes, particularly about academia; Darrell had spent time in Cambridge and Berkeley. He had a wicked sense of humor that I enjoyed immensely. As it grew late, Darrell invited us to stay the night in the tepee, but Ed had to get back to his wife and child in Browning. We walked outside. The canvas tepee was aglow with the light of a small campfire within. Through the doorway I saw Darrell's teenage son, lying in a sleeping bag, watching the coals of the fire, his eyes aglow with waking dreams.

In the cold mountain air, Darrell Kipp and I shook hands heartily. He was a thoughtful man who would not let his guests or himself get away with too much seriousness on a summer night. But he'd planted a host of doubts about my ancestors' role in Montana. I was sorry to go. The long day and the multiple cans of beer suddenly made my head spin; the Indians had reversed things and gotten a Conrad drunk on firewater. I knew I could not drive. Ed Anderson took the wheel of my skunk wagon, *Red Cloud.* Ed may not have been more clear headed, but he would know the winding road back to Browning. After all, it was his home.

The next day Ed sent me out to Star School, a grubby community about five miles from Browning, to meet tribal elder Joe Bear Medicine. The old man's house was clean, and we sat at the dining table. Almost eighty, Joe Bear Medicine was a large man, soft-spoken as a spruce in a low wind. Born and raised on the reservation, he told me of the old days, how he was beaten in school, and of the conflict between the Catholic religion and the Indian ways. He himself was a believer in the Bible but still made use of various plants for Indian medicine.

Joe Bear Medicine said there were fewer full-bloods left in the tribe and fewer people speaking the Blackfeet tongue. "In thirty years the Blackfeet won't exist anymore. They intermarry with the whites—nothing wrong with that. It is human nature. But then they will wonder where the Blackfeet went. It is up to the individual to take responsibility. If you are unhappy, who can you blame? You cannot blame the whites, you cannot blame the Indians. You can only blame yourself. Look at the young ones. They wear braids and they call themselves Indians, but they don't speak Blackfeet. They don't even try to learn it. Me? I don't wear braids. I have short hair. I dress in white man's clothes. But inside, I'm a Blackfeet. And I speak Blackfeet."

Joe Bear Medicine's daughter came in and handed him a manila envelope. From it his gnarled fingers prized a piece of tanned buckskin about a foot long. It was cut in the shape of a miniature buffalo robe and decorated with red and black ink drawings of two tepees, stick-figure men, and bears. "This is a naming pelt. This is how we name people who take an Indian name. It was done for someone who was supposed to come to the annual powwow, but he never showed up. Would you like me to name you?"

I always thought a white man would have to submit to a trial of courage or go on a vision quest before being named; this seemed too easy, some sort of tourist gimmick—and a secondhand name to boot. Before I could politely decline, he confessed that he had been reduced to making a living this way, that it was his only means of income.

"It would be an honor to be named by you," I said.

Joe Bear Medicine's wife came in. We all stood. He spoke in Blackfeet, and Mrs. Bear Medicine translated as we went along. The naming ceremony went like this: "We now give the Blackfeet name to a stranger who has come from afar and is well known for what he does and comes in peace to the Blackfeet, and because of my many experiences in forest fires and having seen many bears, I name him Many Bears."

I was standing with my back to Joe Bear Medicine. When he finished, he gently pushed me forward so that I entered the Blackfeet world with a new name: *A-kok-kiai-wa*, Many Bears. I left fifty dollars with the old man and shook his hand. A good name like that was worth it.

Back at the tackle shop I found Ed Anderson and his wife sitting with a cousin who had driven over from Washington State. Sherry was about thirty, short-statured, with light brown hair. Ed wanted to stay home with his family that evening, so Sherry took me to dinner at the Casino, a twenty-four hour café with electronic poker machines humming away.

Over hamburgers and a Coke, Sherry talked about alcoholism and addictive behavior. She didn't drink because she had once been married to an alcoholic. They lost their infant son in a house fire. Her second husband was better, Sherry said, because he only beat her when he was drunk. She almost lost her second child when this husband, who was cooking in the kitchen at the time, set the child's pajamas on fire. "Burned fifteen percent of the surface of his skin," she said. The doctors did a good job, and the skin graft and scars healed well. That husband took off.

We were interrupted by a teenage Indian who came up and hugged Sherry effusively. He was obviously high on something. His name was Isaac P. Chavez III and he was a drummer in a local band. "Are you playing tomorrow, Isaac?" asked Sherry.

"Yeah, but tonight I'm drunk. I'm just a drunk Indian, right?" he said amiably, to include me in the conversation. "You see, I really am drunk."

"Oh, Isaac, you're playing tomorrow. You shouldn't *do* this to yourself."

"It's *okay.* No problem. Do it all the time." Then he leaned down closer to Sherry. "Hey, do you think you could loan me six dollars?"

"Sorry, Isaac, I can't."

"You mean you don't have six dollars, Sherry?"

"Yes, I do have six dollars, but I need it."

"Hey, I'll pay you back on Monday."

"I can't. But I can smoke you up."

Marijuana? This surprised me after all the talk we had had about alcoholism and addictions. "No thanks, Sherry. I'll see you later." Isaac would get his booze money elsewhere.

With the fall of darkness, the main street of Browning had become a stream of cars filled with Indians. Sherry said the cars cruised all night; sometimes there was trouble. The bar at the War Bonnet Motel was crowded with Indians of various mixes of blood, in various states of inebriation. There were few whites. We had a drink at the bar and talked to Airy Mad Plume. A full-blood, Airy was a trim athletic man, neatly dressed in a cowboy shirt, new blue jeans, and old boots. On his belt flashed an oval-shaped silver buckle with a bucking horse etched in gold—a prize won in a rodeo. Airy had once been a soldier. "I loved the Marine Corps. You know why? Because it was just *me.* Just *me,*" he said slapping his chest. "Full steam ahead!" I suppose he meant that he had been young, in his physical prime. Now, with all the drinks he was putting away, it looked like full-speed backward. Yet he still looked fit and told us he was going to ride in a rodeo tomorrow.

"You're a cowboy?" I asked.

"Me a cowboy? Yeah, I'm a cowboy. Sure! But bear with me, bear *with* me." He was a friendly fellow, but having a conversation with him was like trying to talk to the silver ball running around a roulette wheel. "Hey, I'm American. I'm an American Indian, too. I'm always an American when I'm in America." He finished his drink in a big swallow, then violently slung the ice across the bar, laughing at his own prank.

The part-Indian bartender turned on him: "Hey! Knock that shit off, Airy."

"What shit? I don't see any shit," he said, looking around theatrically.

"I'm not going to serve you if you do that kind of shit, Airy. In fact, I'm *not* going to serve you any more, *period.*"

"Let's get out of here," said Sherry grimly.

We drove back to where Sherry had left her car parked in front of Ed Anderson's tackle shop. I shook her hand and headed back to the War Bonnet Motel.

My room had a garish multicolor shag carpet. I flung off my boots, removed my clothes smelling of trout, sweat, and bar smoke, and got into bed. As I reached to turn out the light, I saw a deep black cigarette burn on the edge of the green Formica nightstand. I thought of Sherry's two children, one killed in a fire, the other burned and scarred for life. How do parents let their children catch on fire?

Then I remembered myself as a small boy of four in San Francisco in 1956. I was dressed in a red Indian costume with yellow plastic fringe on the sleeves. I had a rubber tomahawk and wore a warbonnet with feathers dyed blue and yellow. I was in the kitchen of our first house on Bay Street, watching my mother cook something on a gas stove. When I leaned forward, one of the feathers touched the gas flame, and my warbonnet became a torch. My mother shouted and beat my head with a rag again and again in what seemed an outburst of fury. She knocked the flaming warbonnet to the floor. She slapped my singed and smoking hair with her hands. She stamped on the burning warbonnet with her shoes. I began to cry and she hugged me. Because she was there, because she was not an alcoholic or a pothead, I was not burned.

That was over thirty years in the past. My mother had died two years ago, and all of a sudden I missed her terribly. She was the only person I had ever trusted completely. Then painfully dying of cancer, she wrote a note saying, "I cannot live in this wretched state. I love you all, forgive me," and shot herself with a twenty-two pistol. Maybe that was a reason to come to Montana, and now to cry a little over the past. In a strange motel called the War Bonnet, on an Indian reservation, I realized nobody I knew had a clue where I was at that moment, or even where I'd been all week. I was lonely until I turned out the light.

A. B. Guthrie Jr., author of the classic
novel *The Big Sky,* at his home near Choteau.

Chapter 5

A.B.Guthrie Jr.: Montana's Literary Godfather

"This was man's country onc't. Every water full of beaver and a galore of buffler any ways a man looked, and no crampin' and crowdin'."
A. B. Guthrie Jr., *The Big Sky*

Someone once said that we are all still frontiersmen, only all the frontiers are closed. The one enduring story about Montana's myth of frontier is A. B. Guthrie Jr.'s novel *The Big Sky*. Written in 1947, it is the saga of Boone Caudill, a moody and restless Kentucky sharpshooter who becomes a mountain man in the 1850s—the waning years of the Rocky Mountain fur trade.

My father gave me a copy in 1964, and it was a pretty racy book for a twelve-year-old. Through Guthrie's vivid, even savage depictions of the Wild West, I learned how smallpox devastated the Indian tribes; that Indian men traded women for horses and cut off the noses of adulterous squaws; and that Indian women had sex with white men for money and caught gonorrhea. As the old mountain man Dick Summers recounts to neophyte Boone:

"Light-colored and tall and long-legged and purty as a young filly, and nigh every one of 'em willin', for beads and vermilion or a lookin' glass not as big as your hand. A man got calluses handing the price to the bucks the squaws belonged to. Leastwise, I did them days. I could shine then. And nigh every squaw with the clap and every man catchin' it, and not payin' it no more mind than a sniffle."

I savored exotic passion when Boone fell in love with the Blackfeet maiden Teal Eye and married her: "And she was always ready for him when his body was hungry, not lying still and spraddled, either, like a shot doe, but joining in, unashamed, her legs smooth and warm and strong and her breath whispering in his ear."

And I understood tragedy in the last part of the book: Teal Eye gives birth to a son who is blind, due to smallpox; the boy is also red haired, leading Boone Caudill to believe he has been cuckolded by his best friend, the red-haired Jim Deakins. Goaded by other Indians in camp ("Does the black eagle father the red hawk?"), Caudill kills his only white friend, abandons Teal Eye, and returns to Kentucky. Being neither an Indian nor a white man, he finds little peace on the farm. Homespun clothing and corn bread are a poor substitute for beaded buckskins and fresh buffalo liver. The high mountain winds and bugling elk haunt him from afar. Then Boone learns he has made a great mistake: his mother innocently informs him that her father, a grandfather he never knew, had bright red hair. He has murdered his best friend, slandered his wife, and the wheel of tragedy has turned.

The Big Sky was a best-seller and became a popular film starring Kirk Douglas. The title also became synonymous with Montana, inspiring the "Big Sky Country" logo on the Montana license plate. Guthrie went on to write two more major novels about the frontier—winning the 1950 Pulitzer Prize for *The Way West*—but *The Big Sky* is his best work.

Alfred Bertram Guthrie Jr., known as "Bud" to his friends and family, was now an old man living out the last of his days near Choteau, fifty-five miles northwest of Great Falls. A smoker, Guthrie suffered from emphysema, and his second wife, Carol, was highly protective, turning away all but the most "qualified" fans or visitors. When Carol Guthrie gave me the go-ahead over the phone, I hurried to Choteau to see the eighty-nine-year-old *éminence grizzly.*

It was a long, hot drive with *Red Cloud's* air-conditioning on the blink, so before meeting Guthrie I made for a watering hole. The small town neatly encircled the old county courthouse, yet clearly the epicenter was the Log-Cabin Drive-In, a fifty-year-old hamburger place made of logs painted burnt sienna. At the air-conditioned counter, I gazed up at a four-foot-long varnished brown dinosaur bone that hung from the ceiling and thought about ordering a Stegosaurus Burger, "Medium rare, easy on the Pleistocene sauce." All of Montana and much of the Great Plains was once covered by an inland marsh and sea that now yields rich deposits of dinosaur bones.

The gravel road traversed dry open land, then clumps of jack pine, and eventually crossed the Teton River. The modern house stood alone by the river, and at the door stood a short-haired woman. Carol Guthrie was younger than I expected, maybe sixty. She led me inside to a living room that seemed dark after the day's bright glare, and I made out a somewhat skeletal figure in a chair in the corner.

Bud Guthrie wore a red cotton shirt and khakis held up with red suspenders. There were tubes pumping oxygen into his nose, and his eyes were pale blue, but his rasping voice was still full of intelligence and humor, and his handshake strong. Though Guthrie seemed glad to see me, Carol stayed resolutely by his side during the interview. Every five minutes she'd peer out the window and interrupt to say things like, "What is that darn gardener doing to the trees *now?*"

Guthrie was born in 1901 in Bedford, Indiana, but his parents brought him to the town of Choteau when he was six months old. He grew up wandering the nearby creeks, fishing for trout and shooting ducks, and hearing the old-time ranchers talk about grizzlies, Indians, and rustlers. He worked as a printer's devil for the *Choteau Acantha* and graduated from the University of Montana in Missoula in 1923. He left the state not just for opportunity, but to flee the shackles of Methodist fundamentalism imposed on him by his father, Choteau's high school principal. From 1926 to 1947 he worked on the *Lexington Leader* in Kentucky as a reporter, editorial writer, and finally executive editor. A Nieman Fellowship allowed him to study at Harvard University in 1944–45, where he extensively revised *The Big Sky* before its publication two years later.

Guthrie is chiefly known for six historical novels that give a lusty but unromanticized picture of the settling of the American West from 1830 to World War II. His three finest books were made into films, which Guthrie disliked. He wrote the sixth and last book in the series, *Fair Land, Fair Land,* at age eighty-one. Guthrie told me that, though hampered by the emphysema, he still wrote regularly every afternoon: "I'm not happy if I'm not working." Guthrie's voice took on a moral power in his environmental essays collected in 1988 under the title *Big Sky, Fair Land,* and he was known as a moderate activist.

Just a few miles from Guthrie's house the dry land becomes Pine Butte Swamp, then foothills rising to the eastern front of the Rockies. In 1981 the Nature Conservancy purchased a twenty-two-thousand-acre ranch here. The purchase was originally made to preserve the rich dinosaur finds of paleontologist Jack Horner; now curator of the Museum of the Rockies, Horner discovered a nest of baby duckbill maiasaurs on the Peebles Ranch west of Choteau. But the swampy land below Pine Butte—a rarity in Montana—also happened to be prime grizzly bear habitat. Guthrie wholeheartedly supported the preserve and gave the organization several hundred acres. About ten to twenty bears visited the swamp every year to feed on its berries, tubers, insects, and lush grasses—but they are almost never seen by locals, not even by Guthrie.

Guthrie's son, Bert, is a rancher who views the invisible grizzlies as a threat. A few years ago the Guthries made news when they opposed each other in a public debate over the fate of the grizzly bear. The elder Guthrie, with his eye on the past, sees the grizzly as a symbol of wilderness, to be preserved at all costs. The younger Guthrie, like many ranchers, thinks the grizzly should go the way of the dinosaur. In 1985 a handful of local ranchers pressured two hundred people to sign a petition to remove the grizzly bear from the endangered-species list—the first step toward eradicating the bear as a threat to agriculture and humans. Guthrie responded with a series of provocative letters to the local paper, making himself a pariah but also a hero. (Two years later the ranchers tried to declare the Endangered Species Act unconstitutional, but lost in court.)

When Lewis and Clark crossed Montana they found many grizzly bears feeding far out on the plains. Gradually, man's incursion forced them back into the mountains. "The grizzly became an issue in Choteau when he ventured out of the mountains and onto the plains again," said Guthrie. "Ranchers on the feed lots were careless in disposing of dead sheep carcasses. They attracted the bears, which then began killing sheep—maybe twenty in all. That made the ranchers sore. The bears also raided some commercial beehives. The ranchers wouldn't listen to any suggestions. They just wanted to shoot the bears. I think they did shoot a few. They have a motto: Shoot, Shovel, and Shut Up. I can understand why they would be mad at losing livestock. But they just wouldn't listen to any suggestions. Now that Fish, Wildlife, and Parks are removing the carcasses up into the mountains, we've had no trouble with bears."

"So people in Choteau were hostile?" I asked.

"A sort of hysteria prevailed around Choteau," said Guthrie. "Reports of grizzlies right in town. Untrue reports. People were saying they were afraid to let their children go fishing in the streams around here. Altogether silly. One bear got as far as Fairfield, about eighteen miles from Choteau. A rancher saw it. Word got around that a bear had been seen there. They came with tranquilizers. He was located in a patch of timber—"

"Nowhere near a house," interjected Carol.

"In a windbreak nowhere near a house," continued Guthrie. "He hadn't done a bit of damage. All kinds of people flocked there—with *kids!*"

"This was about six o'clock in the morning," said Carol.

"The kids got out and were throwing *rocks* into the timber," said Guthrie. "They let the kids do *that*. Well, fortunately the authorities got the bear tranquilized. But pestered like that, even a *cow* would charge you if you mistreated her enough."

"Almost sounds like a witch-hunt," I said.

"Here's another example of that hysteria: an old she-bear down at Sperry's ranch had been coming there every summer for years, never did a bit of damage. I even talked to the rancher about it. He said, 'Why, that bear has never done anything wrong.' Well, two years ago she was there with a couple of cubs. And some fool shot the mother bear in the jaw and left her to bleed to death. That left the cubs. They became a problem. A man-caused problem. I think all the ranchers were celebrating."

"The ranchers are hard-nosed," said Carol. "They don't want any government interference—yet they live very nicely on all the government agricultural subsidies."

Guthrie said, "One rancher who grazes sheep up here on Forest Service land under a permit was suspected of killing grizzlies—it was really grizzly habitat—so they revoked his license. There was so much of a stink they had to *reinstate* his license. My contention is that if a rancher is willing to gamble his livestock in definitely hazardous bear territory, then he'd better be willing to take his losses. I never heard of anyone repaying a Las Vegas gambler."

Guthrie took a moderate stance on troublesome bears. "I've always believed in accommodation. For instance, if park rangers find a bear to be repeatedly troublesome to humans, they shoot him. Which is right. They've tried to transport grizzlies, but it hasn't worked out very well. They take him miles away—to the middle fork of the Flathead, for instance—but in two weeks the bear will be back. In the old days, the free lunch was here with all those sheep carcasses. But that's no longer a problem. And the beehives have been surrounded with electric fences—again at state expense."

Bud suddenly coughed, wheezed, coughed again, and rasped, "Forgive me."

I felt a wrench of sympathy, watching this old man gamely hanging on to life.

He caught his breath. "When the people around Choteau got so upset, you should have seen the support we got—and still get—from around the country. Hundreds of letters. The Audubon Society did an interview with me."

"What do other people in Montana think of the bears?" I asked.

"Some years back, school kids in Helena, I think, were asked to choose an appropriate animal to be the Montana state animal. The ranchers were all for the elk. The kids would have none of that; they voted overwhelmingly for the grizzly! We need the grizzly as a symbol, as an indication that wilderness is still here. But we got nowhere with that philosophy. We proudly say we conquered the wildnerness. But we did a lot of damage in the process. We exterminated the buffalo. We raised hell with the forest. We exhausted the gold. Ran out of silver. Ran out of copper. And now we're selling more and more coal, which is our last unrenewable resource. They can't see that an end comes to all this.

"We've also had very little sensitivity to historical preservation. The only building of significance in Choteau is the courthouse. Some kind of bastard Italian architecture. But it's built of native stone, quarried from the butte just out of town. I remember when I was a little boy people used to say, 'It won't last very long because it's sandstone.' Well, it's been there quite a while now—as long as I've been kicking." He gave a wheezy laugh. "That's almost a century!"

Guthrie asked about my search for the Conrads, whose family history he knew through his interest in Fort Benton and the fur trade. He was happy to hear that the replica of the keelboat *Mandan* used in the filming of *The Big Sky* was still on display on the Fort Benton waterfront. "I engineered that," said Guthrie proudly. "It reminds people of the early days of the fur traders—the generation before the Conrads and Powers came out with their steamboats." He pointed across the room to a miniature model of the *Mandan* sitting on his bookcase.

What did Guthrie see in the future for Montana? "There is a feeling—and a fear—that the family ranches are fading out. That the ranches will be owned by syndicates and absentee owners, run by hired hands. That may happen. People think bringing in industry is going to solve their problems. That is a forlorn expectation. What kind of industry? There's no big labor force here. Thank goodness."

"What if the population increases?"

"I'm not interested in seeing Montana get bigger. I want it to get *better.* I want more and better libraries. I want a better school system. A story came out recently that said that parents were satisfied with the school system in Montana. Well, I'd say they were satisfied too easily."

Bud Guthrie was growing noticeably fatigued. When I caught Carol's eye she confirmed with a nod that it was time for him to go back on the oxygen, and time for me to go. As I drove away from Bud Guthrie's world, I thought how important it was that he had expressed in his books both the adventure of Manifest Destiny and the sadder fates it brought to the land, the grizzly, and the native peoples.

Two years later, Bud Guthrie entered the Big Sky. His death left me wondering who would show us the way, who would mark the trail of the West with the right words.

Artist Charles Russell at his studio in
Great Falls with his renowned painting
When the Land Belonged to God. (Courtesy
Montana Historical Society)

Chapter 6

Great Falls: Grave Robbers and Missileers

I have been called a pioneer. In my book a pioneer
is a man who comes to a virgin country, traps all
the fur, kills off all the wild meat, cuts down all
the trees, grazes off all the grass, plows the
roots up, and strings ten million miles of wire. A
pioneer destroys things and calls it civilization.
I wish to God that this country was just like
it was when I first saw it and that none of you
folks were here at all.

> Charles M. Russell, addressing a group of
> Montana businessmen circa 1920

Great Falls, which overlooks the Missouri River, was once the largest city in Montana. The Anaconda Company built a copper smelter here with a 508-foot smokestack, the tallest in the world. The city was supposed to become the Chicago of the plains, but it was shouldered aside by the oil boom that pumped Billings to prominence in the 1950s. With a population of sixty thousand, the city's largest employer is Malmstrom Air Base, which pumps $135 million a year into the economy. Like many a town whose livelihood depends on the military, Great Falls lacks vibrancy and originality.

I was therefore happy to find the Three Pheasant Inn, a charming bed-and-breakfast run by Amy Sloan and her husband, Dave, a twenty-six-year-old air force lieutenant who commuted to nearby Malmstrom Air Base. Dave was a missileer; his job was to go underground and, should the command be issued, turn a series of keys to fire missiles bearing nuclear warheads. His job had combat status, and he went to work in a flight suit. When he wasn't on alert, he worked on the inn. With clever carpentry, antique bath fixtures, and a gazebo in the garden—plus a few moose and deer heads, split-bamboo fly rods, and wicker fishing creels—Dave and Amy had turned their once-dumpy house into something out of an L. L. Bean catalog. My bedroom had a refinished wooden trunk at the foot of the quilted bed, and a decanter of sherry sat on the mahogany dresser.

The founder of Great Falls, Paris Gibson, was a native of Maine who made a fortune producing world-acclaimed woolen blankets in Minneapolis before coming west in the 1870s. While sheep ranching near Belt, he purchased thousands of acres of open prairie land, then contacted his old friend from Minneapolis, the railroad tycoon James J. Hill. Hill commissioned him to buy land for the railroad's westward route.

By 1883, Gibson had platted the Great Falls town site. Two hundred people lived in his upstart city the first year, with Gibson himself inhabiting a tent. When Hill's railroad arrived in 1887, hundreds of settlers disembarked on the stark prairie, and in three years there were almost four thousand residents. Gibson served as the first mayor and later went to Washington as a U.S. senator.

A shaded burg in the middle of Montana's vast wheat fields, today Paris Gibson's city grows stale as it sleeps. Downtown was a checkerboard of old brick buildings and empty parking lots that marked the graves of demolished buildings. One wooden hotel, scarred by a top-floor fire, was scheduled to become HUD housing—if it wasn't torn down. Another was now low-income housing for Indians and the elderly. The energy that once made Great Falls a major western city had been siphoned off to a commercial strip with used-car lots, McDonald's, Fabric Land, Silent Knight Mufflers, a strip joint called the Playground, and Tokyo Massage (where Korean ex-wives of airmen function as prostitutes).

That evening, Dave and Amy Sloan took me over to Malmstrom Air Base for dinner at the officer's mess. Some three thousand people lived on the base; about five hundred servicemen and their families lived off base. A sign at the gate said, "Peace Is Our Profession." After showing ID to a woman soldier at the guardhouse, we pulled up to a museum surrounded by several exhibition aircraft, including the B-25. The base museum was filled with memorabilia describing its raison d'être, the Minuteman missiles. Pushing a button below a map of Montana lit up the two hundred missile sites "hidden" around the state, mostly concentrated around Great Falls.

Dave Sloan dispelled several myths about missileers. For example, when visitors were invited to inspect an underground center, they saw officers wearing guns. "They're not to protect themselves from each other or to force renegade staff to comply with orders. The pistols are only worn in case the visitors try anything funny. After the visit ends, the guns come off. Also, there is no 'button.' Special keys are turned to launch a missile, so it's impossible for one mad missileer to act alone and fire a missile."

A weird thing happened to Dave the first year he was at Malmstrom: a superior officer took a tainted interest in him. "We were on alert together. He suddenly said, 'Let's see what you've got in your pants.' I said, 'What?' thinking he was joking. He insisted: 'Let's see what you got.' Then he put his hand on his pistol and I got scared. The guy was sick. I managed to talk him into putting the gun away. I reported him immediately. He started lying and saying I was homosexual. It turned out that he'd been having affairs all over the base, with men and women.

"They conducted an inquiry, and just before bringing it to a court-martial, he resigned. But simply because I had been involved in a problem—in *his* problem—my own status was under tight scrutiny. The air force doesn't tolerate much. If you show up drunk on alert, or even just make a problem in town while you're drunk, you could be demoted and taken out of combat status."

For laughs, Dave provided me with an anonymous printout he found of the captain's log at G01 Launch Control Center:

> The primary function of the penis is to find and reach its goal, at which time delivering a powerful ballistic load, capable of altering the entire geography of its target and wreaking general havoc throughout the structure of the surrounding environment.
>
> The primary function of a missileer is analogous to the male's performance during sexual intercourse. A computer over which the operator has little control, once turned on, provides detailed instructions for release without further advice from him. The operator has only the most basic knowledge of how the entire system works, nor is such detailed knowledge necessary to the successful accomplishment of the end result. The operator is ready to deliver his package with only a moment's notice and able to consummate the act in minutes (hence the term "Minuteman"). Intimate knowledge of who the target is, or how the target feels, or the future of the target is not necessary. The

operator may never have met, nor ever meet again, the subject of his act. Once the payload is released, the responsibility belongs totally to someone else. All of the action will now occur on the receiving end, beginning at the point of impact. Missile launching is as manly as a one night stand.

Ragin' Cajun

"Pretty kinky, Dave," I said.

"I thought you'd like that stuff," he chuckled.

"Not exactly what you want a woman soldier to read. Might even be considered sexual harassment by the humorless."

"Actually, a lot of the women get a kick out the Ragin' Cajun's rantings."

Dave gave me a quick tour of the base, a nearly self-contained community with restaurants, health clinics, sports facilities, and old hangars converted to recreational centers. Malmstrom Air Base has the biggest police force in the state, about six hundred security policemen. Some were female; women also served as missile launch officers. The police not only maintain security at the base, but protect the hundreds of unmanned missile stations out in the field.

Signs warned us to stay on designated roads.

"Hey, Dave, what would happen if I got out of the car and started walking for that building over there?"

"The one where the jets are?"

"Yeah."

"You want to know?"

"Yeah."

"In about thirty seconds two guys in a jeep would come screaming up to you, jump out, and kick your nuts off. They'd stick an M-16 to your head, lock handcuffs on you, and take you away for further questioning."

"Sounds fair to me."

"Don't mention my name if you decide to try it."

Three hundred men and women in jumpsuits, fatigues, and airmen's dress were chowing down at the officer's mess hall. The women were in uniform, too, but wives wore anything they wanted. Over barbecued chicken and beer, Dave pointed out flight commanders and introduced old friends. It didn't seem like a bad life if you were in your twenties. Dave and Amy had been stationed in Montana for three years now, and he was getting out of the service the next summer, ready to return to the East Coast.

Before I left, he sold me two T-shirts, the proceeds going to the squadron's community chest. The first T-shirt bore a mushroom cloud and

the motto Nuke 'Em Til They Glow. The second depicted a missile emblazoned with a beer can being launched: "Ivan, This Bud's for You!"

By 1890, the era of steamboats and wagon trains had given way to railroads. In moving his power base from Fort Benton to Great Falls, my great-
great-uncle William Conrad remade himself from whiskey trader and
frontier merchant into banker and politician. A cartoon of the day depicted
him as a "collector" chasing banks with a butterfly net, and by the turn of
the century he owned nearly a dozen banks between Livingston and Helena.
He and brother Charles founded the Conrad National Bank in Great Falls,
and expanded into real estate and livestock.

Though William had been a state senator for years and was often urged
to seek the governorship, he wanted to go to Washington. At that time, the
U.S. senator was elected by members of the state legislature rather than by
popular vote. Beginning in 1899, William made four impressive bids for the
Senate but never won; his failures were almost a badge of honor at a time
when Montana politics were at their most corrupt.

At the historical archives, I flipped through the tattered pages of the
Great Falls Tribune, but the Conrad story that caught my eye was not about
politics. The headline for November 26, 1909, was:

BODY OF INFANT IS STOLEN FROM ITS GRAVE
BY GHOULS

Believed That Fiends Are Holding Remains of Infant Son of Mr. and
Mrs. Harfield Conrad for Ransom—One of the Most Revolting
Crimes Ever Committed in Northern Montana—Are Searching for
Clews.

I read on with morbid fascination. In 1909, twenty-six-year-old Harfield
Conrad, William's eldest son, was vice president of the Conrad Circle Cattle Company and a prominent member of the Great Falls community. His
three-year-old son, Arthur, had died of meningitis in April. One morning in
late November the sexton of Highland Cemetery was shocked to find the
child's empty coffin lying by the main gates. Working with the police,
Harfield announced to the papers, "No expense will be spared in running
the ghouls to earth."

A letter arrived asking for a ransom of five thousand dollars. It was signed
"W. C. Hastings." The grave robber ordered Harfield to drive alone in a
light buggy without a top along the Sand Coulee Road at evening.

Harfield's family and the police insisted a deputy sheriff be sent in his place. At the last minute, the body snatchers smelled a ruse, evaded a posse with bloodhounds, and escaped into the hills.

Almost a year passed with no news from the body snatchers. Then, in May 1911, Harfield received a letter asking for just fifteen hundred dollars in twenty-dollar gold pieces. The letter was long, with detailed instructions on how and where the sack of money was to be delivered. Again, it was signed "W. C. Hastings." Harfield and his younger brother Arthur hatched a plan with their old friend, retired sheriff Josephus Hamilton; they would get the bastard. Instead of gold pieces they would leave a sack of iron washers. Hamilton told Harfield, "Look, you take your brother Arthur with you. I'll follow your car on my saddle horse. By the time you drop that bogus sack, I'll ride up and catch the criminals red-handed."

The Conrad brothers set out from the Rainbow Hotel in their car at about 10 P.M., heading toward Fort Benton. Harfield had a shotgun, and Arthur was armed with two automatic pistols. Five miles down the road they saw a light—the signal—and threw out the sack of washers. Continuing down the road about a mile, they were surprised to find another lantern by the roadside. Realizing they'd goofed, they improvised and dropped a handkerchief, hoping the blackmailers would mistake it for a sack. They drove a half mile down the road and again turned around.

When the Conrad boys reached the handkerchief drop, they saw a man's silhouette in the dusk about three hundred feet away. Gunning the automobile, Harfield and Arthur opened fire as they sped by. Reaching the spot where they'd first dropped the bag of washers, they found no sign of Joe Hamilton. A horrible thought crossed their minds. Driving back, they found a riderless horse on the hillside. A little farther on they found a bullet-riddled body. They'd killed the sheriff. The autopsy revealed that the two bullets had come from an automatic pistol—Arthur's gun. Both brothers were devastated, but Arthur was prostrate with guilt and grief.

The body of little Arthur Conrad was never recovered, the ghouls were never captured, and the case was closed. A rather sad oil portrait of the little boy in a sailor suit and high-topped boots hangs today in the Cascade County Historical Society.

In 1914, William Conrad died in his native Virginia, at his rebuilt plantation house, Montana Hall. The Great Depression destroyed the Conrad banking empire, and Harfield's own taste for high living depleted the fortune he inherited from his father. He had grown up the son of a Montana millionaire, but he died in humble circumstances in 1953 in Seattle. When his brother Arthur committed suicide, some old-timers in Great Falls said it was out of guilt for having shot the sheriff years before.

The only true hero of Great Falls was a cowboy and painter named Charles M. Russell, and the city has honored him with a museum. Mostly underground, this modern concrete bunker was packed with Russell's masterpieces of life in the Wild West—Indians hunting buffalo, cowboys roping longhorns, and wounded grizzlies attacking trappers. The real treasures were dozens of illustrated letters.

Next door stood Russell's clapboard house and his log cabin studio, preserved as a shrine. On his easel sat an unfinished painting, as if Charlie had just stepped away for a moment. A grizzly bear skin hung on the wall, a buffalo robe lay on the floor, and there were enough guns, saddles, and Indian artifacts to remind you how the West was lost.

Over the years, Montanans have elevated Charlie Russell to the status of a saint in spurs. His art was everywhere. Reproductions hung in motel rooms, bars, and the offices of service stations. His name was attached to high schools, parks, wildlife preserves, and motels, while an annual statewide contest had schoolchildren write an essay titled "Why I Like Charlie Russell." For Montanans he brings to mind Will Rogers, Norman Rockwell, and George Washington in composite. "Charlie Russell slept here" is something people like to say when bragging about their cabin or ranch house. His masterpiece is the giant mural in the capitol building at Helena, which depicts Lewis and Clark meeting the Indians—from the Indians' point of view. At Sotheby's, Russell's canvases have sold for over a million dollars.

Born in 1864 to a family of St. Louis industrialists, the schoolboy Russell was a disappointment to his Yale-educated father. Young Charlie filled his lesson books with sketches of Indians inspired by the tales he heard about his great-uncle William Bent, a legendary frontiersman who founded the trading post Bent's Fort, in Colorado. Charlie's father thought that a visit out west would cure the boy's frontier fantasies, and at sixteen he was sent to Montana.

Russell worked first for the meat hunter Jake Hoover, who probably killed more bears than any other man in Montana. He then hooked up with the cowboy Patrick Tucker, who got the wide-eyed greenhorn a job with a cattle outfit. Charlie spent ten seasons on the open range with saddle pounders who ranged from amiable gypsies to men with a price on their head. While Theodore Roosevelt found "the moral tone of a cow camp rather high" in 1883, Russell and his cronies generally ended the season whooping it up with whiskey and whores in saloons where, in his words, "a rattlesnake would be embarrassed to meet his mother."

During the winter, no self-respecting cowboy would work at any other kind of job. They usually lived in cheap quarters where a dollar here and a dollar there would hold them through springtime. Russell soon found that sketches of cowboys or a wax figure of a grizzly bear could be traded for drinks at the bar. His early art was just an amusement, a way to tell a story. In 1891, Russell was commissioned to do a painting on the vault door of the Lewistown Bank. He was paid twenty-five dollars for his six hours of work—a month's wages for a cowboy—and his earnings were immediately spent buying drinks for the house.

Russell's eccentric personality brought him as much notoriety as did his pictures. By most reports, he was one of the grubbiest cowboys who ever rode the range. He would wear a shirt until it became filthy with grease and campfire smoke. He and a friend once had a competition to see who could find the largest louse on their bodies. His ripeness finally goaded a bunch of cowboys to strip him and scrub him in boiling water, a fracas that nearly destroyed the bunkhouse.

He also saw some of the harsher aspects of range life, and once helped rescue two girls who had been kidnapped; he and some other cowboys hanged the bad men and left them for the coyotes and crows.

Russell spent one winter with the Blood Indians in Canada. He let his hair grow, learned their language and customs, and sometimes wished he were an Indian. Lamenting the passing of the buffalo and the arrival of the settlers, he felt a kinship with the tribe and the Great Spirit. In his paintings, the recurring image of a pretty Indian woman, Keoma, hints of a romance. Russell painted the Indians as they had been a decade before, mythologizing the last of a noble breed riding across a wild unfenced prairie. In his homespun manner, Russell wrote:

> The red man was the true American They have almost gon but
> will never be forgotten The history of how they faught for thier
> country is written in blood a stain that time cannot grinde out their
> God was the sun their Church all out doors their only book was na-
> ture and they knew all its pages

At thirty-one Russell fell for Nancy Cooper, a seventeen-year-old visiting from the East. When the boys back at the Silver Dollar heard that Russell had given Nancy his horse Monte, they knew they'd lost him forever. Charlie and Nancy married and moved to Great Falls, where he immediately began a series of ambitious oils. His father sent him enough money to build a lovely clapboard house in a fashionable part of town—which made Nancy happy. Painting in a parlor didn't suit a man used to smoke-filled bunkhouses and tepees, so Russell built a log cabin studio next door.

Then—as now—magazine editors knew that the West held a mystique for the rest of the nation, especially as the railroads traversed the Rocky Mountains and the first tourists ventured westward. At that time, Frederic Remington was the most famous western illustrator in America. Remington and Russell had come out west the same year, but the Yale-educated Remington, three years older, and ambitious with his contacts, experienced a phenomenal success as an illustrator for *Harper's Weekly* and *Harper's Monthly*. He visited the West only to gather more material. While Russell still drank with cowboys, Remington lunched with dignitaries at the Players Club and led a gentleman's existence in Manhattan.

Russell had no connections in the East and could barely sell enough pictures to pay for groceries. His prices remained so low that my great-great-uncle Charles Conrad wrote to his wife, Lettie, in 1897: "I saw *Keoma,* the Russell painting in Butte, the owner wanted $150 for it. I think I can get it cheaper. If he talks trade, told John Howard [my great-grandfather] to let him ship it at $95 or $100." Charles eventually bought three other oil paintings by Russell, including *Indian Couch, Indian Scouts,* and *Running Buffalo,* later sold by his descendants.

Getting higher prices for her husband's work became an obsession for Nancy Russell. The Russells made a trip to New York in 1903, and had a little show in a basement gallery. Although the press was kind, few pictures were sold, and Russell was only too happy to get out of New York. "Too many tepees," he said. "The bartenders won't drink with you even. Now I like to have a bartender drink with me occasionally, out of the same bottle, just to be sure I ain't getting poison."

Nancy managed to get Russell to visit New York again, and persuaded Tiffany's to accept two bronzes on consignment. By 1911, Charlie had a one-man show at the Folsom Galleries on Fifth Avenue. The show was billed as "The West That Has Passed," and even the *New York Times* raved. In a bold gesture, Nancy priced several of the pictures at six thousand dollars apiece and sold two. Now the Russells made trips to London and California and found greater financial success, something that gave Nancy pleasure and left Russell merely amused. He was missing the wind in the buffalo grass.

Paris Gibson, the founder of Great Falls, had come to Montana in 1879, just a year earlier than Charlie Russell. Both loved the land, but in different ways. Gibson looked to the future, envisioning a city shaded with elms, and saw the great falls of the Missouri as a source for electrical power; Russell saw only the natural beauty of the land and river. Gibson imagined the plains filling with wheat fields and sheep, while Russell saw the ghosts of buffalo and the vanishing Indians.

Even as the klaxon of motorcars replaced the whinny of horses, Charlie Russell painted away in his log cabin studio. The rough and rugged past became a kind of buckskin paradise in his art. He had known the Indian tribes just a few generations removed from the Stone Age, and they called him a brother. He had seen the great herds of buffalo replaced by the bawling of Texas longhorns and watched men killed over a pair of aces. He had seen sodbusters plow up the old wagon trails and had heard the train whistle wail across the land of the Blackfeet, Crow, and Sioux.

When Charlie Russell "changed ranges" in late October 1926, the whole town of Great Falls turned out in grief. Hundreds of men wept in saloons. Among the mourners following the horse-drawn hearse were a considerable number of Indians who had come to see off a true friend on his journey to the Shadow Land.

For Montanans today, Charlie Russell's vision remains more powerful than Paris Gibson's idea of progress. Russell's words about the destruction wrought by "pioneers" made me uneasy about claiming ancestors like the Conrads, because their vision was Paris Gibson's; as true believers in nineteenth-century entrepreneurship, they ultimately violated the land and its resources, as well as the lives of the Indians.

Southeast of Great Falls, I stopped at a place called Stockett. Once a coal-mining town of two thousand, Stockett now has less than five hundred citizens, and most of them, at some time or other, end up in the American Bar, a classic joint with plenty of deer heads on the walls. Hunting and fishing licenses were sold here; so were ham-and-cheese sandwiches. The proprietor, Smitty, was telling me how he moved out here in 1947 from Illinois, "with the oil people," when in came a husky old fellow in a billed cap.

"Hey, Smitty," said the man as he plunked an ice chest on the bar.

"Hello, Bob."

"Need some ice, Smitty."

"What for?"

"For my ice chest."

"I don't know if we can get it for you, Bob."

"Well, I need it! I'm going down to the Smith River and go fishing."

"What are you fishing for?"

"Just anything I can get. But first I got to go over and get my calf and scrub him up in a lanolin bath, get all the manure off him, get him real clean, give him a nice straw bed, and take him to the county fair. And I'm goin' to tickle his testicles a little bit and maybe he'll give me a kiss."

"Bob, I hope he gives it to you right on the lips."

"I hope so, too."

"Here's your ice. See you around."

"See you round, Smitty."

Back on the main road, I followed the Belt Creek valley up into the Belt Mountains. The wind ruffled the valley's dry grass like fur on a buffalo's back. The farmhouses were old and white, the barns red. The road dropped into the Lewis and Clark National Forest, and the air was suddenly cool among the trees. I passed the old town of Monarch, which still has cabins and a few Victorian houses, and drove by the Lazy Doe, with its sign for "Cocktails and Dining."

Neihart was a small hamlet of wooden buildings that had once been famed for silver mines, several owned by William and Charles Conrad. The old bank was boarded up, the livery falling down, but I could still make out the writing on the false front of the Wu Tang Laundry. Neihart was now populated mainly by people from Great Falls who owned weekend cabins. As I crossed the bridge spanning Belt Creek, I saw a trout jump. I parked south of town and took out my fly rod.

Walking up the creek, I coaxed a strike from a small fish, and released him easily from my barbless hook. From a deep pool surrounded by the twisted roots of an old pine tree, I took two twelve-inchers on a Woolly Worm. Catch-and-release fishing is shaking hands with nature; no need to carry a relationship too far. Letting the second rainbow go, I was content; the fish probably weren't any bigger than that in this creek, and I wasn't trying to set any records. So I sat on the bank for a while, just listening to the water and watching a troop of large black ants haul a big fat white grub over the bark of a tree root. I must have nodded off for half an hour. When I stood up, brushing pine needles from my wool shirt, the shadows had grown long.

Before leaving Neihart, I stopped in at Bob's Bar for a beer. The original Bob has been gone for decades, and it was now owned by Tony, who wears a derby hat and waxes his mustache into a six-inch wingspan. Like many

Montana bars, in addition to liquor, potato chips, and beer nuts, Bob's Bar made a business of selling caps—the kind farmers, truckers, or mechanics wear. One said, "Bob's Bar, Neihart, Montana." Fair enough. Another said, "Retired, Too Old to Work, Too Dumb to Steal, Too Lazy to Move." Still another bore the crude fatalistic message "Shit Happens." Another had no writing whatsoever on it, just the silhouette of a bull elk humping a female elk.

Tony admitted that running Bob's Bar was a quiet life. I believed him. After another cold beer, I said good-bye, and Tony's life got even quieter.

The town of Conrad as it looked in 1906.

Left: Hutterite elder Chris Waldner with young neighbors.

Right: Dorothy Floerchinger at the Fort Conrad site near Marias River.

Chapter 7

From Fort Conrad to the Hutterite Colony

Fort Conrad! What memories I have of it: the busy days of trade; the quiet peace; the stirring adventures there and thereabout in the long-ago days of the buffalo.

James Willard Schulz, *Great Falls Tribune*, 1939

"We're going to build a farming center right here," says that hombre, "and make millions out of cutting this all into small farms and a town site; in another two years you'll see this country in waving grain fields and supporting happy families."
"That sounds all right," says Old Dan. "But I'll bet if anybody gets any riches or happiness out of farming this land, it won't be the families."

Will James, *Cow Country*, 1931

North of Great Falls the land was covered by hundreds of Minuteman missile silos. Driving across the open prairie I suddenly saw a small chain-link enclosure with a few lights and warning devices. No need for armed guards: the missiles are under a cement slab ten feet thick.

Ledger Road took me past the settlement of Ledger—not really a town, just houses clustered around the Farmers Union grain elevator. I turned onto Dead Indian Road. From the wheat fields loomed a huge cement bunker with slanted sides that looked like the base of an unfinished Mayan pyramid. It was an antiballistic-missile site started in 1972 and left incomplete, an enormous palace of poured concrete thirty feet high, with walls ten feet thick.

What I saw was the tip of the iceberg; the ABM center was sunk seven stories beneath the prairie, constructed, it was said, to withstand a first strike by the Soviets. After President Nixon abandoned the project, it would have cost millions to demolish it. So they left it standing in the wheat fields. On the walls were graffiti in fading red paint: "172 Million Dollar Monument to America's Stupidity." There was also a black silhouette of a human being; this painted target had nearly been obliterated by shots from a high-powered rifle.

I stepped inside and set off a deafening explosion: a horde of pigeons and swallows burst from the rafters. Water dripped off the walls, and the chill air was a relief after the hot sun outside. The seven-story-deep cavity had been filled in with earth. With open doors at both ends, wind whistled through the structure. There was enough room in here to house ten basketball courts. With a little thought and a lot of money it could become a museum or school. Today, the ABM center serves as a rendezvous for beer-drinking high school students, some of whom may have lost their virginity here, judging from a few condom wrappers. A mass of tumbleweeds, blown from all over the land, huddled in the center of the cool tomb—a hunk of concrete that will stand for a thousand years.

The country alternated between wheat fields, rolling hills of grass, and coulees where streams did their business in spring, then died. Bland farming settlements clustered around grain silos, more whistlestops than towns. This was the Golden Triangle, the richest wheat land in Montana. The furrow lines ran through the wheat fields like op art. And then, a sign with my name on it: "Conrad."

This was the town William Conrad founded in 1906. In the old days, the tallest structure in Conrad would have been a church spire; now it's a grain elevator. *Red Cloud* bumped over the railroad tracks and rumbled past the Branding Iron, a dinner house offering bowling and cocktails. Another big sign: "Welcome to Conrad, Home of the Conrad Cowboys, State Class B Boys Rodeo." Then came a yard full of tractors, Rocky's Welding, the Prairie Schooner bar, the Ancient Mariner restaurant (closed), and office of the newspaper, the *Independent-Observer*. The smaller the town, the longer the paper's name. On the street corner stood white trash cans marked "Help Keep Conrad Clean" (something my friends have been saying for years). I was tempted to steal one.

The town was a real-estate project developed from the Conrad Circle Cattle Company. Having watched Paris Gibson create Great Falls, William wanted his own agricultural metropolis. "I'm a builder-upper," he once said, "not a tearer-downer." Unlike the colorful mining towns of Montana, which are primarily Victorian, most of Conrad's houses were built in the twenties by farmers. As a result, this white-bread, tree-shaded community is architecturally dull, from Main Street right out to the neighborhoods on the prairie's edge.

I spent the night with my distant cousins Herb and Betty Conrad, a retired lawyer in his seventies and a former schoolteacher, respectively. On the wall of the living room hung the family's prize possession, an original watercolor of a Mandan warrior by Charlie Russell. "My dad bought it when he first came out here," said Herb.

Though they were congenial hosts, I wondered why they didn't own a ranch, ride horses, hunt antelope, or at least fly-fish in the nearby Rockies. They seemed so unrugged, so citified, so un-Montanan. Following a trend among young Montanans, nearly all their children had left the state for cities on both coasts. "None of them wanted to live in Conrad," said Betty sadly. "They always called it 'Dodge,' as in 'Get out of Dodge.' And that's what they did."

The next morning I went out for breakfast at the Home Café and found it bustling at the nine o'clock coffee hour. The conversation consisted mainly of agricultural news.

"You plant your west eighty yet?"

"Yup."

"Your barley comin' in good?"

"Yup, comin' in good. How about yours?"

"Comin' in good, too."

I was reading the newspapers when someone tapped my shoulder. A gray-bearded cowboy smiled down at me. "Heard there was a Conrad in town and wanted to say howdy. I'm Bob Boucher. My dad, Curly Boucher, used to ride for the Conrads' Seven Block."

Over a cup of coffee, Bob said he and his brother Tom now owned the Seven Block brand. From his wallet he pulled a faded old photograph of a cowboy riding herd. Walden "Curly" Boucher had been one of the region's best-known cowboys, and inspired the character Curly in B. M. Bower's classic boy's novel of the West, *Chip of the Flying U.* "Look how Dad sits his horse. He was one heck of a guy."

That's the way Montanans talk about fathers—with respect for men who labored hard and "cowboyed-up" under harsh conditions.

"My horse, Partner, he's got to go over to the vet. Wrecked his leg on a fence and it's come back sore. If you'd like, I'll take you along."

Bob's truck and horse trailer were a nice rig, and in the back of the truck was a three-legged sheepdog. "That's Tippy. She got kicked by Partner a while back and the leg had to come off, but they get along just fine now."

The veterinarian's clinic was on the edge of town. There were already several animals waiting outside, including a llama with an eye infection. Inside we found veterinarian Dick Kinyon working on a horse clamped in the metal gates of the examining chute. A husky balding man, Dick had his arm buried up to the elbow in the mare's vagina. The mare snorted, showed lots of white around the eyeball, and stomped her hooves. Dick withdrew his arm with an audible *slurp* and cleaned up.

"Well, she's not pregnant," he said to the owner. "And she's a little sensitive when I touched her ovaries. But then I'd be a little sensitive if someone were touching *my* ovaries, too. She's fine."

The next patient, the llama, looked highly disagreeable as Dick swabbed her infected eye, but she didn't bite or spit. Llamas have become a cottage industry in Montana for several reasons. Ranchers add one to a flock of sheep because they're tough enough to fight coyotes. They are also being used as pack animals for recreational hikers, while other people breed them for their soft wool. A good llama was worth fifteen thousand dollars, more than many horses.

Bob unloaded Partner, a big chestnut gelding who clomped amiably into the vet's office. Just above the hoof line of his left forefoot rose a crusted red sore. Dick placed Partner's hoof on a two-by-four plank of wood while his assistant wheeled out a portable X-ray machine. Minutes later they had pictures that clearly showed the bone.

"It's deep," said Dick. "No infection in the bone, but it's pretty close. I'll just clean it up." Dick lifted Partner's hoof onto an eighteen-inch-high still rod. "How is he with clippers?"

"He don't get many haircuts, so we'll just have to find out," drawled Bob.

Dick turned on the clippers and began to shave. Partner didn't seem to mind a bit and began to nuzzle Dick's balding head until a gentle elbow to the muzzle told him that was off-limits. Dick covered the wound with Stimuzyne Granulex, an enzyme made from cattle pancreas that eats away at infected tissue. Partner suddenly came awake and jerked his foot away.

"Quit that!" said Bob, raising his hand so the horse could see it and make a choice. Partner went docile.

Dick carefully replaced the hoof on the still rod to finish dressing the infection. "That ought to do it."

"Dick, I thank you, and I'm sure Partner thanks you for keeping him away from the glue factory," said Bob. "Long as he's alive, I know I am, too."

One of the main gathering spots in Conrad was the Keg, a cinder-block bar-restaurant where you could always get a hoagie and a beer and talk about the weather or wheat rust. I was there with cousins Betty and Herb when a curious figure sat down with us. He was a sinewy man in his mid-sixties with a Lincolnesque beard turning gray. In spite of the summer heat, he wore a flannel shirt, black pants, suspenders, and a straw hat. He was Chris Waldner, one of the Hutterite elders from the Birch Creek Colony.

The Hutterites, like the Amish and Mennonites, live in a religious farming commune separated from the world by a stern devotion to the ascetic rules of their sect. They speak a peculiar southern German dialect—"like foreigners," as one local put it—and English is merely a concession to the strange modern world surrounding them. They are communal, virtually self-sufficient on their farms, and rarely spend money in town except on trucks and combines. Although they pay taxes, they are exempt from military service, and their religion discourages them from voting in local or national elections.

Hutterites are not held in high esteem by many citizens in Conrad. Their teenage girls are known to come into the drugstores, spray themselves with the free perfumes and paint themselves with lipstick samples, then leave looking and smelling like French tarts. These cosmetic binges are perhaps understandable when you see them: bound by dowdiness and duty, the girls and women are forced to dress exactly alike, in long dresses with high-necked collars and polka-dot kerchiefs. Some, I was told, even shoplift.

Over the years, Chris Waldner had taken a shine to Herbert and Betty because, unlike many citizens of Conrad, they always treated him kindly. Once Herb did Chris a favor regarding a minor legal matter, and the next day a huge box of fresh Hutterite vegetables arrived at the house.

"Your cousin, Mr. Conrad here, is a real gentleman, and your cousin, Mrs. Conrad here, is a real lady," said Chris in a serious tone. He spoke English well but with a heavy German accent. When Betty explained that I was writing a book on Montana, Chris invited me to visit the colony.

The next day I drove ten miles north from Conrad and swung west off the highway to Valier. While much of the country was suffering from summer drought, the Valier water project, begun by the Conrad brothers, had left this plain a brilliant green. The Hutterites controlled about 80 percent of the water that flowed into Lake Frances, a major reservoir in this area. This empowerment made them a formidable force, and built resentment during droughts. I turned onto a paved road, passed four farms in as many miles, then headed straight for the the eastern front of the Rockies. The asphalt road gave way to oiled gravel, then a sign: "Birch Creek Colony."

I parked *Red Cloud* in a huge open yard encircled by twenty buildings and gleaming aluminum grain bins. Three bearded Hutterite men dressed in black pants and black hats walked by, carrying metal fence posts on their shoulders. The domestic housing at Birch Creek Colony resembled army barracks, with several families living under one long roof. I knocked on a door bearing the initials "CW" and old Chris Waldner pulled it open, inviting me to join him in a plain modern kitchen. His daughter Julia served us iced tea, pie, and watermelon.

"Let me ask you, Barnaby. Are you married?" said Chris, wiping crumbs from his gray beard.

"Not yet."

"Hmm," he said, thoughtfully tugging on his beard. I remembered my cousin Herb's story about the Hutterites being worried about inbreeding. Herb had teased me about becoming a genetic donor. Chris Waldner's daughter did not encourage such fantasies. With her moon-shaped face, like the subject of a medieval drawing, it was hard to tell whether she was twenty-five or forty-five. She was also cross-eyed, but she smiled pleasantly and served me another slice of pie.

As we ate our snack, Chris explained that there were sixteen Hutterite colonies in Montana, with about a hundred souls in each. Birch Creek is one of the largest, with one hundred thirty people working sixteen thousand acres. Every year the colony buys new land, splits the group in half, and starts a new colony, like a hive of bees.

Chris told me the history of his people. The movement was named after the martyr Jakob Hutter, who was burned at the stake in 1536 at Innsbruck, Austria. The Hutterite Brotherhood is descended from the Swiss Brethren, who constitute the oldest of the sixteenth-century Anabaptist bodies, which include the Mennonites. The Anabaptists were former Roman Catholics who did away with infant baptism and practiced baptism by choice by mature believers. The Hutterite founders settled in Nikolsburg in Moravia.

Some two thousand men and women were put to death for their beliefs. Some died on the rack, some were burned at the stake, while still others were dismembered with knives, drowned, or starved in dungeons. The Catholic Church engaged in this persecution with the full blessings of the Austrian state. For the next century the Hutterites were driven from Czechoslovakia and Hungary to Transylvania and Romania. In spite of persecution, they grew to about forty communities totaling over twelve thousand. Early on they acted as missionaries to gain followers, a practice not followed today.

By 1770, the Hutterites were driven to Russia, where they escaped serfdom by petitioning Czar Alexander I, who allowed them to settle on crown lands. Finally in 1874 the Hutterites emigrated to the United States, settling in what is now South Dakota. During World War I they were subject to vicious attacks by local citizens due to their nonresistance stance and their German language. Most of the colonies went to Canada, where they were exempt from military service; Hutterite colonies also exist in England and Paraguay. Born in South Dakota, Chris Waldner was raised on a colony south of Lethbridge, Alberta, and came to Montana in 1945.

From Chris I learned that there were three kinds of Hutterite brethren: Laralites, Milites, and Daralites; their customs vary. The Birch Creek colony is Laralite. About ten thousand Laralites live in Alberta, Saskatchewan, and Montana. The Hutterites are completely self-sufficient and have virtually no crime, violence, or addictions—except to hard work. A Hutterite man receives an allowance of only five dollars a month. At marriage, a woman is given a sewing machine and material to make clothes for her family. The Hutterites build their own houses, and smith their own tractor harrows. The only things they need from outside are medical attention and farm equipment.

What separated the Hutterites from the Mennonites was their practice of "having things in common." Their community is based on Acts 2:44–45: "And all that believed were together, and had all things common. And sold their possessions and goods, and parted them to all men, as every man had need."

Unlike Marxist communism, the Hutterites acknowledged that their kind of life was impracticable for the rest of the world, primarily because a global belief in Christ was impossible. Free from evangelism, they retreat from the secular world.

"Our children don't speak the American language until they are about six years," said Chris. "Then they have to go to school, here at the colony, taught by a certified teacher." Hutterite German is Low German; Chris Waldner spoke both High and Low German.

After finishing our slices of pie, we strolled down to the chicken sheds, where a half dozen girls were sorting eggs on a rubber conveyor belt. As the Hutterite girls performed their duties, they smiled shyly and giggled. The operation was immaculate, and Chris was proud of it. "Ever seen anything like this before?" Thousands of eggs were boxed every day and shipped to market.

Chris opened a door to show me the hens—twelve thousand white-plumed leghorns squawking, preening, and laying. A haze of straw dust obfuscated the thousands of eyes, beaks, and red combs. The chickens produced nine thousand eggs a day and never saw sunlight. The colony also kept eighty dairy cows, two hundred pigs, and twelve hundred ducks. When we'd finished the tour, Chris said, "I've got to do a few things around here, Barnaby, but feel free to wander about and talk to people."

I walked down to the fields and met twenty-eight-year-old George Kleinsasser, a short man whose suspenders brought his black pants high over his belly. He wore his wide black hat cocked back on his head. He had a munchkin look, with bulging blue eyes, a missing tooth, and a friendly, inquisitive manner.

"Are you related to Robert Conrad?" George asked.

"The actor?"

"Yeah! *The Wild Wild West.*"

"Might be distantly," I said. "But he's not from the Montana branch of our family. How'd you know about TV anyway?"

"Oh, I was curious when I was a kid. You know how young punks are. Music, girls, TV. They sneak around. I had a radio once—not now. I get magazines sometimes. You gotta know what's going on in the outside world, too. Right?" George explained that as a teenager he had left the colony for five years, doing odd jobs around Oklahoma and Texas. He'd developed a taste for beer and liked to party.

"I didn't realize you could leave the colony," I said.

"Sure!" said George. "For a while, some guys do. But if you marry outside or have a child out of wedlock, you can't come back to the colony. A woman who leaves is rarely welcomed back, even if she comes back single. You get baptized when you're about twenty-five. Before, you're just a kid. No point in getting baptized until you understand it, right? Like the Catholics—what does a little baby know about God?"

"Why'd you come back to the colony?" I asked.

"Oh, well, you know." George picked a piece of grass and chewed on it. "I had my kicks. After a while the outside world looked like it was falling apart. You know, AIDS and drugs and stuff. Makes you think." George said he came back, repented his waywardness, accepted God, and got baptized. He was married last October to a girl from a Canadian colony. As a married man, he had the right to grow a beard, but it came in sparsely. "I can only grow a goatee," he said, tugging on a wispy beard that was as light as corn tassels.

We walked through the vegetable garden, where cucumbers grew heavy and dark green under the shadow of their thick leaves. "We pickle them. Look, here's sweet peas," said George, picking a dozen pods and putting them in my hand. We peeled and ate them, cool and sweet. A group of young kids, curious as field mice, came around to stare at the alien touring their closed world. The boys were dressed in black with little black hats. The girls were miniature replicas of their mothers, dressed in long dresses, aprons, and kerchiefs. They were all barefoot. They posed soberly as I photographed them. The children followed at a distance as George led me through a grove of birch.

"The German teacher is always the gardener," said George. "He takes care of the kids. They learn how to sing German songs, pray a little bit, and then they come out at about six years old and work in the garden for a few years. When they get older they work in the cow barn, chicken barn, pig barn. At fifteen they go into the fields and eventually learn how to use the big machines." All Hutterite teenagers receive a good butcher knife, rubber boots, and a rubber apron, and everyone helps with the butchering.

Nearby was the cemetery. All the markers bore the names of either Waldner or Kleinsasser—all. Most of the brides, George explained, were brought in from other colonies to avoid the inbreeding that has plagued the Hutterites. I remembered Chris's book on the Hutterites: the names Kleinsasser and Waldner went back three centuries to the beginning of the movement.

George stopped and pointed to three tombstones. "My dad died when I was nine months. Heart attack. My mother died seventeen years ago. I was about eleven. I got a brother here, too. Died right away at birth. We make our own tombstones."

Self-sufficient unto the end.

At five that evening Chris Waldner loaned me a black jacket and broad-brimmed black hat for a church service in the meeting hall. Men sat on one side, women on the other. The preacher—an elected position—read from the Bible. With my feeble German, I picked up only a few words like *Gott* and *Himmel,* but the room was filled with piety and ritual, and when the Hutterites knelt, I, a traditional Episcopalian, knelt with them in prayer. The service lasted just a half hour. Afterward, men and women sat separately at long tables in the communal dining hall. The women served us broccoli, cauliflower, chicken, fresh onions, cucumbers, fried potatoes, and small fried trout that had been caught in the irrigation ditches. The men ate quickly, with barely an exchange of words, and paid little attention to me. In less than ten minutes the men were done, a prayer was said, and they headed into the fields for three more hours of work.

Chris took me back to the meeting hall, where a half dozen teenage girls had moved back the pews and were scrubbing the floor on their knees. When they were done, Chris rounded them up and said, "Now the girls will sing for you." In that light-filled church on the prairie, I listened to the sweetest singing I'd heard in my life. First a German song, then "Show me the way, sweet Jesus, one day at a time"; others in English followed.

When they finished, Chris said, "Very good, girls. You know, they're a homely bunch, but they can sing pretty good."

The girls laughed good-naturedly. I noticed one beauty among them with dark hair, peachy cheeks, and eyes as blue as a Siamese cat's.

Then two girls whispered to Chris in German. He put his hand on my shoulder, smiling. "They want to know if you can sing for them."

I mustered courage and gave them "Yankee Doodle Dandy." The girls laughed and applauded. Encouraged, I encored with "Will the Circle Be Unbroken," and they joined in. They sang one more song for me in German, a plaintive melody that stirred the heart. Chris added the voice of an old man to the sweet harmonies of young virgins singing about prayer and love and the life ever after. Through the church window I saw a dark-hatted Hutterite man driving a combine across the fields of wheat.

Walking back to his house, I asked Chris if he ever watched television. "I got a Bible, books on the colony, and some songbooks," he answered quietly. "That's all I need." Chris and his homely daughter stood in the doorway. On the grass stood a half-dozen little boys, barefoot, their black hats pushed back from their pink faces. "Come back and see us again at Birch Creek," said the old man.

They were still waving good-bye when I headed the Jeep through the colony's gates, and I felt I was leaving a lost world that was as blessed as it was anachronistic.

A year later, I learned that old Chris had become an outcast in Conrad; the local druggist had caught him trying to shoplift an expensive medicine for arthritis.

Give us this day our daily bread, and forgive us our trespasses, as we forgive those who trespass against us.

"I'm glad you like our wide open spaces," said the old woman as I drove her across the prairie near Conrad. Dorothy Floerchinger was born in a homesteader's shack in 1901 and had taught in a one-room schoolhouse. Now she wrote poetry about homesteaders' shacks. As an amateur historian in Conrad, she knew a lot about my family. She was an oracle of the prairie, a big wheat-field granny in gingham talking proudly of her land.

"The prairie is special and it's built a special culture. Just because we don't have big cities with tall buildings, people think we're culturally deprived. Fiddlysticks! I remember a senator from an eastern state once made a statement: 'I think it's time we do something about that culturally deprived area out there in Montana.' Poor devil didn't know we had more artists and writers per capita than any state in the Union! George Montgomery the actor? Born on a homestead east of Conrad. Gary Cooper? From Helena. So was Myrna Loy. Then A. B. Guthrie from Choteau. And what about the artists and writers who were attracted here like James Willard Schultz and Charlie Russell? That gets my dander up."

Dorothy had bright eyes and a pretty smile in a Ma Kettle face framed by pendulous earlobes. She was somewhat deaf but tan and healthy, with sturdy farmer's legs that kept her moving around town as Conrad's self-appointed town historian and chief do-gooder. At eighty-eight she was a great-grandmother many times over and an exemplary version of the little old lady in tennis shoes. "The missiles around Conrad and Great Falls are the one thing that make me cuss," she said. "Why, with the same money we could eradicate poverty and illiteracy in this country."

I had picked up Dorothy at nine that morning in front of the Horizon Lodge, a retirement home overlooking the prairie; she had lived there since her husband, Louis, died almost two decades ago. Her cozy apartment was filled with Montana history books. "I'm a scrapbook person," she said, admitting she'd been up since five thirty to work on her archives. She said she had nearly called to wake me so that I might join her at sunrise. It was never too early to do good or talk history.

Dorothy's family, the Bruners, were Germans from the Rhine Valley who emigrated to America in the 1820s, settling in Iowa. The Bruners wandered west to Idaho, then back to Nebraska, where Dorothy was born. Her father brought her to a homestead east of Conrad in 1913. The Bruners were farmers and struggled to survive in the extreme seasons of the open prairie. Their homestead was simple, and it was years before they had indoor plumbing or electricity. They were among the last to experience the West as an agrarian engine of American opportunity; until 1919 in Montana, you could still homestead on government land. By "proving up" in three years, you could claim the land as your own.

When Dorothy graduated from high school in 1920, she taught in nearby Valier. "The water project—which William Conrad started—was really active then. They were surveying and selling land. The Conrads had brought in those Belgians and Dutch people and a large group from Idaho." That same year, Dorothy got a letter from a man named Louis Floerchinger, a clerk at the school board, asking her to apply for a job teaching school. She accepted. "That was the most important letter of my life. Suppose I had turned him down? Four years later I married him."

Dorothy's late husband, also of German descent, had been an active member of the Farmer's Union, and a committed socialist. Dorothy herself still professed a great affection for the Soviet Union and felt the Soviets were "victims of circumstance," blaming Hitler and even U.S. policy for postwar Soviet suffering. When I suggested that Stalin was an even greater butcher than Hitler, she wouldn't listen to me. "Stalin was forced to make his purges to carry out his plans to help the people." Then Dorothy insisted, "You know I'm *not* a communist." We changed the subject.

Passing an old homesteader's shack, Dorothy pointed and a nostalgic tone came into her voice. "They got by the best they could, living in a building like that. I remember as a little girl how we had to break ice in the well to get water in winter. It was the wind that really got to us. It would howl around the walls of our house. But in the spring the prairie would burst forth in wildflowers. The prairie chickens would hatch and the baby antelope would run. You can't imagine how beautiful it was! Now turn left at the crossroads, young man, and head to the east."

Her eyes sparkled. "I'm taking you to see a real treat," she said. "The site of old Fort Conrad."

I was ready to see the fort named for Charles Conrad. We were armed with a map drawn in 1929 by James Willard Schultz—another one of Dorothy's heroes—who'd lived at Fort Conrad in the early days. Schultz was the author of *My Life as an Indian* and many other books recounting the decade he spent living with the Blackfeet tribes.

The remains of Fort Conrad lay on the Keil Ranch, a ten-thousand-acre spread quilted together out of failed homesteads. Crossing the dry fields, we reached the bluffs of the Marias River and I put my Jeep in four-wheel drive to bump down a treacherous, winding road. Dorothy braced her hands against the dashboard. "This isn't a road, it's a *game trail!*" she squawked.

Reaching the river bottom, we drove within a hundred yards of a train trestle that crossed the slow-moving Marias. I turned off the ignition and we got out. There was silence except for a light wind bringing the scent of green grass, wolf willow, and river mud. Dorothy pointed dramatically across the river. "*That* is where Fort Conrad stood. Schultz made it very clear in his map that Fort Conrad stood on the far side of the river—not the near side, as some later historians had it."

I looked to where she pointed. There was nothing except grass and the river, with no sign of fortifications. "Where's the fort?"

"Floodwaters washed it away long ago. But that's where it stood, right where the river turns, near the base of the railroad trestle. Where we're standing is where the wagons came up from Fort Benton."

In the winter of 1871, twenty-one-year-old Charles Conrad came to this site and built a fort for the Baker Company. His job was to trade goods for furs from the Indian tribes. The fort attracted the Blackfeet but also their northern cousins, the Bloods, from across the Canadian border. It was a key stop in the 240-mile Whoop-Up Trail, a wagon road from Fort Benton to Fort Whoop-Up in Canada. Under federal law, no trader could sell whiskey to Indians in Montana Territory, but it seems reasonable to believe that some of it "leaked" out before crossing the border. I imagined Charles Conrad as a tall, dark-haired young man with a mustache, inviting the Indians to trade, welcoming them to the fort with cups of hot tea or whiskey, and always with tobacco. And here he carried on his romance with Sings-in-the-Middle Woman, daughter of a Blood chief. Out on the plains, such a relationship made sense to a virile young man, but not when they returned to Fort Benton.

I knew little about Charles's life at Fort Conrad, but the author James Willard Schultz—his friend—also lived here and wrote about it. From upstate New York, Schultz was so entranced by tales of Indians and buffalo that he convinced his parents to send him west for the summer. Arriving at Fort Benton in 1877, Schultz met all the Conrad brothers, and formed a lasting friendship with Charles. I was relieved to learn that Charles—called "Spotted Cap" by the Indians—appears throughout Schultz's memoirs as an honorable man when dealing with Indians.

In one of his books, James Willard Schultz recorded the words of Bear Head, who remembered trading with Charles as a teenager. The boy's father, also named Bear Head, had been killed in the 1870 Baker Massacre, in which drunken cavalry officers slaughtered a camp of innocent Indians in error:

> Came the New-Grass Moon (April) of summer, and we all moved to Many-Houses (Fort Benton) and made camp. Next morning we loaded our fifty-five soft-tanned, head-and-tail buffalo cow robes on some horses, unloaded in front of Spotted Cap's (Charles Conrad's) trade house. Spotted Cap, followed by his three hands-out-goods men, came out to meet us, help us unload our many packs of robes and carry them inside. We loved Spotted Cap. He was married to Sings-in-the-Middle Woman, she a member of our brother tribe, the Bloods. He spoke our language, was very kind and generous. Already he had heard that I had taken my dead father's name, so said to me as he grasped my hand: "Bear Head, how happened it? Whose are they, these many robes?"
>
> "My killings, my mother's tannings. Spotted Cap, I want a many shots gun and three hundred greased shooters for it," I answered. (The bullet of the .44-caliber, rim-fire cartridges for the Henry repeating rifle were heavily coated with hard grease, hence the Pikuni name for them.)
>
> He put his arm on my shoulder, hugged me, and said: "Bear Head, though you had not one robe, I would give you a many-shots gun and plenty of greased shooters. Why? Because I loved your father. He was a real man. And I love you; pity you so young, and so many mothers and sisters to care for."
>
> It made me to have wet eyes, that he said to me. My mothers and sisters were crying. Loudly they wept, moaning: "Our brave man, our brave father; he is gone. Gone to the Sand Hills. Haiya! Haiya!" It was some time before we could begin to trade.
>
> "A many-shots gun. Here it is, Bear Head," said Spotted Cap as he handed me a shiny new one. "And here are the greased shooters for it." And he laid six boxes of them on the counter.

It was through Conrad that Schultz met a half-breed, Joseph Kipp, who introduced him to Pikuni (or Piegan) Indians—the Blackfeet. Kipp took Schultz into the Pikuni tribe, where he had all the buffalo hunting he ever dreamed of. In 1878, Joseph Kipp bought Fort Conrad and hired the nineteen-year-old Schultz as his lieutenant. Schultz, Kipp, and Hiram Upham and their respective Pikuni wives and families moved there with a large stock of goods. In 1880 Fort Conrad consisted of two 150-foot-long log buildings built parallel to the river, joined by a stable and corral at their west end. It was a business and social center for the region.

Indians stayed with them during the long winter months, and as they told vivid stories around the campfire, Schultz took copious notes. He also began dressing in a fringed buckskin shirt, leggings, and breechclout. One winter's trade (1878–79) with the Blackfeet and Bloods meant "two thousand buffalo robes and several thousand deer, wolf, beaver and antelope hides."

All went well until a shipper stopped on his way to the fort, and in the night a war party stole all forty-eight of his horses. A few nights later, another war party attacked a wagon train, making off with most of its horses and killing two teamsters. A company of mounted soldiers was sent from Fort Shaw to protect the road north. The commanding officer suspected the Blackfeet, but Schultz and Kipp were convinced it was Assiniboines or Crees or Crows. The soldiers wisely heeded Kipp and set off looking for the real culprits, but in their absence, the thieves struck again, the Assiniboine leader shouting his name from outside the stockade walls: "I am White Dog!" This time Schultz's Indian friends took justice into their own hands, inviting Schultz to join their war party. White Dog was killed and scalped, Schultz was wounded, and several of his companions died before justice was done.

One day Schultz saw the Blackfeet woman named Mutsi-Awotan-Ahki, "Fine Shield Woman." Only fifteen, she had an appealing dignity. Schultz learned she was a cousin of Kipp's wife, Double-Strike-Woman, and he decided to approach the girl's mother. Usually a payment of horses or guns was required for marriage, but the mother exacted only a promise from Schultz: that he be good to her. Fine Shield Woman had never slept in anything except a tepee, and had never been with a man, but without introduction or ceremony, she simply appeared in Kipp's quarters one night.

It puzzled Fine Shield Woman that Schultz was courteous, even deferential to women, because the Blackfeet world was male dominated and polygamous. Females took a subservient role and performed all the most onerous tasks; adulterous women had their noses cut off or were traded for horses.

Schultz shortened her name to Nätahki, a nickname meaning "cute girl" or "pretty girl." In Fort Benton he found a minister of the Methodist Episcopal Church to marry them. Though disappointed that the preacher didn't wear black robes like the Catholic priests, Nätahki was pleased with her elevated status. Not many whites—Schultz and Charles Conrad were exceptions—bothered to legally marry their Indian women. In 1882, Nätahki bore a son, Hart, who became an artist known as Lone Wolf, and painted somewhat cruder versions of Charlie Russell's western scenes.

Schultz saw the old life among the Indians coming to an end as the buffalo were killed off. In the winter of 1883–84, starvation overtook the Blackfeet. Charles Conrad, by then remarried to a white woman, donated a herd of cattle. Schultz interceded on their behalf, writing to Washington, D.C., but it was too late and a quarter of the Blackfeet tribe perished.

In 1886, Kipp sold Fort Conrad to a rancher who made it his headquarters. Schultz tried raising sheep but was harassed by local cattlemen, who burned his house and barn. He and his wife moved to Blackfeet reservation land and built a house and cattle ranch, where he lived for the next seventeen years; he began a new career as a guide in the region that would become Glacier National Park, and published articles and books under the nom de plume Apikuni until his death in 1947.

Recalling life in old Fort Conrad, Dorothy Floerchinger moved her brown hand across the horizon. "This was all once Blackfeet country. They roamed clear down to the Musselshell River in central Montana and all the way over to Fort Peck, controlling about one-quarter of the state of Montana. The smallpox got about half of them. Three epidemics of that. The 1884 starvation killed over five hundred of them when they sat around the Indian Agency. Then they had a measles epidemic. The tribe was devastated. Homesteaders kept pushing the Indians back. It makes me cry."

In the vast plains of windblown grass east of Shelby, Dorothy asked me to pull over next to a stone historical marker on Route 2. "This here's where the Whoop-Up Trail crossed north to Canada," she said. "You can still see the wagon ruts in the grass." Time and the farmer's plow had done their best to erase the past, but the ruts still scarred the prairie on their way north to Fort Whoop-Up.

Built in 1869, Fort Whoop-Up was the first and most notorious of about forty whiskey trading posts that dotted the Canadian plains. Situated at the junction of the St. Mary's and Old Man Rivers, it was a favorite wintering site of the Blood people, a branch of the Blackfeet Nation. There are numerous accounts of how the fort got its name. The most often repeated has Isaac Baker shouting to a wagon train leaving Fort Benton, "Don't let the Indians whoop you up!"

The first whiskey shipment, fifty gallons of pure alcohol, arrived at Fort Whoop-Up in 1869. Four years later that had increased to fifteen thousand gallons a year. The firewater served by the traders was far worse than plain whiskey or rum. One formula called for a quart of whiskey, a pound of chewing tobacco, a handful of red pepper, a bottle of Jamaica ginger, and a quart of molasses, diluted with water and boiled to bring out its potency. Red ink was sometimes added for color, and, it was said, some traders tossed in a small rattlesnake. The Indians reacted strongly to small amounts of the vile brew and became violent with the traders and their own people.

A single cup of whiskey could buy a complete buffalo robe, worth six dollars in the East. The traders encouraged the Indians to develop a taste for tobacco, salt, sugar, flour, and tea. Axes, knives, and firearms soon replaced their stone tools. Indian women yearned for colorful calico cloth, beads, silver, and brass ornaments. In a short time the tribes were addicted to the white man's culture.

The whiskey trade in Canada lasted only five years, ending with the arrival of the Royal Canadian Mounted Police, who closed the whiskey forts in 1874 and controlled the Indians. (Among the Mounties was Francis Dickens, son of Charles Dickens; he is remembered for his drunkenness and insensitivity to the Indians.) The Conrads and other Montana businessmen developed contracts to supply the Mounties. By 1877, the buffalo of Alberta were nearly gone and white men, including the Conrads, moved in with cattle herds. Deprived of buffalo, the Indians killed cattle for food, and tension arose between the tribes and the settlers.

Dorothy directed me to the old Conrad ranch on Dupuyer Creek. The ranch consisted of a big wooden barn, corrals, and a one-story house under cottonwoods. Originally a log cabin, the house had been dressed up with painted clapboard siding on the front half. Behind it hunkered a separate log cabin cookhouse where the cowboys were once fed. I parked *Red Cloud* in the shade of the cottonwoods.

In 1878, the three Conrad brothers plunged into the cattle business with an initial investment of five hundred thousand dollars. By 1884, they had one of the largest herds in Montana Territory. They moved twenty thousand head of cattle onto the Dupuyer Creek ranch, overseen by a manager and thirty cowboys. Beef nourished on Montana grass was recognized as superior to others, and the Conrads raised cattle primarily to fulfill Canadian government contracts. While Charles took an interest in Indians, his brother William was completely unsentimental. Hungry Indians meant money to be made. In 1880, the Conrads supplied over 5 million pounds of beef to feed the Mounties and the reservation Indians. As the open range dwindled due to settlement, large Montana cattle operations were compelled to move north of the Canadian border.

I helped Dorothy out of the Jeep, and the ranch's current owner, Mrs. Earl Peterson, a short, stout woman, welcomed us into the house, a refuge from the heat. The shades were drawn on the windows. In a chair sat a wheezing wraith of a man with plastic tubes in his nose. Earl Peterson had been on oxygen for seven years. Between gulps of air, he recounted his life in short-winded bursts. Born in North Dakota in 1911, he came to Montana when his family homesteaded nearby. He bought the Conrad spread in 1951 when he got married. The ranch is currently seven hundred acres—about 1 percent of the Conrads' original holdings—and feeds only one hundred head of cattle.

A small person appeared in the doorway, silhouetted against the startling sunlight outside. It was a light-haired boy of about seven. He had a stick in his hand.

"Who's that?" I asked.

"That's my great-nephew—*wheeze*—Name's Chester."

"Does he live with you?"

"No—*wheeze*—he comes to visit us for a few weeks—*wheeze*—He's a lot of entertainment for us."

"How does he entertain you?"

"Asking—*wheeze*—questions."

"How does he entertain himself?"

"Same way. Talks to himself. Or he—*wheeze*—catches frogs in the creek." (Montanans pronounce the word "crick.")

It didn't seem fair to make Mr. Peterson talk. I found myself breathing deeply, feeling guilty somehow that my lungs worked easily as his own struggled under a bony chest. I knew he didn't have long to live. I wanted to get out of that house, away from this panting man. The heat of the day had dulled my mind. A fly trapped under the window shade buzzed crankily, crawled silently, then buzzed again.

While Dorothy and Mrs. Peterson chatted about people they knew in Conrad, I stepped outside. A barn, an old commissary, and a blacksmith shop made up the rest of the spread. It could have been anybody's ranch, and I wondered what I'd hoped to find out here in the dry plains of Montana. Mr. Peterson had known little or nothing about the Conrads. Why should he? He was a farmer, not a historian. The Conrads weren't interesting to anybody except a Conrad. What if I had been adopted? Would I still feel this urge to retrace a blood line? How good was that blood anyway? And what did *good* mean in the West—killing buffalo, poisoning Indians with firewater and forcing them to eat cattle? The heat of the sun oppressed me, made me suspect a futility in my search.

When Dorothy came outside, I helped her get back into *Red Cloud,* which the sun had turned into a mobile sweat lodge. The round figure of Mrs. Peterson appeared in the shade of the porch, waving to us as we drove off down the dusty road.

At the town of Shelby we stopped for a hamburger at Kathy's Kitchen, a place whose walls were covered with an artificial paneling in exaggerated wood grain, like the backdrop of a Disney cartoon. The obesity factor was high among the female employees.

In the 1910 U.S. census, Shelby didn't exist. Then the Great Northern Railroad rolled across the plains and put a storage facility here. A saloon was built, followed by a hotel and post office. In 1921, an oil prospector struck oil near Shelby and overnight it became a boomtown. Town boosters promoted it as "the Tulsa of the Northwest." Still, Shelby boasts one great moment in its history. In 1923, the town went fifteen rounds with Jack Dempsey and nearly got KO'd.

It started when two real-estate speculators named James Johnson and Mel McCutcheon decided to pull Shelby's real-estate sales out of a slump. Over coffee at a certain breakfast joint in 1923, Johnson tapped the sports section of the *Great Falls Tribune* and showed McCutcheon where it said someone had offered one hundred thousand dollars to Jack Kearns, manager of Jack Dempsey, if he would send his boy to fight in Montreal. "Mel," said Johnson, "why don't we make an offer for a championship fight? It would put Shelby on the map."

A delegate was sent to New York to sign a contract. Dempsey would fight Tommy Gibbons for a steep price: three hundred thousand dollars. Two hundred Shelby carpenters built a forty-thousand-seat stadium near the Great Northern tracks. Dempsey rented a house in Great Falls, trained hard, and was photographed with the artist Charlie Russell. Dempsey was honest and well liked, but his manager, Kearns, was a crook. When the Shelby promoters had trouble raising the last hundred thousand dollars, someone asked Kearns if he would accept fifty thousand sheep as payment instead of cash. "What the hell am I going to do with fifty thousand sheep in New York?" said Kearns at a Great Falls news conference. "I want these people to live up to the terms of their contract. If I don't see one hundred thousand dollars on July 2, Dempsey will not fight." In a final scramble, James Johnson leased out most of his cattle and oil properties, borrowed the rest, and came up with the money.

On the day of the fight, people came from all over the country. The crowd of ten thousand spectators, said one reporter, was "a mix of millionaires, Blackfoot Indians, cowboys, shepherds, hookers and sportswriters." Most of them crashed the gates. The fight was a tough one for Dempsey, and Tommy Gibbons hung on for fifteen grueling rounds in a dull slugging match. When Dempsey won by a decision, Kearns escaped with the gate receipts in a locomotive hooked only to a caboose. That night, Kearns reputedly slept on the floor of a Great Falls barber shop, clutching the money bags to his chest, and left at dawn for Seattle.

Gibbons was paid seventy-five hundred dollars for his efforts and went on to beat French champion Georges Carpentier in 1924. Dempsey beat Luis Firpo to become a legend, and Kearns stayed rich. The Shelby promoter, James Johnson, went broke, losing $169,000 according to his son, who now lives in California. The great wooden arena was torn down. Today, the Arena Motel marks the site, built with the lumber from the bleachers. The official fight bell hangs in Hogan's Tap Room.

Dorothy Floerchinger remembered the 1923 Dempsey fight for a different reason. "Instead of going to the fight with all those gamblers and scalawags, my husband came to see me and we got engaged."

Shelby's oil boom faded, the population stabilized at about two thousand, and it is still a runty little town. "Shelby has a completely different philosophy than Conrad does—we being farmers," sniffed Dorothy with pride.

We being farmers. The implication was that Shelbyites were less than upright. Conrad, a farming town, had three bars and a dozen churches while Shelby, a boomtown, had the opposite ratio. As we walked along the streets of Shelby, I noticed it wasn't folksy and settled as in Conrad. You had the feeling that people came and went here. I remembered what Cousin Herb had said: that in Conrad, if you did something stupid or crass, teenagers would say, "What, are you from Shelby or something?"

George Bird Grinnell, naturalist and founder of Glacier National Park, with his wife, Elizabeth, in 1923. (Courtesy Glacier National Park)

Chapter 8

Surrounded by Bears in Glacier

Enter Glacier National Park and you enter the homeland of the grizzly bear. We are uninvited guests here, intruders, the bear our reluctant host. If he chooses, now and then, to chase somebody up a tree, or all the way to the hospital, that is the bear's prerogative. Those who prefer, quite reasonably, not to take such chances should stick to Disneyland in all its many forms and guises.

Edward Abbey, *The Journey Home*, 1977

With my new Indian name, Many Bears, I felt compelled to visit the stronghold of the grizzly, Glacier National Park. The eastern portion was once called the Ceded Strip, the land that Charles Conrad helped the Indians sell to the government in 1895. Still capped with snow and glacier ice, the mountains looked like the Swiss Alps—a point that was emphasized to tourists shortly after this region became a national park in 1910.

It was late afternoon when I cruised up through the Swiftcurrent Valley and headed straight for the base of Mount Merritt. Overlooking McDermott Lake stood the Many Glacier Hotel, an enormous wooden building like a giant Swiss chalet. It was booked up. So was the less fancy Swiftcurrent Motel. And the campground was filled. I decided not to worry about sleeping arrangements until later. This is bad camping strategy in bear country, but I was an optimist with a sleeping bag.

In a forest glade I found a hundred campers in multicolored Gore-tex parkas watching a man toss twigs into a popping fire. He was dressed in breeches, knee-length boots, and a Mountie-style hat that went well with his upswept gray handlebar mustache. Dave Casteel is a middle-aged high school teacher from Champaign, Illinois, who serves as a park ranger in Glacier. Every summer he presents "An Evening with George Bird Grinnell." Grinnell represented the U.S. government in buying the Ceded Strip, and is known as the primary creator of Glacier Park.

Portraying Grinnell, Casteel recounted adventures with James Willard Schultz and Teddy Roosevelt, and the last great buffalo hunt on the plains. He recalled how an old Indian had named him Fisher Cap and anointed him with handfuls of sunlight as the two men offered up their puny lives to the Great Spirit. As Grinnell's ghost came to life, Casteel had a way of drawing magic from the high mountain air and the hypnotic, crackling campfire. At one point, a big-eared doe suddenly walked into the firelight. At the end of the talk, Dave Casteel confessed that he had portrayed the naturalist out of character: "Grinnell would never have stood up here and talked about himself. Too modest to acknowledge the great things he did, like being conservation speech writer for Teddy Roosevelt. He was an editor of *Forest and Stream* magazine for forty-one years, wrote twenty-nine books about Indians, and founded the American Ornithological Society. And he was the father of Glacier National Park. He got this area made into a national forest and eventually into a national park. He was responsible for sacking the really crooked Indian agent on the Blackfeet reservation in 1884, the winter so many Indians died through mismanagement. And it was Grinnell who convinced Edward Curtis to photograph the Indians, to record the vanishing tribes. Grinnell's life was so active that he didn't settle down until the age of fifty-six, when he married the widow of a friend. She kept him going until eighty-nine."

The talk ended with hearty applause, but I stayed to hear more about Glacier Park's history. Commerce as much as a love of nature was responsible for its creation. Seeing the potential for tourism, railroad tycoon James Hill forced the park legislation through Congress. By 1917, the Great Northern Railway had spent $1.5 million in Glacier—twice the U.S. government's contribution—and built many of the roads and all the major hotels in a distinctly "woodsy" architectural style. Today Glacier Park attracts a million and a half visitors annually, yet it rarely gets the sluggish Winnebago crowd that jam up Yellowstone's roads.

Unlike Yellowstone, Glacier has few broad meadows and hence no buffalo, but both parks have the grizzly bear, *Ursus horribilis*. Glacier is the largest producer of bears for the whole North Continental Divide ecosystem, with about two hundred bears in the park. "They're all born here, even if they wander out and die someplace else," said Dave Casteel. "There are thirty breeding females in the park. The ticket is knowing how many breeding females you have and how productive they are."

"Could they become extinct?" someone asked.

"Probably not. The state and federal wildlife people would like to take them off the endangered-species list in this area."

"So how productive are they?" I asked.

"A female bear breeds every three years from the time she's six. She breeds in June and gives birth in January or February, generally two or three cubs. She keeps them that summer, dens up with them in the winter, but the third summer she kicks them out in late spring. She literally beats the bejeebers out of them—and chases them away."

"Why?"

"She has to. Because when she comes into heat, any big male that comes around and finds a smaller bear with her is going to kill it and eat it. Then she mates, and the cycle begins again. The first few months are the worst for bear cubs. Everything eats them—wolves, cougar, you name it. After the mother kicks them out, the cubs sometimes den up together that fall, but the next year they go solitary. If a bear lives to age five, he or she will generally live about thirty years.

"Food to a grizzly bear is everything," said Dave. "It controls their whole life. Even their breeding. One year there was this young female that over a period of about seventeen days bred with ten different bears. We took turns watching through the telescope. I was watching her when a great big bear had her practically covered up. She was a small bear, probably only weighed about two hundred pounds. And while she was copulating she was eating. She's face down on the ground and she's eating everything she can reach. I concluded that food was more important than sex to her."

Someone in our group laughed. "Sounds like my ex-wife."

Casteel continued. "Here in Glacier, the land is as much vertical as it is horizontal. We don't have the good soil and food you need for big bears. Down in Yellowstone, a grizzly bear can weigh a thousand pounds. Up here we estimate the big male bears in Glacier weigh about seven hundred pounds. Biggest bear *I've* ever seen here in twenty-three years hasn't weighed over four hundred pounds."

"Don't bears mainly eat grubs and berries?"

"Yes, but they love to eat meat. If they kill a mountain goat they bury it for ten days. If you had to eat a tough old mountain goat, you'd probably use lots of Adolph's meat tenderizer. Bears use ten days and flies. Until it's putrid. They love rotten meat. But a bear's digestive system is shorter than in an herbacious animal. So here's this animal with a short carnivorous gut that eats eighty percent vegetation that's not digestible. You can tell when you see bear droppings on the trail. Huckleberries go right on through, not even bruised. Now you take the food we eat: about thirty percent is digestible. If a bear ever gets a hold of our food he gets a rush from it. Salt, monosodium glutamate, sugar—*it tastes good.* Nothing out there that a bear eats normally tastes as good to him as what we eat."

That explained why camping is no longer allowed in the back country around Many Glacier.

"Picture this," said Dave Casteel, digging in his heels for a juicy tale of horror. "In a beautiful pristine valley up near Iceberg Lake on September 19, 1976, three campers pitched their tents among the meadow flowers. They hiked up the hill to take in the view. Looking down, they saw three big brown bears tearing up their tent. They ran down there, yelling and throwing rocks, but got scared when the bears didn't give ground. After the bears finished eating and left, the guys picked up their stuff and split. They met a couple of other people coming up the trail and said, 'Three big brown bears up there tore up our camp.' But they didn't tell a ranger what happened because they had been camping illegally.

"September 20. Some other people were up *this* valley," Dave pointed to the west. "They camped up there in a nice little meadow near the lake. While they were fishing, they saw three big brown bears tearing up their camp. The bears left and they decided to get out with the remains of their gear. They met some people going up to Bullhead Lake and told them about the bears. But they didn't tell us, because they, too, were camping illegally.

"September 21. People were setting up camp on Fisher Cap Lake when three big brown bears drop in for lunch. One man ran up a tree. The other swam out in the water. The bears tore up their camp and left. The men packed up and returned to the parking lot.

"That afternoon, three young girls drove into the park with a VW camper. They told the ranger at the West Gate they wanted to camp but were afraid of the bears. The ranger didn't know anything about these three bear stories and said: 'Haven't been any bear problems, but talk to Fred Reese, the campground ranger. He'll help you get in the right spot.'

"By the way," interjected Dave, "I had slept outside in this campground every night for eleven years previous to that night and never been bothered.

The girls met Fred Reese and he put them in Site One with their tent, over in Site Seven to cook, and put their car in another spot. They even changed clothes after dinner. They did everything perfectly. But about four in the morning at least two big bears opened up the side of that tent, grabbed twenty-one-year-old Mary Patricia Mahoney by her throat—she never made a sound—and dragged her out of the tent. Took her into the woods and the two bears pulled her into pieces, like dogs with a rag. And they ate her."

"*Ate* her?"

"Ate her," said Dave Casteel. "The other two girls woke up. One climbed a tree. The other got to their VW bus and laid into that horn. *Honk! Honk! Honk!!!* Fred Reese came running out. They couldn't find the missing girl anywhere. But as daylight came, they started finding pieces of her body out in the woods. A little while later, Bob Frausen showed up. He's the East Side manager. And Bob had a shotgun with him. He walked back in the trees. There was a bear back there eating on the girl's body. *Pow!* He killed that bear. Turned around to say something to Fred and there was a second bear. *Pow!* Killed *that* bear. Fell right on top of the first one. Killed them each with a single shot. Never saw another bear."

"But *why?*" said a woman.

"Mary Patricia Mahoney never did a thing wrong as a camper. She died because other people broke the rules. See, most Americans think that civil laws are laws meant to be broken. If it says to drive fifty-five miles per hour, do we drive fifty-five? No. Some idea about personal freedom. The point is, if you're careful or lucky, you can break civil laws and get away with it. You just can't break a natural law without paying a price. For those of us who manage natural areas, we have to state natural laws as civil laws. So we got all these rules. If you feed bears, you put people in jeopardy and bears in jeopardy. Somebody's going to pay the price."

A woman in pink-framed designer glasses and a green parka spoke up: "I was just reading *Night of the Grizzlies* and it says they killed two people in—"

"You should have waited until you got home from this camping trip," said Dave Casteel, grinning. "It's an accurate book. Don't be too alarmed. I sleep on the ground here all the time. But tonight I'm driving back to West Glacier."

When Dave left, I drove out of the park boundary. Just a few miles from the gates I found Chewing Black Bones Campground (named for an Indian warrior, not a grizzly bear). I rumbled across a field dotted with darkened campers and a few tents. When I shut off *Red Cloud,* the only sound was the metallic tinkling of a cooling engine. I whipped out my sleeping bag and wrapped it in a ground cloth against the dew. Then I stuck my .44 Magnum—for protection against bears or humans—under my pillow, took a long look at the stars, and went to sleep.

The following morning I drove west around the southern end of the park thirty miles to Essex—not really a town, but a station on the Amtrak line that runs through the Marias Pass. Here, in 1949, the Great Northern built the Izaak Walton Inn in a pseudo-Tudor style as a rest stop for the railroad crews. Now it's a hotel, popular in winter with cross-country skiers. In summer, train buffs sit on the back porch watching locomotives chug through the dark forest.

Over lunch in the inn's twenty-four-hour café, I met the train master of Essex. An hour later, he issued me a special permit to ride in a "helper" engine, a locomotive that assists heavy freight trains over the steep part of Marias Pass. About four o'clock I saw a helper gearing up to head east, so I hopped across the rails and waved the paper at the engineer.

"Okay, bud, you're on," he said.

I climbed onto the engine. The inside of the steel cab was painted hospital green and was about the size of a small kitchen. The engineer's seat was fixed on the right-hand side, in front of an instrument panel with a transmitter and telephone.

"I'm Art Havens," said the engineer as he shook my hand. He was a grayhaired man just short of sixty. "Used to be we'd take all kinds of people for rides. Heck, I'd take my whole family sometimes. But the company cracked down."

Just then a hefty figure came through the door. Paul Safford, the conductor, didn't seem glad to see me at first, but he brightened when I showed him the paper from the train master. When the fireman, Frank Almanza, got into the second locomotive, we headed off, slowly gathering speed. The mile of freight cars were loaded with transoceanic shipping containers, some originating in Japan, now bound for Europe. It was quicker by train than shipping through the Panama Canal.

Seventeen miles ahead was the summit of 5,280-foot Marias Pass, the lowest passage in the Rockies. The train slithered through the narrow valley separating Glacier National Park to the north from the Bob Marshall Wilderness to the south.

As the forest flew by, I talked with Paul Safford. His job, he said, was "hookin' up and cuttin' off." Paul had joined the railroad just out of high school. "Used to be the railroads were very clannish. You needed a brother or father ahead of you to get a job. Now it's just the opposite: they won't let family members work in the same region. There's no future in the railroad for a young man. The company's constantly whittling down jobs. The nostalgia of a railroad job went out a long time ago. We're just here for the money." Salaries range from twenty-five thousand dollars for novice firemen up to fifty thousand dollars for engineers with seniority.

Two hours earlier Art Havens had been on a golf course in Whitefish when the pager at his waist signaled him to call in. Art had worked for the Burlington Northern Railroad for thirty-three years, starting out when it was still known as the Great Northern. He was just a few years away from retiring.

"I've always wanted to drive a train," I said.

"You want to try now? Go ahead," he said, ushering me into the seat.

"What do I do?"

"Just maintain a balance between the power and the brake—this thing here." Art showed me how to use the hydraulic brake, a gear on the left of the panel. "Pushing it from right to left pumps air into the brakes."

It was strange driving a vehicle that could not be steered; one automatically tried to follow the track. "What do you think they'd do if they knew you were letting me drive this train?"

"Fire me," said Art.

"So why are you letting me drive it?"

"Hey," he guffawed, "who's gonna find out?"

Over the summit, the train gained momentum and we didn't even need to put the train in gear. Our maximum speed was twenty-five miles an hour, but as the track flattened out, Art let me push the power lever from idle to the number-one mark, then all the way up to eight. "Feel the acceleration? Now back off, 'cause we're comin' up to the bridge in front of East Glacier. Okay, now stop it before that block red."

I eased the hydraulic brake forward and we stopped before the red light. "What happens if you don't stop?"

"If I crossed that line, I'd be fired."

Safety is something the railroads work on constantly. "There were about six derailments last month alone," said Art. "Actually, it's rarely from human error. I know eight people who have been killed railroading, six of them in head-on collisions. One was crushed between cars. Another man was run over by a train. You've got track problems, too. The spikes in wooden ties shift, changing the gauge of the track. That's why Burlington Northern is gradually replacing the wood with cement ties."

Most trains don't pull a caboose anymore; it's been replaced by a small red metal box about the size of a television set that hangs off the back of the train. This motion sensor monitors the train's speed and can warn the engineer of problems with the cars or their brakes. This box is known as "Fred," and the corresponding unit at the front of the train is called "Mary." There are also no signalmen on the railroad anymore. Instead the engineer watches block signals, which work like traffic lights.

When we reached East Glacier, Art moved the locomotive onto another track. At about 7 P.M. we hooked up to the tail end of a grain train with over a hundred cars bound for the West Coast. Paul Safford jumped down to move "Fred" aside and hooked the engine to the last car for the steep descent of Marias Pass.

"Our job," said Art, "is to slow this train down when we come off the summit grade. Heavy load here. Notice there's two engines on the front? On the downgrade they won't be pulling; they'll be keeping the train from running away."

"A comforting thought."

"Yeah. Saw that happen once. Bad derailment. The real mess was the cattle cars. Talk about hamburger."

A transmission came in: "Grain Train to Helper. We've got a high yellow."

"Okay, Grain Train," said Art into the mike. "Here we go."

With a lurch we headed west again. Normally when a helper reaches the top of the summit, it unhooks, but the grain train had specifically asked us to stay on for the ride down. Hitting the downgrade, we braked to maintain a constant speed.

Art said a train had derailed just above Essex last winter, spilling a car loaded with corn feed down the hillside. A cleanup crew had done their best in twenty-below weather, but with the summer heat, the corn had fermented into sweet sour mash. The bears had a field day, and got bombed on the alcohol. "Should have seen those bears gorging—like a bunch of drunks!" said Art. Unfortunately, at least one corn-addicted bear had been killed by trains.

As we made our descent, I stuck my head out the window of the locomotive and smelled something like burning wood. It wasn't unpleasant, and I took it in along with deep lungfuls of pine scent. "Say, Art, what's that smell?"

"Burning asbestos," said Art. "From the brake shoes. I wouldn't breathe too deeply if I were you. Woman just won a lawsuit against BN because her husband, an engineer, died from lung cancer supposedly caused by this stuff."

The reset button sounded. "That's to wake up dozing railroaders," Art said. "If the engineer doesn't hit the button or move a switch—any switch on his control panel—then the train's computer assumes you are asleep, dead drunk, or dead, and it automatically slams on the brakes."

Art stopped the train at the base of the grade, and Paul uncoupled the locomotive. A static-laden call came in over the radio and Art translated: "They want us to pick up another grain train in Cut Bank. Summit is our normal turnaround. This is the gravy part of the job. Since it's out of our section, we get an extra day's pay. You wanna go?"

I'd enjoyed the trip, but I wasn't getting an extra day's pay, and after four hours I'd seen enough. "Think I'll head back to Essex on foot."

"Suit yourself," said Art. "You're at East Java right now, about two miles from Essex. Just follow the tracks and watch out for the bears. That corn spill is right nearby."

"You got your bear repellent?" asks Paul. "Old Bruiser's around."

"Is Old Bruiser back again?" asked Art with a twinkle in his eye. "The grizzly that eats backpackers and their bear bells for breakfast?"

"Those are dinner bells for him," chuckled Paul.

I jumped down onto the tracks. "Thanks for the ride, fellas."

"You take it easy now." Art waved and the locomotive chugged away, leaving me in the stillness of the forest. I felt exhilarated at the solitude, but I kept their joke about Old Bruiser in mind. I didn't want to end up as bear bait. I walked down the tracks, listening to my footsteps. I heard a sound behind me and looked back—nothing. I kept walking, humming a Gordon Lightfoot train song: "Went into town for one last deal, and I gambled my ticket away. . . . Now the big steel rail won't carry me home to the one I luh-uh-uh-uvvvv." I picked up a branch as a walking stick, and glanced over my shoulder from time to time.

About fifteen minutes later I saw where that train had derailed, dumping the boxcar full of corn. Fifty yards down the hill I spotted a small black bear with his nose so deep in rotten corn that he couldn't have smelled me if he tried. He was comical, and I watched him feed for a few minutes. He looked up suddenly and shuffled off at a nervous trot.

From the woods lumbered a blondish brown form with high shoulder fur and dish-shaped face. It wasn't Old Bruiser, but it was most definitely a grizzly bear. I instinctively drew back to cut down my silhouette. He was probably a two-year-old, with a lanky adolescent awkwardness about him, but also a sense of power. He nosed the air, then rooted and pawed in the corn with his long claws. I watched him eat for only a minute. With darkness coming, I didn't want to run into any bigger ones on the track.

Up ahead, out of the gloaming, something large and hairy was coming toward me, but it wasn't a bear. It was a young man with a long dark beard and scraggly shoulder-length hair falling under his hat. On his shoulder perched a large ferret, a pet favored by misanthropes. At twenty yards I waved. "Howdy."

No reply.

"There's a grizzly at the corn spill," I said.

The long-haired man passed me with just the slightest glimmer of acknowledgment in his hollow dark eyes, as if I were a hallucination he would rather not encourage. He didn't say a word. I turned to watch his tall thin figure heading down the the track, but only the ferret looked back at me with mild interest. They went around the bend, and I felt that my grizzly sighting had been the more natural of the two encounters.

At breakfast I met Frank Foss, an authentic fixture of Essex. Known as Old Grizz, this mountain man had dropped in to get his mail at the desk of the inn. He was a wide-shouldered human stump in worn clothes that looked as if they had been put on him once and for all, like the bark of a tree. His white hair stood straight up on his head, as if he'd just been struck by lightning. There was a half-inch stubble on his jaw, and the teeth in his grin were sparse. In his late seventies and using a cane, Frank surprised me with a strong grip.

Over a cup of coffee, I learned that Frank's life has been a series of dramatic encounters with animals, people, and machinery. "Used to be six foot two. Now I'm five foot nine and a half on account of the accident and three operations. How'd I shrink? I'll tell you how it happened: working for the *railroad!* Hauling a section of rail, I busted the disc behind the sacker-illy-ack and the lumbar. Hip ripped apart. Now I've got two plastic hips. I'm held together with more scrap iron and baling wire than most jalopies!" He slapped his hip for emphasis.

"Used to do some prizefightin' back east. Powder burn in my right eye made me a sucker for a left hook. How'd I get it? Well, as a kid back in Pennsylvania I was shooting a rat in a woodpile. Rifle steel was overloaded and blew back the bolt. *Pow!* Old Doc Wagner went over my eye with something that looked like a nut pick. He had a shaky hand. Finally he says,

'Frankie, I'm scared to go for the pieces in your iris because I might slip and let water out of your eye.' I says, 'For kee-riste sakes, Doc, don't do *that!* '"

Frank had also been a trapper, woodcutter, hunting guide, and adventurer. "Rode the rails only twice—just to say I did it. Dangerous. You lay down some board or you'll get rocks and cinders shot up into your face like buckshot. One time out of Alliance, Nebraska, I ran into some trouble with a Mexican yard bull. I was riding four cars ahead of the caboose and was half froze. He came up and shined a flashlight in my eyes. Blinded me with that light. Felt a pistol pressed into my belly. Then two younger fellers appeared. That Mex bull pistol-whipped one of them bad. They went to a doctor. Doctor was patching him up and said, 'Somebody ought to kill that guy.'

"Now, that was an idea those fellers took *real* serious. They got into a railcar at night and began to make noise. That yard bull came around shining his flashlight into the car. 'Who's in there?' he yells. Now, they'd picked a car with a real easy-sliding door. The yard bull started to climb in and the second fellow kicked the door shut and caught him—with his head inside. Broke his neck. They wired the door shut and when the train pulled out, he was hanging by the door. Went by a tight cattle guard and broke his legs like toothpicks. He was dead already, but he was a mess when they pulled into the next railroad stop."

Frank invited me to look over his cabin, in a stand of trees about a quarter mile from the inn. Outside stood a seven-foot-high framework with a bucket punctured like a sieve. "Shower when I need it," he said, implying infrequency.

The interior of his cabin would have intrigued the photographer Walker Evans: walls papered with yellowing newspaper and *Life* magazine pages, a potbellied stove, and a bare light bulb hanging over a neat single bed. The cabin scent was a perfume of smoke, bacon grease, and wild game.

"Pretty much live off the land meat-wise," said Frank. "Shoot everything with a twenty-two long rifle. Hell, I can kill a deer or even an elk with a twenty-two long rifle. Just have to know where to shoot 'em. Here, take a look at this." He slid a worn but well-oiled .22-caliber rifle out of a battered leather case. "Had it half my life. Took out that little feller with one shot behind the ear." He pointed the rifle at the skin of a black bear hanging on the wall.

"Frank, I understand they call you Old Grizz around here. Still hunt grizzlies?"

"No more. I've killed three grizzlies in my life," he said solemnly. "Powerful beasts. One gave me nightmares for three years. It started when Old

Gillette came out from New York and wanted to shoot a bear. Wealthy fellow with a dairy farm in Hemmingsport, New York. It was November, about twenty below zero, and somebody had put out a salt lick down near the tracks to attract the elk out of Glacier. Not too sporting, but it worked. One afternoon Pork Chop Johnny, Jonesy, and Muss Moots shot a calf elk. Moots pulled the trigger. They gutted it but it was getting dark, so they covered the calf with pine branches. Intended to come back the next day.

"Well, nearby was a five-year-old boar grizzly with beautiful silver-tipped fur. From the tracks in the snow we knew that this here grizz came up and gorged himself on that elk, then lay down in the snow like a drunk with his gut full of hooch. Couple of local fellers and me went down to the lick for another elk and woke up the bear. Up he pops big as a barn door. Scared one feller so bad he fired off a shot and wounded him. 'Where'd you hit him?' I asks. 'Don't know,' he says. 'You don't know where you shot him?' I says, angry-like. 'Then you had no business shootin' that bear!' Well, of course he was just scared.

"A while later Swede Johnson was leading a horse down Dickey Creek Trail from checking his traps, when that bear appeared in the road. Swede had a rifle on his back, the lead rope in his left hand, and in his right hand a gunnysack of muskrat carcasses he used to bait his marten traps. Tried to ease down the gunnysack and get his rifle, but the bear took off.

"I asked Old Gillette if he wanted to go for the bear and he said yes. I had my two-seventy and a Super thirty-eight on my hip. I told Gillette to get a cartridge in his chamber. 'You'll have one shot,' I told him. We tracked that bear down by the river. I heard a crackling in the brush. We'd stop and listen, move a little closer, and the crackling would stop again. Finally I could see the bear. He was hurt bad, real sick. Had his head between his paws and his snout up against a tree root. Rocking his head back and forth so that his ears hit the snow on either side. Then he'd move forward and I could see big black gobs of blood on the snow, like marbles. All of a sudden he smelled us and took off for the river.

"We ran back to the trail. I told Old Gillette to watch behind us. We found his tracks leading in a semicircle. 'See that old snag on the cliff edge?' I says. 'That's where he is, I'll bet.' So we approached. Suddenly, I seen snow falling from the small trees around the snags. That bear jumped out at us, bellerin' and roarin' with his claws out. Knew I had only one chance so I aimed for the breastbone. Shot him five feet away. That two-seventy just picked him up and put him on his back. I was shakin' like a leaf. So was Old Gillette. The bear was still, but I put another bullet behind his head for good measure. Gillette was snow white and could barely talk. Gillette asked me, 'What am I going to tell the folks back home.' I said, 'You tell 'em you shot him just the way I did.' Expect that's what he did. That bear was nine feet long and weighed five hundred pounds. Beautiful hide, too."

"That's quite a story, Frank," I said.

"It is, isn't it? Haunted me for years," he said, shaking his head. "Never will forget that bear comin' out of the bushes with his claws and teeth ready to tear me to smithereens."

The last thing Frank showed me was the truck he'd outfitted. It was a wooden shell, insulated, with the pipe from a wood-burning stove poking out the top. "Going up to Alaska. Still wild up there, like Montana was when I first come out here half a century ago. Salmon everywhere. Moose! Caribou! Bears! Plenty bears up there still. I might never come back, by God."

I left the old man fiddling with his truck, dreaming of Alaska. Wild country. Plenty bears up there still. A place where you could shoot a bear and leave no dent in the ecosystem. Frank Foss, old Grizz, the mountain man of Essex, as wild as the Montana grizzly—and just as endangered.

Charles E. Conrad, founder of Kalispell. (Courtesy Montana Historical Society)

Alicia Conrad on her wedding day.

Charles E. Conrad, Jr., the half-breed son known as "Edward."

Charles Davenport Conrad, the gambler. (Courtesy Montana Historical Society)

Chapter 9

Charles Conrad Invents a Town

So you see, Father, I am in continual hot water
& I often think that to take one's own life is
justifiable, however, I do not suppose, I would
be so common & broken-hearted to do that. . . ."
          Charles Edward Conrad Jr., in a letter to
                              his father, July 1902

In Kalispell, the town that Charles Conrad founded in 1892, a flock of churches and funeral homes surrounded the Flathead County Courthouse. Once top-notch, the Kalispell Hotel was now reduced to fleabag status. A runty man and woman were engaged in an alcoholic harangue in the hallway, but I checked in anyway. Over dinner at the Ho Won Chinese restaurant, I perused a book about my great-great-uncle and learned that Charles's eighty-nine-year-old daughter, Alicia, had died as recently as 1981. I wished I had met her, because she was the last to know all the Conrads.

In 1890 Charles learned that James J. Hill's Great Northern Railroad was approaching Flathead Lake on its way to Spokane. An arrangement was made: Conrad would pick a town site and Hill's railroad would meet it. Charles and his wife, Lettie, left Fort Benton and went up to the Flathead Valley by coach. Charmed by the gentle landscape, Charles called it *Kalispell*, after the Indian tribe.

At 6 P.M. on New Year's Eve 1891, Hill's westbound railroad construction crew joined rails with the eastbound crew on the fledgling Main Street, making Hill the first man to build a railroad across the continent without government aid. After a parade, a silver spike was driven into the joined rails by Mrs. J. J. Kimmerly, the first white woman to settle in the valley. Then came a hearty pounding from Nicholas Moon, one of the earliest settlers. Moon was a bachelor who shunned women when he was sober but found prostitutes the perfect end to a good toot. Soon after the spike-driving celebration, Moon sold his ranch, had one last whing-ding in Kalispell's redlight district, and announced, "I'm heading for British Columbia where there is some peace and quiet. There's jest too many petticoats on the clothes-lines in this town."

In 1892, Charles opened a branch of the Conrad National Bank in a one-room frame house on Main Street. In time a brick building was built. He also bought seventy-two acres of land and commissioned a twenty-two-room Norman-style house with eight bedrooms—the grandest house that that part of Montana had seen, from the modern indoor toilets to the Tiffany-glass windows and a wood-paneled billiards room. The stables could have accommodated a small cavalry.

Alicia Conrad remembered her father reading Kipling aloud, telling fairy tales to the children at bedtime, and sometimes singing "Swing Low, Sweet Chariot," a memory of his youth in Virginia. Afternoons were for riding sleek saddle horses or driving a team of matched grays called Fog and Mist. There were camping trips and hunting parties in the fall. Charlie Russell, Teddy Roosevelt, and George Bird Grinnell were guests.

There was one social group Charles Conrad never forgot. Alicia remembered Indian leaders visiting the house in their finest regalia, and at dinner they would be served on the finest china, linens, and silver. After dinner, Charles would lead them into the Great Hall. Here the Indians squatted in a semicircle around Conrad, who sat tall and rigid, his back to the fireplace. The lights were dimmed so that only the flames illuminated their faces and dark glowing eyes. A pipe or good cigars might be passed as they spoke of old times: Fort Conrad, intertribal skirmishes, the great buffalo hunts. Conrad spoke Blackfeet well, but sometimes sign language was best. Alicia crept down the front staircase in her nightgown to peer at her father surrounded by a "half-circle of Indians seated in the semi-darkness, with the lights from the flaming fireplace highlighting their bronzed and glistening faces, giving them a look of dignity . . . ."

To the town of Kalispell, Charles seemed the model husband and father, doting on his children: Charles Davenport, Katherine, and little Alicia. But there was always one dark spot—his relationship with Charles E. Conrad Jr., the half-Indian son, known as Edward. The cruelest blow came when he named his white son Charles Davenport Conrad, as if the firstborn weren't good enough to hold up the name. I suspect it was Lettie Conrad's doing, as the middle name is from her side of the family.

I could find little about the Indian boy's early life except that after his mother, Sings-in-the-Middle Woman, died in the late 1870s, he was sent at age four to Catholic boarding schools in Montreal. Conrad corresponded with Edward and occasionally visited him on business trips to Canada, but he never invited him to the house at Kalispell. Once he took his daughter Alicia, then seven years old, on a trip to Hot Springs, Arkansas, where he had arranged to meet Edward. Alicia remembered stepping into the lobby of the hotel as a tall, dark, handsome apparition appeared; her father said, "Alicia, dear, this is your brother, Edward." Alicia was fascinated by her exotic sibling, and vice versa. To her delight, he picked her up and carried her around the hotel lobby on his shoulders.

Hoping to give Edward an occupation and steady income, Charles traveled to Montreal and set him up in a partnership called the Porter-Conrad Importing Company, with a man named A. T. Porter. All seemed promising until September 1899, when Porter abruptly wrote Charles about Edward: "He is not intentionally bad or dishonest but simply has a mania for spending money, which he cannot resist. And it is due to his intense self-conceit. He cannot bear to be surpassed in anything. If a man spends ten dollars, he must go him one better, and do it with a flourish. If a friend drives a fine horse, he must have a finer. He simply cannot and will not be outdone. It is conceit that rules his every act." Porter went on to reveal that Edward not only had been spending company funds hand over fist, but had been drawing advances against his hundred-dollar-a-month salary, and was often absent from work.

Porter also reported that Edward had "got into a love-scrape" with a French girl, Marie Blanche Lionais. "She is considered a very beautiful girl, moves in the best French society, and is irreproachable in every way. Her family are quite prominent—all well-to-do, and some of them wealthy." For several months, said Porter, the lovers had been meeting secretly until her father caught on and made things unpleasant for Blanche at home. When Edward plucked up his courage and asked for her hand, Mr. Lionais consented to an engagement if Charles Conrad himself would grant permission to his son.

Charles did approve, but Edward's money problems continued. In need of a loan from his father, Edward wrote an impassioned letter to his stepmother, Lettie, addressing her as "My dear Mrs. Conrad":

I do not know whether my father tells you of my letters; I hope he does, you could be such a good help to him, for there are subjects that the quick natural conception of woman is more true, unselfish & lenient; the latter I want, especially. I want an advocate; I need it. I have been a black sheep, and like the prodigal, returns, after spending his wealth—that of the Scripture has been a costly payment for experience—whilst, mine is on a very small scale, and not so wicked, in fact, it has been honorable, only with too many friends and too much heart—that I have spent my money and more. But now I see the fatality of such living. If it was not for the bright prospects of my business, my love for a good woman (with your consent, she could be such a good helpmate—my better half) my duty towards you and yours, and also my partner, I would not stop a minute in this place, but start anew, without the aid of anyone, in another country.

Edward's command of English was impressive. He went on, taking a different tack:

In the short time I have known you, my greatest respect and admiration have been won without resistance; and I feel proud when some of my friends permit you to be called my mother; I hope I do not offend. It is so nice, it is a world in itself—the word, "mother." When I see the exchange of affection between child & mother, it often makes my eyes water. Give my love to Alicia & tell her my sweetheart is making a doll for her and hope father is well.

Believe, I remain,
Yours very sincerely,
Edward

Lettie did intercede for Edward, because he soon received a check for over eleven thousand dollars. He married Blanche at Montreal's Catholic cathedral in June 1900, with the the archbishop performing the ceremony. Charles Conrad, who attended with his wife, gave his son a ten-thousand-dollar house.

Married life did not stop Edward from gambling and entertaining beyond his means. In a series of bitter letters, Porter said that it was impossible to work with Edward, so Charles bought out Porter, and by February 1902, Edward was writing on letterhead of the Conrad Importing Company. As he fell further into debt, Edward's emotional state remained as precarious as his business. In September, Blanche herself wrote her father-in-law, begging him to visit Edward, as "I don't know what he'll do . . . ."

Charles was in no shape to travel, having suffered from diabetes for almost ten years. Insulin had not been discovered, and the disease ravaged his body. A few weeks before his death, he purchased ten acres of land on a promontory where Lettie and he had last ridden their horses and drew a sketch for a mausoleum, specifying dimensions and materials. His legs caused him great pain, which he bore stoically as the family gathered. William came from Great Falls, and John hurried by train from Seattle. Charles died on Thanksgiving Day 1902, aged fifty-two, and the news flashed across Montana that one of its pioneers was gone.

Edward was in Chicago and did not know of his father's death. His highest priority was money and his failing business. On December 2, he wrote to Lettie on hotel stationery saying he would come to Kalispell to speak to his father about financial matters: "I shall go incognito under the name of Joseph Edwardes—you need not fear of I [*sic*] making any mischief, I shall be a total stranger." Not wanting to embarrass his father, the half-breed son dared not even use his real name.

Mistakenly assuming that Edward knew of Charles's death, Lettie sent a telegram that said only: "If you wish to come incognito do so at once. Mr. Curry awaits you as my representative. I cannot see you. Answer, Mrs. C. E. Conrad."

I imagine Edward stepping off the train at Kalispell and taking a carriage down Main Street, passing the Conrad National Bank, and arriving at Charles Conrad's great house. He walked up the steps to his father's mansion for the first time in his life, and was ushered into the sitting room by the stern family lawyer. Here Edward learned that his father was dead, and that the funeral had been held two days earlier. I see him looking about at the house that was never his home, hearing movement upstairs and wondering if it was his stepmother, Lettie, or his white siblings, two of whom he had never met. Then he was driven to the train station for a long, lonely ride back to Montreal.

Charles's will left one-half of his $2.5-million estate to his wife and the other half equally divided among his four children. Edward was twenty-six, with his white siblings somewhat younger. The will created a trust for eleven years that would pay each child, including Edward, $150 a month until final disbursement was made. According to the will, "that certain half-breed Indian known as Charles E. Conrad, Junior, who has been educated by me in Canada and who now resides in the City of Montreal" was entitled to his fair share—but all previous loans were to be deducted when the trust ended.

Over the years, Charles had advanced his Indian son over forty thousand dollars—a large sum of money; he hadn't done likewise for his white children. "That certain half-breed Indian" was a chilly way to describe a first-born son, and the will reflects a final effort to teach Edward that in death all things shall be reckoned, at least financially.

Edward was not happy with the terms of the will and asked for cash immediately. Alicia, as executor, wrote to her stepson: "Are you going to wake up from this false dream you have been living in?—Go to work and be a man! Live within your income and be ready to receive your inheritance in the eleven years your father left you to make a man of yourself. And hold your head up so I can be proud of my other son!" The letter was the best advice anyone ever gave Edward.

Instead, Edward boldly hired attorneys in New York who acted through a local Kalispell attorney to declare Charles Conrad's will invalid, but a Kalispell judge ruled that nothing would change. The defeat sent Edward into a deeper financial panic. Finally, on the advice of her brother, Lettie bought out Edward's interest in the will for fifty thousand dollars and forgave the forty thousand dollars in previous loans.

Edward returned to Montreal able to pay debts, but also knowing that his source of income was gone. Edward's marriage and business disintegrated, and in September 1905, at the age of twenty-nine, Edward committed suicide.

Years before, in the days of the disappearing frontier, Edward's Indian mother, Sings-in-the-Middle Woman, had thought her half-breed son would be better off educated as a Catholic and as a white man than left to starve with her tribe on the reservation, stranded in a world without buffalo. Charles Conrad gave his half-Indian son a famous name, an education, and plenty of money, but never the things he craved—a real home and a father's love.

After Charles's death, Lettie Conrad maintained the house and controlled the family fortune in partnership with her brother-in-law William until his death in 1914. The day Lettie named her son, Charles Davenport, president of the Conrad National Bank marked the downfall of the Kalispell branch of the Conrads.

Unlike his ambitious father—but very much like his Indian half-brother—Charley did not consider earning money to be of high priority in his life. He liked liquor, women, and hunting. At his apartment in downtown Kalispell he gave wild parties and was Kalispell's most eligible bachelor until he married Kokoa Baldwin, daughter of a prominent lawyer. After the wedding, the wild parties continued—without her.

One morning Kokoa rode her horse to the Conrad National Bank, handed the reins to the janitor, and stormed into the lobby. Her husband was at his desk, in full view of the customers. Leaning into Charley's puffy face, she screamed, "I'll teach you not to go whoring around with other women!" Then she thrashed his face with her riding crop until bystanders pulled her away.

Kokoa filed for divorce in 1915 and went down to Hollywood, lured by the dream of starring in the silent pictures. An excellent rider, she got bit parts in westerns with Tom Mix and William S. Hart but never achieved stardom. A new marriage to a man in the film industry failed, and she returned to Kalispell to open a shop and seek child support. When she died under mysterious circumstances, there was talk of suicide.

Charley married a complacent woman who tolerated his increasing appetite for alcohol. In 1930, Charley's twenty-one-year-old son, Billy, went off alone on a hunting trip and didn't come back. The next morning Charley found him in the woods, dead from a shotgun blast through his chest. It was called a hunting accident, but again everyone suspected suicide. It gave Charley another excuse to drink.

During Prohibition, Charley was supplied by rumrunners who came across the border from Canada (an ironic reversal of how his father had started the family fortune as a whiskey trader). As president of the Conrad National Bank, he exercised poor judgment with loans, even taking personal kickbacks, and the bank went steadily downhill. When Lettie died in 1924, Charley and his two sisters inherited half a million dollars total from their mother. Alicia and Katherine naively allowed Charley to invest in hare-brained schemes, including a corporation whose product was a cream for Negroes to straighten their kinky hair. During the Great Depression, all the family's timber and farm land was sold or mortgaged to pay taxes.

Charley had one last scheme: in partnership with a local tavern owner, he proposed to turn the family house into a bar and casino with a discreet bordello on the upper floors. When Alicia heard this rumor, she secretly bought the house in 1935 with a small down payment. Charley was furious. In 1940, a group of Kalispell businessmen bought the Conrad bank and allowed Charley to stay on as a figurehead president out of respect for his father. He died of lung cancer the following year.

Alicia would live another forty years in the house she saved, part of that time in poverty. In 1914, she married Wally McCutcheon, a handsome, charming cad who spent most of his time trying to get control of her share of the estate while carousing in the best whorehouses of Butte. As Alicia's money dwindled, McCutcheon turned nasty. He mortgaged their ranch, and when the debt fell due, they lost the property.

In 1921, Alicia gave birth to Alicia Ann, known as "Timmie," but fatherhood had no rehabilitating effect on McCutcheon, and their 1924 divorce proceedings documented his drinking, gambling, whoring, and violent behavior. Before hopping a train to Kansas City, McCutcheon said bitterly to a friend, "I've squeezed this orange dry." The family never heard from him again. Without a husband, Alicia struggled to support her little daughter.

The next morning I went to the Outlaw Inn to meet my cousin Timmie—that is, Alicia Ann McCutcheon Vick. I found her in the motel dining room, a woman in her sixties with short brown hair and a warm smile. Her owl-like brown eyes twinkled with ironic appraisal behind thick glasses. Timmie had been dealt a hard life early on, but now seemed comfortable, even happy with her second husband, Richard Vick, a retired radio-station manager. Richard owned a framing shop in Missoula, and they had driven up especially to meet me.

Though distant cousins, Timmie and I connected right away as she spoke of Alicia Conrad, who had been dead for a decade. "Mother was not what you would call a happy person, though she had a tremendous ability to enjoy things in the moment. She had a dramatic sense of fantasy. She liked to go outside in storms and feel her dress whip around in the wind. She loved graveyards and probably should have been an actress or writer. When she married my stepfather, George Campbell, I was seven."

Timmie's stepfather was a tall, gaunt man who had been to Yale and flown in the Lafayette Escadrille. Secretive and controlling, he made a living managing ranches for absentee owners and buying out destitute homesteaders. "George Campbell was an archconservative who believed everyone should be able to take care of himself. He didn't believe in Social Security. Even though he received the checks, he never cashed them. After he died, we found them stuck in his books like bookmarks. He didn't know anything about children and made me call him 'Mr. Campbell' until I was in my thirties. He didn't like me and I didn't like him, but later we became friends. I took care of him after he had a heart attack."

George and Alicia had moved into the Conrad house in 1935, but he refused to put any money into its upkeep. The house and grounds soon declined. Brambles filled the garden, and the hedges grew ten feet high, hiding the house from the street. The roof leaked. When plaster fell from the ceiling and a chamber became uninhabitable, Alicia and George simply closed the door and moved to another room. "It was like the House of Usher. They never discarded anything that ever came into that house," said Timmie. "There were whole rooms stacked with newspapers. It was a firetrap. They ended up living mostly in the dining room."

The mansion declined so much that it was known as the Haunted House. Eventually, even George and Alicia found it uninhabitable and moved into a mobile home in the garden. George kept Alicia apart from the world for the last ten years of his life, until he died in 1973. "My mother was not grief stricken when he died," said Timmie. "It really liberated her. "

"That's a weird story," I said.

"Well, we're a weird family," laughed Timmie. "My mother's brother, Uncle Charley, was a gambler and invested in strange business schemes. At first, my mother had a three-hundred-dollar-a-month allowance, but then the trust ran out. It was gone by the time I came along. I was married young, had a child, and divorced young. My daughter, Dede, lived in the Conrad house until she was eleven. We both have memories of living in that big house and being ashamed because there was no means of taking care of it. We were broke. It was terrible."

In the late 1970s, the reclusive Alicia Conrad suddenly announced that she wanted the house turned into a museum. Her grandson Chris Vick approached the city council, and it became a hotly debated topic in Kalispell. "The city council members who were against the house then are now eating crow, because it is the largest attraction in Kalispell. It is the *only* attraction. With eighteen thousand paying visitors a year, it's self-sufficient."

After brunch, the three of us drove to the Conrad Mansion. The gardens were in full bloom, with orange and yellow zinnias encircling the great dark-shingled house; blooming wisteria framed the wide veranda. The house had become a monument not only to Charles Conrad but to the *idea* of Charles Conrad, the myth of the red-blooded Virginia gentleman who was tough but decent to the Indians and helped tame the West for white people, making a bundle in the process. The volunteer docents on duty recognized Timmie and welcomed her, but I sensed a peculiar rivalry. Timmie was a descendant of the Conrads, but she was from the prosaic ancien régime— that is, from the time when the house was actually lived in, and on the decline. Timmie was dressed in a simple pantsuit—a civilian—while the women wore Victorian blouses and long dresses, high priestesses to the shrine of western vigor and gentility.

In any case, they let us in free. As the women guides gathered the other visitors, Timmie took us off on our own tour of the house, deconstructing the shrine aspect. "This is not the original table. My Uncle Charley got it. And that wasn't there," she said, flicking her wrist at a chair. We stopped in the hallway and Timmie pointed to an empty space. "The large chest and mirror and grandfather clock were stolen about twenty years ago. It was Labor Day weekend and my parents were in Missoula for medical checkups. The thieves brought a moving van up to the house and loaded it up. The FBI got in on it—but never caught them." The thieves also made off with a number of valuable Charles M. Russell watercolors.

The ground-floor rooms were cozy, with warm wooden paneling, photographs of the famous buffalo herd, and a large oil portrait of Theodore Roosevelt. Sitting on Charles's desk was a photograph of his Indian son, Charles Edward, and nearby stood a picture of his white son, Charles Davenport. Timmie looked at the pictures of her two uncles and shook her head. "Edward's picture was never displayed when I lived in the house. I always felt sorry for that boy. I can't understand why my grandmother insisted on naming *her* son Charles, too. It was a terrible thing to do. Lettie couldn't have been as perfect as my mother thought she was."

"It wasn't a very happy family," said Richard Vick.

"No, not a happy family," said Timmie. "I suppose it had something to do with their way of making money, and becoming robber barons, so to speak. That would create tension. I don't think Lettie was much of a hater. She seemed to be well liked, but she was a strong-headed woman."

Richard turned to Timmie and said, "You don't want to give the impression that Alicia—your mother—was some timid soul living in her mother's shadow. She was one of the first people in Kalispell to own a Harley Davidson."

"She rode it?" I asked.

"In a black turtleneck sweater," said Alicia. "She also went skinny-dipping in Lake McDonald, which wasn't done. She also did the flapper thing. She was the first woman in Kalispell to get her hair cut short. So she was a rebel. Later she and George went around in a Pierce Arrow, but they were eccentric recluses by then. He had a lot of power over her."

Upstairs in the central hall was an impressive panel of Tiffany glass. A trio of buffalo heads hung in the billiards room. Timmie nodded at a bedroom door and laughed. "This room was for Charles's eldest daughter, Aunt Kate. She weighed two hundred and sixty pounds. She always loved to eat cream, butter, and sugar. Her arms were so fat it was hard for her to comb her hair. She married someone called Egbert Van Duzer—what a name!—a cashier at the Conrad bank. She called him Bertie. She was addicted to chocolate and had boxes of it delivered every day.

"Poor Aunt Kate, popping all those chocolates in her mouth and growing fatter by the moment. They had to take the banister off the stairs in the house to ship her out on two stretchers to the hospital. She had a ruptured appendix, but by the time the doctors cut through all that flab, it was too late. She took up two spaces in the mausoleum." Timmie giggled wickedly. "All those chocolates! I shouldn't be laughing."

Up in the attic was a playroom and a room filled with a dozen stuffed birds and animals. "They belonged to Harry Stanford, Lettie's younger brother," said Timmie. "Uncle Harry was a taxidermist and a friend of Charlie Russell. They'd sit on the porch and drink whiskey together and talk about animals and Indians. Russell sent Harry about two dozen illustrated letters, which appeared in the book *Trails Plowed Under.* Harry used to send Russell stuffed animals so he could paint from them."

"What did Harry do for a living?"

"Harry was Kalispell's first police chief," said Timmie. "One spring the town was having trouble with a bunch of young Indians riding through backyards tearing down clotheslines as a prank—the way kids steal hubcaps today. Well, Harry took a two-by-four, hid himself in an alley, and when the next Indian rode by—*whang!*—he took care of him."

"Couldn't do that today," said Richard.

"Harry was a character," said Timmie. "He had a telephone hanging on his wall which he hated. He would never answer it. Finally one day it rang and he tore it off the wall and threw it into the street."

"Harry never married?" I asked.

"Oh yes, Harry married. To a woman eleven years older than he was. She had been a prostitute," said Alicia casually. "That was in Fort Benton. She was a dear woman, Aunt Jo, but she had a stroke in later years and her eyes were completely crossed. After she died—I was about nineteen—he would sit in a rocking chair on the porch and cry because he missed Aunt Jo. Mother and I used to get a great kick out of it because he had been really mean to her in life. He would never even give her an indoor bathroom at their house!"

"Is it documented that your Aunt Jo was a prostitute?" I asked.

"Only by my mother," said Timmie. "Aunt Jo had a sad life in the early days of Fort Benton. But mother would have embroidered on it. Too bad, because Aunt Jo was a nice old woman. And Harry! Well, I loved Uncle Harry dearly. He was the closest thing I had to a dad. Harry had nicknames for everyone. He called my mother 'Slats.' He called my brother 'Alligator Bait.' He called me 'Bee.' I don't know why. Maybe I looked like a bee," laughed Timmie softly. "When I was young, a long time ago."

Wolf biologist Diane Boyd with her dog, Max,
at Moose City.

Chapter 10

The Woman and the Wolves

There was a bounty of twenty-five dollars on grey wolves laid by the Judith Round-up Association, for wolves are bad on young calves. Russell and I slipped from the leather. Our guns belched smoke, and one wolf bedded down. The other stood his ground and snarled. Charley slipped a cartridge into the magazine of his gun, dropped to his knee, and when the smoke rolled away there lay two grey wolves. We skinned them out and were fifty dollars to the good. We tied the wolf pelts to our pack horses, and rode on.

Patrick Tucker, *Riding to the High Country*, 1933

Moose City, a settlement located northwest of Glacier Park, appears on no map of Montana. When I asked directions in a gas station at Columbia Falls, a man said, "Fifty miles up that dirt road. About twenty yards from the Canadian border."

As there are no phones in Moose City, I was going on a hunch to meet a woman who knew about wolves, the most controversial animals in Montana today. One hundred years ago, there were wolves all over the territory. Today the only wolves most Montanans see are in Charlie Russell paintings. Wolves were an integral part of Montana's ecosystem until cattle replaced the buffalo. No one cared if wolves killed buffalo calves, but when they took down a Hereford calf or a merino lamb, some white rancher lost money.

Wolfers baited dead carcasses with strychnine, which killed not only wolves but also coyotes, bears, cougars, magpies, and other animals. The

Conrads were linked to wolves in a way typical of the last century: they wanted to exterminate them. In the late 1880s, Ashby Conrad, one of my great-great-uncles, ran successfully for councilman of Billings on the anti-wolf program. This made political sense in a region dominated by cattle and sheep, but it is not something to be proud of. Thanks to bounty hunters, Montana now has barely a dozen wolves running within its boundaries. Recently, the Park Service began a program to reintroduce wolves to the state, raising the hackles of ranchers.

I followed the dirt road that parallels the North Fork of the Flathead River, which defines the westernmost boundary of Glacier National Park. It was a road filled with surprises: coming fast around one corner, I skidded to within ten feet of a big black Angus cow standing smack in the middle of the road. A half hour later, a logging truck nearly sideswiped me.

At Polebridge, a community consisting of a general store, a saloon, and a few cabins, I bought a Coke and asked about Moose City. "Up ahead, half hour," was all the gum-chewing girl could tell me. The road was soft from the morning rain, and it was tricky driving. I was headed far north, and it felt as if the summer would end in a week. The forest seemed to stretch endlessly up into Canada. With the exception of the logging truck, I had passed only one other vehicle in an hour. When I reached the United States–Canada border—posted with a small sign—I turned right, splashing down a muddy road that wobbled across a pasture. Ahead stood a cluster of five log cabins. I headed for one with a smoking chimney, and knocked on the door.

Diane Boyd was a tall blond woman in her early thirties with a friendly handshake as rough as a carpenter's. Her face was rosy and windburned rather than tan, and had a tomboy aspect. She was dressed in a sweatshirt and blue jeans. Since she had no phone and I hadn't written, I explained who I was and what I was doing. She sized me up carefully, then invited me in.

Her cabin was crude but cozy, divided into two rooms with a big stove in the center. Her shelves held papers and books including *Wolves and Men* and Ernest Thompson Seton's *Rolf of the North*. On a table sat a cassette player and tapes by groups like Crosby, Stills, and Nash. On the back wall hung large metal traps, a few fox furs, and a caribou skull with antlers, a curiously rough contrast to the sleek little Toshiba word processor on her desk. Driving through Columbia Falls, I had noted that many stores or houses flashed signs like: "This Establishment Supports the Timber Industry" and "This Family Supported by Timber Dollars." Diane Boyd has a similar sign on her wall, but it has been doctored to read: "This Family Supported by

Timber WOLF Dollars." She offered me a mug of coffee and M&Ms from a bag.

Diane Boyd has devoted a third of her life to studying wolves. Born and raised in Minneapolis, she studied at the University of Montana, then with the wolf expert Dave Mech in Minnesota. There was only one wolf in Montana in 1979 when she came back here to complete research for her graduate studies. "The wolf had been radio-collared, and we wanted to compare her habits with coyotes and their spatial use. I came for two years and stayed for ten."

She lived first in a log cabin near the U.S. Customs station, with other wolf and grizzly bear researchers. Then she became a caretaker at Moose City, a little ranch setup with no commercial enterprise. Studying wolves year-round, she had only one permanent companion, a dog named Max, though occasionally friends or fellow researchers came for visits.

"Listen," Diane said, "I was just on my way out to pick up some traps I keep about twenty minutes down the road at the new cabin I'm building. You want to ride along?" Outside by her truck she held up a heavy metal trap with pointed spikes, a wolf trap. "This is what I use. I know it looks awful, but you get minimal damage with this because it only touches on a couple of points. It seems ironic that this tool—the trap that wiped the wolf out of the West—is now the one we use to do our research with, to learn all we can to benefit and preserve the species."

The Wolf Ecology Project for which Diane works is based out of the University of Montana at Missoula. "Bob Reed began collecting wolf-sighting reports all over Montana starting in 1973. Some were phantom wolves— you know, somebody's husky or a big coyote—but then real wolves were trapped in 1979 and one female was radio-collared. Kishnina was her name. The battery failed, but the next winter we still found tracks and it turned out Kishnina had pups. That's when the Wolf Project started for real. There was no money at all. I was living on a hundred and fifty dollars a month and I couldn't set up a research project. A professor gave me some money out of his pocket and I bought a used Honda Ninety from the Forest Service. I caught up with Kishnina and her pups. One of those pups grew up and began to hang out around my place. I had two dogs then, and I think the wolf pup was just lonely. The dogs knew he was not a dog. He was on the bold side, but never killed any stock. He could have killed my dogs any time he wanted. He was just curious."

In 1984 the program got more funding and the team documented a population increase, with three separate packs. "There are seven wolves in the

Camas Pack, although the pups that were born this spring died. Probably due to a virus. The Headwaters Pack has had three adults for several years, but they just had their first litter this year—eight pups. The Wigwam Pack had eight wolves until this spring, but when I went over there with my traps I only got one wolf and I think that's all there is. Something happened to those wolves. We may find out more this winter when we can track them better in snow."

Year-round Diane Boyd tracked the wolves from an airplane that lands in the hay field near her cabin. The plane had just flown in that morning, dropping off a federal trapper. "I have twelve wolves radio-collared on the air right now."

When Diane finds a wolf in one of her traps, she knocks him out using a jab stick—a four-foot pole tipped with a drug-filled syringe. She has never been bitten by a timber wolf. When drugged they don't move much, but they are vaguely conscious. The drug, Ketamine, is a veterinarian's aid and wears off quickly; thirty minutes later the wolves try to get up. In the old days researchers used PCP, the same drug many ghetto kids used for a high.

"I heard that PCP affected their brains, gave them bad trips," I said.

"I'm not a chemist and I don't do drugs," said Diane. "So I can't tell you."

"Do you take flak from ranchers?"

"All the time. At first it was hard for me to report a problem wolf, one that ate livestock, because it would have to be destroyed. But I had to do it or the local ranchers would get upset and want to get rid of all the wolves. In the long run, the best thing for the wolf is for me to stand in the middle. Ironically, when you talk to radical pro-wolf people they think I'm a redneck. And when you talk to radical wolf haters they think I'm a hippie environmentalist. A friend of mine who works for Fish and Wildlife says, 'The wolf has only two enemies: the wolf haters and the wolf lovers.' A lot of wolves die because of the polarization of these groups."

"You've got a pragmatic approach," I said.

"I'm a scientist, so I try," she said. "My pet peeve with media people is that they want to characterize me as an eccentric woman living in the wilds—this Wolf Woman image. It's bullshit. I'm a serious biologist. I'm concerned about the wolves. The only way to help them is to study them in their element and deal with both sides of the issue."

I mentioned the intense conflict over the use of the northern forests by timber, petroleum, recreational, and environmental factions. "I *am* environmentally oriented," said Diane. "I admit I don't like to see development, but it's inevitable. Certain kinds of development are compatible with wildlife and certain kinds aren't. Logging per se does not hurt wolves. If done right, it stimulates undergrowth, and it can increase deer and elk numbers, which increases wolf numbers. But the public access created by this offsets any benefits. Snowmobilers, hunters, et cetera, come right on in. All our wolves that have been shot or harvested legally—they've been shot on roads or seismic lines."

"Doesn't it hurt you when you lose a wolf?"

"Some biologists think of a wolf as a member of a population, whereas I think of them as individuals. If I lose an animal that we've been studying and developing a long history on, I do react to it emotionally. It's kind of like losing a friend. But I'm a scientist. A mortality doesn't ruin a study; it's an important factor *in* the study. It's important data in figuring out what's limiting wolf numbers. For example, if you can get to a dead wolf soon enough, you can study the reproductive tract or some other aspect of the wolf that you can't do with a live wolf. When hunters have shot a wolf, I walk up and ask where they shot it, if they saw others, and I ask permission to measure it. I'm objective. Some of the hunters are curious about the wolves and actually want to know more about them. The hunters are proud of their trophy. They're beautiful animals. I'd feel worse if people were blasting them because they despised them.

"Right or wrong, there's value in a trophy. The value in an elk a lot of times is the trophy head, although they're also great to eat. The value in a grizzly, for a hunter, is the hide. Value in a wolf? A lot of people don't see it. But I see an aesthetic value in every animal in the woods. It's good that hunters see a value in them at all, or else they wouldn't want them around, because wolves are competitors for other game like deer and elk. So even if hunters see them as a trophy or a nice hide on the wall, it's still better than having a negative value on the animals."

"Why aren't there more wolves here?" I asked.

"Wolves need lots of space. One pack runs along a river drainage fifty miles long and four miles wide in the winter. There are hundreds of prey animals in that area, enough to support two or even three packs. But wolves are territorial and they won't permit other packs in that space. They control their own numbers. You'll never see an area overpopulated. They just won't reproduce." Self-enforced zero population growth. Now, Diane said, the wolves number about twenty-five animals.

Last spring Diane was collaring wolves in Glacier Park. "We were radiotracking them closely, so I knew the mother had abandoned the denning area and gone up into Canada for five days; that's when we knew the pups were dead. We couldn't tell what killed them, as the bodies were decomposed. The sutures on the skull weren't fused at all. They may have been stillborn, or less than two weeks old. I imagine we'll learn something when I take blood samples from the wolves. Some of the samples we took in 1986 showed positive blood titers for *Parvo* virus, so we know they've been exposed."

"What kind of virus is that?"

"I think it's a mutated feline distemper. It's very easily transmitted and it's new in the population and the wolves don't have immunity to it yet. Dogs probably brought it in. A dog poops in the park and the virus is in the droppings and the wolves get it. You know, dogs die right and left in downtown Kalispell of this virus; it's really common."

Diane drove the truck up a side road and parked in front of a nearly completed cabin. She had built the foundations two years ago and then put up the roof and walls last summer with the help of a carpenter friend. We went inside her house, welcomed by the scent of freshly sawed wood.

Living in the woods can be unpredictable: once Diane strapped a deer skull up in a sapling to cure and a bear uprooted the whole tree. One of her dogs was killed by a cougar. She's seen eight cougars and captured one in a wolf trap by accident. "Caught him by the back foot. Usually you catch wolves by the front foot. It took five minutes to knock him out so I could release him. He kept swatting at the jab stick with his paws."

She's also trapped two wolverines. Largest member of the weasel family, the wolverine (*Gulo gulo*) is, pound for pound, the fiercest animal in North America. Wolverines will take down deer and even climb a fifty-foot tree to gobble up baby eagles. "You let them out of the trap and they try to eat you," said Diane. "No fear at all. I trapped one old female wolverine that was blind in one eye with a scar running out of the other one. A crabby old bag, only twenty pounds, but vicious. I gave her enough drugs to put down a big coyote. The minute she could move again, she went for me. I got away. The next day I went back and tracked her in the snow. She'd gone back to the trap site and pissed all over everything for spite."

That fall, Diane was going to spend a few weeks in northern Minnesota, which has the greatest wolf population in the lower forty-eight states, to trap for a research project. "Not to brag or anything, but my trapping reputation is pretty good. I have to be there by Labor Day. Then I'll have to come back to help out the people in Babb [Montana] get some wolves collared. Trapping ends in mid-October when freezing weather and snow sets in."

When the snow starts swirling, she begins to write. As a graduate student she published an article on cougar predation of coyotes in a scientific journal; she's also written on wolf-prey characteristics in her area. "One of the papers I'd like to publish sometime is an article on predator-predator interaction in a carnivore complex where you've got grizzlies, black bears, cougars, coyotes, and wolves. They do eat each other. I like all predators. And I'm a hunter myself. I have no problem killing a deer or an elk which I eat, and my dog gets a bone. But I would never want to hunt a predator. I respect their cunning and hunting skills."

Diane is always amused at the unreal view most people have of carnivorous animals. "A few years ago a friend was teaching a class on wilderness up here on the North Fork to these vegetarian kids from California with this Walt Disney view of the wild world. They were talking about how glorious that movie based on Farley Mowat's *Never Cry Wolf* was: 'Like, wow, wolves don't have to go out and kill caribou, they can live on mice!' I had to say, 'Come on, kids, it's not real. Wolves need large amounts of red meat, not just mice.'

"I guess I'm kind of a troublemaker. Anyway, that night the students were playing cards and I saw a mouse in the kitchen. So I put out some traps. They were appalled. I said, 'If you want to live with mouse turds in your oatmeal in the morning, fine. But I don't want to.' I caught that mouse. The next morning I took some of their organic lettuce and wholewheat bread and made a little mouse sandwich. The mouse's nose hung out one end and the feet and tail hung out the other. I put it on a pretty china dish, garnished it with a lemon wedge and parsley, and I left it on the table. One of the guys—the biggest sap in the group—saw this and I guess he went crazy. He picked the plate up and threw it across the room. I said, 'Hey, they ate mice in Farley Mowat's movie—get with it, guy!' He didn't like that at all, but I had a lot of fun."

Outside Diane handed me a pair of gloves, and I helped her pull twenty traps out of a dirt pile where she had stashed them to shed human scent. We loaded them into the back of the truck. Driving back to Moose City, Diane told me a last story about wolves and predator-predator interaction. One summer she hired a college student named Curt, who had never been out in the woods before. They had just trapped a wolf, drugged him, weighed him, and taken blood samples. When a wolf is trapped, it emits an odor out of fear. There was also blood on its leg from the trap. Suddenly, Curt glanced up and said, "Diane, look. There's a bear." A young adult grizzly was coming their way. It stood up and swayed, smelling the wolf blood and human odor. It kept coming. The wolf was still groggy, defenseless. Diane couldn't leave the wolf until it revived enough to get away from the bear. Diane said, "Curt, go back and start the Jeep."

As Curt tried to start the old Jeep, the grizzly bear angled slowly toward the wolf. Diane started banging on her clipboard and yelling. Finally the engine started up and the wary bear took off. Curt wedged an axe handle down on the accelerator to keep the engine revved. But the bear appeared again and began to circle around.

"We had put the wolf into a dangerous position and we had to get him out of it," Diane said. She picked up the eighty-pound wolf and dragged him to the Jeep. The wolf was barely conscious, snapping his jaws weakly, when they dumped him into the backseat next to Max, her dog. "Max wasn't quite sure he wanted a drugged wolf next to him."

They drove two miles and unloaded the wolf on a cool mossy bank where he could wake up safely. As they watched the wolf revive, from a distance, Curt turned to her and with youthful candor said, "I don't believe it—I'm workin' for a crazy woman!"

Crazy like a wolf, I thought.

Back in Moose City, we unloaded the traps. Dusk was coming and I had to go. There was plenty to admire in this dedicated biologist, her work intrigued me, and I promised I'd send her a card. The whole way back, I imagined wolves—pack after flourishing pack—running through the deep snow that would come this winter.

Top: 1882 photograph *After the Chase* by L. A. Huffman.
(Courtesy Montana Historical Society)
Bottom: Flathead Indian trader Colonel Doug Allard with
trophy bull from his buffalo herd.

Chapter 11

Flathead Valley: A Home Where the Buffalo Roam

Some Indian legends say that the first buffalo came
out of a hole in the ground. When the seemingly
impossible happened and the buffalo were wiped
out, there were Indians that claimed that the white
man found the spot, hazed the herds back in it, and
plugged the hole.

Montana historical road sign

South of Kalispell the northern forests give way to the Flathead Valley. In late afternoon light the neat farmhouses seemed transformed into holographic projections of Maxfield Parrish paintings. Wheat fields begged in operatic tones to be harvested by raw-boned men of faith and strapping pregnant women of virtue and humor. The horizon opened up into a vast expanse of water.

Thirty miles long, Flathead Lake is the largest natural freshwater lake in the West. Supposedly it was home to a monster similar to the one in Loch Ness; numerous sightings describe it as a giant serpent with fishlike scales. Nevertheless, the wooded shore was dotted with getaway houses, boat docks, and cherry orchards. Zooming by, I waved to a pair of purple-lipped children selling buckets of fresh huckleberries. Two deer bent their slender necks to clip the grass, near a golf course signposted as "Home on the Range." At the southern end of Flathead Lake I entered the Flathead Indian Reservation.

Moiese is home to a national treasure, the National Bison Range. Just beyond the gates stood the modern visitors' center. Inside was a spiffy display with audiovisuals on the American buffalo, and a plaque said that the buffalo grazing here descended from the private herd Charles Conrad once kept in Kalispell. I like to think Charles helped save the buffalo—especially since the Conrads derived their early fortune from buffalo robes and tongues sold through the Baker Company.

Early in the nineteenth century, an estimated 40 million buffalo roamed westward from the Mississippi. After the Civil War, white hunters began systematically killing the animals, sending the skins eastward for blankets, clothing, and industrial belting material in factories. As hide hunters swarmed the West, the herds diminished with astonishing speed. Professional hunters with heavy-caliber Sharps rifles would set up a stand downwind and kill hundreds of the unwary beasts before the herd became alarmed.

In 1874, the U.S. Congress tried to pass a law that would prohibit the killing of a buffalo cow by anyone except an Indian and make it illegal to kill more animals than could be used for food. But President Ulysses S. Grant was more concerned with controlling hostile Indians and vetoed the bill.

General Phil Sheridan, who coined the phrase "The only good Indian is a dead Indian," was Grant's chief agent in handling the Indians. He encouraged the buffalo hunters who did "more to settle the vexed Indian question than the entire regular army has done in the last thirty years." As Sheridan told a group of legislators: "They are destroying the Indians' commissary; and it is well-known fact that an army losing its base of supplies is placed at great disadvantage. Send them powder and lead, if you will; but for the sake of a lasting peace, let them kill, skin, and sell until the buffaloes are exterminated. Then your prairies can be covered with speckled cattle and the festive cowboy, who follows the hunter as the second forerunner of an advanced civilization."

An 1883 survey found less than two hundred buffalo in the entire West. Miles of prairie glistened with their bleached bones. For years afterward, entrepreneurs made money by shipping carloads of bones eastward to be processed into fertilizer. The Montana cattle boom coincided almost directly with the slaughter, and soon the prairie was torn up by plow horses and homesteaders.

The salvation of *Bison bison* began in an extraordinary way. A Pend d'Oreille Indian named Sam Walking Coyote wintered with the Piegan Indians on the Milk River in eastern Montana and took part in a buffalo hunt. The herd thundered off, leaving six orphaned calves, which followed Walking Coyote's horse back to the Indian camp. The Piegans thought it was lunacy, but Walking Coyote tended the orphans throughout the winter of 1878. Four survived. In the spring he and his stepson Joseph headed west, arriving at the Catholic mission of St. Ignatius with the buffalo calves trotting behind. By 1884, Walking Coyote's calves had bred and grown to about twenty in number.

A Flathead Valley rancher of French and Indian descent named Charles Allard saw a profit in threatened extinction. With a neighbor, Michael Pablo, he purchased ten of Walking Coyote's buffalo for $250 apiece. Sam Walking Coyote, the true savior of the buffalo, took his $2,500 and rode his pony south to Missoula. A few days later, his body was found under a bridge over the Clark Fork River, the cause of death never determined.

When Allard died in 1896, he left a thriving herd of three hundred bison. A roundup was conducted (in which cowboy artist Charlie Russell participated), and the herd was divided between Pablo, Allard's widow, and various heirs. Charles Conrad knew that the animals were good stock and purchased Mrs. Allard's share. Another group was sold to the Canadian government for their preserve.

Conrad moved his buffalo to a ranch west of Kalispell, and they multiplied. The dominant bull was called Kalispell Chief, but the leader of the herd was a magnificent cow called Frizzle Top. It was Frizzle Top who decided when the herd would move on to new grazing grounds, often pushing down fences of irate neighbors. When Conrad died in 1902, his estate listed the number of buffalo at forty-six, among them eleven mature bulls.

As the demand for purebred buffalo grew, Lettie Conrad corresponded with zoo curators, conservation officials, and wealthy estate owners in the East. Chief among them was the naturalist William Hornaday of the Smithsonian. In 1908, Hornaday arranged for Lettie to sell thirty-four bison at $250 apiece to the American Bison Society of New York City. (As a gesture of good faith, Lettie threw in two calves for free.) Through the society's efforts, the U.S. government was persuaded to set aside land for the National Bison Range at Moiese, and today the preserve is nineteen thousand acres, managed by the National Park Service.

The refuge's manager, a dark, stocky man named John Malcolm, told me, "There are about seventy thousand buffalo in the world today. Could be ten times as many in just a short time if people wanted them, because they breed easily enough. There are some big buffalo ranches in the Dakotas and Oklahoma and, of course, a couple in eastern Montana. We have about four hundred buffalo on the National Bison Range, and every year we have to cull the herd."

"How do you do that?"

"We round them up on horseback in October. Then we make a selection and sell them at auction. The buffalo roundup has become kind of an event; actually I'd like to downplay that because the tourists kind of get in the way."

Driving *Red Cloud* through the rangelands, I soon found a group of buffalo—an old bull surrounded by a half dozen cows cropping grass. They were sleepy-looking animals and close enough for me to snap a few pictures from my Jeep. The novelist Ivan Doig recently wrote an accurate description of a bison:

> A buffalo up close appears to be two animals pieced together: the front half of a shaggy ox and the rear of a donkey. There is even what seems like a seam where the hairy front part meets the hairless rear half. But although they are a cockeyed-looking creature—an absentminded family where everybody had put on heavy sweaters but forgot any pants, is the first impression a bunch like this gives— buffalo plainly know what they're on the planet for. Graze. Eat grass and turn it into the bulk of themselves. Protein machines.

Buffalo meat contains certain fats that actually reduce cholesterol in humans. In the old days, Plains Indians were observed eating eight pounds of meat in one sitting with no digestion problems and no obesity. Charlie Russell once wrote that America should have named the buffalo as its national dish on Thanksgiving Day rather than the turkey because "the nickle weares his picture dam small money for so much meat he was one of natures bigest gifts and this country owes him thanks . . . ."

Red Cloud bumped over the dirt road winding up Red Sleep Mountain, passing bands of antelope and skittish mountain sheep with large curled horns. Coming down into a valley, I spotted the perfect buffalo herd for a photograph. The problem was their distance from the road. I looked around—no rangers in sight. So I broke a cardinal rule of the National Bison Range: *Do Not Leave Your Car.* Stealing across the field, I slunk to within fifteen yards of the grazing herd. There was some risk to this, for every year some tourist in Yellowstone Park gets gored or trampled by "tame" buffalo.

I snapped my pictures and was heading back across the field when a ranger's car appeared a half mile away. A minute later he pulled up as I was getting into my Jeep. I felt guilty, worse than if I had been speeding on a freeway, and I remembered Glacier Park Ranger Dave Casteel's little talk about the consequences of breaking natural and civil laws. I was an environmental delinquent.

In my rearview mirror I could see the ranger talking on the radio; then he walked up and leaned on my window. He was a young fellow wearing a flat-brimmed hat. "Good afternoon, sir. Could I see your driver's license, please?"

I handed it over. He walked to his car, talked on the radio, and then came back to my window. "You're the fellow that was talking with John Malcolm, weren't you?"

"Yes, sir."

"You know it's against regulations to get out of your car, don't you?"

"Yes, sir."

"Normally, I could give you a fifty-dollar fine. But in this case, I'll let you go with a warning."

"Very kind of you, sir."

I waited until he had driven around me, heading off to keep the law and protect rubes from getting their buttocks launched by charging buffalo. Then I slowly cruised through the range, enjoying the dark woolly herds of buffalo, thanking Walking Coyote for his vision, and wondering if my ancestors had understood how lucky they were to have known the great herds on the unfenced Great Plains.

Doug Allard's presence in St. Ignatius was unmistakable. The billboard hits you first: "Colonel Doug Allard's World Famous Flathead Indian Trading Post and Museum Just Ahead." Allard's roadside empire was an impressive two-story log trading post and museum, gas station, and motel. Nearby, a thick-barred corral held a half dozen shaggy buffalo dozing in the sun. I had buffalo business to talk with Colonel Allard.

The trading-post items ranged from arrowheads and T-shirts to museum-quality Navajo blankets and finely beaded Crow ceremonial vests selling for thousands of dollars. A kindly Indian woman led me back to an inner sanctum. Doug Allard rose from behind his desk, a hefty fellow in his fifties dressed in shorts and a sport shirt. His jet black hair was pulled back in a foot-long ponytail, while a neatly trimmed mustache fell jauntily around his toothy smile.

Doug Allard's title—colonel—is not military in origin, but an honorific given to auctioneers. "I took a mail-order course from the Florida School of Auctioneering. I have fun using the title. Nobody around here knows why

I'm called colonel—I was a staff sergeant in the Marine Corps—but people around here actually *like* to call me that."

Doug had charm, humor, and a fair load of buffalo blarney. "Okay, I'm a Flathead," he said, "but like most of the people on this reservation I've got white blood in me, too. My white ancestors were of French descent. My great-grandfather Charles Allard Sr. came here as a young boy, established a ranch down here, and married an Indian woman. He was the one who owned the buffalo.

"My great-uncle Charlie Jr. was kind of the wild man of the region. He was half Indian. At one time he owned everything from the end of Flathead Lake down to just about Ronan. Lost it all in a horse race during the 1920s. He liked the ladies, too. One day I was sitting here when a little old lady came into the shop and asked, 'Are you related to Charlie Allard?' I said, 'Yes, I am.' Her eyes just glowed and she said, 'He was the greatest love of my life. I was seventeen when Charlie came to town with the circus. He was the most handsome and gallant man I ever met. He invited me into his wagon and we spent hours together. I knew right then that I always wanted to be with him. He promised to meet me the next day and we would elope. I packed my bag and waited. He didn't come. The circus had pulled out that morning. I never told my parents or even the man I later married. I'm eighty-six years old, but I've never forgotten the enchanting moments I spent with your uncle Charlie Allard.' Then she left. Isn't that sweet? *Enchanting moments.*"

"Sounds like a cad. What ever happened to Uncle Charlie?"

"Alcoholic. Died in Warm Springs of the D.T.'s. Warm Springs is Montana's nuthouse, by the way. But he was the head honcho rounding up the buffalo, and he'll always be remembered for that."

A huge buffalo bull head hung above the door. "What's his story?"

"You saw the buffalo herd I keep out there in the corrals? From the National Bison Herd at Moiese; they auction a few off every year to cull the herd. I shot this big young bull two years ago because he was picking on my favorite old bull. We ate him, of course. He's a descendant of the original Pablo-Allard-Conrad herd."

Doug's Indian-art business started as a hobby, but he became highly successful at organizing auctions of Indian art in the Southwest. "It's a competitive market. There are over a hundred and sixty Indian stores in the Phoenix area alone. When I go down there with Indian stuff, it's like taking sand to the beach, but people love to go to auctions. Always looking for a bargain. Sometimes they find them, sometimes they don't." When the business flourished, he built a museum attached to his trading post. "I'm the first Indian to ever build a museum—on a reservation or off," he said proudly.

Our conversation was momentarily interrupted by the entry of an Indian woman of extraordinary beauty wearing a white tennis dress. She handed Doug an envelope and a few bills to pay. "Hi, sweetheart," said Doug, tucking an arm around her waist. "This is my wife, Debbie." Debbie shook my hand and apologized for the quick visit, but she was off to the courts for a game of singles.

"Wow," I said after she left.

"Gorgeous, isn't she?" chuckled Doug. "She's twenty-eight—half my age. I am a lucky son of bitch. I've never married anyone older than thirty, and I've been married three times with eight kids," said Doug proudly. "But Debbie's the best. She does all the photography for the auction catalogs and keeps the books. She's a good woman and a great shot. Nailed a deer in the vegetable garden last year. One reason I don't play around is that she'd probably nail me with that rifle!" He chuckled heartily.

"She's Indian all right. The first men in our family married Indian women," said Doug. "Since then, my father and his brothers and sisters—none of them married Indians. Because my Indian grandmother was an *anti-Indian*. She told me when I was a kid, 'Get an education and get off this reservation, or you'll become another drunk Indian just like your Uncle Charlie.' All my childhood friends are dead due to alcohol—except one guy who quit about fifteen years ago."

After high school, Doug spent a year in the Korean War, graduated from college at Bozeman in 1956, and worked in San Francisco, first in meat packing, then insurance. "I lived down there from '56 to '72. From the Beat generation to the hippies. Nice town, San Francisco. Haven't been back in a while because most of my business now is in the Southwest."

The tribal council elected Doug as executive secretary of the Flathead tribe in 1978. "It's the most powerful position on the reservation, especially if you have a chairman who you can work closely with. It was a hell of a job, but we got some things done. At that time there was very little employment policy, no clear job descriptions, and no pay scales. A tribal employee could be fired on the spot—no employee's rights. We restarted the post and pole yard, which is the only successful tribal business we've ever had. I was general manager of it."

The Flathead reservation consists of the Salish, Pondera, Kalispell, and Kootenai tribes. In the 1830s, the tribes sent delegations to St. Louis to search for "black robes"—Jesuit priests—to teach them about life after death. Settling among the Flatheads in 1849, the Jesuits taught the Indians farming, domestic skills, and Christianity. Prior to 1855, their tribal domain consisted of the whole of western Montana plus parts of Canada. When pressured by the government, Pondera chief Alexander and Kootenai chief Michel agreed to move to a smaller reservation. In 1910, by executive order, the Flathead reservation was allotted to the Indians and opened to homesteading. Whites bought up much of the land. In 1935, the tribes voted to govern themselves under the Indian Reorganization Act.

"One reason the Flatheads seem to be more progressive than many other Indian tribes is that we assimilated into white society," said Doug. "We've had more educated Indians here because we have more white blood than other Montana tribes and the white parents pushed for the education."

"Why did the Flatheads marry whites more than the Blackfeet did?"

"Flatheads were just less warlike as a people. We had no qualms about intermarrying with the first Hudson Bay fur traders and the French from Frenchtown. All our names are French and Scot. I'm not saying that breeds are smarter than full-bloods, but we've become culturally more white than Indian. The downside is that the youngest person on this reservation that can speak our language is in his forties. Our language will be dead in a couple of more years."

"That's a shame."

"It is, but it's just the way things are," said Doug. "People don't really understand the basic truth about being an Indian. As an American citizen, I can do anything you can do. I'm also free to do anything that an Indian can do—and you can't do that. Living on this reservation, I don't have to pay state income tax or run my business according to state law. In the old days, being a member of the tribe might have entitled you to about twenty-five dollars a year. Now any enrolled tribal member gets about a thousand or fifteen hundred a year."

"Welfare?"

"Dividends, if you like. Personally, I think they should put it into a long-term trust or business and really build up the money, because I don't need any handouts. I have the biggest business in this town, I have more money than anybody in this town, I have the best house in this town, I have more possessions than anybody in this town, and I'm a bigger bullshitter than any of the whites or Indians in this town! I can outtalk them, outsell them, out-buy them—out-*anything* them! When I was kid, I was just another breed in an Indian town. I came back to show both whites and Indians that I could make it—by working harder than any of them. And I still work hard."

"Sounds like the American dream," I said.

"Why not? This is the free-est nation in the world! What are people *complaining* about? Listen, in San Francisco, I used to wear a suit and a tie to my job. During the hippie-yippie years I'd go out to Sather Gate at Berkeley and debate all those goddamn radicals. I was the crew-cut-and-suit guy and they'd boo me. They'd say, 'Hey, Mr. Straight Arrow, you got your uniform on there, huh? Pocket full of credit cards and driving a Cadillac, huh?'

"And I'd say to them, 'I'm not the one in uniform. You guys are. You're all dressed in dirty bib overalls with long hair and beards. Your women all got sloppy dresses. You know why you all dress that way? Because you're a bunch of ugly, depressed people! You've got no imagination or energy! You can't dress like I can and look as good as I do! You're putting on all this hippie shit, free love, and flower-power crap because you've found a cop-out culture that you can hide behind!'"

Doug Allard chuckled. "Of course, I didn't really *mean* that. I was just trying to get their goat. I used to have a lot of fun with them, though. Jerry Rubin and his yippie pals were there. Jerry was a real anti-everything guy. He was a smart guy—we got to be friends—but I used to really piss him off. Look what he's doing now—networking and making millions!"

"He's cut his hair, and now you're wearing a ponytail and beads, Doug. What does that mean?"

"Oh, Jesus!" Doug chortled, tugging at his long black ponytail. "If those hippies could see me now!"

Surrounded by woods and meadows at the base of the Mission Mountains, St. Ignatius was a more attractive town than Browning, with none of the ghetto aspects. Just past Starvin' Marvin's gas station rose the central attraction, the large mission church, dedicated to the saint. I parked my car and went inside, the only visitor. At the rear of the church was a large panel of the Virgin and Christ Child portrayed as Indians—a lovely dark-haired maiden with a papoose strapped to her back, both encircled by halos. To the right stood Joseph as an Indian chieftain with a halo around his warbonnet. I said a prayer—for the buffalo and Flatheads—and left.

Five miles south, I hit the tiny settlement of Ravalli and a roadside joint caught my eye: "The Bison Inn—Buffalo burgers and huckleberry hot cakes." In smaller print the sign grew poetic:

Cherish the freedom in Montana
The buck stops here, so does the doe,
Good food and fare, I'm telling you so.
You stop, too, my friend,
Don't just pass us by
You'll be glad you did.
Our food do satisfy.

Inside the Bison Inn were photographic blowups of buffalo bulls in head-on combat. You could buy coyote and fox pelts, jars of huckleberry jam, and buffalo jerky. I ordered a buffalo burger and a huckleberry milk shake to go. Back in my Jeep I drove west through the twilight, looking for a place to stay. I bit into that buffalo burger stuffed with onions, and warm juice dribbled down my chin. The Indians called buffalo "the real meat"—anticipating the jargon of modern advertising—and they were right.

Don and Ron Kinsman at the "mountain men" rendezvous at Wise River.

Chapter 12

Missoula: From Brains and Eggs to Black Powder and Flintlocks

Bill Bullard was feeling good, and started to tell us his right name: "My name is Buckshot, better known as Whirlwind of the Plains. I've been hooked by buffalo bulls, bit by rattlesnakes, and scalped by Indians. This is my night to howl and I'm going to HOWL!"

Patrick Tucker, *Riding to the High Country*, 1933

Missoula was the capital of the lumber industry in Montana, and from its surrounding forest came timber for the mine shafts of Butte. Missoula is still a pokey lumber town, but as home to the University of Montana—"the Berkeley of the Rockies"—it has a hip element to it.

After a day of research in the library, I wanted to eat lumberjack food, so I went to the Oxford Café. The Ox is a Missoula institution, a fairly grubby bar that has been in its present location since 1955. (Its predecessor, the Old Oxford, started down the street in the 1880s.) There were a few barflies and half-respectable winos at the bar, including a long-haired Indian and his woman talking amiably with the barman. A woman was a rarity in here until a few years ago. At the lunch counter two summer students in running shorts ate berry pie. In the back, card games were going full tilt, with all the men still wearing their work hats.

I wasn't there to drink or gamble; I was there to eat gray matter. As any Missoulian knows, the thing to eat at the Ox's lunch counter is calves' brains and eggs, known as *He needs 'em*. It's a meal that really should be eaten in cold weather rather than summer. When you say, "Could I have some brains, please?" the waitress yells over her shoulder, "*He needs 'em!*" And a bunch of calves' brains go splat on the grill. If you split an order with a friend she yells, "*Two half-wits!*" One notch down is diced ham and eggs: "*Brains for a poor man!*" Fried liver is "*Inside job!*" Order a hamburger and she says, "*Stretch one!*" Ask for it with cheese and she adds, "*Put a saddle on it!*" With a slice of onion? "*Stretch one and pin a rose on it!*"

The Oxford was more than just a place to eat for Mike Mansfield—Montana's most famous political figure—when he ran for the U.S. Senate in 1946. It became his unofficial campaign headquarters, a place where he could rub shoulders with the loggers, miners, doctors, lawyers, professors, and students. The owner stumped for Mansfield, and as one local biographer said, "Two or three times a week he would order brains and eggs. We had that expression *He needs 'em,* but for some reason or other the waiters never hollered that out when Mansfield ordered brains and eggs. I was always holding my breath thinking they would . . . ." The cerebral Mansfield, a Democrat, went on to become Senate majority leader and ambassador to Japan.

My kinsmen Richard and Timmie Vick had invited me to stay at their house in Missoula—a tiny, neat dwelling with a single tree in the front yard—to meet their son, Dick Vick.

Cousin Dick looked like a lumberjack who had eaten brains and eggs all his life. He was powerfully built, with a dark beard that framed full rosy cheeks. His blue eyes had a cheerful sparkle, but a tattoo on his arm bore the Latin motto Illegitimi Non Carborundum ("Don't let the bastards grind you down"). Dick had worn many hats in his thirty-eight years, none staying in place for long.

Over a vodka tonic, I learned that after university he had worked in a number of jobs, even as a bouncer at the Top Hat bar in Missoula. He now ran his own art gallery and framing shop. His wife, Liane, worked at the university, and their house, just across the street, was decorated with Indian artifacts. Dick has followed various religions, from Christianity to Judaism, but his current path is that of the mountain man—life and salvation through black powder and flintlocks.

In fact he was leaving that weekend for a rendezvous of modern mountain men. The first rendezvous were held in 1824, sponsored by fur-trade entrepreneur William Ashley, a partner in the Rocky Mountain Fur Company. Each year in early summer, a caravan of trade goods, guns, ammunition, and flat casks of alcohol hauled overland to the rendezvous site. The mountain men and a few Indians would congregate to sell beaver pelts, compete for marksmanship, tell tall tales, drink, and occasionally murder each other.

"You got to come on a rendezvous with us," said Dick, clapping a big hand on my shoulder. "You savvy?"

That Friday, Dick, Liane, and I packed up their camper with tents, coolers of food, and black-powder rifles. We drove south past Anaconda and through the Deerlodge National Forest until we struck the Big Hole River. Near Wise River we turned off onto a dirt road that ran through the forest for a mile. As we entered a green meadow, our camper abruptly became a time machine.

In the clearing stood six Indian tepees, and pitched among the trees were thirty canvas tents in the style of the 1830s. Squaws tended smoldering fires, and from the far end of the meadow came the sharp burst of black-powder muskets. The clock had been turned back a century and a half. *Rendezvous!*

The men wore buckskins and hats made of beaver, rabbit, fox, badger, even skunk; it looked as if animals were hitchhiking on peoples' heads. The women wore squaw dresses of deerskin, or long gingham dresses and bonnets. Dick outfitted me in a buckskin shirt, a *trappeur's* wool hat, moccasins, and a greasy buckskin jacket for the evening chill. I wore a pair of black sailor's pants that buttoned up the front. "Those are legit," Dick explained, "because the style hasn't changed since about 1825 and this is exactly what mountain men wore to stay cool in the summer."

It took almost an hour to set up Dick's big canvas tent and cast-iron stove. Dick laid out his trade goods on a blanket: glass beads that dated to seventeenth-century Florence, a knife with a brass-studded handle, a black bear's skin, fox pelts, and an Indian-style lance. He was now ready to barter and trade.

A man in moccasins and a full-length coat made from a Hudson's Bay blanket moseyed up to us. He wore wire-rim spectacles and a battered beaver top hat garnished with rattlesnake rattles. A flintlock musket rested easily on his shoulder.

"Howdy, Hoss," said the man.

"Howdy, Rattler," said Dick.

"Nice-lookin' trade goods," said Rattler. "More than passable bearskin you got there, by gar."

"So 'tis. So 'tis."

Even the lingo was retro.

Rattler told me he'd been going to mountain-men rendezvous for twenty years, and was an active member in the Wise River Club. "It's a damned good club. We put on a rendezvous every year and get people from Idaho, Utah, and Wyoming—pert' near all the Rocky Mountain states." Rattler good-naturedly revealed his twentieth-century identity as an employee of the Louisiana-Pacific sawmill in Deer Lodge, running the cut-off saw. "We're what you call a stud mill, and cut mainly lodgepole, some Douglas fir and spruce."

His car's license plate was "RATTLER," and not surprisingly, his hobby was herpetology. He used to make hatbands, belts, desk sets, and assorted doodads out of rattlesnakes. "Everything I made was guaranteed for a year. But too many other guys got in the business and started putting junk on the market. I didn't want to be associated with them."

He never studied the science in college, but he knew as much from thirty years of field experience as some academics. "So I began doing the lectures, to educate kids at schools and 4-H clubs. I try to dispel all the tall tales about snakes. Like the one that a rattlesnake won't cross a hair rope. Hell, they'll cross any rope or anything! Then there's that old story about the cowboy who finds two snakes and kills one of them and rides on twenty miles. Then the other snake follows him out of revenge, finds him that night in his sleeping bag, and bites him to death. That just isn't true.

"First, rattlesnakes don't mate for life. Second, they can't travel more than a few miles in a day. And third, they don't seek revenge. A snake conserves his energy. The only reason it goes from point A to point B is for food, water, shelter, or a mate thing. Why do snakes sun themselves? Well, it sure isn't to get suntan. They can't go into hibernation with any waste in their stomach or intestine because it would turn into a solid blockage and kill them. Because a snake is cold-blooded, it has to have sunlight to clean its system."

"So what's it like to be bitten by a rattlesnake?" I asked.

Rattler's face lit up as if I'd asked about losing his virginity. "The first time was what they call a dry bite. He didn't give me no venom. Why not? Maybe it was just a warning. The second snake that bit me first struck the stick that I was trying to pin him with, see. So he'd expended all his venom by the time he bit me in the finger.

"The third snake that bit me was on this knuckle." He raised his left hand. "I had a noticeable swelling in five minutes and a real acid taste in my mouth. *I knew I had venom in me.* By the time I got back to the truck, my whole hand was swelled. I had to spend three days in the hospital at Butte. When the venom really hits, you sweat real bad and you're hotter than hell. Then you get the chills and they throw these preheated blankets on you. The doctors said, 'When he goes sour, we're going to have to be right on top of it.' They hooked me up to a heart monitor and gave me adrenaline shots to get my heart moving fast enough to keep that poison *moving*. It will go all the way through your system until it reaches your kidneys and flushes out. It's when the poison *stops* that it does damage. It's a hemotoxic poison that breaks down cell walls.

"That hospital bill was sixteen hundred dollars. They told me if I got bit again it would kill me. That was in '80. I got bit again in '87. That bill was *eleven thousand dollars!* Eight days in the hospital. I damn near died—*twice!* Definitely made a believer out of me. I'm allergic to rattlesnake venom. If I get bit again, doctor says I'd be dead in five minutes."

"Do you still keep snakes?" I asked.

"Sure, I still keep rattlesnakes," he guffawed. "But I don't handle them anymore except with a stick. I let the stick work for me."

When it comes to rattlesnakes, I thought, a wise man knows how to delegate, even to a stick.

Dick took me over to a firing range lined with paper targets in the shape of deer and buffalo silhouettes. He handed me a .50-caliber ball-and-cap rifle that was almost five feet long. "Now, the first thing you've got to remember when loading is this: 'Powder, patch, ball.' Say it."

"Powder, patch, ball."

"Good. 'Cause if you screw up the order you're in real trouble. And don't overdo the powder. Or you'll blow your shoulder off."

The first time you load a black-powder rifle it takes forever. You lean the rifle's octagonal barrel against your chest and measure out an eighty-grain load of powder into a brass measuring pipe from your powder horn. You dump this down the barrel. Then you put a patch on the muzzle mouth and press a lead ball into it. You use a short ram stick to push it out of sight. Then you take your ramrod and shove it three feet home. You replace your ramrod under your rifle barrel. You open your cap box and slip a cap onto the nubbin of the hammer. You cock your hammer, put the gun to your shoulder, and release the back trigger, which is your safety. The weight of the long barrel makes the puny little muzzle bead sway over the target. You take a breath, release it, then pull the trigger. *Ka-whammmmbo!*

It's a lunging kick, not the sharp brutal smack of a modern weapon. Smoke enwreathes you, and the powder smells good in your nostrils. You might even hit the target, by gar.

Powder, patch, ball. I fired and reloaded twenty times in two hours. I scored surprisingly well on the targets, but I couldn't improve my reloading speed. In the old days, the real mountain men could fire, reload, and fire again from a galloping pony in less than a minute.

When night came to our valley, we ate roasted buffalo meat and the whiskey flowed. Dick pulled out his guitar, another man blew a harmonica, and they sang old songs around the fire. All evening long rifles, buckskins, beads, and furs changed hands. A rendezvous attracted a mix of history buffs, redneck ecologists, ex-hippies, and former motorcycle-gang members. It appealed to a romantic longing for a lost age. There was rarely any theft, and it seemed a healthy if escapist hobby, even environmentally correct.

The gun maker was the top artisan at a mountain-man rendezvous. At this get-together, he was Kyle Fingersohn, a young man in wire rims, longish hair, mustache, and a brown felt hat. Kyle was still a student at Montana State University in Bozeman at age thirty, but his profession is making fine rifles. He gently, proudly thrust a rifle into my hands the way a father might a newborn. In the firelight the maple wood grain of the stock glowed like veins of whiskey and blood. When I took a bead on a star visible through a gap in the pines, I felt its good heft.

"There are three schools of gun builders," he said. "The first group builds guns that are so beautiful and costly that nobody wants to use them. You're talking twenty thousand dollars. I mean, they're just *immaculate*—but even two hundred years ago there weren't any guns like that. I mean, no way! Another school of thought is to make a gun and age it to make it look antique, like it's two hundred years old and used. And the last school is to build a usable gun that looks just as it would have been, brand-new, two hundred years ago. That's what I do. But I'll do custom guns, too."

Kyle has made about twenty guns in the last two years and charges between five hundred and a thousand dollars for his pieces, depending on the quality. Flintlocks, he explained, first appeared in the sixteenth century, made by French gun builders, and they remained in use until the 1880s, long after cap-and-ball and other percussion firearms appeared. In the early eighteenth century, the French traded a high-level flintlock to the Indians. "I love these eighteenth-century guns. Some were carved with the same beautiful flourishes that appeared in furniture of the period." When the

French presence faded in the fur trade, the guns were supplanted by cheaper British models. "The worst were trade guns contracted from Belgian gun makers. It was a wonder that some fired at all.

"I read a lot of old journals kept by mountain men. We know that some of those guns were smooth bore. You could put anything in them, from heavy ball to carpet tacks if you were desperate. You could shoot geese or bear with the same gun."

"Do you ever hunt with black powder?"

"That's all we *do* hunt with!" he guffawed. "I wouldn't shoot a bear, because I'm not sold on bear meat. It's greasy. But I like to get a deer or elk."

The best marksman at the rendezvous was Badger Bob, whose prowess I'd admired earlier on the firing range. He was a short, powerful man, and with his long nose, beady eyes, and shaggy beard, he somewhat resembled his animal namesake. A Cajun by birth, each year Badger Bob returns to Louisiana to work on oil rigs until he has a year's grubstake on which to live wild in the Rockies. Badger Bob and his woman spent one winter in the Wise River area, living in just a canvas tent. "Sometimes the temperature hit fifty below zero," he drawled.

"What'd you do then?"

"Put a lot more wood on the fire."

During a lull in the music, Badger Bob and Ron Kinsman, a policeman from Butte, staged an old-time wrestling match. Badger dove for Ron's buckskinned legs, but he spread them wide, flipped Badger on his back, and jumped on top. In an incredible display of strength, Badger shoved Ron up and off him. They rolled and Badger leapt, pinning the policeman. The crowd roared with pleasure, a jug of whiskey was hoisted, and the music started up again.

The next morning, Saturday, the mountain men were slow to stir, but as I hunkered over a cup of coffee with my cousins Dick and Liane, I heard the first *thwack* of a hatchet blade over at the tomahawk range. I spent the morning throwing "tommy-hawks" into a stump with a couple of twelve-year-old boys in coonskin caps; by afternoon I was back at the firing range. Powder, patch, ball—*ka-blam!*

Evening brought more frolic and whiskey around the campfire as the fiddler played old tunes. Dave, an elder mountain man with a grizzled face and no front teeth, suddenly leapt into the firelight in a borrowed gingham dress and bonnet, dancing a crazy jig. His bosom was bolstered with two Pepsi cans. Rattler made a grab for his pop-top falsies, knocked them askew, and

Dave squealed in falsetto. Ron Kinsman linked arms with him, and other mountain men and women joined in for a fiddler's hoedown.

Looking at the bearded faces and the laughing women in beaded buck-skins, the world of automobiles, taxes, and fax machines seemed far away. Montana's open land was what brought the first mountain men west, and its legends continued to feed the imagination of these neo–mountain men and women. Were they kidding themselves? There seemed no harm in it, and it was fun. My cousin Dick Vick clapped me on the shoulder: "This is a crazy world, isn't it?" By the end of the evening the whiskey had flowed enough that Dick could sing an old Doors song, "People Are Strange," and it didn't seem out of place.

In the morning, the rendezvous was over. Dick made a few last-minute trades and came out seven hundred dollars ahead for the weekend. "Good trade," he said. For a second I flashed on Dick's great-grandfather Charles, trading buffalo robes and wolf pelts with the Indians at Fort Conrad. Over a century had passed, the buffalo were gone, and there was no call for beaver hats, but it was still good trade, by gar.

1890 photograph
*Going to the
Roundup.*

Miles City Main Street in the 1890s. (Photos by L. A.
Huffman, courtesy Coffrin's Old West Gallery, Bozeman)

Chapter 13

The Miles City Bucking Horse Sale

These twisters of to-day are made of the same
leather as the old-time ones. It ain't their fault
that the country's fenced an' most of the cows are
wearin' bells.
            Charles M. Russell, from "Bronc Twisters,"
                        Trails Plowed Under, 1927

One could easily sneeze and miss the town of Ryegate on Route 12 between Shawmut and Cushman. It consisted of a grocery store, Fleck's Bar,
about thirty houses, and a 1908 post office that served farmers and ranchers
who came because of the railroad, which is now gone. Each spring, after the
calves have been branded and castrated, Ryegate celebrates with the Testicle
Festival. Weeks before the festival, signs are posted around the town, but
half of them disappear as God-fearing little old ladies sneak out at dawn to
tear down the "pornographic" announcements. Yet the festival can't be
killed, and people drive from all over to eat thousands of deep-fried calf testicles and swallow pitchers of beer at Fleck's Bar. The ritual has been immor-
talized in song by local singer Greg Keeler:

> It's Ryegate, Montana's Testicle Festival time
> Where you can pig out on calf nuts for hours and it don't cost a
>   dime.
> There's artists and ranchers and drunk two-step dancers and
> grannies who've just reached their prime

At Ryegate, Montana's Testicle Festival time.
Now that Hutterite up at the bar,
He's had too much liquor by far
But he swears he can sober up quicker than most folks might think.
He'll buttress his gut walls with batter-fried calf balls
Then barf 'em back in the sink
Hell, barfing's no sin, it's a good second wind for more drinks.

Though I saw no Hutterites buttressing or barfing, I did try a few Rocky Mountain Oysters, as the greasy little critters are called, and I did meet some friendly people in Fleck's Bar.

Another unusual Montana event, the Miles City Bucking Horse Sale, led me hundreds of miles east in a marathon drive of ten hours. The straightness of Montana's roads can almost hypnotize, so it was good to take my eyes off the yellow center line occasionally, even if only to note road kill on the asphalt. There was an abundance of dead animals. In just a few minutes I passed a rabbit, a deer, a fox, and two pieces of unidentifiable, Firestone-flattened fauna. Magpies darted out onto the road to peck at the flesh. Even ground squirrels came out for a cannibalistic nibble on their fallen brethren, then got flattened themselves.

Grasshoppers, wasps, flying ants, mayflies hit *Red Cloud*'s windshield in yellow, brown, and green splats. Two butterflies mating in midair sent an ochre explosion across the glass. At the side of the road stood little white crosses that commemorated the victims of road accidents. In the fields sat white cubes that looked like stacked hatboxes; they were hives for the bees that pollinate the alfalfa, and produce honey. Bees, too, added splats to my windshield.

I whizzed by Square Butte, Coffee Creek, Lewistown, Grassrange, Roundup, Sumatra, and Ingomar—momentary pockets of civilization in the vast prairie. Many of these towns were just a handful of dwellings clustered around a gas station and dingy café; less lively communities were marked by abandoned bank buildings and craven homestead shacks that shimmied in heat mirages. Transience is key to an understanding of the West.

From Forsyth, I followed the Yellowstone River valley, a band of green bottomland that snakes through a parched vastness. Up ahead, rising from the cottonwoods, was a white-painted water tower emblazoned "Miles City."

The main street of Miles City buzzed with pickups and horse trailers. I glanced up at the cornices of the old brick buildings, hoping to see John Conrad's name carved in stone; a century ago he'd owned a store here. No such luck. The town has suffered so many fires over a century that a local bumper sticker says: "Last one out of Miles City put out the fire."

I drove *Red Cloud* to the rodeo grounds and took a seat low in the bleachers. The Bucking Horse Sale has been an annual happening in Miles City for about seventy-five years. Unlike at regular rodeos, the bucking horses at this event are auctioned off to various professional rodeo stock companies. Mostly big-boned crosses between quarter and draft horses, these were powerful kickers with hairy fetlocks and huge hooves. Many had never been ridden before and had never felt a flank strap. They bucked unpredictably and hence were more dangerous than seasoned professional rodeo stock.

The first horse blasted out of the chute, jumped four feet in the air, and landed on its side with a loud thump, slamming the cowboy into the dust. Unbelievably, the rider lurched to his feet unharmed, and as the pickup men shooed the horse out of the ring, the auctioneer went into his speed-lip act: "Do I hear two hundred for this high-stepping bucking horse—two hundred—do I hear two-fifty—two-fifty, now three hundred, three hundred, now . . . ."

The horse was sold for one thousand dollars. The second horse gave an exciting but conventional bucking tour around the arena and drew bids of sixteen hundred dollars and a round of applause. The third horse came out of the box at full speed, ran head-on into the wire fence, and broke his neck. It was a gruesome sight. The horse twitched on the ground in death spasms until two men tied a rope around its hind feet and hauled it away behind a truck. Somebody bought the horse for five hundred dollars as a "canner"—destined for dog food.

After a dozen horses had been bucked and sold, the fences were opened on either end of the arena, offering access to the large race track. Jockeys ran Thoroughbreds, and bets flew. I won a quinella, earning seven dollars on a two-dollar bet, bought lunch, and lost the rest of my winnings.

Members of the Lewis and Clark Expedition stopped at the town's present site for about an hour when their passage was blocked by a massive buffalo herd. After the Custer Massacre, the Sioux were driven out of the area, and a fort was established where the Tongue River meets the Yellowstone. When the Northern Pacific Railroad arrived in 1884 there were twenty-two hundred inhabitants.

As the smaller towns in the area have died off, Miles City has become a retirement and health center for aging ranchers. Its population is now at nine thousand, and dropping. Since the townsfolk were reluctant to welcome any industry other than ranching, the young people continued to leave for jobs elsewhere. Some people think this whole area will return to the buffalo and coyotes. In fact, a number of books (particularly *Where the Buffalo Roam,* by Ann Matthews) promote this theory. But during a cowboy event like the Bucking Horse Sale, to express such an idea is asking for a fight.

The Olive Hotel was an orange brick building overlooking the cottonwood trees of Riverside Park. A good crowd was drinking on its front porch. The transom window above the door glittered with Victorian crystal, and the lobby floor bore the original tiles; the rest of the hotel's 1899 interior had been modernized in an unfortunate manner. To beat the heat until sundown, I took a shower, then rested.

I went out into the streets as dusk soft-pedaled the heat. Bands played country tunes from flatbeds planted at each intersection for three blocks. Neon saloon signs glowed invitingly: "The Bison Inn," "The Montana Bar," and "The Trail Inn." Among them wandered cowboys and cowgirls in black or gray Stetsons, strolling arm in arm. You can always tell a real cowboy because his jeans hang down over his boots two inches farther than a city slicker's, and on a Saturday night he wears his newest pair, not ones that are bleached and patched.

The Range Riders was marked by a gaudy red, white, and blue sign depicting a rearing horseman. Twenty people sat or stood at the bar; the same number played cards or billiards in the back room. Above the back bar hung photos of cowboy greats being bucked into glory—or a hospital.

A seedy cowpoke with a beard and snakeskin hatband walked in, surveyed the room, then asked the woman behind the bar sotto voce, "Anything, uh, goin' upstairs?"

The obese woman bartender suffered from a case of what Montanans call Buffalo Butt. "Not anymore, thank God," she said with mild annoyance.

I asked an old fellow sitting next to me what, in fact, *had* gone on upstairs. He sucked on his cigarette and wheezed, "Oh, they had a couple of girls doing sex dances. They'd do other things, too. For money, you understand. That is, until the fire."

"Fire?"

"Started in a back room. Old wiring on the fritz. Come down runnin' and yellin' 'Fire!' Fires in this town ain't all accidents either. Time they found this feller had drilled a light bulb and filled it with gasoline. So's when they come in and flip the switch—ka-boom! 'Nother time this feller paid a couple of kids to burn his place down for the insurance. Police caught the kids liftin' the cash register out of their car trunk. Explain that one, huh!"

"Getting back to what was going on upstairs," I interjected.

"Oh, you mean sportin'. Boy, they was some hot ones in this town. All gone."

"All gone?"

"Preachers run 'em out of town."

The most wondrous place in Miles City is the Montana Bar. The tiled floors, the printed-tin ceiling, and the elegant wooden back bar are original. Built in 1902, this classic bar is an untrashed shrine of the West. There were no doodads or molded plastic Bud Lite ads to junk it up; just one good painting of a nude woman, two longhorn steer mounts, and a buffalo head hung high on the walls. The Montana Bar had nearly caught fire three years earlier when the building next door went up in flames. In my most scientific opinion, it was saved by God.

In the front window of the bar stood a stuffed Audubon bighorn ram that was mangy and nearly hairless. Named for the painter who came up the Missouri River in 1843, *Ovis canadensis auduboni* fell prey to diseases carried by domestic sheep, and the last of this bighorn subspecies was killed off in 1916. So it went in the West.

I fought my way to the bar through a crowd of shouting folk. There was a contagious, raucous joy in the evening, as young men brayed for whiskey and old ranchwomen laughed and showed the gold in their molars. Among them I found the poet laureate of the rodeo circuit, Paul Zarzyski.

Jaw jutting like a Hapsburg's, Paul wore a thick brown mustache on a long face with rough skin, and his teeth were deeply stained by chewing tobacco. A midwesterner, he was once a star on the University of Montana rodeo team and wrote a poem about God and his mother conspiring to get him to quit riding the broncs—a formidable tag team that failed. Now in his mid-thirties (old in the sport of rodeo), he still rode the bone-jolting broncs. "It just gets in your blood." He admired bards from John Keats to Gary Snyder, but chose to work in the cowboy genre, a school that juggles doggerel and sentimental clichés, with amusing if trite results. Yet Zarzyski's work crow-hops with original metaphor, ringing alliteration, and leathery humor. His poem "Zarzyski Meets the Copenhagen Angel" fit the evening perfectly:

> Her Levis, so tight
> I can read the dates on dimes

in her hip pocket. Miles City,
a rodeo Saturday night.
She smiles from a corner bar stool,
her taut lower lip, white and puffed,
pigtails braided like bronc reins.
She leads the circuit, chasing cans,
a barrel racer in love with her horse,
her snuff, and a 16 second run.
We dance close to LeDoux's "Daydream Cowboy."
I'm Zarzyski, rhymes with whiskey,
I tell her—a lover, a fighter,
a Polish bareback bronc rider.
And these Copenhagen kisses jump and kick
higher than ol' Moonshine, himself.

Moonshine was a famous bucking horse. Copenhagen is chewing tobacco, or *snoose,* as it's known in Montana. Kissing a man with a lip full of
snoose is not for the squeamish.

The nighttime activities around the Bucking Horse Sale used to be
wilder. In the old days you could drink anywhere and there really was girlie
action upstairs at the Range Rider. People would wander out into the night
and snooze in the cool grass of the park, even make love on the courthouse
lawn. There were fistfights and pistols fired through the tin ceilings of bars
long gone. In recent years the city fathers have clamped down on the action.
Now it's a hundred-dollar fine for taking a beer into the street.

"It's all the goddamn churches that got together," said one cowboy. "They'd
like to kill the Bucking Horse Sale and all the fun it inspires in the bars. But
they cain't. There's just too goddamn much cowpoke blood in this town."

By 1880, there were an estimated 428,000 head of cattle in Montana
Territory. Most of this stock grazed in the western part of the state, where
water from the Rocky Mountains provided vast meadows of grass. As the
buffalo were killed off and the Indians herded onto ever-shrinking reservations, the arable western region grew populated. Only the eastern plains
were wide open to entrepreneurial cattlemen. In 1881 two books whetted
the appetites of East Coast investors: Brisbin's *The Beef Bonanza; or, How to
Get Rich on the Plains,* and Strahorn's *Montana and Yellowstone National
Park.* The authors assured readers that investments in Montana livestock
could produce reliable profits of over 15 percent annually. Other journals,

like the *Breeders' Gazette,* explained how a five-dollar steer could be fattened for a season or two and then sold for sixty dollars.

Companies from Chicago to New Hampshire moved in. The Niobrara Cattle Company, for example, drove ten thousand head from Nebraska into the Powder River Country south of Miles City. Montana ranchers divided into two groups. The earlier-established ranches raised shorthorn cattle, while the newcomers to eastern Montana, mostly Texans, ran longhorn cattle. The older group were "she stockmen," who used the ranges for breeding purposes, while the Texas outfits were "steer men," who brought yearlings and two-year-old steers north to be fattened on Montana grass for two seasons before sending them to market. The speculating newcomers ran bigger herds, overcrowded the range, and aimed for a quick profit.

By 1880 twenty-six-year-old John Conrad had sold his Baker Company shares and entered the cattle business. John was not a rancher by temperament. He was a profit-minded capitalist with ambition, the president of and largest shareholder in a cattle company capitalized at five hundred thousand dollars. The Hurlbut-Conrad Cattle Company was based out of Johnson County, Wyoming (about 125 miles south of Miles City), but held its board meetings in Chicago. John also owned other brands, and ranged cattle north of Miles City, mainly on the Tongue River, with cattle camps on Prairie Dog, Goose, and Big Dry Creeks.

In 1885, the year after the final buffalo hunt, the open-range stockmen formed the Montana Stockgrowers Association. That same year, several newspapers cited Conrad as the largest independent cattle owner in Montana. The 1885 edition of Warner-Beers's *History of Montana* listed him with fourteen thousand head.

The profit was good, but there was plenty of downside. Prairie fires, blizzards, and wolves decimated herds. Rustling was a real problem and difficult to police. In 1884 a group of stockmen from central Montana rallied under Granville Stuart (author of *Forty Years on the Frontier)* to form a vigilante group nicknamed Stuart's Stranglers, which killed at least fifteen outlaws. Another vigilante group on the lower Yellowstone ran a sinister train down the Northern Pacific tracks that stopped periodically to hang or shoot rustlers.

Ranchers rarely owned all their rangeland, and the U.S. government (unlike that of Canada) did not lease public lands for grazing purposes. So cattle companies squatted on their "accustomed range" and protected themselves as best they could. If an interloper crowded his stock onto someone else's range, local ranchers ostracized him, sometimes at gunpoint.

In 1885, John Conrad moved six thousand head of cattle with the STV brand eastward across the Musselshell River onto rangeland claimed by the powerful Niobrara Cattle Company. The Niobrara manager ordered his men to drive Conrad's cattle away. Conrad's men boldly drove them back. The irate manager announced that any further trespassing would be met with Winchesters.

John was furious. According to the *Fort Benton River Press* of November 18, 1885, "Mr. Conrad has very properly appealed to the courts, which will undoubtedly decide that the range belongs to all, and that no company can claim exclusive right to land which belongs to the government." John wasn't successful in court, and that fall, Miles City stockmen condemned him for violating range "law" and warned that they would not handle his stock at the big 1886 spring roundup.

John showed up anyway. Day after day his silent crew of six-gun-toting cowboys ghosted along right behind the roundup's line of march. Each afternoon, as the official roundup cast loose the herd that had been cut, Conrad's STV punchers invariably found their cattle and roped them in. Thus, without officially belonging to the roundup, they benefited from it. I liked hearing that my great-grandfather had gumption, even if he didn't play along with the other cattlemen.

Then came a great lesson. In the winter of 1886–87, blizzards dropped the temperature to minus sixty degrees and killed over 80 percent of all the cattle on the northern plains—an estimated 362,000 head. Granville Stewart wrote of the disaster, "A business that had been fascinating to me before suddenly became distasteful. I wanted no more of it. I never wanted to own again an animal that I could not feed and shelter." The disaster eliminated all but the most powerful companies. It also turned some ranchers into sheep men, and by 1900 there were 6 million sheep in Montana, making it the nation's number-one wool-growing state.

But my great-grandfather never went in for sheep. He stayed in the cattle business for at least three more years. In 1890, he sold five thousand head at sixty dollars a head, putting three hundred thousand dollars in his pocket. By 1891, he had sold the last of the STV brand to a Canadian firm and was out of the cattle business forever.

The era of the open range gave America its most enduring hero: the cowboy. The average saddle tramp was usually a bachelor in his twenties, and, though it is rarely mentioned, many were black or Mexican. A cowpuncher was overworked and badly paid. He suffered from sunstroke and mosquitoes in the summer and from frostbite in the winter. He was thrown from broncs, and his injuries ranged from concussions to broken collarbones. He earned little more than a dollar a day and a steady diet of beef and beans. His few days off would be spent carousing in towns like Miles City, where liquor, the card tables, and prostitutes would strip him of his wages. Most town folk looked down on the cowboy as an unreliable adventurer, but he led a colorful and unfettered life. Even a *Billings Gazette* of 1890 referred to him as a "knight of the lariat." For the next century America lapped up a heroic, whitewashed version through dimestore novels, songs, and, later, films and television shows. Owen Ulph, writing in *The American West* (1968), elegantly summed up the cowboy as most of us think of him today:

> The Stupendous Western Cowboy Legend can be subdivided into four major fantasies: the Myth of the Great Outdoors, with its reputation for cleansing and purifying the human spirit; the Fable of the Life of Perpetual Action and Adventure, with its tempering effect on masculine character; the Illusion of Existence as a Permanent Fancy Dress Ball, with its constant inspiration to romantic individualism; and the Mirage of the Regal Splendour of the Courtly Ranch as a dazzling center for sustaining frontier chivalry.

On Sunday evening I met a cowboy named John Moore on the Olive Hotel veranda for a Coke. He was in his late thirties, with the lean physique of a college sprinter. Moore wore a clean shirt and jeans, round-toed work boots, and a dust-free gray hat. When he took off his tinted glasses, his green eyes glittered.

Moore saw the cowboy as an endangered species. "Even some of the local Montanans are out to get the real cowboy, to put him on the back shelf in the name of progress. They want to take away his rights. There's a lot of anti-cowboy and antilandowner sentiment in this country. They're turning the cowboy into a museum piece. They are attracted to the image, the icon, by a mixture of admiration, envy, and hate. They can't stand the power he represents. They want to dethrone him, to see the idol shatter. There's a real desire to emasculate the cowboy."

A newspaper writer, novelist, and preacher, Moore was fiercely proud of eastern Montana life and its traditions. Moore's grandfather had been a horse trader who owned a livery stable and raised seven cowboy sons. Moore's father, Johnny Moore, rode for the Chapple Brothers Cannery, which made a business out of capturing the thousands of wild horses that roamed the vast unfenced spaces around Miles City. The horses, often turned loose by failed homesteaders, were destined for dog food. Roundup days began at 4 A.M. and ended after sixty-mile rides. Most horses were destined for slaughter, and horsemeat was not uncommon fare on the range. Sometimes they'd solve a food shortage by "chasing slicks": they'd look for a few studs that needed cutting, a fire would be kindled, and the testicles would be roasted.

When the cannery pulled out of Montana, many of the cowboys bought up land controlled by the company. Johnny Moore and two partners began running horses from their headquarters on Sunday Creek. They were soon sending bucking horses with names like Deadman, Crying Jew, Ironjaw, Wagonbox, the Wasp, Singing Canary, and Dark Journey to rodeos as far away as Madison Square Garden.

Johnny Moore and his five brothers also put together a forty-thousand-acre ranch in which author John Moore still owns an interest. "It's an old-fashioned outfit. We use pickups and good horses to do our work—no motorcycles or snowmobiles."

When Moore wrote about his family in a novel, *The Breaking of Ezra Riley,* he evoked the toughness needed to survive in the harsh dry land of eastern Montana. The average annual rainfall for the Miles City area is a little over thirteen inches, but in recent years it has been almost half that. One large corporate ranch operating northwest of Miles City was once able to run fifteen thousand head of cattle; now it's only three thousand as grass and water diminish. Land values have plummeted. In 1979, ranchers were asking over a hundred dollars an acre; today they get as little as forty-five dollars. Store owners see cattlemen window-shopping rather than buying, the bankers scrutinize loans more carefully, and alcoholism and stress-related diseases have increased. If drought conditions continue, an exodus of people from the region may occur.

John Moore knew more than just the range. At seventeen he left the family ranch and went to the newsroom of the *Miles City Star.* During the seventies, his hair grew long and he drifted around the country, visiting gurus and communes. He lived in the Tenderloin in San Francisco and ate meals at church shelters with bums.

"I've had guns shoved in my belly and knives held to my throat. I worked for a crop duster, got chemically poisoned, and was within half an hour of death. Had hallucinations for twenty-four hours. Later I got a liver disease and was healed miraculously. The Lord healed me in the middle of the night and I sweated out about six pounds of fluids. My wife jumped out of bed not knowing what was going on. I was very self-destructive at one time with the drinking and the drugs. I did it all, from organic hallucinogens to needles. Not any more. Once in a while I still get a real craving for pot. But I don't do it. I had enough encounters with the brink of death that I figured I could cross the line if I wasn't careful. I wasn't a typical cowboy. I'm not your typical Christian, either."

After serving in the air force, Moore went to work at the *Great Falls Tribune.* "I introduced serious rodeo journalism—something that really hadn't been done before. Most journalists in Montana aren't from here. The newspapers themselves are owned by out-of-state chains. So these journalists come out from Ohio or New York and treat rodeo like some freak cultural event instead of a sport born out of tradition. I treated it as both and got some attention for it. I grew up around rodeo stock and know what's happening. Eventually I got tired of it. But I always like the Bucking Horse Sale."

The original sale, said Moore, was put on by cowboys and gradually taken over by the Jaycees. "They're really just a bunch of beer salesmen. They promoted this thing as a big drunken party to sell beer and we got bad press. That's why the open-container law came in. They didn't know anything about horses. For about ten years they tried to do away with it entirely. The Bucking Horse Sale revived when they went back to promoting it as a great horse auction. There's only one Miles City Bucking Horse Sale in the world. It's unique."

Between ranching, preaching, and his family, John had few spare moments to write, but felt that the greatest compliment to his writing would be for it to be accepted as authentic by other cowboys. His latest book, *Letters to Jess,* had been published by the Christian division of Macmillan. "They're letters to my son about the fading West, spiritual parables learned from ranching. One of my deepest concerns is that agriculturists and Christians alike have missed the mark with the environment. We have conceded that area to the radical environmentalists, who are gaining strength and power, and some of them are absolutely crazy. They're coming out of a Hindu theology, whether they realize it or not. Neither the church nor the agriculturists have taken a responsible stance."

"How's that?"

"In the mass production of chickens, for example, or the way they raise veal. I'm also looking for some realism. On the left wing you've got the animal-rights people who are romantic about something they don't understand. On the right wing you've got some of these old ranchers who are out to make a buck and that's about all. They're not stewards of the land, they're just cut-throat mercenaries," said Moore.

"What I'm trying to do as a writer is show how far removed and out of touch we are from the environment. These animal-rights people don't want anything to die. But everything's gonna die sometime. Even at the Bucking Horse Sale, eighty percent of those horses are going to be dead in the next few months. Animals get sent to the cannery. I mean, that's just the way it is. That's life. Meanwhile, you've got people all across the nation who want everything to live except unborn babies and the aged. They're ready for abortion on demand, yet they're trying to ban deer hunting. They're spiking trees, and they'll try to kill you for rounding up mustangs. Radical environmental groups outnumber us and outgun us with money and power. To beat them at their own game, landowners and cowboys are going to have to be better environmentalists and land stewards than they are.

"We're conservative ranchers. We don't believe in dryland farming this fragile ground. The government for years paid some of our neighbors to plant their pastures with wheat. Now it's paying them to plant them back to grass. We've never been paid for our mistakes. We don't expect to be."

"So how do you feel about people moving into the state?" I asked.

"I'm not really against new people coming in and enjoying Montana," said Moore. "After all, we're all transients. I get fed up with some of these Indians that get political—especially the Sioux when they start saying, 'This is our land.' Like heck it is. The Sioux came out here from Minnesota. All they ever did was to wipe out agrarian Indians and take their land. I get real tired of hearing about the Noble Red Man thing from outsiders. We forget how demonic the Indians were in many ways, and how much cruelty there was in their culture. They cut the noses off of women who committed adultery. Look, I'm not into redskin smashing or anything. The Indians weren't saints. Nor were the people that settled this land."

"How do you feel about the new people—the movie stars, for example—moving into Montana?" I asked.

"Western Montana got Californicated about ten years ago. Eastern Montana doesn't get all of those new people, because this country is too damn *tough* for them. One day this year on our ranch it was a hundred and twelve degrees in the shade. It was so damned hot that you couldn't face the wind for more than thirty seconds. It just burned your face. Then this February I saw a wind chill that was seventy-five below zero. That's a temperature swing of almost a hundred and ninety degrees! What kind of animals and people survive here, let alone flourish? There's no such thing as *flourishing* in eastern Montana. You have to be tough to survive. That goes for people, too. There's a saying around here: 'Forty below zero keeps the riffraff out.'"

South of Miles City on Highway 59 I was enjoying the scenery and singing along to music on the radio when a blinking red light appeared in my rearview mirror. Officer Hazeldon from Miles City had clocked me at seventy miles an hour. "I'm going to have to fine you five dollars," he said with apparent regret.

In Montana, you pay speeding tickets right on the spot and they won't go on your record. I forked over the money. Until recently, the speed limit was seventy on the main freeway and it was even legal to drink while driving; you just weren't supposed to get drunk. In fact, some people defined lengths of journeys by liquid volume rather than linear time: "Yeah, it's about a six-pack from here to Missoula."

Even with this monetary spanking from Officer Hazeldon, it was one of the most pleasant exchanges with a police officer I've ever had. We talked about the Bucking Horse Sale and even about John Moore; he and Moore were members of the same athletic club. I asked how the roads were from here to Ashland, on the Cheyenne reservation. "Not bad," he said. "But you don't want to spend too much time on the reservation. Not after dark. Sometimes the Indians can be unfriendly."

"In what way?"

"I don't know if you heard about it, but two years ago there was a young man from Miles City, Marty Etchemendy, who met some Indians outside a bar. They beat him unconscious and threw him in the trunk of their car. They drove him all the way to Gillette, Wyoming, where they tried to stick a crowbar through his skull."

I was about to make some dumb crack about an Excedrin headache, but Miles City is a small town and I had the feeling that nobody, including Officer Hazeldon, was too happy about what had happened to one of its more likable citizens. On October 17, 1987, two appropriately named brothers, Vern and Lester Kills-on-Top, subjected Etchemendy to thirty hours of beatings and torture. "When that didn't kill him, they took a twenty-two cartridge—they didn't have a gun—and held it in a vice to detonate it into his skull. It was one of the bloodiest murders around."

I registered this story in my braincase, thanked the policeman for his advice, and followed the Tongue River, a favored river of the Cheyenne. The late spring rains had brought new green to the grass and the willows along the riverbank. The sagebrush ran up to naked red hills. I slowed to weave through a dozen cows wandering loose on the road. My tires rattled over cattle guards flanked by green fields glowing velvetlike as the sun waned and reddened. Four antelope stood watching me from a hill while a cagey buck ran down the back side. *Red Cloud* stopped grumbling when I hit smooth blacktop and zoomed past Decker, a coal-mining town on the Montana-Wyoming border. After Sheridan, Wyoming, I drove twenty miles south to Buffalo in search of the first general store John Conrad started after breaking away from his brothers in Fort Benton.

In the tiny Gatchell Museum near the old courthouse I found a beautiful scale-model diorama of early-day Buffalo. Riding down Main Street was a tiny Teddy Roosevelt in buckskins leading ox-drawn wagons. (Teddy, who had a ranch in North Dakota, visited in 1884 while hunting in the Bighorn Mountains.) Featured prominently was a one-story general store, John H. Conrad & Co., and beside it a log cabin bearing the name "Stebbins, Conrad Bank." Framed on the museum's wall were old checks for fifty dollars written on the J. H. Conrad & Co. account. I saw my great-grandfather's handwriting for the first time—a large bold script with the sweep of an ambitious hand.

"Where are the Conrad buildings now?" I asked the woman curator.

"Oh, they're long gone. They'd be where the present bank building and Masonic Hall are today on Main Street."

The area around Buffalo was a site for the fur trade between Indians and whites as early as 1811, but permanent buildings took root only after the Ninth U.S. Infantry constructed Fort McKinney in 1879 to protect immigrants on the Bozeman Trail. John Conrad secured a contract to supply the soldiers, started the small bank, and with two partners established general stores at Sheridan and Powder River Crossing.

The Conrad Company carried a stock so large and varied that it became well known throughout Wyoming Territory. On the shelves were high-buttoned shoes, corsets, red flannels, calico, and sheetings. Staples like flour and sugar came in hundred-pound sacks, and coffee beans were bagged green, ready to be oven-browned by the industrious housekeeper. Dried fruit came packed in boxes. There were also cookstoves and parlor stoves with nickel-and-glass doors; neck yokes and iron shoes for the oxen; copper-toed boots for children; lanterns and five-gallon cans of kerosene. You could order a brand-new wagon from Studebaker or a Sunday bonnet.

John took partners into his ventures because he was constantly traveling around the territories and in the East. In Chicago he met his future wife,

Mabel Barnaby, during the 1884 Democratic National Convention. Just nineteen, Mabel had accompanied her father, J. B. Barnaby, a Rhode Island merchant and politician who was impressed by the ambitious twenty-nine-year-old cattle king. Five months later, they were married in one of the most ostentatious weddings Providence had ever seen. Newspaper headlines like "A Providence Belle Married to a Western Millionaire" suggested a merger rather than a romance.

After the honeymoon, John and his wife spent the winter in Chicago, where they bought a house, and traveled to Wyoming that spring. As rough as Buffalo must have been, with mule skinners, trappers, and cowboys riding in for whiskey and two-fisted frolic, there was an effort to launch civilization: carriage rides, concerts by the military band at Fort McKinney, a masquerade ball, and parties in white tie and tails.

I hadn't intended to spend much time in Wyoming, but I was learning that state borders were arbitrary divisions in the Old West. Even today, citizens of northern Wyoming were as likely to read the *Billings Gazette*, Montana's largest newspaper, as any Wyoming paper. John Conrad still remained a shadowy figure in my imagination, but I had picked up his scent and was eager to return to Montana.

A half hour later in Sheridan, a ten-foot-tall neon sign of a bucking bronc tempted me to stop for a beer at the Mint Bar. The interior was covered with polished gnarly wood and decorated with stuffed animals: arctic fox, moose, owls, and a rattlesnake skin nine feet long. Tacked to the ornate back bar was a notice common in these parts:

LOST: DOG

Description: Three legs, missing one ear, broken tail, recently castrated, answers to the name "Lucky."

There was no old hotel in Sheridan, so I checked into a motel, the Trail's End Inn. There are probably a hundred motels or bars around the West called Trail's End. The fact is, there is no such thing; where one trail ends, another begins.

John Conrad's store in the town of Billings,
circa 1885. (Courtesy Montana Historical
Society)

Chapter 14
Billings: The Rise of a Cow Town

In Billings, Montana, I broke my hand every
Saturday night due to the influx of local citizenry
who lived in the outskirts and came in to have fun
and at the end of it wished to fight.

> Ernest Hemingway, drunkenly fibbing that
> he had been a whorehouse bouncer, in a
> 1950s recording session

    A road sign at the city limits said "Bright Lights, Big Sky." With eighty thousand people, Billings is the unofficial capital of eastern Montana and—with 10 percent of the state's population—the largest city in the state. Yet it still has the feel of a big cow town. A current U.S. senator, Conrad Burns, comes from Billings; his only previous public experience was as a Yellowstone County commissioner and a radio announcer of livestock reports, but it was enough to take a seat away from Senator Melcher, a former veterinarian.
    Since I couldn't find a small old-time hotel that looked safe, I splurged and checked into the rather tony Northern Hotel. My sixty-dollar room on the eleventh floor was painted mauve and decorated with flower prints instead of Charlie Russell scenes. After a long bath, I went upstairs to the Petroleum Club, a rooftop dining room named for the two oil booms that quickly pumped up Billings's skyscrapers, then collapsed along with the town's economy. The restaurant was empty, except for two businessmen talking quietly.
    "So how's Bill doin'?"

"Well, he didn't make a well."

"Dry?"

"Hit sand."

"Hell, I remember twelve, fifteen years ago they was drilling a well right off the back of this hotel. Took longer to drill here than a fifteen-thousand-foot well."

"What happened?"

"Hit water."

I headed outside for a nightcap. After passing a brightly lit restaurant, upscale clothing stores, and a shop specializing in western memorabilia and rare books, I felt the neighborhood change abruptly; two blocks from the hotel a trio of hookers propositioned me. Two were black; the third might have been Hispanic. They wore cheap, garish dresses and shivered in the cool night breeze. They looked out of place in a state where the population is mostly white, and where hookers are now rare.

I walked south along Twenty-eighth Street, past pawn shops displaying saddles, firearms, and hunting bows in their windows. Near the railroad tracks, a drunk Indian was hugging a lamppost. He reached out to me with a forlorn hand, but the dead eyes in his acne-scarred face could not achieve focus. On the corner of Twenty-seventh Street and Montana Avenue I found John Conrad's old store—or at least where it once stood. It had been torn down for spiffy law offices.

The Empire Bar was a dingy place, and you could see the whiskey working in the faces of the Indians and whites ranged along the bar stools. The man to my right was hunkered down at the bar. He wore a faded plaid work shirt and a grimy green baseball cap with a little white button on top. He lifted his face abruptly, revealing a beard like bear fur and the dented nose of a boxer. There was a dirty abrasion above his right eye and a fresh gash in his left cheek. He was very drunk. "Hey," he said, "are you an asshole?"

"Don't think so."

"'Cause I'm an asshole. I'm a real tough asshole. Are you tough?"

"Not as tough as you are."

"Yeah, 'cause you wanna try sumthin', you just go ahead, take the first shot. Name's Marlon Cole, and I'm a tough asshole from Miles City."

"Glad to meet you."

"You think *I'm* tough? You ought to meet my wife. She weighs two hundred pounds. I mean, she's not just tough, she's *nasty!* We're in a bar, you know, and this Indian chick is makin' trouble and I'm down on my knees on the floor—on my knees in pain, getting kicked in the ribs—and my wife, she just grabs that Indian chick by the hair. Like *this*."

With surprising swiftness Marlon Cole grabbed a hunk of my hair and tipped me sideways. I grabbed the bar rail for balance. "And she just whomps that Indian chick back and forth against the bar. Bam, bam, bam!" He shook me for emphasis the way a terrier does a rabbit. This was painful. I grabbed his rough-knuckled hand to keep it from tearing my hair out by the roots. My other hand tightened on the bar.

Marlon suddenly released me with a sigh and continued his story as if nothing out of the ordinary had occurred. "I mean, man, if you'd mess with me—she'd mess with *you*. I mean, I come in late, you know, beat-up or drunk, she doesn't just *cozy* up to me. She grabs me and beats the hell out me! Hits me on the side of the face—like *this*." His fist flashed an inch from my face and then retreated. "I mean I'm tough, Golden Gloves contender and a 'Nam vet, but she's tougher than that. Sheeee-it."

"Where is she now?" I asked, taking a quick look around the barroom.

"Somewhere. I don't know," he slurred. "Somewhere pissed off at me." The woman bartender passed by polishing a glass, and Marlon beckoned to her. "Say, babe, can I have a drink?"

"Marlon, you've had enough. No more tonight."

When she left he gave me a pleading look. "Can I have a drink, old buddy? Please?"

I bought two bottles of beer from the male bartender and, against my better judgment, passed one to Marlon. He put down about half the beer before the woman bartender came back and confiscated it. Marlon protested, whined, and began calling for someone named Louie, who was playing pool. He was a skinny man with glasses and thin dark hair combed over a pasty bald spot. You could see the outline of his T-shirt through his polyester-blend white shirt. It was hard to believe he and Marlon Cole could be friends, or have anything in common, except that they both seemed to be regulars at this bar. Louie interceded. "Come on. He's not bad off. He can do it."

The woman bartender eyed Marlon the way a Yellowstone Park ranger sizes up a garbage-eating bear, but Marlon got to keep his beer after all. He held it protectively to his chest, clutched in a dirty hand that was missing most of the thumbnail. He complained to me that he'd been run out of another place, the Crystal Bar, earlier that evening. "Threw me out on the street, the bastards." His left hand hovered gingerly over the gash on his cheek. "I mean, look at this, man. It's not too bad, is it?"

The inside of the wound looked like a slice in a venison steak. It would need stitches. "Looks pretty bad to me."

"Well, it would, wouldn't it? I mean, it would to *you*. 'Cause you're not a tough *asshole* like I am."

I'd seen enough toughness for one evening. I stood up, but he took hold of the lapels of my jacket and jerked me forward. He was very strong, and his eyes grew strange as hobnailed jackalopes bunny-hopped though his brain waves. I tried to pull back, but his grip tightened. Before he could explode, I had a small, brilliant thought. "Marlon, I think I see her," I gasped. "Near the pool table. Your wife."

His blue eyes widened in fear. "My *wife?* Where?" he whispered.

"Back there."

His grip began to loosen.

He released me and turned, squinting into the darkness beyond the brightly lit pool tables. Before he could grab me again, I hurried out of the bar.

Billings was named for Frederick Billings, an executive of the Northern Pacific Railroad, which arrived in 1882. Before the railroad, the tent-and-shanty community on the Yellowstone River was called Coulson. A bank, a newspaper, a post office, a bakery, and plenty of saloons opened to serve the population of five hundred. The first Fourth of July was celebrated with races and fireworks on the railroad's right-of-way. About a thousand people attended the raucous ball; a teenager was killed during a horse race with a friend when his mount shied into the speaker's stand. The first cattle were shipped out on the Northern Pacific that September, and the deputy sheriff, Muggins Taylor, a former Indian fighter, was shot by an alcohol-crazed wife beater. Taylor was replaced by John "Liver-Eating" Johnston, whose name, reputedly, came from having eaten the liver of a Crow Indian. (Johnston always denied the story, saying he had eaten the liver of a deer to spook greenhorns.)

To control the stench of garbage, hogs were set loose in the back alleys; when they broke open kegs of oysters in brine kept on a hotel's back porch, they were immediately slaughtered. A company to operate the horse-drawn Billings Street Railway was formed. A few cases of diphtheria and typhoid appeared. Ice-cream socials were held by the ladies at the Congregational church. President Chester K. Arthur, General Phil Sheridan, and an army escort stopped briefly in Billings in 1883 on their way back from Yellowstone National Park. And Joseph Zimmerman strung a wire from his clothing store to his home to establish Billings's first telephone line. When Chief Plenty Coups of the Crows heard a voice from the earpiece of the telephone, he declared it "big medicine."

In 1886, seminary pupils performed the operetta *Cinderella* at McKee's Opera House. The same year, Calamity Jane showed up for laundry work at the Headquarters Hotel. Chief Bobtail of the Crows came to town and threatened to scalp a U.S. deputy marshal who had ordered stockmen to quit feeding their herds on the rich grass of the reservation; the cattlemen had been paying the Crows in fresh beef, and without buffalo, the Indians were hungry. Five years later, the western side of the Crow reservation was opened to white settlement to accommodate miners and ranchers.

By 1887 my great-grandfather had purchased a log cabin house in Billings for his wife, Mabel, and established an impressive store in the First National Bank Building. His store's letterhead now listed locations in Miles City as well as Buffalo, Sheridan, and Fort McKinney, Wyoming—a growing spiderweb of commerce. Billings was an excellent place to build a business and to establish a political base. There were over fifteen hundred people living there in 1888, surrounded by an estimated 150 major ranches in the area. By then it was a boomtown with two banks, an electrical lighting system, graded streets, and new houses springing up every day. The Northern Pacific connection had made the town the sheep-marketing capital of Montana and Wyoming.

An 1888 *Chicago Inter-Ocean* article on Billings praised John Conrad in hyperbolic style: "Probably there is no man in Montana who has contributed more to the upbuilding of this territory than this estimable gentleman. . . . The success achieved by Mr. Conrad is due to his indefatigable and tireless work, business sagacity, and keen financial management, supplemented with large means and pluck to carry out successfully every business effort undertaken. Personally he is held in the highest esteem throughout the territories, and is a plain, modest, unassuming gentleman . . . ."

Modest? Unassuming? These were not words I would have used to describe my great-grandfather. *Ambitious* came to mind first. It was no coincidence that this article was reprinted in the *Billings Weekly News*—for consumption by local customers and future voters.

Beginning in 1887, John was in constant contact with former territorial governor Samuel Hauser—a financial octopus who wielded tremendous power in the banking, railroad, mining, and cattle industries. Hauser was one of the Big Four, along with railroad tycoon Charles Broadwater and the copper kings Marcus Daly and William A. Clark. The concept of "conflict of interest" in politics and business didn't exist in Montana. Hauser had been in Montana since the gold rush days at Bannack, and recognized useful ambition in Conrad; it was nice to have a smart young man around. And when coal deposits were discovered down at Red Lodge, John made sure the former governor got a cut of the action.

In 1888, the year of the constitutional convention, the population of Montana Territory was approximately 185,000, and 15,000 were Indians. (The voting population was only about 40,000.)

In June, John wrote to Hauser: "After talking with some of my friends I have made up my mind, should it meet with your approval and entire satisfaction to try for the Governorship this fall. I can get eastern and northern Montana to go solid for me in the convention. And I believe I could win. So would like you to consider it. As I would not under any circumstances make a move in it unless you thought it best."

Hauser must have approved, because a month later the *Billings Gazette* wrote: "We predict that in the event Mr. Conrad enters in the race for the governorship there will be no flies resting on his shoulders during the canvass."

One fly John did allow to rest on his shoulder was Marcus Daly, who controlled many of the copper mines in Butte as well as the smelter in Anaconda; the copper king needed coal from Conrad's mines. In late July, John joined Daly and a private railcar of his associates on a short rail trip down to Red Lodge to look over the coal situation. On the return leg they stopped over in Billings for a few hours. Daly invited John to continue on to Butte by train. They shared Daly's private stock of cigars and brandy, and John spent the weekend schmoozing in Butte to promote coal sales and his political profile.

However, the other Democrats from Butte and Helena had another candidate in mind for Montana's first governor under statehood: Joseph Toole. Previously a congressional delegate from the territory to Washington, Toole brought far more experience to the job than Conrad. The Democrats needed a seasoned politician to run against the Republican candidate, Thomas Power—the Conrad family's old rival from Fort Benton days.

When the Democrats convened at Anaconda in August 1889 under the leadership of William A. Clark, most stayed in Marcus Daly's grand new hotel, the Montana. After Toole was introduced as the gubernatorial candidate, John Conrad was nominated for lieutenant governor. With his height, strong brow, and large mustache, Conrad cut a handsome figure in his dark suit from a leading Chicago tailor; this, surely, was no cowboy.

The copper kings began delivering the votes. Daly's political machine in Anaconda naturalized hundreds of Italian workers so they could vote for the Democratic ticket, while in Butte, Clark let it be known that miners who voted Republican would be dismissed. The candidates crisscrossed the state by train to rally support, but John was absent during the last two weeks of September; he was in Rhode Island attending his father-in-law's funeral. And this was a factor in the narrow loss to his Republican rival. The Democrats and Joseph Toole managed to beat Thomas Power for the governorship, but that fall Montana's legislature declared Power and another Republican as the state's new U.S. senators.

Hauser, himself a former governor, had hoped to be senator until the Democrats turned against him. Miffed, he distanced himself from the party. William Clark's paper, the *Butte Miner,* wasted no time in lambasting him: "Mr. Hauser is doubtless ashamed of his defeat, but the Democratic Party of Montana should be proud of it. Of course Mr. Hauser will go over to the Republicans—indeed he has already gone—but like Benedict Arnold he will die in a political garret unhonored, unsung and unwept."

That was more or less Hauser's political fate, but he and John Conrad kept up their close if secretive business relations. My great-grandfather planned to run for the governorship in 1892, but unexpected events— among them his wife's infidelity and the murder of his mother-in-law— would soon change his life in Montana.

Perched high up on the rimrock near Billings International Airport sits the Yellowstone Museum, a log cabin affair. Montana is covered with folksy museums like this. One display case holds a buffalo exquisitely carved out of a bar of soap, a sort of shower-room scrimshaw. Sioux and Cree beaded moccasins hang alongside Liver-Eating Johnston's billy club—notched four times for the Indians he killed.

There is also the knife that belonged to Big Nose George Parrott, who robbed trains and killed two members of the posse that eventually caught him. They hanged him from a telephone pole, but the rope broke. Half-choked, George urged the mob to shoot him, but they tried to hang him again. He got hold of the telephone pole with his legs and shimmied up it until he got tired and fell, breaking his neck. A doctor took the body away and pickled him in a barrel of brine, then sliced off pieces of his flesh for medical study. George's skin was made into a medical bag and a pair of two-tone shoes. The top of his skull was sawed off and used as a stop for the doctor's front door. In nineteenth-century Montana, there was only selective respect for the criminal dead.

Ernest Hemingway enjoyed trout fishing and bear hunting in northern Wyoming and near Cooke City, Montana, but he had an unpleasant experience in Billings in November 1930. Hemingway, John Dos Passos, and a cowboy named Floyd Allington were driving back from a camping trip in Yellowstone Park on a two-lane gravel road (now Interstate 90) when oncoming headlights blinded them. Hemingway swerved to avoid a collision. The Ford flipped into a ditch, pinning him upside down behind the wheel, and breaking his right arm.

St. Vincent's Hospital in Billings was staffed mainly by Catholic nuns. Hemingway was placed in a private room with a view of the rimrock. The fracture was a bad one. The surgeon made a long incision and tied up the sheared bones with kangaroo tendons. Hemingway endured the pain, but was depressed that he was unable to finish the manuscript of *Death in the Afternoon,* and worried about having to cancel his trip to Africa that spring. On doctor's orders, he was forbidden to walk around the hospital. He lay immobilized for a month as the arm swelled, burst, and drained.

During these insomniac hours, he listened to a portable radio, and amused himself by making up obscene versions of a Rudy Vallee song, "Betty Co-ed has lips of red for Harvard." He also got to know a pair of wounded sugar-beet workers, a Russian and a Mexican, who lay groaning across the hall. They had been shot in an all-night restaurant. The bullets had been meant for the Mexican, a small-time gambler; the Russian was just an unlucky bystander. The Mexican refused to name the gunman, insisting he had no enemies. The gambler's friends sometimes stopped by Hemingway's room to speak Spanish and drink whiskey.

Hemingway's favorite nurse was Sister Florence, a gentle nun who loved baseball and prayed fervently for her team during the World Series. He let his hair and beard grow, and with his hospital tunic belted at his waist he posed for a photograph as a cossack. When Hemingway was released after seven demoralizing weeks, he was still weak and his friends worried for him, but he had in mind a short story: "The Gambler, the Nun, and the Radio." And he made it to Africa after all.

Calf roping at the Oldtimers
Rodeo in Absarokee.

Marge and Alice Greenough
at the rodeo in Absarokee;
Alice was one of the greatest female bronc riders of
all time.

Chapter 15

Red Lodge: Alice Greenough and the Pigs of Bearcreek

Let's give this cowboy a big hand while he's still conscious.

rodeo announcer

Red Lodge is an old coal-mining town at the base of the Beartooth Range. Though it has become a low-key ski resort, its well-preserved brick storefronts and good saloons make it one of the prettiest, most authentic towns in Montana.

Near the log cabin that serves as the Carbon County Museum, a good-sized black bear padded behind summer cabins. When the critter tipped over a garbage can, I walked to the cabin's front door and knocked. A woman answered.

"Hi," I said. "Just thought you might like to know there's a black bear in your garbage."

"Oh my, is he back again? Thanks for telling me." The woman found a broom and came outside. "Shoo, bear! Get away from here!" The bear took off into the bushes. "He's a nuisance," she said. "But a cute one. Usually only comes at night."

Red Lodge is so named because Crow Indians camped here many years ago and painted their council tepee with red clay. The first white settlement began as a way station on the hundred-mile road down to Meeteetse, Wyoming. The discovery of coal and other minerals brought the railroad, mining entrepreneurs, and my great-grandfather, who opened a bank and store here in 1889. So many new buildings went up that there was a shortage of lumber; the new streets filled with mud during the rains. There were plenty of bars, and a row of whorehouses known as "the Castles." Finn Town and Little Italy sprang up, while native-born Americans lived in a fancier neighborhood, "Hi-Bug Town."

An article entitled "In Cold Blood" from an 1890 copy of the *Red Lodge Picket* gives a picture of the times:

> The denizens of Red Lodge were thrown into a wild state of excitement Thursday night by the assassination of Vic Arland, of Arland, Wyoming. About 12 o'clock Vic Arland was sitting in John Dunivin's saloon talking to a crowd of friends about old times and in a twinkling of an eye his life was snuffed out by a shot from some cold-blooded assassin standing on the outside of the saloon. The ball pierced the man through the heart and killed him instantly. Dr. F. R. Musser was immediately sent for but it was useless as the man never made a struggle and was dead by the time he struck the floor.

Two years later, the dream of Red Lodge began to fade when Samuel Hauser, John Conrad, and other stockholders in the coal company became locked in a financial battle, which penalized the miners themselves. The *Billings Gazette* reported: "Nearly all these men are married and have large families and they have just enough money from their labor to keep the wolf of starvation from the door. It is impossible for the majority of them to seek new fields of labor and they must bend to the yoke."

Only seven of the town's two dozen saloons stayed open. In 1893, John's store—which depended on the miners' business—went into receivership, and the bank was under attack as well.

A woman at the historical society gave me a photocopy of a century-old map and sent me looking for Conrad's store. I followed the map carefully until I stood in front of the lot; it was now a YMCA swimming pool swarming with brown-bodied kids. Once, not so long ago, I'd been a kid running around a pool with boundless energy. Now I was running around a murky swamp of history and absent ancestors. Smelling the chlorine and watching the kids being told not to run by an exasperated lifeguard, I felt time's power in my own life, now ending its fourth decade.

I had a drink at the Carbon County Coal Co. bar, which was formerly the Finnish Opera House, built in 1897. There were three customers at the bar, until a middle-aged dwarf walked in. He waddled, as dwarves do, and his high bulbous brow seemed full of angst. The stools at the bar were high, but he nimbly clambered up one of them and ordered a beer. No one paid him much attention; he was no doubt a regular. I wanted to ask him what it was like to be a dwarf in Montana, but the question didn't sound polite, so I drank my beer in silence.

That night I went to the Red Lodge Café and, with some trepidation, sampled a plate of roast bear meat. Tasting something like pork, it was over-cooked and greasy, and I had qualms about having eaten a beast that could ride a bicycle in the Moscow Circus.

On my way back to the old Pollard Hotel, I stopped in at the Snag, a bar with swinging saloon doors. At the end of the bar sat two old-timers. One said, "I remember about twenty years ago settin' here when one of the trainers from the Red Lodge zoo parked a truck outside. He was on his way to a circus. 'Whatcha got in the truck?' I asks. He says, 'I'll show ya.' Goes out and comes in with a baby elephant and a chimpanzee. The chimp gets himself up on the bar stool for a glass of juice just like a regular customer. The elephant picks up a pool cue and begins to shoot, side-pocket and all. He'd been trained to do that. You should have seen the double-takes on the people walking by! That's when there was fun in this town."

"And money," said the other old-timer.

"Now there's no fun and no money. So let's have another drink."

Some cowgirls get the blues. Others get black and blue, and break their ankles, arms, and collarbones while flying off saddle broncs.

Alice Greenough was the greatest woman rodeo rider the West has ever seen. The first to be honored by the Cowgirl Hall of Fame, she is also in the Cowboy Hall of Fame. Alice also won the Cowgirls International Buck-jumping Contest in Sydney, Australia, in 1934 and 1935. She and her sister Marge are part of the most famous rodeo family ever. Their father, Ben "Pack-Saddle" Greenough, came to Montana in the 1880s and won the first professional bronc-busting contest in the state. Five of Ben's eight children went into rodeo, and to this day, Red Lodge is known as "the Home of the Riding Greenoughs." It was Alice who started the Carbon County Museum and filled it with memorabilia from Red Lodge's history.

Alice and Marge normally live in Tucson, Arizona, but I found them near Red Lodge, at the Oldtimers Rodeo in Absarokee. Every pickup in town was parked outside the rodeo gates. With barely a thousand people, Absarokee is a place where farmers and ranchers collect their mail, get a drink, and pray. The grandstand was the size you'd find at a small high school football field, facing an arena lined with chicken wire. There were only two chutes for rough stock and another for calf roping. This was how rodeo was done fifty years ago: a cozy way to get your bones broken.

I arrived during a heartfelt tribute to an old cowboy, Hi Whitlock, who'd been buried that morning. A riderless black horse was solemnly led around the ring with a pair of old boots and spurs stuck backward in the stirrups, to the sad song "Empty Saddles in the Old Corral." From the announcer's booth Alice Greenough said a few words about her late friend. "Hi was always there. He always knew what to do, even in difficult situations. He was a stock deputy. He was always a gentleman, and a gentle man as well. Never raised his voice, always got the job done. And God bless him—wherever he ends up."

When Alice finished, I joined her and sister Marge on the front row of the bleachers. In their mid-eighties, both women were trim and surprisingly unwrinkled. You could see they had once been pretty, and tough. In cowboy hats, boots, and western-style pantsuits, they still looked ready to ride. Alice, the elder sister, didn't give up riding broncs until she was fifty-seven.

We watched the Oldtimers Rodeo together. The agility and strength of the cowboys—some in their sixties—was admirable, but the second bronc rider came out of the chute on a horse that twisted around and smashed him into the gate. The man was flipped and thrown hard to earth, like a wet rag slapped on a table. As men crowded around the fallen rider, the flashing red light of the ambulance started up behind the stands.

Alice has seen her share of accidents, including two women killed in rodeo. "That stopped quite a few other gals from getting into it. In 1930, I broke my ankle in El Paso and they tried to cut my leg off," drawled Alice. "Got my foot hung in the stirrup. Twisted my foot right out of the boot. They messed around, put it in a cast, then started talking about amputation. An old German doctor come across the border there from Mexico. And he was on the elevator when they were taking me to the X-ray room. He said, 'You're not going to take that girl's leg off. I've got a bunch of ivory pegs with me. I can peg those anklebones together.' After they fixed me up, I was called 'the Girl with the Ivory Ankle.' Sometimes when I walk too much one of those ivory pegs works out from the bone and I have to push it back."

Alice's father, Ben, was one of Red Lodge's more remarkable citizens. He had cut firewood for Calamity Jane, lived with Custer's Crow scout Curly, and built Liver-Eating Johnston's homestead in Red Lodge. "My dad never took a drink or smoked a cigarette in his life, and he wouldn't let anyone smoke in the house or drink on the ranch. He lived until 1957. After Mama died I came home and lived with him, and I was kind of his left-hand gal." Ben ran an ice-skating rink in Billings every winter. "He was a beautiful figure skater. Never defeated. He learned to skate from a manual. I took him to New York in 1939. They'd just get off the rink when he started his beautiful turns. My dad and I did a lot of exhibition work together."

Ben Greenough was born in an orphanage in New York City and ran away when he was fourteen years old. He went to Miles City, Billings, and finally Red Lodge. Once, Alice remembered, they were at Madison Square Garden and Ben took off in a taxi. "He went back to the orphanage he left sixty years before and said, 'Maybe you've been wondering where I went. Well, here I am.' They declared it a holiday, and he spent all day telling the kids western stories about rustlers and Indians and bears. He told them the truth because he didn't believe in telling windy stories."

At the turn of the century, Ben Greenough broke saddle and packhorses and shipped them to Illinois. He also had a five-year courtship by mail with an Illinois woman that led to marriage. In 1917 he took a rural mail route out of Billings, but he had so much to do on the ranch that he often sent fourteen-year-old Alice instead. Alice rode thirty-seven miles on horseback every day for two summers and three winters in which the temperature sometimes dropped to forty below zero. During the First World War, she drove a six-horse team on a gang plow.

In her twenties, she and Marge hit the rodeo circuit. "The hotels would be filled, so we slept in tents most of the time. We lived off our winnings, and all the cowboys shared. If one fellow had ten dollars, he gave you five for gas or food. When we'd get ready to go off and rodeo, Dad would say, 'Mind your own business and don't let anyone get the best of you.' Then he'd walk away a few yards, turn, and say, 'Listen, Alice, you take Old Willy with you.'"

"Who was Old Willy?"

"That meant *willpower.*"

Another friend by that name was the cowboy writer and artist Will James. "I met him first about 1925. He had a home and studio up on Pryor Creek near the Crow reservation. Then he moved up to Billings to a stone house under the rimrocks. Bill was around the roundup wagon on our ranch a lot. He was a good hand himself, a real cowboy, even though he was just a little wiry fellow. Once he asked me to dance and he was pretty drunk and they was playing the tango. Well, I had never danced the tango and I got my steps kind of mixed up, and he hauled off and slapped me and said,

'You can't tango at all! You can't dance!' So I hauled off and hit him and said, 'You can't dance either!' About four or five old cowboys got hold of him and shook the tar out of him. He spent the rest of his life apologizing to me."

"What would he say?"

"He'd almost cry and say, 'Alice, why would I do a thing like that? I think a lot of you.' Bill was a heck of a nice fellow until he started with that awful drinkin' and carousin' with that secretary that he had. He had the best little wife in the world, that little Alice James, but that darn secretary was just his downfall. When he died they cremated him and flew an airplane over the Pryor Mountains and scattered his ashes. I was at the funeral. I had my dad with me, too. Some of those ashes fell on my hat brim. It meant something to me. I got a few pieces of the bone and ash and put them in a little bottle which I kept above the fireplace. But someone came along and took it, along with some gold nuggets my dad gave me."

Alice won bronc-riding contests at the Boston Garden in the thirties and at Madison Square Garden in 1941. Then she became a stunt rider for the movies. "I had all the offers in the world to stay in Hollywood. I might have become a star. But I didn't like the people and I didn't like Hollywood. Course, not being a gal that smoked or drank, it was hard to mix. I had a contract to do stunt riding for Metro-Goldwyn-Mayer, but I just walked off and went to Spain and Australia."

Both widowed now, Marge and Alice live next door to each other in Tucson and "never get lonely," with old rodeo friends passing through. "The old-timers are different from these new cowboys," she said "We call ourselves the Wild Bunch and get together every year to reminisce. I'm still driving stagecoaches for Hollywood movies made in Tucson. Paramount and Metro-Goldwyn have bought a huge lot out there for westerns. It's all nonunion and they're getting along fine. Just fine."

The town of Bearcreek, seven miles from Red Lodge, once had a thousand miners digging coal in its environs; it went on the map in 1943 when an explosion in the Smith Mine killed seventy-seven men, Montana's worst mining disaster. Now only thirty-seven hardy souls live in the ghost town. I drove to Bearcreek to bet on pigs at the Bear Creek Saloon.

"It was called the Hooty Owl," said the owner, Pits De Armond, "until somebody came in and shot the stuffed owls down off the top of the back bar with a two-seventy. You can still see bullet holes in the tin ceiling." Pits was a big mustachioed man of about forty, wearing a large, sweat-stained Stetson. "We're still pretty lenient about guns in here."

When Pits and his wife, Lynn, bought the Bear Creek Saloon, they knew that even with good Mexican food they had to be different to survive. So they began "porki-mutuel" betting on pig races at Bear Creek Downs. Every Saturday and Sunday at 7 P.M., Pits, Lynn, and their pig wranglers urged a few dozen customers to wolf down enchiladas and margaritas and step out onto the back balcony to participate in the Swine Sweepstakes. There were betting windows, a formally announced post time, and even video playback for those glued to the friendly bar scene inside. The cost of a betting ticket was two dollars, and no more than five tickets could be bought on any one race. A win ticket paid three dollars, an exacta five, and a trifecta ten. Most winnings, I remarked, seemed to get spent at the bar.

"That was kind of the idea," said Pits.

From the balcony I had a good view of the pig track, a thirty-yard oval. The pigs in the starting chute were white, gray, black, and pinto, and wore little jackets bearing their racing numbers. The program listed names like Soo City Soo, Hamlet, Barbie Q, Corndog, Oscar Meyer, Jimmy Dean, and Lucky Links. Lured by food at the finish line, they ran around the track in about fifteen seconds. The fact that there were fifty different names entered in the ten races and only twenty actual pigs in the corrals didn't seem to bother anyone.

Pig racing wasn't the only way to draw customers. The Cowboy Golf Classic, played in the sagebrush-covered hills south of the saloon, had a scoring system that allowed participants to deduct two strokes for every rattlesnake they killed, and four strokes for every rattler that bit them. Another popular event was the Big Drop. A buffalo was placed in a corral painted with a numbered grid. If the buffalo made his "big drop" on your number, you could win up to a thousand dollars. This all seemed a lot more fun than coal mining.

Western novelist Thomas McGuane.
(Courtesy Winston Conrad)

Chapter 16

Thomas McGuane: Writer of the Purple Sage

Whiskey is the cowboy's color TV.

Thomas McGuane

The noon heat carried the scent of sagebrush down from the rimrock in a perfume that could cure a hangover. In a corral near the West Boulder River, I found Thomas McGuane training his pretty sorrel mare, Louie, to cut a white-faced cow out of a herd. This was the start of a hoofed chess match: the cow desperately tried to rejoin the others, but the mare sank on her hocks and gracefully sidestepped and mirrored every move the cow made, blocking her return. Left, right, then hard left again. The horse dominated the cow, pushing her backward to the other side of the corral.

If this were the open range, the cow would be roped for branding or doctoring. But this was work elevated to sport, practice for cutting-horse competition—a relatively new event in the equine world of America. Released, the baffled cow scuttled for home. McGuane patted Louie's neck and headed for the barn.

A few minutes later, McGuane walked into the kitchen of his ranch house and squeezed his wife, Laurie, saying, "Darling, I'm so happy. It's a perfect day."

Laurie McGuane was a striking woman with dark brown hair, a long nose, and a taut figure with the jare of a racing sloop. Athleticism was a big part of their marriage—shooting, sailing, and horses—and both McGuanes have been cutting-horse champions of Montana in different years.

At fifty, McGuane was graying and handsome, with dark eyes that gave off an ironic spark befitting one of America's leading satirical novelists. Still wearing his spurs, McGuane settled his lean six-foot-three-inch frame into a chair, ran his hand through short thick hair, and began opening the mail before lunch. One of the letters said that a publisher in Paris wanted to translate three of McGuane's novels—and would pay good money.

The McGuanes recently moved over from Paradise Valley to this ranch near McLeod, population thirty-five. The log cabin house was furnished simply, with paintings by Charles Burchfield and their friend Russell Chatham, a baby grand piano, and a three-foot carved mobile of a fish. McGuane's writing studio is a cabin down near the river. There is a marble slab near the river's edge engraved with the names of all the McGuanes' deceased dogs and other small pets. McGuane calls his three-thousand-acre spread the Raw Deal Ranch, but on a day like this, when the clouds stampede across the big sky and the royalty checks roll in, it seems anything but that.

When McGuane's fifth novel, *Nobody's Angel,* came out in 1979, a Los Angeles *Times* critic praised him for being as "meticulous with his metaphors as a Renaissance poet" and called his book a "thinking man's western." Pegging McGuane's books as westerns, however, would be like calling Faulkner's books southerns or John Updike's easterns. McGuane's novels and stories center around a Montana cow town called Deadrock, which functions for McGuane as Yoknapatawpha County did for Faulkner. Unlike pulp hack Louis L'Amour, who dished up hang-em-high clichés of the Old West, McGuane writes about the contemporary West with a satiric bent. His tales are populated with psychopathic cowboys, adulterous horse trainers, pistol-packing ranchwomen, jet-setting ranchers, speed-freak coyote hunters, and hookers working out of trailers. It's *The Big Sky* warped by a century.

McGuane's second book, *The Bushwhacked Piano* (1971), established him as one of the most poetic—as well as the funniest—writers of his generation. The novel is the manic hegira of misguided Nicholas Payne, who enters the Montana rodeo circuit to win his girlfriend away from her country-club parents. Payne nearly loses his life to a jealous voyeuristic cowhand named Dwayne Codd, undergoes a horrendous operation for hemorrhoids, and eventually flees to Key West in partnership with a multiple amputee named C. J. Clovis, who is intent on harnessing the insectivorous appetite of bats for profit. McGuane's novel illuminated America's varicose geography with alternate moments of slapstick and paranoia. A vignette in a Montana motel:

All the windows were open to the cool high-altitude evening; under the blanket of his rented bed, Payne had the sudden conviction that he was locked in one of the umbral snotlockers of America. On the pine wall overhead, a Great Falls Beer calendar with Charles Remington reproductions of wolves, buffalo and lonesome cowpokes who tried to establish that with their used-up eyes and plumb-tuckered horses they were entitled to the continent . . . .

McGuane's hybridization of the names Charles M. Russell and Frederick Remington was deliberate.

An avid consumer of western lore, McGuane feels that Montana is a land of dying legends. "Many of the colorful old-timers died in the sixties, and this part of Montana never had a very glamorous history. You know: homesteaders, barbers from Kansas, or dentists—small people living out their small lives against a bigger backdrop." His hand motioned to the Crazy Mountains in the distance. "Some of them are kind of hangdog in the presence of these snowy peaks."

Nevertheless, McGuane's books always contain references to the old days. "The hardest thing for the locals to remember is the Indian presence here— that the area beyond the McLeod schoolhouse was a camp used continuously for four thousand years. They don't really think of the Indians as people like themselves. So you hear locals saying, 'You know, people have only been here since the 1870s.' This place can get pretty insular. Sometimes I get tired of hearing about grizzly bears and the environment and conversations that amount to 'Yup' and 'Nope.' I often miss the honeycomb of humanity of a New York or San Francisco."

When Indian graves were discovered on McGuane's property, he let them lie in peace. "They were victims of a smallpox epidemic in the 1840s. My hired man is half Sioux and half Irish and gets a little superstitious fooling around with Indian stuff."

Though wry, and usually forgiving, McGuane's heroes are not immune to violence. "I used to be kind of a bar fighter myself," admitted McGuane with a certain amount of pleasure. "One time when I had long hair, I was shooting pool in a bar in Bozeman and this guy kept needling me, with stuff like, 'Hey, sister, what are you doing tonight?' When he finally made his move, I hit him with a pool cue on the side of his head and knocked him about three bar stools down. I went across the street and called the bartender to find out whether or not he'd died. I'm not promoting violence per se, but if someone else brings it to your door, you've got to blow him out of the box in round one."

McGuane, like his characters, has a highly personal sense of justice and righteous revenge. Once a social-climbing banker who was trying to ingratiate himself with the local ranchers took it upon himself to shoot and kill McGuane's beloved Labrador, who was seen wandering on a neighbor's ranch. "The first thing I did was get him fired from the local bank. Then he moved over to a little bank in Belgrade, Montana, as a teller—and that bank failed. Forced him to move back to Minnesota. Couldn't sell his house for three years. I understand he's destitute. I might have to think of another way to get him again. Sometimes you have to be relentless. You have to understand that I loved that dog desperately."

It has been said that Montana has more artists and writers per capita than any other state in America. "That's just because our population is so low," jokes McGuane. "All we need is one of each and we win." (Montana is almost twice the size of Great Britain, yet its population is less than eight hundred thousand.) McGuane was never interested in creating a Montana literary movement, but after he moved to Montana, a tribe of actors, writers, and artists followed him. His newest neighbors include newsman Tom Brokaw, beefcake photographer Bruce Weber, and authors such as grizzly expert Tom McNamee and African elegist John Heminway. McGuane himself just sold a couple of hundred acres to *Batman* star Michael Keaton. "There's no coterie up here," McGuane insisted. "Writers don't hang out together to discuss the future of literature." But Jim Harrison, William Hjortsberg, and Russell Chatham often join McGuane for hunting and fishing trips.

Born in Michigan in 1939, McGuane grew up comfortably middle class, son of an Irish Catholic slum kid who rowed on the Harvard crew and started a successful Detroit-based auto-parts company. After studying at Michigan State and the Yale School of Drama, McGuane won a writing fellowship at Stanford under Wallace Stegner. As a teenager McGuane had spent every summer he could in Montana and Wyoming, hitchhiking or working on ranches. "We were under the spell of Jack Kerouac in those days—*On the Road,* you know. I guess I always wanted to be a cowboy—a pretty silly idea." He chuckled gently, spinning the rowel on one of his spurs. McGuane's self-deprecating humor is sane and attractive, in pleasant contrast to the reputation he had in the seventies as a wild cadet in the drug, booze, and womanizing cavalry of American letters.

His first novel, *The Sporting Club* (1969), was about an exclusive Michigan trout club brought to ruin by a dueling millionaire and a raunchy motorcycle gang with a yen for dynamite. It was also a story of class struggle, male rivalry, and bare-ass ribaldry. The book was greeted with thunderous critical acclaim, but with less enthusiasm by McGuane's staid family. "The book was kind of racy for the times. One of my favorite uncles called up my mother and asked, 'Where did Tommy learn those *words?*' "

After selling the movie rights, McGuane bought a ranch in Paradise Valley, south of Livingston—the model for his fictitious town of Deadrock. Between novels and screenplays, he threw himself into the world of rodeo, sometimes earning more from his saddle than he did from his pen. Despite their comic lunacy, McGuane's books are firmly grounded in a knowledge of horsemanship, hunting, and fishing, pastimes he pursues with passionate skill. Wintering in Key West, Florida, to escape the ferocious Montana blizzards, McGuane took up saltwater fishing with a devotion that spilled over into his third novel, *Ninety-two in the Shade* (1973), nominated for the National Book Award.

Writing the screenplay for *Ninety-two in the Shade* whetted McGuane's appetite to engage a more lucrative world—filmmaking. "I was just like any other sucker in American literature that goes to Hollywood. I really felt I *belonged* in Hollywood," he laughed, shaking his head. His first original screenplay was *Rancho Deluxe,* starring Jeff Bridges. "I was fascinated by the mythological West and its relationship to the present. So I wrote a modern western about cattle rustling and survival in the lousy Montana railroad towns that I actually lived in." McGuane wanted Robert Altman to direct it, but when Altman became caught up in other projects, the producer finally said to McGuane, "Anybody can direct a movie. You do it."

"I enjoyed directing, but I went through hell with the English financiers and lost control in the editing room. I'm still proud of parts of that film, but aspiring to work in the movies is like aspiring to work as a copilot. Hollywood is made up of a lot of copilots."

He wrote two other original scripts: *Tom Horn* for Steve McQueen, and *The Missouri Breaks,* about a small-time outlaw, Jack Nicholson, who meets his match in a strange shaman character played by Marlon Brando. As McGuane remembers it, this film eventually became a vanity battle between the two movie stars. "My original idea was to make a low-budget western with Warren Oates and Harry Dean Stanton. We would all work for free and shoot it cheap and dirty up in Montana in about a month. When I sold the deal to a studio they said, 'We really like the script. But we want movie stars. We don't want those guys you like.' So they lined up Jack Nicholson and Marlon Brando. The producers then came back to me and said, 'Listen, we're paying each of these guys a million dollars. We've got to have big scenes for these guys. Your script has no big scenes; it's about a bunch of outlaws being killed off like coyotes.' I said, 'That's what the film's about.' The producer shook his head. 'No, no, no, Tom. It's about *Jack* and *Marlon*. That's what it's *about*, Tom. If you don't like it, go back to your ranch."

In the meantime, McGuane realized that Hollywood and the high life can leave weeping sores on an original writer's psyche. "Looking back, I wish I'd had a squarer swing at things," he says. McGuane's own life during this period was turning into a comedy of eros spiked with drugs and infidelity. McGuane's marriage to Becky Crockett (now Mrs. Peter Fonda) was jolted by affairs with actress Elizabeth Ashley, then with Margot Kidder, whom he married for nine months. McGuane met his present wife, Laurie Buffett (sister of country-and-western singer Jimmy Buffett), while lying semicomatose on the floor of a Key West bar. Laurie wisely waited six months to call him.

In 1978, McGuane wrote *Panama,* a novel about the alienating forces of fame and drugs. "It wasn't just me. It was what I saw happen to my friends who were actors and musicians." Also set in Key West, *Panama* tells the tale of a paranoid rock star who, in one incident, is so racked by love that he nails his hand to his girlfriend's front door. The book throbs with dislocated pain. "It's my only novel told in the first person, because I wanted to get into the head of an individual under great stress."

One of his strongest novels, *Nobody's Angel* (1979), bears a dedication that is intimate and revealing: "For my beloved Laurie, still there when the storm passed." Those were trying years for the McGuanes. His sister died of a drug overdose at twenty-six, and his parents died as alcoholics. In *Nobody's Angel,* a Montana rancher named Patrick Fitzpatrick tries to save his disturbed sister, Mary, but she commits suicide anyway.

McGuane stopped drinking. "I was so menaced by my own family's history that when I got nervous about being what is euphemistically called 'a hard drinker,' I decided it was time to quit," says McGuane. "I didn't really have the addictive side to it, but I did have personality changes. Once clear, I became addicted to *not* being addicted." As McGuane straightened out, he settled down to ranching and being a father to his four children. "They're true Montanoids."

In addition to breeding horses, McGuane and his wife enter about twenty-five competitions a year, often winning purses of five thousand dollars and up. Though the sport does reduce his writing time, McGuane says, "I can't write all day long. Cutting horses to me are a sort of art issue anyway. They're a challenge." To escape Montana's brutal winter, each fall the McGuanes trailer their horses to Point Clear on Mobile Bay, Alabama, where they shoot, train dogs, and fish for tarpon in the Gulf of Mexico— pastimes McGuane has written about beautifully in a collection of sporting essays, *An Outside Chance* (1982).

It is fiction, though, that most accurately charts McGuane's talent. A collection of short stories, *To Skin a Cat* (1986), revealed McGuane's voice to be more resonant than ever. The stories range from the tale of a salesman who steals the neighbors' dogs to a deeply moving account of man dying of cancer who goes grouse hunting for the last time. A novel, *Keep the Change* (1989), also displayed maturity, but lacked the wacky brilliance of the first books. As McGuane says about refinements in his style, "One of the first things to go, strangely enough, was the very stuff I made my reputation on—the pyrotechnics."

At the end of our talk, Tom McGuane excused himself, saying he wanted to get in a few more hours of ranch work. He suggested I cast a fly in the West Boulder, and drove me upriver in his truck to a good stretch of water. "The brown trout are gorging on hoppers," he said. From the glove compartment he pulled a plastic box filled with dry flies. "Here, try this little yellow-bellied fly. And fish that long pool assiduously."

Fishing is meditative, and, wading Tom McGuane's river, I thought of where he was going as a writer. His ambition and skill had brought him celebrity and appetites that had hurt him, but he had changed his life, *engineering* a new McGuane out of his tumultuous youth. Even as his hair grayed, there was a new streamlined aspect to the man and his writing—less razzle-dazzle, more hewn. He's still a contender and all his books are in print. (Three years later his big novel *Nothing but Blue Skies* thrust him into stardom, again.)

The frog-bellied scent of the shady river drew me in, and I saw a trout rise in a deep pool upstream. My wading boots bumped over the unseen riverbed. As I began to cast, there was another rise near the far bank. Of fishing, McGuane once wrote: "In looking for one fish you find another, and maybe in the end you find it all."

A Grizzly sow and her cubs near Yellowstone.
(Courtesy Montana Historical Society)

Chapter 17

Those Crazy People from California

My daddy was a banker in a mining town,
he was murdered on the night I was conceived.
Collecting on a mortgage from a miner's wife,
he died with his pants around his knees.

> Greg Keeler, songwriter, circa 1988

North of Gardiner I turned *Red Cloud* off the highway, crossed a metal bridge, and headed up a dirt road toward a settlement by the banks of the Yellowstone River. Today's Corwin Springs was once called Electric, and before that it was known as Horr. In 1883, two brothers organized the Horr Coal Company. Harry, known as Major Horr, once shipped a one-ton block of coal to the world's fair in New Orleans, and he is credited with writing the first dime novel about Calamity Jane. Despite his promotional flair, he and his brother Joseph failed to get the mines productive until 1887, when a handful of Livingston businessmen stepped in. Two years later, Major Horr sold part of his interest in the mines to John Conrad, who became president of the company.

By 1892, the Horr operation was producing four hundred tons of coal a day, and the thirty-six coke ovens billowed smoke night and day. (It took 1.7 tons of coal to make one ton of coke.) The real discovery was the Number Seven Mine two miles up the mountain, a find that would create the town of Lake. The coal was hauled out of a thin concentrated vein in the mountain, dumped into a long wooden water flume, and washed a mile downhill to the coke ovens at Horr.

John Conrad set up a general-merchandise store at Horr for the miners, and began to build a tramway up to Lake. When a bank panic swept the country in 1893, John was hit hard. The problem was his little bank at Red Lodge, whose cashier had just been charged with embezzlement. Though John was never implicated, the bank closed. To buttress his reputation, he made a personal assignment to satisfy bank creditors and claimed that the problem would have no effect on the coal company. For over a year, however, there was no work at the mines or the coke ovens, and the store shut down. The coal company was sold at a court auction, but John remained as manager of the mines for four more years. In 1896 Lake was renamed Aldridge and the mines operated twenty-four hours a day.

Outside a one-story bungalow shaded with tall trees, I met John Michlovich, a rangy farmer in his early seventies. He pushed his sweat-stained hat back from his tanned face, exposing a pale brow. The name Conrad rang a muffled bell in him. "Too bad my dad isn't with us anymore. He knew all that stuff. Dad said this house was built for the Aldridge mine superintendent."

"That might have been my great-grandfather," I said. "What year was the house built?"

"Trouble is, I just don't know," said Michlovich, pushing his hat even farther back and scratching his scalp. It was a hot day with no breeze. A shadow slid swiftly across the road, a buteo hawk banking toward the Yellowstone. Michlovich himself had been born up the hill at Aldridge in 1918. When the mines and the town finally closed in the twenties, his family moved down here to farm. Farming, not history, was what he knew. I thanked him and headed down the road toward the buildings that had once made up the old community of Horr.

Red Cloud rattled over a cattle guard, passed a sign that said "Royal Teton Ranch," and entered one of the strangest new communities in Montana. The Church Universal and Triumphant's thirteen-thousand-acre spread runs from the Yellowstone River up over the mountains to the border of Yellowstone Park, and contains the ghost town of Aldridge. Until 1981, the ranch was owned by billionaire Malcolm Forbes. When Forbes put the land up for sale, wilderness groups lobbied the U.S. Forest Service to buy it as a key piece in the Greater Yellowstone Ecosphere. The Forest Service dillydallied, and eventually Forbes sold it for $7 million to a relatively unknown religious sect out of California.

The new ranch owners, known locally as CUT, have been called a New Age church, a radical survivalist cult, and "those crazy people from California." Nominally Christian, they believe that their leader, Elizabeth Clare Prophet, is a messenger from God who communicates with "Ascended Masters" of the human race, including Muhammad, Confucius, Christ, Saint Germain, Shakespeare, and Sir Thomas More—a.k.a. El Morya. With an additional twenty-three thousand acres in three parcels in Paradise Valley, the church is the second largest landowner in Park County, inspiring an active distrust among locals, and federal investigations for illegal firearms and environmental abuses.

Known to her followers as Mother Clare Prophet—and to the local press as Guru Ma—this fiftyish woman holds tremendous sway over her disciples. When the 1988 Yellowstone Park fires threatened to sweep over the mountains to their ranch, she sent several hundred members of her church to chant and pray on the fire lanes. The fires receded due to "divine intercession." Several times she predicted that the earth would end in a nuclear Armageddon. All the predictions, of course, were true; God simply changed his mind at the last moment.

The Church Universal and Triumphant complex occupied modern buildings and the old houses that once made up the mining settlement of Horr. The church had maintained the older buildings impeccably and brought in trailers to accommodate an ever-expanding population. At the headquarters, I met Ed Francis, Clare Prophet's husband, who acted as spokesperson and chief of staff. He was about forty, a clean-cut, dark-haired man in khakis and a blue short-sleeved shirt. An earnest boyish aspect nearly offset the crafty brightness of his eyes.

"For a minute I thought that blue frame house you can just see through the window—over there—might have been your great-grandfather's," said Ed Francis. "But after you telephoned we ran a check on it. It was built in 1906. Too late for your ancestor. Naturally, I'll arrange for someone to take you up to Aldridge whenever you're ready. Now, what can I tell you about us?"

"Let's start with your wife."

"She's a person, just like a lot of other people, but we believe that she is what we call a *messenger*. The church was originally started by her first husband, Mark Prophet. By the way, Prophet was his real name. He was born in Chippewa Falls, Wisconsin, and was a fundamentalist Christian when he was first contacted by a particular Ascended Master whom we know as El Morya. Mark didn't believe the messages at first. Over a few years he had a personal interaction with this master and started publishing what we refer to as *dictations*—direct personal messages from El Morya and other Ascended Masters. It's different from channeling. There's no trance involved. It's a conscious transference of a message. In the 1950s Mark moved to Washington, D.C., and started the Summit Lighthouse."

The purpose of this group, said Francis, was to publish the teachings of the Ascended Masters. After marrying in 1961, the Prophets bought a house in Virginia and gathered people to read their teachings. In 1966 they went to Colorado Springs, and the movement grew even after Mark Prophet died in 1973.

"We believe that Mark ascended," said Francis. "You probably heard that."

"No. I just learned about your group last week."

"Anyway, he trained Elizabeth as a messenger. And she *is* a messenger. She began receiving dictations in 1964, and she is the primary spiritual inspiration for the church. And it's grown considerably since then."

Ed Francis wouldn't reveal the membership figures, but he claimed that the Montana group was small compared with the thousands of members spread all over the country. "Most know about us from the mail. And that's one thing that distinguishes us from a lot of these so-called cult groups. We don't proselytize on street corners. We publish our material; here's our catalog. And here's a biography of Elizabeth Prophet and a history of the church."

He handed me the publications. One book was on the lost years of Jesus. "How does Christ fit in?" I asked.

"We believe that the life of Christ as reported historically was censored and molded to meet the political needs of the people who were forming the church and forming an alliance with the Roman Empire. A lot of things were deleted. For example, in the Bible there's a seventeen-year gap. Nothing is said about what Jesus did between the age of twelve and twenty-nine. It's silent. It's like he was being a carpenter all that time! He was doing much more than that.

"Our church has some unorthodox beliefs, but our basic value system is pretty traditional American Christian. We view Christ as a *way-shower,* a person who demonstrated a path of salvation. We believe that every person has a spark of divinity in them, that Christ is a potential that every person can achieve, and that life is an evolutionary process. And we believe in reincarnation. We don't see it as being incompatible with Christianity."

"Most Christian churches don't believe that doctrinally," I said. "Reincarnation, that is."

"But many Christians in the *past* believed in it. Saint Francis used to teach reincarnation—publicly. I read that in an encyclopedia. I was surprised. It's been suppressed by the Catholic Church. The early Christian Gnostics believed in a lot of the things that we believe in, but they were suppressed. We believe that Christianity took a turn—doctrinally—away from what Jesus believed."

"So, are you a New Age church?"

Ed Francis smiled. "Jesus is still the major religious prophet and example of this age, but the earth graduates into a new awareness of itself and its potential. Jesus was the prime exponent of the Piscean age, which is coming to an end. We're on the verge of the Aquarian age. We do not believe that the Christian faith, as it is taught today, is going to save the world. We don't believe that just because Jesus died on the cross, you're saved. That's what reincarnation is all about. You have to achieve your own victory."

"How do you do that?"

"We believe everyone has done bad things and good things in the past and that these become part of a person's life record, which we call karma. Part of the purpose of living is to eventually balance that karma. In the past you've probably been a murderer or a thief or done things that are not in accordance with God's law. In other words, you have to pay your debts to people, and to life, and to the universe if you want to get out of a worldly existence."

Francis's cosmic recipe struck me as a peculiar mixture of Christian guilt and Jainist escape, extending the karmic guilt over previous lives—as if one weren't enough.

"We believe there is another existence, a spiritual existence that you can graduate into—and that is the purpose of physical life—but it doesn't just happen because someone died on the cross for you."

"Is it possible to skip grades during one lifetime?" I asked. "To go from a very low karmic level—of, say, a murderer—to an enlightened state?"

Ed Francis smiled enigmatically. "There is no easy path to salvation. You can't pay back karma that you've incurred in a thousand reincarnations, in one fell swoop."

"I guess that would be too easy, right?"

"Reincarnation gives you a chance to start over," said Francis. "The only thing that will get you going in the right direction is to start living a good life and be good to people. There is also the matter of a person's destiny. We believe that every soul has a destiny. You came into life to fulfill that purpose."

I had been glancing at the publications. "And who are the Ascended Masters?"

"Ascended Masters are basically people like you and me that have balanced their karma, fulfilled their destiny, and ascended. Our version of going to heaven. Jesus ascended. Mary also ascended into heaven. There are others. That process is the spiritual part of you permanently leaving the physical octave and ascending into a new spiritual life that is outside the cycle of reincarnation. You become a person who is not subject to time and space. You become an immortal person, which we believe is everybody's destiny."

"How many Ascended Masters are there?"

"Lots, but not all are active with us."

"You mean some go off duty?"

Ed gave me a tolerant smile. "Not exactly."

"What about Shakespeare?" I asked. "Is he an Ascended Master?"

Ed Francis smiled. "Yes and no. We believe that the person who wrote the Shakespearean plays eventually made his ascension and is a person whom we refer to as Saint Germain. However, we don't believe that the actor Shakespeare wrote the Shakespearean plays. There's a healthy academic debate about this."

"So you believe they were really by Bacon?"

"Yes. There's evidence that Francis Bacon wrote the Shakespearean plays and that the actor Shakespeare took credit because he had the goods on Francis Bacon. We believe that Bacon used the name Saint Germain in another incarnation, in France."

All that spiritual transportation. "What do you actually do here at the ranch?"

"Everyone has a job or function. The main purpose of our staff is to administrate the headquarters of our spiritual community. We do all our own publishing. That's half the people. We've had our own private school since 1970, which uses the Montessori method. And we've got a restaurant across the river. We do traditional ranching: raising alfalfa, oats, and barley. We also have intensive farming—vegetables. We use all our vegetables to feed our church members."

"How is the Church Universal and Triumphant different from a group like the Moonies?"

"We have a religious hierarchy, but no veil of secrecy. We believe that the Constitution of the United States is a divinely inspired document and that America is a place that has a special destiny. And we strongly believe in the rights of people to worship as they please. They have a right to join our church, too, and not be harassed for it. It's part of the good and the bad in this country." Ed Francis emphasized that church members do not go through the programming and brainwashing that Moonies do.

The church has strict rules on conduct between the sexes. "Basically it is a celibate path until marriage. You're not supposed to carry on a physical relationship without a commitment." In the last seven years they have had about forty marriages a year. Members marry whomever they wish—unlike Moonie marriages, Ed Francis points out, which are basically to get Koreans into this country. Members of the cult learn that diet, physical desires, and spiritual well-being are all related—a reasonable belief.

"We are conservative politically, but we have some attitudes that tend to the left. For example, nuclear power: we are against it and see it as a potential disaster. We're concerned about hormones in meat and chemicals in vegetables. All our farming is organic. We eat a largely vegetarian diet, but we serve some red meat from cattle or sheep. I hunt and eat a fair amount of elk myself."

"So how did you get involved?"

"I grew up Methodist. In college at Colorado Springs, I was a religion major and had some friends who attended some of the Church Universal and Triumphant meetings. I read a lot of the material over nine months. I was actually skeptical to begin with."

"What if I wanted to join your church?" I asked.

"You could join the Keepers of the Flame Fraternity the first day and get sent lessons in the mail. It would take about two years before we would allow you to become a communicant. We want you to be ready to embrace the tenets of the church. We screen out window-shoppers. And we tithe. We ask our members to give ten percent of their income. If you're not prepared to do that, then you shouldn't join."

Francis stated that there was some turnover, but nothing like the Moonies. The constituents were a broad cross section, from young singles to married couples with families to the very old. "One woman just died at ninety-three, and she'd been connected with us for twenty years. We have people of all races and from different countries. The people on our staff have been with us from five to twenty-five years."

"I understand you're getting a lot of flak from the Livingston locals right now about your bomb shelters," I said.

"We get along well with most of our neighbors, but so many things have been exaggerated. We have about three hundred and fifty people on the ranch. We have about a hundred or so closer to Livingston. Our total plan for the ranch is to have about six hundred people. The state did an EIS—an environmental impact statement—on the ranch; here's a copy for your files. The verdict is 'no major impact.' The people that are not in favor of us being here have labeled the EIS as inaccurate."

"They're probably concerned that you're so close to Yellowstone Park."

Ed Francis shifted in his chair. "Environmentalism has political overtones that we don't agree with. It's an excuse for stopping any kind of development. Of course, some areas should just be left to nature and nothing else. But private land is private land, and people should have reasonable use of it." In most cases, Ed said, the church has allowed access to hikers, and they provide guided elk hunts (for a fee) on their land that abuts Yellowstone Park.

"How long will your church stay in Montana?"

"A lot of people around here think we're a flash in the pan, that in five or ten years we'll sell out and move on. I'd say, 'Don't count on that.' This is a permanent location for us. Montana is one of the last places that offers an opportunity for people like us. We don't intend to build a city here, like the Mormons did at Salt Lake. This is a retreat, but the church also has a subdivision up by Emigrant which is called Glastonbury."

"Sounds very English."

"It is. In Arthurian times, supposedly, the Holy Grail was taken from the Middle East to Glastonbury, an ancient seaport in England that was one of the first outposts of Christianity. We kind of believe in the King Arthur legends. Joseph of Aramathea, a tin trader who sailed to the British Isles, stopped there. Glastonbury eventually grew into an abbey and was destroyed by Henry VIII when he drove the Catholics out."

"I take it Henry VIII isn't one of your Ascended Masters."

"I don't think so," said Ed Francis. Then he brightened. "That's not to say he couldn't become one, though."

"In another lifetime?"

"Sure. He could balance his karma. But Henry VIII, of course, was responsible for killing the particular individual whom we believe founded this organization, Sir Thomas More, who we believe is El Morya. We don't accept the idea that things happen by chance."

"Do you think it's just chance I'm here?"

He smiled. "Maybe, maybe not. Depends on what you make of it."

Horr had once been a mining town; now it was a spiritual center housing hundreds of CUT members in trailers. If the Church Universal and Triumphant lived up to its name, what would this valley look like in another hundred years? "Welcome to El Morya City, Population 35,000."

Just a few weeks later a church member named Vernon Hamilton was arrested in Washington State for using a false identity to purchase fifteen semiautomatic assault rifles and 120,000 rounds of ammunition. Hamilton had twenty-six thousand dollars in cash and gold coins on him when arrested. During a search of a church-owned car, investigators found a letter from Hamilton addressed to Ed Francis that described an elaborate scheme to obtain the false identification Hamilton needed to buy the weapons. They also found documents indicating that Hamilton intended to buy $130,000 worth of weapons, enough to arm two hundred men. The weapons would include .50-caliber rifles capable of piercing armored personnel carriers. Church leader Elizabeth Clare Prophet, her husband, Ed Francis, and two other members were subpoenaed to appear before a grand jury in Spokane in mid-August.

Hamilton went to jail, while Ed Francis did one month in a minimum security prison in Spokane. After being released with an electric bracelet, Francis confidently told a newspaper reporter, "I don't happen to be a worry wart. If I have problems, I pray."

Ed Francis arranged for me to be driven up to the ghost town of Aldridge by Edwin Johnson, a tall thin man with a long face and prominent chin. We set out in a church-owned four-wheel-drive Jeep, climbing up a dirt road that took the mountain at a steep angle.

"This is a pretty rough road," I said.

"And this is the good part," said Edwin with a grin.

We rocked from side to side. On one steep turn, Edwin had to drop back and make a grinding run up the slope. As we bounced along, Edwin told me about his life. Raised in a middle-class family, he went to college, then became a ski bum in Colorado before joining the church. "I was into drugs for a while, and the church really helped me clean up my act. My parents are Lutherans, but they like the church because they see how much it's done for me." Now, at forty-three, Edwin does ranch work and guides fee-paying elk hunters on CUT property. Three years ago Edwin married a fifth-grade teacher at the church's school.

A half hour later when we parked the Jeep at seven thousand feet, we were just a few miles from the border of Yellowstone Park. Edwin strapped on a webbed pistol belt with a Colt .45 automatic in the holster. "Lot of grizzlies up here right now. They're really going crazy on the huckleberries. You want to make a lot of noise so we don't surprise them."

Within a few feet of the Jeep was a purplish lump of something that looked like chewed-up huckleberry pie. "Grizzly scat," said Edwin with distaste. "About two days old." As we walked we found more. "That one's from yesterday. And this one's from a few hours ago."

"Boy, *this* one's really fresh," I said. "It almost *steaming—*"

"Hold it." Edwin had his pistol out and cocked a shell into the chamber. I heard a slight rustle in the trees to my left. "You think they're still here?" I wanted very much to see a grizzly bear.

"I sure hope to hell not," said Edwin. "I hate bears."

"Why?"

"I just don't like them. Never have."

"I'd like to see one."

"Huh." he snorted. "Be my guest. The thing is, you don't want to get too close to a bear or you bump into his aura."

"Bump into his *aura?*"

"Yeah, his aura. That annoys them. Makes them attack. You don't want to have to shoot a bear, because you'll get buried alive in paperwork by the state."

We hiked up the incline until we came to cabins and the remains of shacks clinging to the hillside above tiny Electric Lake. "Well, here's Aldridge," said Edwin. "Most of the buildings have been pushed over by the snow. A lot were taken out with that fad for weathered wood in the sixties. You know, for people's dens or bar decorations. Too bad; probably looked more interesting then."

So this was all that remained of a town of three hundred miners. We walked over to the remains of the wooden trestle above the coal mine. I imagined my great-grandfather standing in this very place a century ago, a tall man in knee-high boots and long buffalo-fur coat, his bristling mustache rustling above a cigar as he barked orders. Smoke funneled up from a hundred cabins. Impatient mules brayed as they stood in the traces of the coal wagons. The men shoveled coal down the wood-and-metal flume to the coke ovens at Horr, cursing in a half dozen languages.

Today there were still a few cabins with their roofs intact. I walked into one that had a cooking stove and a couple of bedsteads with rusty springs.

The walls were lined with yellowed newspapers from almost a century ago. The writing was not English. Czechs, Serbs, and Austrians were the dominant immigrants in this camp, with a smattering from Ireland and Canada. The coal miners were aggressive men who risked their lives for a few dollars and high odds of getting black lung.

There were no unions until 1897, but in 1896 the miners threatened to hang the new superintendent, J. E. Strong, if he didn't leave the camp in four hours. Paid by the ton, they accused Strong of short-weighting them on their coal. Two months before, J. E. Strong had come out from Alabama to replace Conrad as mine superintendent. (Whether John stepped down or was fired is unknown, but he remained a stockholder.) Strong had even threatened to replace the miners with cheap Negro labor from the South.

According to the *Livingston Enterprise* of March 7, 1896, "Mr. Conrad remained in camp and lost no opportunity to incite discontent among the employees, even going to the extent of giving orders in direct conflict with the recognized authority. The interference was unbearable to the new superintendent and he asked Conrad to leave camp. Conrad was popular with the miners and this caused the trouble."

Strong and three allies barricaded themselves in a cabin with rifles. A mob of seventy-five Austrian and Hungarian miners encircled the cabin. The frightened Strong telephoned the sheriff of Livingston, who arrived with a posse that made seven arrests.

The miners went back to work, and Aldridge kept producing coal at large capacity. In 1899, experts reported that the upper seam of coal was rich enough to pay out $30 million in dividends over the next decade. Ten years later Aldridge was on its last legs. All across the country, from Pennsylvania to Butte, miners were striking. Hydroelectric dams were providing electricity for industry and domestic use, while gas and oil use was on the rise. The era of coal and coke had passed.

When I'd seen enough, we headed back to the Jeep.

One valley over from the Church Universal and Triumphant lay the Sargent ranch. Len Sargent had been my geometry teacher at Taft, a boarding school in Connecticut. One summer in the 1950s, Len Sargent drove out to Yellowstone Park and bought himself a two-thousand-acre ranch in Cinnibar Basin near the town of Gardiner. Len's first clue that the ranch needed a lot of work was when he fell through the cabin's wooden floor and nearly broke his leg. When Len retired from teaching in 1970, he married at age fifty-eight, and moved out to Montana.

I was a teenager when Len invited me and seven other Taft students to work on the ranch for the summer of 1971. For room and board, we worked hard four days a week and had three days off to explore the most beautiful country on earth. We built Len a sturdy Quonset-hut barn, dug and sunk hundreds of fence posts, and baled tons of hay. We hiked up into the mountains abutting the park, surprising moose and elk, and caught sixteen-inch trout in a creek with our bare hands.

We also managed to wreck the irrigation buggy, almost burn down the bunkhouse, and generally wreak havoc on the farm machinery. Amazingly, no one was killed. Later, a moose fell into the swimming pool and couldn't get out until we put a wooden ladder in the water. One afternoon I saw my first grizzly. He was high up on a ridge, just below the tree line. Through binoculars I watched him tear apart a rotten log for the grubs inside, and saw the silver-tipped fur on his muscular shoulders glint in the sunlight. Fleeting youth, fleeting wilderness.

Now, standing on the porch of the ranch house, Len Sargent seemed nearly unchanged, a handsome, active seventy-eight-year-old with a full head of hair and no moss on his brain. His wife, Sandy, he was quick to point out, "is a lot younger." Len, too, had been drawn to this country by an ancestor. "I have a connection with Yellowstone Park that goes way back. One of my ancestors, N. P. Langford, was one of the six Bozeman business-men who camped in the park in the 1870s, marveled at the geysers, and suggested it become the first national park in the world. My relative came out as a territorial tax collector in Bannack but ended up the first superin-tendent of the park. He wasn't a very good one because he was usually back east lobbying for money to run the place."

Len and Sandy ran about a hundred head of cattle on their ranch, but its real value lay in its natural wildlife and proximity to Yellowstone. "We gave a conservation easement on our property to the Nature Conservancy. It means nobody can ever change this land. No subdividing, no commercial timbering, and only elk and deer can be hunted in season. No hunting moose, sheep, bear, or lions. Whoever buys this land is stuck with these re-strictions. There is a slight tax benefit to this, but you don't do this sort of thing for the money."

Over the years, Len and Sandy have lobbied in Helena and in Washing-ton to preserve land in the greater Yellowstone area. John Wilson of the Montana Land Alliance once told me, "Len has probably done more for Montana's environment than any person living today." The Sargents also helped found the Greater Yellowstone Coalition, which is dedicated to acquiring land around the park that would complete the ecosystem.

"We're not saying it all should be park, but I think my ancestor Langford was shortsighted. He should have made the park bigger. This ecosystem extends about a hundred miles in radius from the borders of the park. Elk herds and bears migrate across these lands."

Len was upset that Montana's current delegation to Washington had been unable to reach a consensus on a wilderness program. "All these politicians seem to be posing for votes instead of looking ahead to the big picture. If we can get a strong bill now, it will be a step in the right direction. A lot of the six million acres eligible for wilderness in Montana is what we refer to as 'rocks and ice,' which no one wants anyway. Yet our congressional delegation only wants about one million."

Some of the people opposed to wilderness are ranchers, but most are in the timber business. "Timbering in this area is usually clear-cut. People say we have to keep the timber industry going, but it's heavily subsidized by the government. These same people also want us to cut government spending. How can you cut and subsidize at the same time? Where's the logic? I'm all for free enterprise, but I'm also for *reality*."

The Sargents have tried to maintain a courteous relationship with their big neighbors, the Church Universal and Triumphant. "We now have a whole lot more people here than the Yellowstone ecosystem can stand. For years we argued in local politics for zoning, but people around Livingston, and Montana in general, rejected it. They see it as an infringement on their property rights. The church did careful research before choosing Montana—because it has such weak zoning laws. So now Montanans are finding out what freedom is all about. And I think they regret it."

How long did he think the church will last?

"Well, Christ started a kind of cult and it's been doing pretty well for two thousand years," said Len. "I suppose it will depend on how important Elizabeth Clare Prophet is to the continuation of the church."

"I heard a rumor they have guns."

"That's true. There have been gun rumors. But do you know anyone in this part of the country that *doesn't* have guns?" Sargent's weathered face wrinkled in a smile. "I'm really more concerned about the bomb shelters, the housing project, and the population they're bringing in than about the guns."

That night we heard a bear prowling around the house. The next morning we found that a grizzly had visited the caretaker's residence and clawed away six feet of metal siding. The caretaker, Philip Herne, said, "Oh, I saw him, all right. The way I got rid of that bear was by pouring a glass of water on him from the second-story window. But look what he thought of *that*." He pointed to a huge pile of grizzly scat on the front lawn.

"Well," said Len, "we're just glad there are still a few bears around."

After breakfast, Len sent me down to call on some aging neighbors, Jack McDonald and his wife, Margaret. Jack was a cheerful old fellow in overalls, worn plaid shirt, and cap. If he had any teeth, he'd forgotten to put them in that morning. Born in 1911, he grew up in Aldridge, where his aunt was postmaster and his uncle worked in the company store. "That was after your great-granddad was running the show."

McDonald's father, a Scots Canadian, had come into Montana with the Great Northern Railway. "My father homesteaded here before 1900, then went over to Aldridge as a miner. He mined in the winter, but in the summer he took his horse over and worked in the park."

"Were people proper at Aldridge?"

"If they weren't, I never did hear of it," said Jack McDonald.

"Wasn't there a murder up there?" asked Mrs. McDonald.

"Oh, sure. A lot of them deals was when the Bohunks would come to this country and send back for wives from the old country. There was them marriage brokers that would take care of the details. Some of them poor devils didn't know what they were getting into," Jack laughed. (*Bohunk,* derived from *Bohemian,* was a catchall nickname for anyone from eastern Europe.)

"Nor the poor girls," said Mrs. McDonald.

"Who shot the buffalo?" I pointed to a big buffalo robe on the wall.

"I got him in the sixties. Just slipped into the park and took him," said Jack, with no remorse about violating game laws. "Buried his skull in an anthill. Cleaned up real good."

On the other wall was an enormous grizzly bear skin—the biggest I'd ever seen. It must have been ten feet long.

"Who got the bear?"

"Mrs. McDonald killed it," said Jack. "Tell him about it."

"We were working over at the Silvertip Ranch in the sixties, near Cooke City," said Mrs. McDonald. "I was there alone in the cabin when the bear came one night and raised cain. A real mess. I telephoned *him*," indicating her husband with a nod. "He was up there at our daughter's. He said, 'You'd better get him.' We had bacon and butter on the back porch. It was just getting dusk and I heard the dogs barking. I looked out the window of our cabin and there he was standing up, big as life. I had a thirty-ought-six and shot him at ten yards. He just come down with an *oomph* and then ran off into the timber. Shot him in the chest. The bullets are soft tip and blow up. I didn't hear no splashing in the creek. So I went back to the cabin and got a gaslight. I found him dead among the trees."

"He was the third largest grizzly killed in the state of Montana," said Jack proudly. "They measured him out."

A big bear had been killed to save some bacon and butter. If eight hundred breakfasts were protected in this manner, by next year there would be no grizzly bears left in the continental United States. Still, why bother to protect animals that eat our breakfasts—and sometimes us, too? For the hell of it? Or because, as humans, we believe in something greater than ourselves? Later I came across John Murray's words in *The Great Bear:*

> We shelter these bears in their preserves and parks, finally, as the ancient Greeks honored their sacred mountains, groves and animals, as a refuge of the spirit, testifying that our greed is not unrestrained, our growth not without limit, our grasp of the holy not entirely lost. Those who have packed far up into grizzly country . . . know that the presence of even one grizzly on the land elevates the mountains, deepens the canyons, chills the winds, brightens the stars, darkens the forests, and quickens the pulse of all who enter it. They know that when a bear dies, something sacred in every living thing interconnected with that realm, including those resident human souls, dies.

My great-grandmother,
Mabel Barnaby Conrad,
was accused of
adultery.

John Conrad in
1906, before the
Yukon gold rush
broke his spirit.

Chapter 18

Helena: Greed, Murder, and Divorce

Cries of gold or men about to hang
trail off where the brewery failed
on West Main. Greedy fingernails
ripped the ground up inch by inch
down the gulch until the hope of gold
ran out and men began to pimp.
Gold is where you find it in the groin.

> Richard Hugo, "Helena, Where Homes
> Go Mad," 1973

The outskirts of Helena consist of strip architecture and fast-food places—the complexion of most towns in America—but when I turned up a street called Last Chance Gulch, gold-rush Helena of a century ago came alive. Gold, and gold alone, was the reason for Helena's creation. On July 14, 1864, four down-on-their-luck miners decided to try one last section of Prickly Pear Creek, which they jokingly called Last Chance Gulch. By day they killed rattlesnakes, and at night they lived in fear of a silent grizzly bear that came down to feast on streamside berries. Then they hit it rich. One miner, an Englishman named Reginald Stanley, recalled the creek: "From its shallow, gravelly beds . . . gold could be panned wherever tried." Within days of the discovery, the world rushed in, turning the valley into a bustling shantytown of log cabin banks, gambling houses, and overpriced hotels.

And for those itchy-fingered claim jumpers who couldn't abide by frontier laws, there was always the hanging tree in Dry Gulch.

By 1870, $6 million in gold dust per year was being shipped out of the Helena region. Soon the shanties built on mining claims gave way to national banks built of solid granite, while the hotels served Puget Sound oysters and French champagne. On the hills above Last Chance Gulch, pioneers built ambitious Victorian mansions reflecting the ebullient merchant optimism of the nineteenth century. "Every newly made millionaire of the place seemed to be striving to outdo all the others, of whom there were many," wrote one observer.

In 1889, the year Montana Territory became a state, Helena had more millionaires per capita than any other city in the Union. Helena's population was less than eleven thousand, but the city was known as the Queen City of the Northwest. Helena fell from grace in a series of disasters: the bank panic of 1893, diminishing gold mines, the Great Depression, terrible fires, and the earthquake of 1935; then a half century of declining population, falling beef prices, and the flight of industry. Opportunity fled the so-called Treasure State.

No longer an El Dorado or millionaire's playground, modern Helena (population twenty-five thousand) remains a charming historic city caught in amber. Were it not for the various government offices, it might decline further, but its inhabitants enjoy its smallness and the proximity to the mountains.

I stopped *Red Cloud* in front of a hotel on the Gulch called the Iron Front. Built in 1887, its prefabricated cast-iron elements made it a forerunner of modern steel-and-glass curtain wall construction. (In 1889 my great-grandfather Judge Hunt and thirty fellow Republicans had gathered in the hotel's ballroom to form the first state house of representatives.) Today the hotel is flanked by pawnbrokers and questionable bars, so I locked my car and lugged my most valuable gear up the stairs. Later, Helena people would say, "You stayed *there?*"

Two men stood ahead of me at the check-in desk on the second floor. Both were covered with dirt and grime. They handed the old clerk some vouchers in exchange for rooms.

"Where'd you come from?" I asked.

"Off the railroad," said a scruffy, red-haired fellow with a mustache and a week's stubble. He was wearing an old-time blue and white striped railroader's hat and dusty overalls.

"You an engineer?" I asked.

"Naw, we're hobos."

"Really?"

"No kiddin.'"

They took their room keys and went down the hall, leaving a greasy scent behind. The old man behind the desk watched their departure for a few seconds, then shook his head with disgust. "They're not hobos. They're bums. Not even good bums. In my day there was a difference between a tramp, a hobo, and a bum."

"What's the difference?"

"Tramp and hobo would work for food or shelter. Bum wouldn't."

"Then where'd they get the money for a room?" I asked.

"God's Love."

"Where?" I asked.

"Those vouchers they had? Got 'em from God's Love. Churchy handout place down the street. When God's Love fills up they give 'em vouchers and they come over here. Keep's 'em from drinkin' it up. Bums."

For seventeen dollars, including a five-dollar deposit on the key, I was given a quiet, seedy room with a sink—shower and toilet down the hall.

On the grass in front of the state capitol stands a grand equestrian statue in bronze. It was erected in 1905 by Montanans of Irish descent. Most modern-day Montanans can't guess who this lime-spattered horseman with upraised sword is. Then they read the nameplate: "Thomas Francis Meagher." And they still haven't a clue.

Born in Ireland in 1823, Meagher was a political rebel and was sentenced to hang by the British Crown. At the last minute, he was banished to the penal colony of Tasmania. Three years later he escaped, made his way to New York, and became an American citizen. During the Civil War, he organized an Irish brigade and became a general. Lincoln appointed Meagher as secretary to territorial governor Sidney Edgerton in Bannack. When Edgerton left Montana, Meagher became acting governor. A political opportunist of the first order, he was such a heavy drinker that one editor accused him of "being drunk nearly every day since he has been in the Territory," turning the executive office in Virginia City into "a place of rendezvous for the vilest prostitutes."

Meagher also seemed to have a phobia about Indians, and constantly badgered the government to send out more troops. After the Sioux killed trailblazer John Bozeman in the Gallatin Valley, Meagher immediately raised civilian troops, and named himself their leader. The Indian "invasion"

234 Ghost Hunting in Montana

never arrived, but Meagher's motley militia ran up bills totaling some $1.1 million.

Meagher died under mysterious circumstances in Fort Benton. After dinner with the merchant Isaac Baker (the Conrads' employer), he announced he was retiring to his berth aboard the steamboat *G. A. Thompson*. A sentry heard a splash and awakened the crew for a rescue, but patrols along the riverbanks failed to locate Meagher's body. Heart attack? Drunkenness? Suicide? Murder? No one knows.

Helena's capitol building was constructed in 1902 with the generous help of another Irishman, the miner Thomas Cruse, who took the full issue of $350,000 in bonds after other investors spurned them. Cruse was a poor immigrant until he hit it rich in the mines of Marysville (now a ghost town north of Helena). He spent his later years as one of Helena's great philanthropists and financed Helena's cathedral just in time for his death.

The Montana legislature still meets only every other year—an indication that the state's political life is fairly simple, uncorrupted, and quite folksy. Since agriculture is a main part of the economy, many representatives are ranchers and farmers. There are also a few Indians—notably Bill Yellowtail, who represents Bighorn County, which is largely dominated by the Crow Indian Reservation.

Upstairs in the house chambers hangs Charlie Russell's masterpiece, a twenty-five-foot mural of Lewis and Clark encountering Indians. Breaking with the traditions of historical commemoration, Russell painted the Indian warriors prominently in the foreground, magnificent atop their wheeling ponies, while the white explorers appear small, on the right hand of the mural. For Russell, the Indians symbolized Montana in its natural state, while the visitors from the East, no matter how noble the intentions of Jefferson's emissaries, represented impending loss and degradation. Today, one might see Montanans, both white and Indian, as a kind of tribe resisting encroachment from outside interests.

Below the old bank buildings that had been built on gold dust, I found the arched doorway to a large brownstone building, the Montana Club. It, too, had been founded on gold, power, and cigar smoke. Started in 1885, it quickly became the sanctuary for the Montana establishment. Here ranchers, bankers, railroad tycoons, and copper kings decided the political future of the state before their private railroad cars whisked them off to Chicago or Seattle. William Conrad was a member, and Judge Hunt was named president one year. The first clubhouse opened in 1893, with a former slave named Julian Anderson as the bartender. The building was destroyed in 1903 by an arsonist who turned out to be Anderson's fourteen-year-old son; the boy admitted he did it "to see the fire horses run and help the firemen work." The club members forgave the old man for the sins of his progeny, and Julian held his job for exactly sixty years. By 1916, women were admitted to membership—no doubt reflecting the fact that Montana voters had just elected Jeanette Rankin as the nation's first woman in Congress. She was the only person in Congress to vote against America's entry into both World War I and World War II.

A secretary let me wander through the wood-paneled club, first to gaze at a photograph of Judge Hunt as president, then to peek at a reproduction of Charlie Russell's brilliant picture of a buffalo herd, *When the Land Belonged to God*. The club commissioned Russell to paint the picture in 1915 for three thousand dollars, but when it was delivered, one club member called the lead animal "a miserable bull." Hearing this, Russell drawled, "Well, mebby he is a bum bull, but he's the best buffalo bull I ever painted." When the club faced financial difficulties in recent years, the Montana legislature appropriated $750,000 to buy the magnificent original, now hanging in the Montana Historical Society.

On Helena's fashionable West Side, a neighborhood of large Victorian houses and mansions, I found 702 Madison Avenue, a russet-colored clapboard Victorian with a carriage house in the rear. John Conrad lived here after he narrowly lost the race for lieutenant governor in 1889. Leaving Billings, he moved Mabel and their three children to the bustling capital, with its shops and even boasting an opera house, not only to satisfy a wife tired of living in dusty cow towns, but to reposition himself for a run at the governorship in 1893.

The present owner of the house, a grandmother whose son served in the state legislature, let me look through the house. With the exception of new wallpaper and bathroom fixtures, little had changed in a century. The three stained-glass windows from Tiffany were still in place in the dining room; even the original wood-burning stove engraved with a steamship emblem remained in the kitchen, next to a modern gas stove. The mantel of the parlor fireplace bore a curious dragon motif. In a reverie I imagined my great-grandparents here in 1891. Young Mabel was seated, pretending to read a book, while John impatiently jabbed the fire with a poker and muttered about political intrigue in Butte and his striking coal miners at Red Lodge. It was not a happy scene. Already there were rumors that the Conrads' marriage was rocky. Centered in the beveled glass of the front door was the letter *D* for Marcus Downs, the man who had built the house. Later people joked that it stood for *divorce*.

John Conrad's marital problems came to a head in the spring of 1891, when his mother-in-law, Josephine Barnaby, was murdered. While visiting friends in Denver, the widowed Mrs. Barnaby received a mysterious package bearing a Boston postmark. Inside was a bottle with a cryptic note: "Wish you a Happy New Year. Please accept this fine old Whiskey from your friend in the woods." After Mrs. Barnaby fixed two hot toddies for herself and her traveling companion, both women became violently ill. Mrs. Worrell recovered, but Josephine Barnaby died from poisoning.

Though Mrs. Barnaby was estranged from her two daughters, telegrams were sent to Mabel Conrad in Helena and to twenty-one-year-old Maud Barnaby, then unmarried and traveling in Europe. The investigation in Denver revealed that the "whiskey"—actually colored water—had been laced with 132 grains of arsenic, enough to kill at least sixty people. Local tabloids were filled with speculation and innuendo about Mrs. Barnaby's will, which left ten thousand dollars to Mrs. Worrell, ten thousand dollars to an Adirondack guide named Ed Bennett, and twenty-five thousand dollars to her personal physician, Dr. Thomas Thatcher Graves of Providence.

Dr. Graves was more than just Mrs. Barnaby's doctor; how much more is open to conjecture. Graves had been a major in the Union Army during the Civil War, then graduated first in his class from Harvard's medical school in 1871. Mrs. Barnaby trusted him so much that she gave him full power of attorney for her investment transactions. When her husband, J. B. Barnaby, died, leaving most of his $1.7-million estate to their two daughters, Dr. Graves advised Josephine to contest her husband's will. Resentment grew between the widow and her two daughters. The lawsuit was successful. Mrs. Barnaby was grateful and even allowed Graves to hire a lawyer, his friend Colonel Daniel Ballou, to write her own will.

The moment John learned of his mother-in-law's death, he took a train from Butte to Denver. He spent the day speaking with the police before heading east to Providence. Although he sent Pinkerton agents all over the East Coast to track down suspects, from the start John was gunning for Graves. As fact and gossip about the murder swirled eastward, reporters swarmed to Graves's Providence home, pestering the doctor and his wife, Kitty. When a group of reporters asked her, "Did your husband kill Mrs. Barnaby?" Graves lost his temper. Later it was revealed that several newspapermen were under special contract to John Conrad.

Summoned on a pretext to the Barnaby house in Providence, Graves found John drinking with a man who claimed to be his brother, Charles; in fact, he was a Pinkerton agent. A good bit of whiskey flowed. During the court testimony, Graves recalled that Conrad badgered him to sign a written statement saying he had sent a bottle of whiskey to Mrs. Barnaby—and offered him twenty-five thousand dollars to do so. When Graves refused, John lost his temper in spectacular fashion. Graves recalled, "He flew into a perfect passion like a mad bull and raved and stormed about the room and kicked the furniture and swore that if I didn't help him he would have me arrested and bring me in irons to Denver." John shouted at the doctor, "The East is your country, the West is mine! If you are taken to Denver I will pack a jury on you, you will never have a fair trial—with my money I'll buy up a jury and you will be convicted anyway!"

The next day, John apologized and showed Graves a telegram from the Denver police asking the doctor to come give testimony. (Actually, it had been sent by the Pinkerton man employed by Conrad.) Three days later when Conrad, Graves, and "brother Charles" stepped off the train in Denver, Graves was arrested for murder.

The tabloids had a field day with a sensational murder trial. John Conrad had a lot at stake. A murdered mother-in-law was scandal and hence a liability in his next run for the Montana governorship. On the other hand, if he could convict Dr. Graves with "western justice," he might reap some political benefit. The six-week-long trial offered only unflattering glimpses of John's volatile personality. At first he played the part of the grieving family man trying to do justice for his kin. A newspaper reported that he "battled hard with his emotions, broke . . . and he burst into tears."

While being cross-examined, John suddenly stood up in the witness box, pointed at Colonel Ballou (the attorney who'd written Graves into the will), and shouted: "And there, gentlemen, is your co-conspirator in the plunder of the estate and your co-plotter in the murder!"

The presiding judge rapped his gavel twice and said, "Mr. Conrad, only Dr. Graves is on trial here—you cannot make irresponsible statements like that!"

"Even if they're true?" asked John.

"Be quiet, sir!"

"In Montana," John growled, "we aim to get at the truth!"

"Sir, be quiet or you'll be held in contempt and will be going back to Montana sooner than you expect!"

The courtroom audience was aroused by this interchange, and not necessarily against Conrad's boast of frontier justice. After all, both Colorado and Montana had found vigilante justice rather expedient—even if a few innocent men got hanged in the process. When the defense attorney called John to the stand he freely—even proudly—admitted that he had paid all the travel and hotel expenses to bring some thirty-eight essential witnesses to Denver. He also admitted that he had "secured the attendance" of two yellow journalists (one of them aptly named Mr. Tricky).

A key piece of evidence was the stamp used to mail the bottle—an orange-colored fifteen-cent Daniel Webster. John's Pinkerton agent had gone to Boston, where the package had been postmarked on March 30, hoping to find a clerk who might remember the sender. No luck. But he learned that all nine thousand post offices in New England had stopped selling the orange Websters the year before—all except the post office at Providence. That would point the finger at Dr. Graves, or at his wife, Kitty.

A beautiful but deeply disturbed young woman, as a girl Kitty had once been found wandering nude in a meadow at midnight, babbling lines of Ophelia from *Hamlet*. She was still a teenager when Graves began treating her for various nervous disorders, then brought about a "miraculous" recovery, and married her within a year's time. At the time of the trial Kitty's mental instability was unknown. She was called to the stand only once, and the prosecution barely trifled with her—in spite of the fact that she often filled her husband's prescriptions.

The jury took just an hour and a half to reach a verdict: Dr. Graves was convicted of murder in the first degree and sentenced to hang. John held a victory party with champagne and caviar at the Windsor Hotel; Kitty Graves suffered a complete mental breakdown and was delirious for nearly a month. Editorials and even poems appeared in newspapers all across America as people continued to argue whether the doctor was guilty or innocent.

But Graves didn't hang. An appeal was made and a new trial scheduled for early September 1893. On September 1, Graves seemed in a cheerful mood and had a pleasant lunch with his wife, who had recovered somewhat. When Graves failed to report for breakfast the next morning, a guard entered his cell and found the doctor dead. A newspaper suggested he had poisoned himself with arsenic obtained by soaking flypaper in a glass of water, but there was no official autopsy.

A long letter from Graves to his wife was never made public, but a bitter, open letter to the people of Colorado stated that the trial had cost him everything he owned. He claimed that the only way to ensure that his wife and mother would be looked after financially was to "take this way out." He ended the letter with his "solemn Masonic oath" that he had nothing to do with the death of Mrs. Barnaby. Kitty Graves collected the twenty-five thousand dollars from Mrs. Barnaby's will, and some time after being released from a sanitarium she left Connecticut, never to be heard from again. It had cost John thirty-five thousand dollars to lock up Graves and bulldoze justice into the package he wanted.

Whether Graves was guilty—or merely taking the rap for his wife—I was dismayed by the account of the trial and my great-grandfather's conduct. The teenage pioneer, the enterprising merchant, the ambitious political candidate had revealed himself to be an unscrupulous, vengeful, jury-packing bully who would stop at nothing to get his way. He was not very likable, and following his trail around Montana seemed shallow, perhaps unwarranted.

As if this were not enough, I found these headlines in the September 27, 1893, issue of the *Butte Miner*:

SENSATION AT HELENA

John H. Conrad Sues His Wife for Divorce
on the Ground of Adultery

The article stated that John Conrad had begun proceedings for divorce and had named three corespondents, "giving dates and places in great number." The first culprit was a wealthy Michigan lumberman, while the second was a Denver man charged with "offenses at Helena in 1892 and at Denver during the trial of Graves." The third, Joseph Baker, was the most painful discovery: Baker (Isaac Baker's nephew) was Conrad's business partner and a former brother-in-law.

Then came the article's comical kicker:

Last night, it is current report on the streets, there was a big row at the house in which Conrad, his wife, the coachman and Chinese cook participated, the coachman using a stick and the Chinaman a skillet. Conrad came out of the melee in bad condition and left the house for a lawyer's office, where the complaint was made out and filed to-day.

Mabel denied the accusations and countercharged Conrad with "adultery, cruelty and intoxication," asking for a divorce and custody of their three children. She further charged John with having committed adultery with five women, habitual drunkenness, and "extreme cruelty." She stated that she had "a large fortune in her own right and that her husband, through pretenses and threats and unkind conduct succeeded in getting large sums of money from her, aggregating upwards of $50,000." In 1895, the Conrads divorced and Mabel took the children—Florence, Maud, and my grandfather, Barnaby—to Europe. There she married an American gentleman named George Choate Kendall and moved to a château in France.

John Conrad's political dreams faded with the divorce and his business failures. In 1899, he gave up his coal mine at Aldridge. The few letters he wrote to other members of the family were on hotel stationery from Chicago and Seattle. With the exception of his appearance at Charles's funeral in Kalispell, he disappeared from view.

Then up popped a 1905 article from the *Livingston Enterprise* saying he had struck it rich with mining claims in the Windy Arm region of the Yukon: "It is believed it will turn out to be richer than any of the Klondike properties!"

My great-grandfather had left Montana for good and moved on to the goldfields of the Yukon, the latest frontier. He was now calling himself Colonel Conrad—an affectation that went back to his Virginia roots and his father. Near Whitehorse, British Columbia, he founded the town of Conrad City, where three hundred miners worked his "vastly rich" Venus and Montana Mines. He hiked these mountains in a pair of tweed plus fours and a wolfskin overcoat. All-night poker games were held at his log cabin house at Caribou Crossing. He had married again—to a music teacher from Iowa—but she would not go to the Yukon. They lasted only a year, producing one son, William, who was given his mother's maiden name after the divorce. (In 1990, I visited eighty-three-year-old William Robinson in Muscatine, Iowa; after an evening of off-center reminiscence, he wept, saying I was the first member of the Conrad family he had ever met.)

John was almost sixty years old then, with a flowing gray beard that he said he would not cut until the Venus Mine was a success. The beard kept growing until the company went broke in 1912. He died in 1928 as an impoverished alcoholic in a Seattle hotel room. His own son, my grandfather Barnaby, did not attend the funeral, and the Montana press barely noted his passing. Today, his great mines in the Yukon lie dormant; at the ghost town of Conrad City the trees grow up among the fallen cabins and broken dreams.

Despite his failures as a husband and father, I found that I still admired John for having set great goals. He didn't have the subtlety to be a quiet back-room player like his brothers William and Charles. He was a grand-stander, a gambler, and an expansive optimist—until whiskey got him. In my search through Montana, I had come to understand him better than I knew his son, my grandfather. I thought of the great pain John must have felt when his dreams of Yukon gold went sour. It wasn't just the gold he was after, but the *glory* of finding gold, and this I understood. He had lived his life not just for the bottom line, but for the chance to leave a mark, to create something lasting, to make others know and respect his name. I was left questioning that respect, wishing things could have been different, and wondering what I would do with my own life.

Finished with research on John Conrad's life in Montana, I turned back—with some relief—to the life of my maternal great-grandfather, William Hunt. As the district attorney for the territory, Hunt was still living in Fort Benton when a posse cornered a notorious horse thief named Con Murphy at an abandoned ranch house near Helena. A sheriff was shot through the hand before Murphy was captured.

Hunt immediately took a stagecoach to Helena, to meet the posse and the prisoner. It was winter, and while the sheriff brought Murphy by sleigh, several hundred old-timers formed a vigilance committee. They waylaid Murphy and his guards in a snowy pass, put a rope around his neck, and hanged him. The anonymous crowd went quickly back to Helena.

Judge Hunt arrived late that night in Helena and confronted the sheriff about the horse thief. "If you want Murphy you'll find him in the building next to the jail," said the sheriff. Hunt went into the engine house and found Murphy's stiff body wrapped in a tarpaulin. The engine house stood directly opposite the courthouse, and the symbolism of misplaced justice struck Hunt sharply: "A sense of outrage arose in me. Surely, I thought, the law must be strong enough to avenge the lawless act, and I, as the proper law officer, must invoke every process."

Hunt ordered the sheriff to make a full inquiry and summoned a grand jury. He personally conducted the examination of witnesses, but made little headway. The deputies claimed they'd been disarmed by a faceless mob. Nobody would volunteer a name. Finally, Hunt called to the stand an ex-sheriff who had accompanied the vigilance committee.

"Did you see the hanging?" asked Attorney Hunt.

"I did," said the ex-sheriff.

"Did you do any act in helping to hang the man?"

"I did not. I was a spectator."

"Who put the rope around Murphy's neck?"

"I cannot say, it was getting dark and I could not recognize the man."

"Who produced the rope?"

"I saw a man hand it to another, but who had it I do not know."

"Did you see the men pull the rope?"

"I did."

"Who were they?"

"Well, you know, it was a very cold evening and all the men were so wrapped up that you could not see enough of their faces to identify them. I would hate to say that I recognize any of them."

"Well, Sheriff, describe to the grand jurors how some of the men looked."

"Some had moustaches; some had dark eyes, some light; some were tall, others were short; but you know yourself, Mr. District Attorney, that with only a small part of a man's face showing, you cannot positively swear who he is."

"But you can certainly tell us more definitely who some of the men were," insisted Hunt. "What did they look like?"

The former sheriff paused a minute and looked about the room calmly. "Well, as far as I could see, several of them looked to me a good deal like some of the gentlemen in this Grand Jury."

A roar of laughter went up in the courtroom and Hunt's face grew crimson. He recalled, "The old sheriff, who was intimately known by every one of the grand jurors, sat unperturbed, but with a stern look which indicated some satisfaction over the crisis."

The jury foreman excused the sheriff from the stand. "The witness and I left the room and upon returning I was informed that by unanimous vote the investigation was ended and that no bill had been found," wrote my great-grandfather. "Thus the execution of Murphy passed into the history of Montana as an instance where the publicly constituted authorities refused to disaffirm the decree of an unwritten code of the resistless, restless race of pioneers."

After this setback, Hunt moved his family from Fort Benton to Helena in late 1885 in an open buggy—a three-day journey over 150 miles of dirt road. That spring he sent his pregnant wife, Gertrude, to stay with her parents in Washington, D.C., where she bore a son, known as Willie. The Hunts were reunited that fall and moved into a house in Helena near lower Main Street.

When Hunt finished his term as attorney general, he intended to return to private practice, but after the 1888 Republican convention, he won election to the territory's house of representatives. As the movement for admission to statehood gained support in Washington, Montana politicians looked for an honest judge to serve the state district court at Helena. Hunt was elected and sworn in by Governor Joseph Toole on November 8, 1889, the day of statehood. "The honorable title of Judge became mine," wrote my great-grandfather. "And on the next day, with some formality, I opened the District Court for the First Judicial District of the new State of Montana."

One afternoon I drove the two miles out to Kenwood, a suburb of Helena where Judge Hunt had built a house for his growing family. This had once been open country; now it was a neighborhood of undistinguished but well-maintained homes. I didn't have an exact address—no street numbers were used in the 1895 city directory—but at the corner of Hauser and Glendale stood a large Victorian house towering over the newer ranch-style houses. And high up on the side of the brick chimney was a metal design in the shape of an *H*. Judge Hunt described the house in his memoirs: "With about half an acre and plenty of unoccupied land about us, we had dogs, chickens, a cow and a horse. As the children grew older, they went to the public school about three-quarters of a mile away. I can still see the little girls in their red hoods plodding through the snow, followed by Chester, our faithful Chesapeake Bay dog. The children were never sick."

My grandmother Helen Upshur Hunt was born the year of Montana's statehood. Nearly a century later, at the age of ninety-two, she told me about life at this house: "I remember we were always playing in the 'boulevard,' a dirt road that ran in front. The Rockies started right behind our house, which was near the entrance to the mountain trail. Every year the Indians came—twice a year—and camped nearby. We had four dogs. One day we saw that all the dogs were gone. We were worried because the dogs were close to our hearts. Father rode out to the Indian camp in the buggy with me along. I remember all the tepees and campfires. It was dark and in the firelight I saw Father talking to the Indians. A boy went around behind a tepee and brought out the four dogs, which went wild when they saw us. Father had to pay something to get the dogs back."

In contrast to the free-spending Conrads, Judge Hunt lived on a tight budget: "Judicial life was agreeable, though only by close management could we keep within my moderate salary. However, when the panic of

1893 came and nearly all the banks in Helena failed, there was comfort in knowing the salary would protect us."

On holidays, Judge Hunt would take his family on hunting or fishing trips in the mountains, driving the wagon while friends and some of the children rode horses alongside. He was an avid fly-fisherman, always dressed in a tweed jacket and necktie. He often went down to the Big Blackfoot River "where fly fishing for trout was very fine." (This was the same river that inspired Norman Maclean's *A River Runs Through It.*) All his children, including my grandmother, learned fly-fishing, and the skills were passed down to my father and my uncle, and finally to me and my cousins.

An able judge, Hunt was soon elected to the state supreme court, but by 1897 he felt that presiding over law courts was tedious. Yet within a year his life—and the very government of Montana—would be scalded as the copper king of Butte, William A. Clark, unleashed an unprecedented wave of political corruption.

I needed the country now. I drove north out of Helena, following the Missouri River as it wound through mountain gorges interspersed with rich meadows. At about 6 P.M. an inordinate number of bugs began to splatter against my windshield. This would be a nuisance to most people, but it told me there were bugs on the river, and bugs on the river meant that trout would rise to a dry fly. By the time I reached the town of Craig, I could see trout dimpling the river.

I turned off the highway and passed through Craig in less than twenty seconds, rattling east across a steel bridge. I wiggled north along the riverbank, then pulled into a recently mown hay field. I didn't bother with waders as it was a warm evening and the Missouri wasn't a cold river. I took out my rod, tied a small caddis on the leader, and slid down the muddy bank. In half an hour, I had hooked two nice fish about fifteen inches long, and was thoroughly enjoying the evening.

The sun was going behind the mountains when I saw the lazy gulp of a big fish just ahead. I cast, saw the take, and lifted my rod tip. The fish took off in a long deep arc, and I let him take line off my reel. He came to my hand finally, a hefty brown trout who smacked the fleeing sunlight with his spotted tail. The left flange of his upper jaw was missing, and he seemed to regard me with more disdain than fear. I let him go in the darkening water.

The big fish and the enchanting country overwhelmed my desire to return to Helena. Catching two smaller trout, I climbed back up to the Jeep and pitched my tent at the edge of the trees. I built a discreet fire, skewered the trout on green branches, and roasted them until the skin bubbled brown and the tails turned as crispy as bacon. I ate the trout and tossed the bones into the fire. Sitting in the door of my tent with a tin cup full of whiskey and canteen water, I watched a three-quarter moon rise over the Rockies. As moonlight illuminated the river and the trout rose, I breathed the night deeply and felt I had every treasure in the world.

On a pack trip near Cabin Creek with
guide Sandy Pew.

Chapter 19
Riding to the Tree Line with Booger Blitz

It pleases me plenty to know that thair is so
maney men and wimen that will quit a gas wagon and
a good road and ore wilen to look at the world
with a horse under em.

Charles M. Russell, in a letter, 1921

To really plug into Montana, you have to leave the road on foot or horse-back. At the Red Rock Canyon trailhead just a few miles south of Big Sky, three saddle horses and three packhorses were tied to an enormous, state-of-the-art, sleekly painted black and red truck and horse trailer. A tall thin man in a high-crowned hat, tight jeans, and a pair of knee-length fringed chaps called "chinks" came toward me in a clank of spurs.

"Hi, I'm Sandy Pew," he said, shaking my hand in a tight grip. His blue eyes smiled from the reverse raccoon tan pattern that ski instructors get from wearing sunglasses. An outfitter based near Bozeman, Sandy guides cross-country ski trips, as well as canoe, backpacking, and horseback expeditions.

Sandy's other client was Lee Feldman, a New York business consultant. With his shaggy mustache, broad-brimmed hat, and full-length yellow slicker, Lee bore a strong resemblance to Wyatt Earp. He also had a sureness with the horses, learned around eastern stables. Only his fancy suede, shot-gun-style chaps betrayed him as a nonwesterner.

Sandy assigned me a pretty gray mare called Kissimee and a packhorse called Booger Blitz, who lived up to his name. "Unlike any other horse I've ever owned," said Sandy with a mixture of love and frustration. "Used to be a racing quarter horse. Once he was in a two-year-old race in Wyoming. Heading for the home stretch he just stopped in his tracks and stared at the grandstand. Didn't even pay attention to the jockey whipping him; he wanted to look at the people! When the same thing happened in the next race, the man sold him. As you'll see, he's the class clown of this horse string. Loony at times but a good horse."

It began to rain just as we finished packing. We buttoned our slickers and headed up the trail, leading our packhorses. Running along with us was Trapper, an Australian sheepdog who darted in between the plodding hooves with impunity. We followed a mountain stream bordered by mossy rocks, vines, and wildflowers in profusion. The trail was steep. Packhorses sometimes try to stop and eat, which inevitably jerks the rope in your hand. Booger had a trick to beat the system. Every few minutes, he trotted up next to Kissimee, gained slack in the lead rope, then snatched clumps of grass before the rope came taut against his halter. Like most mares, Kissimee didn't like having a gelding poking his nose up her rear end, and her ears flared back. Occasionally, Booger's feeding trick drew the rope under her tail, which irritated her enough to kick at him, but that was life, and nothing much came of it.

As we lined out on the trail, Lee Feldman whipped out a pack of cigarettes and lit up. I don't smoke myself, but I enjoyed that initial gunpowdery scent of match head and tobacco igniting. Lee may have been trashing his lungs, but he was litter conscious, and after his nicotine fix, he stubbed the cigarette out on his chaps before pocketing the butt.

The storm clouds parted and the sun lit up a mountain meadow full of lupine and wild daisies. The spruce, white pine, and lodgepole pine glistened. By five we reached a ranger's cabin, whose windows were laced with barbed wire—bear protection. We put the mares in a wooden corral, while the geldings roamed free with hobbles and bells. Sandy instructed us on feeding each horse four pounds of oats. We built a fire outside and poured three scotch-and-waters, then roasted chicken with Cajun sauce and mixed wild dandelion leaves with our domestic lettuce.

As night came Sandy tended the campfire with care. "Last year an outfitter I used to work for had a major fire problem: one of his employees was leading a group and allegedly forgot to put out a campfire properly. That fire burned hundreds of acres on the edge of Yellowstone Park. Fellow contested the charge. Said there were other outfitters in the area. Forest Service still socked him with a bill for two million dollars."

"Two million? Didn't pay it, did he?" I asked.

"Can't. Doesn't have the money. Besides, it was a bum rap," said Sandy. "He was a darn good outfitter, too."

In the morning when we went to gather the horses, we found Booger with a dozen porcupine quills stuck in his muzzle. "Damn. Porked again," said Sandy. "Some horses never learn."

I held Booger's halter while Sandy pulled the quills out with pliers. The horse jerked away each time Sandy yanked, but in five minutes the muzzle was clean except for a few tiny bubbles of blood. "These are just little quills. The bigger ones are about the diameter of knitting needles and really hurt."

Sandy forced Booger's mouth open. His teeth looked like one octave of a yellowing Steinway. "Uh-oh, one right through his tongue. Hang on to his head." The quill's point had worked all the way through the other side. Sandy grabbed it and yanked. Booger barely seemed to notice, but as he walked away, his lips worked like a trumpet player checking his chops.

Crossing the high mountain meadows of Cabin Creek Valley, Sandy— who has guided groups from the Smithsonian Institution—identified the wildflowers blooming in profusion. "That one with the purple cone flower is wild onion—and they're good to eat. The dark purplish blue flower is larkspur. If a cow eats half a pound of that it will die. Now, that grass there isn't native to this area—it's timothy. Carried in by sheep and horses before they limited grazing up here. And that tiny white flower is valerian."

We pitched our tents near a spring pouring from a rock in Sage Basin, ninety-two hundred feet up. As the hobbled horses cropped lush grass, we also ate well: blackened salmon steaks, wild onions in the salad, and a cheesecake that I chilled in the stream inside a Ziploc plastic bag. The half-moon rose and we went to sleep.

I awakened just after dawn to hear something banging on one of the plastic paniers (pronounced *PAN-yers,* Montana style). I looked out my tent and found Booger Blitz looking for oats. A couple of well-aimed rocks sent him off with his bell clanging.

At seven I heard Sandy's voice: "I hate to wake you guys up, but there's a moose out here."

I stuck my head out of the tent in time to see an enormous cow moose striding across the meadow into the timber. She was antlerless and looked like a cross between a horse and a camel. Booger also saw the moose and trotted over to talk to her, but she didn't like his looks and split.

After breakfast we took the horses on a day ride along Wapiti Ridge. Booger led the three unloaded and untethered packhorses in a wild stampede ahead and around us. We passed a U.S. Forest Service marker at 9,475 feet, and we spied another female moose lying downhill from us in the shade of trees. Back at camp I decided to shed my snakeskin of sweat, dust, and horsehair by going downstream and scrubbing myself with environmentally safe peppermint soap. The water was so cold I felt as though I'd been chastened with an icicle.

Walking after dinner I found a young bull moose down in the trees. I sat and watched the great beast with its bulbous nose and heavy horns still in velvet as it cropped grass in the growing dusk. The fire had burned down low by the time I returned; Sandy and Lee were talking about religion, newspaper unions, and old girlfriends. Before getting into my tent, I looked up at the stars. In the clean air of Montana, the lunar crescent gave off more light than a full moon over Los Angeles or Manhattan. People in cities rarely take the time to look at the sky, but here every star and astrological formation was as clear as a planetarium model. A meteor fell in a swift streak of flame across the sky.

By seven the next morning Sandy had already dismantled his tent and fixed breakfast for us. We were moving camp. Once again, peppermint soap and icy stream water bludgeoned me awake. We saddled up and rode down a ridge lined by wind-twisted white pine and fir whose branches were covered with green moss. Some had been blackened by lightning.

A grayish bird flew into a tree and screeched at us. "Camp robber or Canadian jay," said Sandy. "In California they call them whiskey jacks."

"In New York we call them corporate lawyers," said Lee, puffing away on a cigarette.

Our horses picked their way carefully over trees fallen across the trail. "Not used much, this trail. Low priority," said Sandy. "Forest Service only clears it once a year." Sandy chopped through one fallen tree with the hatchet. At another windfall, Sandy tied a rope around the log and used his horse to pull it aside.

At a bend in the trail we surprised a large cow moose and her light brown calf. She snorted, then stole away through the woods. "You sure don't want to get between a mama moose and her calf," said Sandy. "Fiercer than a bear with cubs. They'll charge you, bite you, butt you, stomp you."

Kissimee had grown tired of Booger shoving the lead rope under her tail, so Sandy and I switched packhorses. My new partner was a sorrel gelding named Toby, a passive horse with a dazed, insecure look in his eye.

"We're going up into the Lee Metcalf Wilderness today," said Sandy. (The region was named for a Montana congressman instrumental in environmental protection.) Our goal was Expedition Peak and the lakes below it. By five we reached the first lake, as clear as a swimming pool in Beverly Hills. The second lake was even more inviting, but seeing another outfitter's tent, we pushed on.

Halfway to the next lake something happened. Maybe Toby got the rope up under Kissimee's tail. Maybe Kissimee just stung herself with her own hooves. All I remember is doing a somersault and landing flat on my back in the trail. A *wreck,* in cowboy parlance.

"You all right?" asked Sandy, getting down off his horse.

I stood up slowly and brushed myself off. "I'm fine."

I had been lucky with the soft landing. On either side of the trail were skull-sized rocks ready to break bones. Toby hadn't even moved, and stared at me with an innocent look. I got back on Kissimee and we headed up the trail.

Reaching a small creek that spread out below into a green, spongy meadow, Sandy said, "Great feed for the horses!" with the enthusiasm of a miner discovering nuggets of placer gold. We set up camp and started a fire. Lee hiked up to the crags above and returned a half hour later with a bowlful of snow, which we covered with scotch to make adult snow cones. We roasted chicken and talked about horse colic, buffalo ranches, and the great bull-trout fishing on the Flathead. While I washed the dishes in the amazing peppermint soap, Sandy switched the horses on the tie line, putting Breezy, Trail, and the gray mare known as Music out to pasture in hobbles. I got into my tent and fell asleep in minutes.

Around 6 A.M. I awakened to overhear a conversation through my tent wall:

Sandy: "Good morning."

Lee: "Morning."

"Three horses are gone."

"Gone?"

"Heard their bells last at 5 A.M. Could be halfway down the trail by now. "

"Aw, shit."

By the time I'd struggled into my jeans and boots, Sandy was already mounted on Kissimee and heading down the trail at a fast trot. Lee and I made coffee and cleaned up camp, secretly glad we weren't outfitters. "If the horses have an hour's head start, it could take Sandy an hour to catch them."

"And that long to return," I said.

"So let's eat breakfast," said Lee.

About forty minutes later, Sandy appeared with all the horses. "Lucky—found them down at Blue Paradise Lake. Ran into an old outfitter who saw them. Also, saw some fresh bear scat. Black bear."

Sandy and Lee went out for a trail ride while I stayed with the horses and read. The sky grew overcast. I crawled into my sleeping bag for a nap. I awakened a few minutes later and looked out the door to see the ground hopping with millions of white mothballs. In a few minutes the hailstorm was replaced by steady rain. Only after Sandy and Lee returned and unsaddled did Sandy discover that he had left his sleeping bag out to air. Now it was soaked. "I'll just have to use horse blankets tonight," he sighed.

In the morning, we saddled up three horses and rode to Expedition Pass. Above the timberline, the country looked more like tundra—a wide sloping meadow with rock clusters. In the rocks, marmots sounded their warning cry, a high-pitched whistle that rings and echoes. From Expedition Pass, we could see eighty miles over range after range of mountains. Back at camp that evening, gumball-sized hailstones drove us under the blue tarp.

As we drank scotch and tended the fire, Sandy told a tale about former clients. "Once took a group of four women from New York backpacking. Their leader was this high-powered publisher. We stopped on the trail the first day and she whips out this plastic funnel-like thing. A female urinal spout so she could go by just undoing her zipper. Never seen anything like it. She said, 'I've always wanted to see what it was like to piss like a man.' Then she asks me, 'You want to try it?' And I said, 'No thanks, I already know how.'"

Over dessert on our last evening together in the mountains, Sandy and I found that we shared the same crazy idea. "I've always wanted to canoe the whole Yellowstone River," he said. "To re-create Captain William Clark's return voyage. You know, when he separated from Lewis?"

God, how many hundreds of miles were we talking about? The Yellowstone crossed nearly the whole state of Montana, but I heard myself say, "Let's do it."

"Have you got the time?"

"Plenty, after the Montana Centennial Cattle Drive in September."

"Then I'll do it as a friend, not as a paid guide," Sandy offered.

"You're on, pardner."

We shook hands.

"This I'd like to see," said Feldman, puffing away on his ubiquitous cigarette. His skeptical tone served to strengthen my resolve.

By then it was too late; the idea had been planted. A week after our pack trip ended, I called Sandy from the road to learn that he'd purchased topographical maps of the whole Yellowstone drainage, bought new paddles and waterproof bags, and cleared his schedule for the month of September.

"Don't break your arm on the cattle drive," he drawled. "Makes it real hard to paddle."

William Conrad, banker and founder of the town of Conrad.

William A. Clark, who "stole" the 1899 U.S. Senate campaign.

Marcus Daley, the tycoon of Anaconda.

My great-grandfather, Judge William Henry Hunt.

(All courtesy Montana Historical Society)

Chapter 20
The Copper Kings of Butte

By his example he has so excused and so sweetened
corruption that in Montana it no longer has an offensive
smell. His history is known to everybody; he is as
rotten a human being as can be found anywhere under
the flag; he is a shame to the American nation, and
no one has helped to send him to the Senate who did
not know that his proper place was the penitentiary,
with a ball and chain on his legs.

   Mark Twain on Senator William A. Clark, 1907

On a mountaintop overlooking the city of Butte stands the largest dashboard ornament in America, *Our Lady of the Rockies*, a ninety-foot-high
stone statue of the Virgin Mary, her arms outspread. Butte is also famous for
being the hometown of daredevil motorcyclist Evel Knievel, and for its
faded mining title, "the Richest Hill on Earth."

Butte also has been called the Ugliest Town in the West, but I disagree. It
is the most culturally and architecturally diverse city in Montana and, with
a population of more than thirty-seven thousand, the third largest city in
the state. Driving down from Homestake Pass, the first thing you see is the
Berkeley Mine, a mile-square hole in the mountainside right next to the
town. Hundreds of houses once stood here, but in its greed for copper, the
Anaconda Copper Mining Company literally dug away whole neighborhoods like Dublin Gulch and Cabbage Town.

Montana Street was flanked with old Victorian houses that looked
transplanted from San Francisco. On the hill above me rose the gallowslike

structures of mining frameworks. Street names followed geology: Quartz, Granite, Mercury, Platinum, and Copper Streets. In its heyday at the turn of the century, Butte produced about a quarter of the copper used in the entire world. It once had a population of seventy-five thousand, with twelve thousand miners and laborers toiling twenty-four hours a day in mile-deep shafts. The mineral riches of the West were brokered on Wall Street, and financiers such as George Hearst and John D. Rockefeller would slip in and out of the city in their private railroad cars.

With the copper gone, Butte is an impoverished city, a haggard metropolis of crumbling architecture frequently prey to arson. Unemployment figures are in the high teens, and environmental problems have made the area a major Superfund candidate. In spite of the successful opening of a sports center to train Olympic athletes at high altitudes, this is not a healthy town.

Still, it has gumption, pride in its past, and an unkillable spirit. "Butte is the most Western of American cities," wrote a journalist in 1903. "It gives the impression of an overgrown mining-camp awakening suddenly to the consciousness that it is a city, putting on the airs and proprieties of the city, and yet often relapsing into the old fascinating reckless life of the frontier camp." Butte was once a miniaturized New York in the Rockies, full of Welsh, English, Mexicans, Finns, Germans, Austrians, Slavs, Greeks, Serbs, Chinese, and Jews. The Cornish miners were known as Cousin Jacks, while the Serbo-Croats and other eastern Europeans were called Bohunks. At least twenty languages were spoken in neighborhoods called Finn Town, Corktown, Parrot Flat, Dublin Gulch, and Meaderville. Its Chinatown was one of the largest in the western states, complete with opium dens, noodle parlors, and a slave trade.

I wandered through the crumbling red-light district along Galena Street, peering in at the underground cribs now exposed by the wrecking ball. On any given Saturday night at the turn of the century four thousand men and women could be found milling about with gold dust and lust in their pockets. Charlie Chaplin, who played the city with a vaudeville troupe in 1910, remembered it vividly in his autobiography:

> The red-light district of Butte, Montana consisted of a long street and several side streets containing a hundred cribs, in which young girls were installed ranging in age from sixteen up—for one dollar. Butte boasted of having the prettiest women of any red-light district in the West, and it was true. If one saw a pretty girl smartly dressed,

one could rest assured she was from the red-light quarter, doing her shopping. Off-duty, they looked neither right nor left and were most acceptable."

The heart—or perhaps the liver—of Butte was the landmark M&M Bar. Built a century ago, the bar acquired its shiny art deco aluminum exterior in the 1930s. Inside, the long wooden bar faces a busy lunch counter and a smoke-filled gambling parlor. At the counter I tried a traditional Butte dish, the *pasty*, a thick pastry shell stuffed with chopped sirloin, potatoes, and onions. The dish was brought to this country by the Cousin Jacks—the Welshmen and Cornishmen who pioneered hard-rock mining in Butte. In the old days, when a miner found a pasty in his lunchbox, he'd exclaim, "Ah, a letter from 'ome."

"The bars in this town do thirteen months of business in a year," said the bartender at the M&M. "We do a month's worth on Saint Patrick's Day." For predominantly Irish Butte, March 17 is a bigger celebration than the Fourth of July. At breakfast that day, the bar at the M&M is lined with veterans sipping eye-openers. By midnight some ten thousand people will have consumed a ton of corned beef and cabbage, one hundred fifty cases of whiskey, and over one thousand cases of beer. The parade at noon is what you'd expect in any small town: the volunteer fire department, Rotarians, a couple dressed as Mr. and Mrs. Leprechaun, school marching bands, and campaigning politicians. Even Saint Urho makes an appearance—a bearded man dressed in white robes and a bishop's miter. Just as Patrick drove the snakes out of Ireland, in olden times Saint Urho cleansed Finland of grasshoppers, the farmer's plague. In the parade, the saint leads a giant papier-mâché grasshopper transported by two pairs of stumbling human legs. Once the parade ends, the drinking begins in earnest, and by late afternoon it's permissible to kiss anyone you like, or to punch out anyone you don't.

In spite of the varied background of its citizens, Butte was always dominated by the Irish, from its publicans to its labor bosses. In the fifties the comic Lenny Bruce noticed that anyone who lived in New York eventually "became Jewish" but that in Butte even a Jew eventually "became Irish." One example of this adaptation process was the Muslim tailor who thought it would be good for business to change his name to Muhammad Murphy.

A favorite local story has a priest calling on a dying Irishwoman. The priest grows frustrated with his failure to bring her spiritual comfort. Finally the woman tells him, "Father, it's not the thought of dying that bothers me. It's the thought of leaving Butte."

Butte began in 1864 with a gold strike in Silver Bow Creek, but it was copper that put Butte on the map. The men who profited most from this were William A. Clark, Marcus Daly, and F. Augustus Heinze. Copper made them among the richest men in the world, and when the copper kings began to feud, it rocked the economy and politics of Montana.

Born in 1839, William Andrews Clark personified the rags-to-riches story. He spent his childhood in Iowa, studied law, taught school in Missouri, then became a miner in Colorado. He arrived in gold-rush Bannack at age twenty-four in 1863, wearing a red shirt, patched pants, and an old army coat that had one tail burned off by a campfire. Small-framed, with a high voice and a ferretlike appearance, this tense red-haired man seemed an unlikely Montana pioneer. Clark made fifteen hundred dollars his first summer at Bannack and bought horses and a wagon to haul goods all over the dangerous Northwest—always working alone. By 1872 he'd started a bank in Deer Lodge.

Clark invested heavily in silver and copper properties in Butte and convinced a group of Coloradans to join him in a smelting enterprise. His mineralogical savvy and ruthless business practices soon won him control of half the copper mines and assorted banks in Butte. He built the first smelter and stamp mill, started the first water company and electric company, and owned an electric railway. He also owned newspapers, including the *Butte Miner* and the *Great Falls Tribune*. He donated money to the YMCA and built a ten-acre park for the people of Butte.

A powerful capitalist at a young age, Clark had flair and a vision of the glory money could buy, even in a rough mining town. He dressed well, wore his hair rakishly long, and kept his beard impeccably trimmed. "Inordinately vain," wrote C. P. Connolly, "he loved the flattery and adulation of women. He was a Beau Brummel in the midst of the awkward inelegance of the West." Eventually he would keep homes in New York, Washington, and France, and die one of the richest men in the world.

Today in Butte, however, the bronze statue in front of the mining college depicts not Clark but his equally ambitious rival, Marcus Daly. A stocky, likable tycoon with a full-cheeked face and droopy mustache, Daly had immigrated from Ireland in the 1850s. As a young man he went to California and worked the great Comstock Lode in Nevada. His practical mining skills impressed the wealthy Walker brothers of Utah, who hired him in 1876 to assess a mine in Butte.

Striking out on his own, Daly invested in the Anaconda Mine, a silver operation on the southeastern side of the hill, and turned to even more powerful financiers from San Francisco: George Hearst (father of William Randolph), Lloyd Tevis, and the Turkish tycoon James Ben Ali Haggin. The mine was the purest body of copper sulfide the world had ever seen; Daly and his partners made millions.

At that time, ore was shipped by boat all the way to Swansea, Wales, for smelting. In 1883–84 Daly constructed the Washoe smelter twenty-six miles away at a town on Warm Springs Creek that was first called Copperopolis, then Anaconda. It became his personal fiefdom, the classic "company town."

For a decade Daly and Clark were adversaries in a statewide battle for political power. No one is quite sure how the bad blood started. Some say it was over a mining claim in Butte, others that Clark called Daly's mining partner, Ben Ali Haggin, a "nigger," referring to the financier's dark skin and Levantine origins. Perhaps Daly simply didn't like Clark, who was a stone-hearted popinjay. In 1888, Clark ran for territorial delegate to the U.S. Congress. As Montana was strongly Democratic, he should have won handily, but Daly, a fellow Democrat, undermined him by urging his miners to vote for Republican Thomas Carter. Clark was livid.

In 1894 Montanans were asked to vote on a permanent capital for the state of Montana. Clark spent one hundred thousand dollars to promote Helena, while Daly spent five times that sum pushing Anaconda. This time Clark won: the voters chose Helena.

Clark's dream was to become the U.S. senator from Montana in 1899— to arrive in Washington at the dawn of the twentieth century—and his ambitions caused the most infamous political scandal in Montana's history. His opponent in the 1899 U.S. Senate race was my great-great uncle William Conrad. After thirty years on the frontier, Conrad was a prosperous cattleman and banker from Great Falls. Far and away the favorite Democrat, he was politically untainted and enjoyed Marcus Daly's approval.

Clark began a strategic campaign to rock Daly's political machine. As the state capitol wasn't completed in Helena, on New Year's Day 1899 the ninety-four member legislature assembled at the Merchants Hotel: seventy-four Democrats, fifteen Republicans, four Silver Republicans, and one Populist. For months Clark's attorneys and henchmen had been snooping into the private lives and business affairs of the legislators, hunting for weaknesses. They bought up mortgages on the legislators' ranches and businesses, then offered them a choice: vote for Clark and the debt is forgiven; vote against him and lose the property. Clark bought Democratic votes for an average of seven thousand dollars per delegate. Republicans were more expensive: the chairman of the Republican caucus received a whopping fifty thousand dollars.

In the first few days of the voting session, Clark appeared occasionally in the lobby of the Helena Hotel, but he was so badgered for bribes that he would agree to meet only by appointment in his room. As his son Charlie Clark stuffed thousand-dollar bills into envelopes, he joked, "We will send the old man to the Senate or the poorhouse."

Helena became hysterical with greed. The purchase of votes was talked about as freely as the weather. Under heavy editorial pressure from Daly's *Anaconda Standard,* the two legislative houses established a joint committee to investigate the many allegations—as sensible as asking a drunk to give himself an inebriation test.

On the first ballot only seven votes went to Clark. Three days later he picked up fourteen more, but Conrad, the main challenger, still had thirty-five votes, with others scattered among Republicans and other candidates. Concerned by Clark's steady gains, Daly's *Anaconda Standard* declared:

> To Every Man Who Is Getting Ready to Sell Out to W. A. Clark, Greetings. When You Make Your Deal, Get the Real Stuff—Cash in Hand—If You're Going to Be a Criminal, Be It in Style. Demand Cash Every Time.

Few could resist Clark's money. From a high score of thirty-eight votes on the second ballot, Conrad's total shrank to thirty-three on January 21, when Clark tied him for the first time. A grand jury was called to examine the bribery evidence, but Clark's money had already reached the jurors (at ten thousand dollars apiece), and they duly reported that there was insufficient evidence for a trial.

On January 28 when the final ballot was cast, some legislators broke down sobbing as their price was shouted at them from the gallery. With passionate disgust the orator of the session said, "I am sorry it is necessary for the manhood of Montana to be dishonored in order that any man may attain his end."

That day, the copper king was elected by fifty-four votes to Conrad's twenty-seven (with the other votes scattered among several candidates).

Clark himself did not show up to hear the outcome. Not even the Clark men felt elation; the price in human spirit had been too high. Clark's election cost an estimated $431,000—the equivalent of about $10 million today.

The disillusioned Conrad brothers left Helena the day after the last vote. During the afternoon and evening, the bars of Helena served drinks on the house, courtesy of Senator Clark. Clark's champagne bill for the night was said to be thirty thousand dollars—barely the price of three good men.

Clark didn't get away with it for long, thanks to my favorite great-grandfather. On May 5, a legislator presented Judge Hunt and the Supreme Court of the State of Montana with a written accusation against Clark's attorney, John Wellcome, charging him with bribery and demanding his disbarment. After a legal tussle involving the attorney general and the bribed grand jury, Hunt and the supreme court decided to hear the evidence.

One day in early August, Judge Hunt's family physician, Dr. William Treacy, asked to see him. The doctor invited Hunt into a back room and announced that he had a personal interest in the Wellcome case. My great-grandfather was surprised at political talk from a physician. Dr. Treacy made himself clear: "I wish you to understand my position. There is a party over here and they have got one hundred thousand dollars. They want to put it up if that case can be thrown out of court."

Judge Hunt was stunned, then outraged. "Doctor, I would not for all the money there is in the United Verde Mine and the Butte mines put together, with every dollar that Daly and Clark have got, sacrifice my conscience to the extent of granting a man five minutes' continuance in a lawsuit if I did not believe it was right. That case must go ahead. They don't know me, Doctor."

That evening the persistent doctor approached Hunt again at his house, and was nearly thrown out physically. Clark partisans unsuccessfully approached Hunt's fellow supreme court justices as well as the attorney general, who angrily rejected Clark's offer of one hundred thousand dollars.

On December 4, Republican Senator Carter petitioned the U.S. Senate to challenge Clark's legitimacy. The Senate committee started investigative proceedings, and in February 1900, Judge Hunt and his fellow judges testified in Washington along with dozens of other witnesses, including William Conrad. Dr. Treacy himself testified that he had only been "joshing" when interviewing Judge Hunt and the attorney general.

Back in Montana, newspapers controlled by Clark lost no time in slandering the judges, making Judge Hunt the "principal target for scurrility."

The U.S. Senate investigation found that Clark had indeed obtained his election through bribery. But before he could be unseated by a vote in the Senate, Clark cleverly resigned on May 15, 1900, giving a last speech that blamed Daly for Montana's political scandals. He concluded by saying: "I was never in all my life, except as by such characters as are now pursuing me, charged with a dishonorable act, and I propose to leave my children a legacy worth more than gold, that of an unblemished name."

At the time of the Clark hearings, Marcus Daly was slowly dying of Bright's disease, and had just merged his Anaconda Company with the Amalgamated Copper Company, a corporate giant run by Henry H. Rogers, president of the Rockefellers' Standard Oil Company. Capitalized at $75 million, the copper trust was called "the biggest financial deal of the age," by the *New York Times*. Daly's death in November 1900 ushered in a new era in which Montana's politics would be dominated by megacorporations rather than powerful entrepreneurs. Daly had owned not only the *Anaconda Standard* but newspapers in Bozeman, Livingston, and Virginia City, and Amalgamated immediately bought a half dozen more papers around the state.

Clark, who already owned the *Butte Miner* and controlled the *Helena Independent,* prepared for the next U.S. Senate election by purchasing the *Great Falls Tribune.* He formed an alliance with another copper magnate, the rabble-rousing F. Augustus "Fritz" Heinze, who controlled the hearts and minds of the Butte miners. With Heinze's support, in 1901 Clark ran for the U.S. Senate again on an anti-Amalgamated platform and ousted Republican Carter. Once again, Clark treated the city of Helena to free champagne.

The game changed when Clark got to Washington and met his match in Henry H. Rogers. Next to John D. Rockefeller, he was the most powerful man in America. Physically impressive, with piercing green eyes and a fierce silver mustache, in private life Rogers occupied the front pew at his church for forty years. He bailed Mark Twain out of ruin, and the author considered him one of the greatest gentlemen of the day. But in matters of business Rogers was ruthless.

When the newly elected Senator Clark arrived at his New York offices, Rogers gave him a clear choice. "Mr. Clark, I have no objection to your taking your seat in the U. S. Senate. But, Mr. Clark, you have formed an alliance with Fritz Heinze in Montana which is absolutely unacceptable to me. Heinze is causing us great difficulties in Montana. I intend to destroy Heinze, Mr. Clark. However, I have no particular desire to destroy you if you demonstrate a willingness to cooperate with me. I will, however, use my influence to prevent your being seated as the next senator from Montana unless you terminate your arrangement with Fritz Heinze immediately."

Clark listened in shock as Rogers continued. "I have ample power in the U. S. Senate to accomplish this and I have enough confidential information about you, the disclosure of which would render the task quite simple. . . . And I might add, any attempt by you to resume a relationship with Heinze in the future will be disclosed to me through my own apparatus, and I am prepared to move against you in the future so as to interrupt your term in the Senate at any time during the next six years. Do I make myself clear?"

No one had spoken this way to William A. Clark since he was a schoolboy, but he recognized the terrible power Rogers represented. Within twenty-four hours, Clark sent a telegram to Heinze severing their business and political relationship. Mystified and angry, Heinze launched an all-out battle against Amalgamated that divided Butte into warring factions. In a few years, Heinze cashed out to the copper trust for $20 million and moved to New York, where he lost most of his fortune on Wall Street.

Clark served six undistinguished years in the Capitol, and rarely went back to Montana. He spent $25 million building a railroad from Salt Lake City to Los Angeles and San Pedro, completing it in 1905. It was the only railroad in the United States owned entirely by one man (without issuing corporate stock), and it eventually became part of the Southern Pacific. He was also the sole owner of the United Verde Mining Company and founded the town site of Clarksdale, Arizona. He acquired the *Salt Lake Herald* and made large profits in the sugar-beet industry in Los Angeles, while his oil wells in nearby Long Beach gushed millions.

In 1884 Clark commissioned the most extraordinary house in Butte, a rusty red Victorian mansion with thirty rooms, nine fireplaces, ninety doors, and many gables and turrets. The interior was a bourgeois tour de force of stained-glass windows and marquetry in oak, cherry, burled walnut, and mahogany; the price tag was $250,000 (about $5 million today). After his tour as senator, Clark rarely came back to Butte.

The house's present owner, Mrs. Ann Cote Smith, was a pretty woman in her sixties, with a husky voice deepened by cigarette smoking. Her father was a professional gambler; her mother, who owned the Milwaukee Bar on Montana Street, had bought the Clark house in the fifties for about fifty thousand dollars. Today it is a National Historic Place. As Mrs. Smith gave me a tour of the house, she spoke admiringly of "Senator Clark."

After the last tour group left, I asked Mrs. Smith to recommend a hotel. "Why don't you stay here?" she said. "I have to get up early tomorrow to drive to Helena for a Montana Historical Society gathering, but you're welcome to have the guest room. Just be sure to wake up before the first tour comes through at nine." In gratitude, I took Mrs. Smith—now Ann—out for dinner. Back at the Clark house I fell asleep immediately. I awakened only once in the night, hearing some poltergeist running through the radiator pipes. Maybe it was the copper king himself, agitated that a descendant of Conrad and Hunt had been invited into his house.

Clark was an incurably vain man, a dandy obsessed with his social standing. A Francophile, he taught himself to speak French and then German. He let his thick graying red hair grow long like a poet's, and wore his beard and mustache impeccably trimmed. In 1904, he announced that, three years earlier, he had secretly married his pretty young "ward," Anna LaChappelle, a Butte girl half his age, whom he had been educating in France. There was talk of "a bird in a gilded cage." It was learned that Anna had borne him a daughter in 1902. (Their second daughter, an octogenarian recluse, still lives in New York.)

In 1906 Clark began to build an ostentatious palace in New York. Six years later the 131-room mansion, at 77th Street and Fifth Avenue, was finished at a cost of over $3 million. The style was called Baroque Beaux-Arts, but one critic later said, "If architecture is frozen music, this edifice is frozen ragtime." It was a far cry from his log cabin at Bannack in his early days as a tobacco peddler. He bought art by Turner, da Vinci, Gainsborough, and Reynolds—as well as twenty-two Corots and a Rembrandt. (No Charlie Russells, though.)

Even in this palace, Clark was never able to rid himself of the stain of bribery and corruption. After suffering through a dinner with the tycoon, Mark Twain wrote in 1907: "To my mind he is the most disgusting creature that the republic has produced since [Boss] Tweed's time."

When Clark died in 1925 at eighty-six, he left an estate conservatively estimated at over $200 million. His will ordered the ostentatious Manhattan mansion to be destroyed, and it was. He left little money to charity, although his children later endowed a number of institutions. Virtually nothing went back to Montana—the state from which Clark had taken so much.

After the departure of Clark, Daly, and Heinze, the town of Butte became ensnared in the coils of the Amalgamated Copper Mining Company, which changed its name back to the Anaconda Company. It dictated not only Butte politics, but the politics of Montana. Opposing this giant were the powerful unions and labor bosses of Butte. The antagonism peaked in

1917 when IWW organizer Frank Little was lynched under a train trestle by a group of masked men. This was just one of many conflicts that led to seven years of intermittent martial law in Butte.

Dashiell Hammett was in Butte as a Pinkerton agent to monitor the 1920–21 miners' strike, when Wobblies were pressuring Anaconda for higher wages and better working conditions. In his 1929 novel, *Red Harvest*, Hammett called the town Personville—nicknamed "Poisonville"—and wrote:

> The strike lasted eight months. Both sides bled plenty. The Wobblies had to do their own bleeding. Old Elihu hired gunmen, strikebreakers, national guardsmen and even parts of the regular army, to do his. When the last skull had been cracked, the last rib kicked in, organized labor in Personville was a used firecracker.

By the 1970s Butte was brought to its economic knees by two rival factions—the overbearing company and a miner's union that featherbedded and refused to lay off members even as copper prices dropped. Profits dwindled along with productivity, and both sides squelched the entrepreneurial spirit in Butte. Anaconda had sold the mines to Atlantic Richfield Company, and in 1983, with copper prices languishing at an all-time low of sixty cents a pound, Arco shut down the mines. One thousand union members lost their jobs. Only the reincarnation of Marcus Daly, they said, could save Butte from its chronic 17 percent unemployment rate.

When a self-made millionaire contractor, Dennis Washington of Missoula, came down to bid on the Anaconda Company equipment as scrap, he saw a way to make money where the unionized company had failed. Civic leaders were so eager to lure Washington's Montana Resources, Inc. (MRI), that they put together an $11-million credit line that included money from the state's mineral severance tax fund. Montana Power reduced power rates to MRI by as much as 15 percent, and the town of Butte slashed MRI's property taxes for three years. Most importantly, only the die-hard union members grumbled about the nonunion jobs Washington offered them.

By 1986 MRI had put almost three hundred miners back to work in the open-pit copper mines at good wages and with a chance to participate in a profit-sharing plan. Productivity rose, absenteeism and theft were down, and the general spirit was optimistic. MRI became Butte's fifth largest employer.

But the mining that made Butte rich has left it poisoned. Water in the pit was as caustic as battery acid. The mine tailings, pulverized rock from deep within the earth, held metallic poisons—copper, lead, manganese, arsenic, and more—that appeared miles away in streams, drinking water, and sterilized soil. Superfund sites dot the country for a hundred miles down the Clark Fork River, the easternmost tributary of the Columbia River, which is the main drainage for most of western Montana. After a 1986 study by the Centers for Disease Control found elevated levels of arsenic in the hair, blood, and urine of children in the small town of Mill Creek (twenty miles downstream from Butte), the EPA evacuated the town, destroyed all the houses, and fenced off the area.

Ironically, Butte's disastrous environmental situation may make it a mecca for environmental cleanup technology. It's a patient that can only get better, not worse, so nobody minds if experimental high-tech remedies fall short. In a curious alliance between local and federal government agencies, Butte's future still lives off of its mining past. Uptown Butte, with four thousand buildings, has been designated a National Historic Landmark district, making it bigger than the historic area of Boston, New York, or Philadelphia. The National Park Service wants to preserve the district to illustrate the West's mining heritage, much as Lowell, Massachusetts, was used to preserve a classic New England industrial town.

For breakfast I walked down to West Granite Street and went into a place called Gamer's. As I came through the door, a man who could have been a stand-in for the older Fred Astaire came bounding toward me with an outstretched hand and a big smile. "*Heyyy*, look who's here!" he sang, shaking my hand. The whole restaurant seemed to be grinning with him. "*Sayyy*, we've been waiting for you to show up!" He guided me across the floor with a hand at my back. "Got a special place for you right here at the counter!"

"Thanks, but do you know me?"

"*Course* I do! You're the one whose going to eat the *best* breakfast he ever had in his *life!* Sweetheart," he crooned to a waitress at the counter, "take care of this handsome young fella! *En-nee thing he wants and plen-tee of it!*" The man slapped his hands together and did a little jig before dashing across the restaurant to greet another lucky customer with the same enthusiasm.

At eighty-plus, Carl Rowan didn't look a day over sixty and had the springy-noodle physique of a tap dancer. He did everything differently in his restaurant: You want coffee? "Sure, pour it yourself—it's a free country! But don't forget to offer your neighbors a cup and chat with them awhile! They're nice people from Ohio!" You want a soft drink? "Get yourself a glass and some ice, walk to the machine over there, and make yourself a big fat Coke!" You want to pay your check? "Go to the cash register, ring it up yourself, and make change for your five-dollar bill. We trust you—even if your pretty wife here doesn't! Aw, sure she does. Go on, give her a *big fat kiss!* I'll bet she won't mind. Now *I'll* give her a *big fat kiss!* Say, beautiful, let's go *dancing* tonight!" he said, sashaying across the room. Carl Rowan has been doing this at Gamer's since 1944.

The cash register at the counter faces *toward* the customers; several generations of kids have learned to make change on it. "Never had a problem except once when they came out with those Susan B. Anthony dollars," said Carl Rowan. "I lost forty-two dollars in one day. Everybody thought they were quarters! Basically people are honest—and it's something they remember. We're probably the only restaurant in the nation that lets people make their own change, and people remember that. They come back and bring their kids."

Carl admitted that once there had been another kind of problem. "One night after I had gone to bed in the back I woke about midnight and heard the cash register open. I'd left the front door open, waiting for my son to drop off some laundry. I walked out barefoot and saw this great big fellow. 'Hold it right there!' I said. 'Jim, keep me covered.' I walked right up to that big fellow and made him put the money back. Then I sat him down at that table right over there and gave him a talking-to. He said he'd never done anything like that in his life. He was down on his luck from Anaconda, just walking by, and saw the door open. He said he was ashamed.

"Then he asked how I had the nerve to face him down. 'I could have shot you and your friend Jim,' he says. 'I doubt it,' I said, 'Jim's handy with a rifle.' I finally got up and said, 'Jim, follow me as I show our friend the door.' And the man left. The funny thing is, there's nobody named Jim. I was completely alone. I just made him up!"

As I said good-bye, Carl handed me a sack. "*Sayyy,* take a big fat doughnut with you for the road. Then come back and see us!"

Anaconda's raison d'être is a 585-foot-high smokestack looming over ash-colored foothills sterilized by a century of smelting copper. As you drive into this dying town, you wonder how it ever could've been considered a candidate for the state capital. Dominating the hill is the smelter, known as the Stack. If you were good, the miners say, you went to heaven; if you were bad you worked under the Stack for eternity. As one miner put it, "When I was a kid I always thought there was God, country, and Anaconda. I thought they'd all be here till I died. Now Anaconda's gone, so you wonder about the rest."

Surrounded by quaint Victorian houses and old street lamps, the brownstone carcass of Marcus Daly's Montana Hotel still stands at the center of town. Built in 1888 for three hundred thousand dollars, the four-story structure was modeled after government buildings in Brussels and Vienna. Inside, the Tammany Bar had once shown off hand-carved mahogany columns; the mirrors remained flawless for eight decades. Half the rooms had had marble fireplaces. Daly lived here with his wife, sometimes inviting his miners to drink with him in the splendor of the Tammany Bar. "Marcus Daly was a man's man and a miner's miner," the Irishmen would say. This hotel was also where John Conrad tasted a moment of glory in 1889, when the Democratic Party nominated him as the candidate for lieutenant governor of the soon-to-be-state.

The Montana was one of the great hotels of the West until the Great Depression. Ten years ago, however, the owners caved in to financial pressures and "developed" it, with miserable results. The entire center was gutted to make an open-air arcade of shops—most of which failed—and another great piece of Montana architecture was lost.

The reddish stone facade with "1888" carved in the arch above the main entrance now leads to a drafty courtyard—to nothing—and the hotel stands as a pathetic footnote to a broader tale of rape and plunder. Marcus Daly had scoured the mountains for copper, and smelted the ore with the coal John Conrad sent him from the Aldridge mines, but like the state's economy, the Montana Hotel was built with nonrenewable resources. Now it, too, had been destroyed by its transient owners.

As I love old hotels, it felt natural to wish time could reverse itself and then move forward in the right way. *Welcome to the newly refurbished Montana Hotel—a recent addition to the Conrad Historic Hotels chain. And remember our flagship hostelry, the Grand Union of Fort Benton—where the past is always a pleasure.*

When I left Anaconda, my steering wheel acted like a renegade Ouija oracle, taking me on a random detour along the Pintler scenic route north of Philipsburg. There was a storm overhead, so the pine forests did not beckon me to pitch a tent for the night. Away from the shadow of the Stack, cows lay patiently in a field as a heavy rain fell, and I struggled to keep the windshield from fogging up.

A dead deer lay by the side of the road. As I drove past, the doe's hind leg moved in a violent jerk. I braked, thinking she had been hit recently by a car and was still alive. A compelling humanitarian vision came in a flash: I would put this flopping animal out of her misery with the .44 Magnum I kept under my seat. I had bought it to protect myself from radical bears or Charlie Manson's third cousin, but it could be a tool of mercy. I reversed the Jeep and pulled abreast of the deer.

Through the rain-fogged passenger window, I discerned a strange canine ghost hovering above the carcass. It was a coyote, so intent on pulling the deer's entrails out through her anus that he seemed barely to notice me. His muzzle was stained bright red with blood. Putting the pistol aside, I reached for my camera, but the coyote ran behind my car, skulked across the road, and disappeared down a ravine.

I went up the road half a mile and waited for the coyote to return. When I drove slowly by, there was a new scavenger, a black crow sitting on the haunch of the carcass. Then I understood. This was the true West.

Tucked into Judge Hunt's memoir was an original letter I valued. It was from Marcus Daly, written in 1900 from Washington during the scandal over Senator Clark's election. "Your reputation and good name since you have lived in Montana is such that the tongue of the scandal monger cannot reach you or your family, and you should adopt a course of independence and disregard of criticism and not be at all worried by it. I regretted that the judges of the Supreme Court were brought to Washington to testify, or were brought into a connection with this filthy pool, but since I have been here, I am very much pleased that it did happen."

Apparently, the children of Daly and Hunt often played together, and at a children's party, Daly gave all the children cash as presents; under attack in the U.S. Senate, the Clark forces tried to construe this as bribery. Both Daly and Hunt were furious at the pettiness of the allegation, but Hunt knew that by exposing Clark's corruption, he had seriously jeopardized his political future in Montana.

After Hunt's six-year term as a justice ended in 1901, President McKinley appointed him the new governor of Puerto Rico, a colony recently wrested from Spanish rule. In San Juan, my great-grandfather examined every aspect of the country, from labor relations to transportation and financial reform. He spoke out strongly for education and the legal system as the Americans transformed this feudal backwater into a democracy.

After McKinley was assassinated, Theodore Roosevelt encouraged Hunt to stay on as governor. Hunt's shaky health improved in the tropical climate, and after three years he considered returning to the United States. In a meeting at the White House, Roosevelt told him: "I would like to appoint you to the Supreme Court, but there is no vacancy there now." Instead, in 1904 Roosevelt made Hunt the U. S. district judge for Montana, where Hunt found that "old friends in Helena greeted me cordially; the warmth of their words of welcome made me feel the strength of my attachment for the state and friends."

When William Howard Taft—an old friend from Yale—was elected president in 1908, he appointed Hunt to the Court of Customs Appeals in Washington, D.C. Even at a distance Hunt continued to exercise such influence over Montana's judiciary and politics that Montana's Senator Joseph Dixon complained to a colleague that "Hunt has the President's ear exclusively."

Hunt thought Washington would be his "last stand" job-wise, but under Woodrow Wilson he was assigned to the Second Circuit Court out of New York. There he presided at the trial of William Rockefeller and others charged by the government with having conspired to violate antitrust statutes through the great octopus of the Amalgamated Copper Company, which now controlled Montana politics. It must have brought back disquieting memories of Montana's battling copper kings Clark, Daly, and Heinze.

Hunt had just taken a judgeship with the Ninth Circuit Court based in San Francisco when the Republican Party of Montana asked him to enter the 1916 race for U.S. senator. Since 1913, U.S. senators from Montana had been elected by a popular vote, rather than by the legislature. My great-grandfather had never lost his fire for national politics, but it would mean resigning from his life appointment as a circuit court judge, and there was no guarantee of winning. Nearly sixty, he had spent thirty years in public service and had accumulated no wealth. With regret, he turned them down.

In 1921 a concerted effort was made around the country to have Judge Hunt named to the U.S. Supreme Court, but the first vacancies were given to Taft and a distinguished former senator from Utah. Both men had supported Hunt's candidacy—and vice versa. In 1928, Judge Hunt retired on full salary and promptly went into private practice in San Francisco. He worked until his late eighties, stopping only after his wife fell ill and needed attendance. In 1940 he confessed in his memoirs, "I could have done much more than I have. Naturally some regrets force themselves into my mind as I watch the world receding. . . . I use the word 'regret' with full understanding of its meaning."

Certainly he never regretted refusing the hundred-thousand-dollar bribe from William A. Clark. When he died in 1949, aged ninety-two, his estate was barely ninety thousand dollars—even less than what Clark's men had offered him a half-century before. Many times I have cherished his honorable decision, hoping that I would be capable of doing the same thing.

As a small boy Judge Hunt had shaken the hand of Abraham Lincoln; in his prime he had known the friendship of Roosevelt and Taft and met every president up to F.D.R.; as an old man he watched newsreels of the atomic bomb over Hiroshima and heard talk of sending a manned rocket into space. Yet my grandmother told me that as Judge Hunt neared death, he reserved his greater enthusiasm for his youth on Montana's frontier. He vividly recalled his first steamboat journey up the Missouri when a great buffalo herd plunged into the current a hundred yards from the bow. The brown beasts filled the air with their bawling, blocking the steamboat's passage for an hour before scrambling up the far bank and thundering across the great plains.

"We will never see that again," he said.

Crow Indians at Pryor in 1906.

Chief Plenty Coups—Crow Tribe.
(Both courtesy Montana
Historical Society)

Chapter 21

Crow Fair: Surrounded by Indians

When the buffalo went away the hearts of my people
fell to the ground, and they could not lift them
up again. After this nothing happened.
        Chief Plenty Coups, Crow Tribe, circa 1900

From Billings south to the Pryor Mountains, the land opened into miles of dry grass with sparse pine in the rolling foothills. I followed the lazy flow of the Little Bighorn River past Custer Battlefield National Monument until I reached Crow Agency, headquarters of the Crow Indian Reservation.

The Crows migrated from what are now the states of North and South Dakota into Montana and Wyoming about four centuries ago, abandoning their agricultural pursuits to became hunters and warriors. Unlike the Blackfeet, the Crows had historically been friends of the white man. Their first friendship treaty was signed with the fledgling government of the United States in 1825. In 1851, the U.S. government acknowledged Crow ownership of 38 million acres, but reduced it to 8 million in 1868.

Today the Crows possess just 2.5 million acres, mainly in Big Horn County, and the reservation is still twice the size of Rhode Island. Most of the five thousand enrolled members of the tribe live on the reservation. The Crows have a constitution and govern themselves, yet are U.S. citizens.

Every August, the Crow Indians celebrate with a weekend powwow that reaffirms their identity as a people. For three days, Crow Agency becomes one of the larger towns in Montana, six thousand people and hundreds of white tepees rising above the cottonwoods. From kids chasing each other on bicycles to old squaws preparing the evening meal, nearly everyone was Indian and spoke Absaroka (Crow). Weaving between tepees and trucks, I stopped my Jeep and waved down a pair of young men carrying a red and white ice chest filled with sodas. "Where's Bill Yellowtail's tent at?" I'd been picking up Montana's grammar.

"Just past that old burned tree."

I had never met Bill Yellowtail, but I'd heard about him from a mutual friend. A graduate of Dartmouth College and currently a rancher near Pryor, he was a naturalist, an expert fishing guide, an outspoken environmentalist, and a state senator in Helena. Yellowtail was the pride of the Crow people.

I approached a tepee with an adjacent dining area covered by a large tarpaulin. An old Indian—in his nineties—was sitting at a long table drinking a glass of lemonade. His face was beautifully lined, marked with kindness, wisdom, and a sense of humor. I introduced myself and asked his name. "I'm Tom Yellowtail, Bill's grandfather," he said softly. "Why don't you sit down?"

Tom Yellowtail, whose father was called Hawk with the Yellow Tailfeathers, had a reputation as a medicine man who knew the old ways. In 1971, a Shoshone medicine man named Rainbow endowed Tom with the powers to conduct the sun dance. In the original ritual, young men would pierce their chests and cheeks, and attach their flesh to rawhide ropes suspended from a central pole. They would hang for hours, even days, chanting, dancing, and seeing visions, until the ropes tore from their flesh and they fell to the ground. "The sun dance ceremonies were banned on the reservations in the 1890s," said Tom. "The white man said it was because of the torturing and piercing, but it was really to stamp out our religion. There weren't any dances for a long time at Crow, not until 1941."

No flesh was pierced in the modern sun dance, and it has been transformed from a preparation for war into a healing ceremony. Dancers formed a circle around a buffalo head suspended on a central pole. The men danced up to the pole and back almost continually for three days without food or water; many fell unconscious and had visions. "When that happens, we say that the buffalo spirit has hooked him with his horns and is giving him a reward," said Tom. The outward warrior had become the inner warrior.

In other healing rites, Tom Yellowtail passed eagle fathers over the dancers and prayed to Acbadadea—the Maker of All Things—and to the Medicine Fathers, spiritual beings that inhabited a world between the earth and the world of Acbadadea. "The prophecies say that when enough people have forgotten to follow the way to their maker, then the world will end."

A large man, maybe six foot three or four, in blue jeans, a work shirt, and cowboy boots, came around the side of the tepee. Bill Yellowtail was paler than I thought he'd be, but then his mother was a white woman. At forty-one, his hair was salt-and-pepper gray. Behind wire-rim glasses his eyes were alert and his smile broad. "Welcome to Crow Fair," he said. "How about some lemonade?" Bill Yellowtail had a down-home way of speaking and used phrases like *By golly, Holy smokes,* and *Darned tootin'.*

We sat and the family gathered: Bill's second wife, Maggie Carlson, who is white; Bill's teenage daughter from a first marriage to an Indian woman; and a cousin, Leslie, who was as redheaded and freckled as a Scot but completely Indian in identity and dressed in beautiful beaded buckskins.

Everyone deferred to the patriarch, Tom Yellowtail. He was a good storyteller, recounting how he'd roped a deer from his horse, how he'd shot thirty-three ducks with only three shells, and how once he'd caught a pheasant with his fishing pole. "It was in June, and my nephew and I had gone fishing at a lake when a big storm came up. We headed back without one fish. We were walking home in deep grass by the river when a pheasant flew up. We didn't have a gun, but I threw the fishing pole up to my shoulder and said 'Bang!' At the same time, that big pheasant flew into some overhead electrical wires and broke his neck. He fell just as if I'd shot him, dropping right on the path. I turned to my nephew and said, 'Pick it up. You will have the bird that I caught for you.' When we got home, the women were surprised, because they had their skillets ready to fry fish."

When someone mentioned muskrat as food, Tom said, "It tastes a bit like porcupine or beaver. They all eat tree bark." Someone else asked if there were old stories about berries. Laughing mysteriously, he said, "There may well be. There may well be." Tom's late wife, Susie, was the first Indian to become a registered nurse. She also chaperoned several of the Miss Indian America contest winners, rode a horse in Nixon's inaugural parade in Washington, and was one of the few women elected to Montana's hall of fame.

The name Yellowtail has been famous on the Crow reservation since the turn of the century when Tom's older brother, Robert Yellowtail, emerged as a powerful leader. Robert fought a seven-year battle to save the reservation from homesteaders in 1917. A self-taught lawyer, he served as interpreter and attorney for the great Chief Plenty Coups, who spoke no English. In 1934, Robert became the first Native American superintendent of his own reservation for the Bureau of Indian Affairs. After World War II, he fought a ten-year battle with the government to keep it from building the dam on the Bighorn River. Eventually, however, it was built and named for him. He also sued the Bureau of Indian Affairs to win control over valuable coal resources on the reservation—and won.

One of Robert Yellowtail's first acts as superintendent was to revive the Crow Fair. Previous agents had replaced the traditional festivities with a white-bread version of a fall harvest fair. Yellowtail brought back the dancing, feasting, horse racing, and gambling. He also engineered the renaissance of a buffalo herd on the reservation. With his remarkable wife, Dorothy, he took part in his last Crow Fair parade in 1987 at the age of one hundred, and died shortly afterward.

As the sun set, Indian drums started and the Yellowtail clan left their tepee to join the dancing. Crow Fair swirled with dust stirred up by cars and horses. A central arena for the dancers was surrounded by stands selling hot dogs and burgers. The ground was strewn with paper plates and soft-drink cups, and the portable toilets had become unmentionable nightmares. There were only a few white tourists, clutching their Nikons. I stepped into a tent to buy an Indian specialty, a greasy food called *fry bread*.

As I ate, I noticed a swishy Indian man wearing mascara and posing self-consciously near one of the food stands. Warriors of the Plains Indian tribes were the ultimate in machismo, but a century ago, an honored member of the Crow tribe would have been a drag queen called a *boté* or *badé*. The Crow word describes a man who dresses in women's clothing, specializes in women's work, and forms emotional and sexual relations with other men. The early French explorers and traders called them *berdaches*—a word derived from the Arabic *bardaj*, or male concubine.

Anthropologists have documented berdaches in over 130 tribes across America, but they held special status among the Crows. Boys who at an early age showed a preference for women's clothing and work habits were allowed to make a choice at age twelve or thirteen. They became expert in sewing and beadwork, in butchering and tanning hides, and most importantly in tepee making. They were also integral players in religious ceremonies. In preparing for the sun dance ceremony, a berdache would be sent to cut down a tree to make the central pole of the sun dance lodge and say, "May all our enemies be like me."

When reservation Indians were subjected to the white man's morality, the berdache tradition was squelched. As one nineteenth-century government doctor observed: "Of all the many varieties of sexual perversion this, it seems to me, is the most debased that could be conceived of."

More sympathetic was Major General Hugh L. Scott, who, as a young cavalry officer, saw berdaches among the Crows camped at the Bighorn in 1877. Some forty years later, Scott returned to review the reservation for the Board of Indian Commissioners, and he took time out to visit the last of the true Crow berdaches, *Miakate,* or Finds-Them-and-Kills-Them, also known as Woman Jim.

Scott went to a cabin near the Bighorn River and found Woman Jim sitting outside, recovering from a case of blood poisoning. "She had a woman's calico dress on and her hair dressed woman fashion," wrote Scott, who estimated "her" age as sixty-five. Scott asked the berdache why he wore woman's clothes.

"That is my road," replied Woman Jim. "Since birth."

Had anyone coerced him into becoming one? "No! Didn't I tell you—that is my road?" answered the berdache forcefully. "I have done it ever since I can remember because I wanted to do it. My Father and Mother did not like it. They used to whip me, take away my girl's clothes and put boy's clothes on me but I threw them away—and got girl's clothes and dolls to play with."

Scott described Woman Jim as "most jolly" and having "a simple air of complete satisfaction with herself, perfectly unconscious of anything abnormal." Born in 1854, Woman Jim was the leader of the *boté* clan. In 1889, a government doctor had described the thirty-three-year old berdache as a "splendidly formed fellow of prepossessing face, in perfect health, active in movement and happy in disposition." He was five feet eight inches tall and weighed 158 pounds, and his genitalia were "in position and shape altogether normal."

Woman Jim enjoyed prestige among the Crows for his tent-making ability, but also due to an incident in his early youth. In 1876, the berdache became a Crow warrior for the day, joining General George Crook at the Battle of the Rosebud, which occurred just eight days before Custer's more famous demise. Woman Jim and approximately 175 Crow warriors volunteered because of the dangerous proximity of their traditional enemies, the Sioux and Cheyenne, at the Little Bighorn. On the morning of June 17, 1876, Crook's thousand men were attacked by Sioux and Cheyenne forces. The Crows, with Woman Jim at the forefront, played a major role in the defense of the soldiers. One soldier said, "If it had not been for the Crows, the Sioux would have killed half our command before the soldiers were in position to attack."

The story of that battle comes to us from an old Crow woman, Pretty Shield, who spoke with author Frank Linderman (*Red Mother*) fifty years after the battle. "Ahh, they [the men] do not like to tell of it," she chuckled. "But I will tell you about it. We Crows all know about it. I shall not be stealing anything from the men by telling the truth. Yes, a Crow woman fought with Three-Stars on the Rosebud, *two* of them did, for that matter; but one of them was neither a man nor a woman. She looked like a man, and yet she wore woman's clothing; and she had a heart of a woman. Besides, she did a woman's work. Her name was Finds-Them-and-Kills-Them. The other woman was a *wild* one who had no man of her own. She was both bad and brave, this one. Her name was The-Other-Magpie; and she was pretty."

According to Pretty Shield, both the berdache and the "wild" woman brought glory to the Crows. The-Other-Magpie rode her horse, singing her war song, and waving her coup stick at a fallen Lakota warrior. Just as The-Other-Magpie struck the Lakota with her coup stick, Woman Jim killed him with a rifle shot. The-Other-Magpie took the dead man's scalp and waved it proudly when she returned to the village. Pretty Shield remembered: "Yes, and I saw her cut this scalp into many pieces, so that the men might have more scalps to dance with. . . . The men do not like to tell this, but I have."

As the Crow tribe submitted to the white man's teachings on the reservations, the tradition of the berdache faded. In 1926, Woman Jim, a.k.a. Finds-Them-and-Kills-Them, who once was famed for sewing buffalo hides into tepees, won a ribbon at the Yellowstone County Fair for his bedspreads. He also received first prize for his collection of wild roots, berries, and meats prepared in the traditional Crow manner. Three winters later Woman Jim died, last of the real berdaches.

Leading the midmorning parade at Crow Fair were uniformed veterans from World War II, Korea, and Vietnam who carried the flags of Crow Nation, the state of Montana, and the United States. Bill Yellowtail, dressed in a cowboy hat and jeans, followed on horseback. Trucks and wagons ferried old women, young princesses, and children outfitted in buckskins so brilliant with beaded geometry they could have inspired Kandinsky. Men dressed in ceremonial headdresses and breechclouts, with faces and chests painted, rode spirited ponies. As the artist George Catlin wrote a century and a half ago, "No part of the human race could present a more picturesque and thrilling appearance on horseback than a party of Crows rigged out in all their plumes and trappings—galloping about and yelping in what they call a war parade." While the parade lacked yelping, for a moment I forgot that these Indians were from the Pepsi generation.

That afternoon I drove over to the fairgrounds for the All-Indian Rodeo. Indians were among the most enthusiastic rodeo performers in Montana. I watched a young Indian flip off a bareback bronc, get kicked in the head, and fall limp in the dirt. Medics managed to revive him, but he was taken away in an ambulance. It reminded me of my decision to back out of the rodeo a few weeks before, and I felt lucky.

On the way back to Crow Fair, I stopped to buy a newspaper at Garry-owen, a town named for an old Irish tune that was the regimental marching song of the Seventh U.S. Cavalry under General Custer. The Battle of the Little Bighorn brought Custer face to face with ten thousand hostile Sioux and Cheyenne gathered under the medicine man Sitting Bull and Chiefs Two Moon, Gall, and Crazy Horse. Two Moon said the battle lasted "as long as it takes a hungry man to eat a meal." The Indian women grotesquely mutilated all the soldiers' corpses, except Custer's. It is said that two Cheyenne women punctured his eardrums with a sewing awl so that he would be able to hear better in the next life.

In his day, Custer had been a Civil War hero—the youngest general in the Union Army. His adventures on the plains inspired dime-store novels, and he often traveled with newspaper correspondents. He thought a triumph over the Indians might become a springboard to the presidency itself. "Custer Died for Our Sins" and "Custer Had It Coming" are slogans that appear on T-shirts worn by both Indians and whites who tour the Custer Battlefield National Monument. Today's revisionists have turned one man into a scapegoat for a nation's errors and ignored the history that led up to the battle. Only a fool would see the Custer massacre as a triumph for the Indians, who outnumbered Custer's troops twenty to one. The massacre merely intensified the public's hate and misunderstanding of the Indian.

At the time of my trip there was a bill before the U.S. Senate (H.R. 848) to change the name of the Custer Battlefield to the Little Bighorn Battlefield and to supply a monument to the Indian dead (at a cost of between $2 million and $7 million), although only about fifty warriors were killed in this battle. Until his recent death in 1991, George A. Custer IV, a grandson and a retired soldier himself, fought against changing the battlefield's name, but endorsed creating a monument to the Indian dead. In an open letter to the Montana Historical Society, he pointed out that the true culprits of the day were the nineteenth-century politicians who concocted Indian policy—not the imprudent general who carried it out. He accused the modern Congress of "feel good" politics, and urged politicians to use the money in another way—to improve the plight of Indians across the country with more realistic aid like education and jobs. "Honor the Indian with meaningful change," he wrote. "Honor the General by keeping his name."

Custer may not have been the Indian hater he's made out to be. In *My Life on the Plains,* Custer wrote: "If I were an Indian, I often think that I would greatly prefer to cast my lot among those of my people who adhered to the free open plains, rather than submit to the confined limits of a reservation, there to be the recipient of the blessed benefits of civilization, with its vices thrown in without stint or measure."

That evening I wandered over to the tent of Pius Real Bird. The Real Birds were a big clan on the Crow reservation, and controversial. A summer earlier, Crow tribal chairman Richard Real Bird had suspended his brother, Kennard Real Bird, after he punched out a Billings attorney in a cafeteria at lunchtime, giving him two black eyes. Bigger problems had come this summer: twenty-six leaders of the Crow Nation appeared before a U.S. magistrate in Billings. A federal grand jury had charged individuals and the Crow Tribal Housing Authority with conspiracy, bribery, embezzlement of tribal funds, extortion, fraud, and lying. Several defendants, including Richard Real Bird, were represented by the grandstanding San Francisco attorney Melvin Belli.

Pius Real Bird invited me to join thirty of his friends and family at a buffalo roast. At the long table, I sat next to a member of the Wannabe tribe. A Wannabe is a white man who wants to be an Indian. This one was tall and wore a black Indian-style hat above a mustache and long brown hair woven into braids. His name was Karl, and he had just come over from Germany to buy Crow land. "What's your line of business?" I asked.

"I help people," he replied in a smug way.

Answers like that don't inspire confidence. Nevertheless, after dinner we walked over to the arena together to watch the dancing. We sat on the upper bench of the six-tier bleachers. A couple of fat Crow women squeezed in and we made room. Then their even larger friend wanted a place. Karl, who had his back comfortably planted against a pillar, begrudged them a scant three inches on the bench. Karl turned to me. "*Ach!* Dey are only doing dis because ve are vite. You must be strong."

Then a fourth fat Indian friend appeared. It was going to be impossible on the bench. "Dat's dat," said Karl. "Now I don't move no more." He had established his Siegfried Line. His obstinacy worked. The fat friend had to push her way over to the other side.

The Indian dancers came out, first in competitive dances, then in intertribal free-for-alls. There were Pawnee and Sioux, Cheyenne and Blackfeet.

They swirled and hopped in feathered costumes and buckskins. Some were dressed traditionally; others wore bright silks and even fluorescent feathers in fuchsia, chartreuse, and Martian green.

"Hey-yah, hey-yah, hey-hey-yah. . . ." The singing and drumbeat took on a monotonous aspect, because the only instrument was the drum and the songs barely had a melody.

"What do you suppose they're saying?" I asked.

"Oh, de usual," Karl replied laconically. "'May de Great Spirit protect our families and tribe and bless our tomahawks as ve split de skulls of our enemies.' Dat sort of thing." After an hour I'd seen enough and left Karl, the Wannabe Indian, still trying to establish territorial rights with the fat Crow women. I returned to my tent and fell asleep to music that would have terrified a Montana settler a century ago.

In the morning, we all gathered for breakfast at the Yellowtail clan's tent. Bill Yellowtail's red-haired cousin, Leslie, arrived at breakfast with news of Karl. "The Wannabe left, and good riddance!" she announced, reaching for pancakes and bacon. Karl, it seemed, had been to the Crow reservation several times before and had been currying favor with Tom Yellowtail. Karl considered himself something of a mystic healer and was involved with a group of Germans who were fascinated by American Indians. (German children still read the Indian stories of Karl May, a turn-of-the-century German author who wrote book after book on Indians without ever visiting America.) Karl had even paid for Tom Yellowtail to fly to Germany that summer and tour Europe, giving talks.

"That trip turned into a nightmare for my grandfather," said Leslie. "Karl treated him real badly. He's an old man—he's eighty-seven—and has to take these pills at regular intervals with his meals. Well, Karl wouldn't let him eat. 'You eat when I eat,' he said. Or he'd make my grandfather fast. He even pocketed the money he earned at speaking engagements."

Karl had asked Tom Yellowtail to sell him Crow land to start a spiritual healing center. Plus he wanted Tom to adopt him into the tribe and to give him his medicine. When Tom refused, Karl became furious. "'I brought you all de way over here. You owe me something for dis trip, old man,'" said Leslie, mimicking the German's accent. The old man arrived back at the reservation tired and haggard. "That really pissed us off, to see him so down."

Moments after I had left Karl at the dancing last night, Leslie and her brothers tracked him down. One brother gave Karl's braids a jerk and said, "Listen, you Wannabe. Lay off our grandfather or you'll get what's coming to you." Then he grabbed Karl's hat brim and yanked it down over his eyes. They left him sputtering in German.

"What's Karl doing now?"

Leslie sighed, munching on a strip of bacon. "Oh, somebody saw him hitchhiking with his suitcase on the road to Billings. I guess it's back to Frankfurt for that Wannabe."

Though Crow Fair would go on for another day, Bill Yellowtail and his wife had to leave. After breakfast he asked if I'd help him take down his tepee. First, Bill removed the holding pins from above the doorway. We rolled back the canvas, leaving the twenty-five-foot poles standing naked. It was like a game of pick-up sticks: we removed them in sequence until Bill gracefully brought down the main tent pole.

When the truck was loaded, Bill said, "By golly, there's a yellow-sulfur-dun hatch coming off the Bighorn. And Bill Bryan's meeting me down at Fort Smith tomorrow. What do you say we wet a line?"

Bill Yellowtail deftly maneuvered the Mckenzie boat down the Bighorn River, and I looked over the gunwale just as the shadow of a big trout darted through strands of wafting aquatic grass.

Casting from the stern was our mutual friend Bill Bryan. Built like a full-back, with graying hair and fierce blue eyes, Bill had the hoarse voice of a cigar-smoking back-room lobbyist. An environmental activist and political consultant, Bill and his wife, Pam, owned a travel agency called Off the Beaten Path, which specialized in the Rocky Mountains.

The Bighorn River is one of the greatest trout streams in the West, and one of the most unusual. Thirty years ago, the river was a slow, warm-water river filled with nothing but suckers and carp. But when the Yellowtail Dam was built high up in the Bighorn Mountains, it created a lake that stacked the water three hundred feet deep. The outflow, taken from the bottom of the lake, issued water cold enough to change the whole aquatic ecosystem of the Bighorn. Warm-water fish departed, while the brown and rainbow trout in the stream grew enormous.

As with any situation involving water, there were political problems. The U.S. Forest Service saw the value of this piscatorial jewel and wanted it open to the public. The Crows, always eager to gain new revenue and control the destiny of their reservation, claimed that the government had no business on the Bighorn. Why shouldn't the Crows regulate it? The issue was debated in courts for years, and the current situation was still not satisfactory to either party.

"Holy smokes, Bryan, have you got Moby Dick on your line?" said Bill Yellowtail. I looked back to see Bryan's rod bowed in a throbbing arc; twenty yards away a two-foot-long rainbow leapt twice out of the water. There were so many rises all around the boat that I couldn't put the fly over a specific fish. I heard Bill Yellowtail coaxing Bryan's fish to his net. When I looked back, he was releasing a three-pound brown trout. "Heck of a monster, ain't it?"

When my own fly disappeared in a whirlpool, I lifted my rod tip and felt the pulse of a fish, while the reel screeched. The fish gave a tremendous jerk, and I'd lost it and my fly. Bryan caught another fish, but I missed two more good strikes. Up ahead another party of fishermen was working the east bank, so we pulled to the other shore, tied the boat, and went on foot. Slipping along the muddy bank, I spooked a grouse that rose with a motorlike buzz.

I cast over rising fish, but I couldn't get them to take the fly. There was too much natural food on the water. Then a good fish rose and slurped my fly, and a few minutes later I held a twenty-incher gasping in my hands. I released him.

Bill Yellowtail made fishing seem easy. Every time I looked over, he was playing a new fish. As darkness fell, I walked up closer to him. "Any tips, Bill?"

"Why not try up ahead?" he suggested. "Sure might do some good casting just below that big ol' bush on the right." I cast and cast as the sky filled with night. I was casting blind into the dark, drifting mirror of the river. "Looks like you're fishing by Braille," said Bill Yellowtail.

I sensed the strike more by sound than sight. I lifted my rod tip firmly and set the hook in a big fish. It turned left, then right, swinging its weight into a long parabolic curve that gained momentum. The fish broke water in an angry thrash and set off across the river in a reel-screeching run. This was a fish I didn't want to lose.

"Holy smokes," Yellowtail exclaimed. "Sounds like you've got Leviathan on the line! Don't rush him."

I didn't rush the battle. I didn't want it ever to end. There were stars in the sky and the air was cooling with the night and I had the biggest fish of the summer on the end of my line. My heart was pumping so richly it felt as if Bordeaux gushed through my ventricles. The wholeness of the trip and the season and my own self-worth were tied up in this big fish's fight in a way that would have tickled a Jungian psychoanalyst. I *needed* this fish.

Bill Yellowtail was standing next to me now, chuckling with pleasure as the trout came to bay. When it rolled with exhaustion, Bill netted it easily.

He held the fish gently in his hands to show it to me. "Now, there's a beauty, by golly," he said. "And caught in almost complete darkness." Bill hefted the rainbow. "He'll go five, maybe five and a half pounds."

It was the biggest trout of my life. Bill removed the fly and held the rainbow in the current. When it was strong enough to swim away on its own, Bill straightened up with a sigh. We stood for a moment, taking in the night sounds and the stars in the deep blue sky.

"Makes you kind of thankful, doesn't it?" said Bill. "I could do this every day of the week."

The next morning in Hardin I left my Jeep in the motel lot and Bill Bryan took me to Lame Deer on the Northern Cheyenne reservation. In addition to his travel agency, Bill Bryan operated Silvertip Consulting, a firm that specialized in political action and environmental concerns. The Northern Cheyenne were the only Indians in the Rockies who didn't have their own public high school on the reservation itself. The 350 high school students were bused twenty-two miles away to Colstrip, one of the wealthiest school districts in the state, thanks to coal mining and energy production. Although the rich Colstrip high school has a swimming pool and other top-notch facilities, the Cheyenne kids were a minority and felt unsettled, apart. They wanted their own school. "The Cheyenne have rich coal reserves themselves, but accepted low royalty leases with various companies," said Bill. "One of the things I've done for them is get those leases voided. There's no mining on the reservation right now. Gain control of your resources and you control your future."

Bill met for an hour with tribal members about creating a new school district, then enlisted me for another kind of mission.

"I'm trying to find Susie Tall Wolf," said Bill in his hoarse voice. "She's a Cheyenne married to a friend of mine in Bozeman who's going through a hard time right now. He broke his leg farming. Susie left him a week ago and is hiding out. If we're lucky, we'll find her at her sister's. If not lucky, we'll find her in a bar."

Many Indians who live off the reservation get a homing instinct, and this wasn't the first time Susie had gone into hiding on tribal land. "She's an alcoholic, and when she runs out of cash, she'll prostitute herself to make some money for booze," said Bill. "Eventually her husband retrieves her, straightens her out, and they're happy for a while. Then she runs off, repeating the pattern."

The inability of many Indians to function off their reservations reminded me how dramatically different the culture of Indians and whites had been a century ago. Today their worlds are closer, but not necessarily better.

Bill and I drove to her sister Agnes's place in Ashland. Agnes was a fat-bellied, thin-legged woman who obviously enjoyed a drink now and then.

"Where's Susie?" asked Bill.

"She's down at the Buffet Bar," said Agnes in a friendly way. "I'll give her a call and tell her you're here."

We loaded Susie's packed suitcase into the trunk of the car. When we drove over to the Buffet Bar five minutes later, Susie Tall Wolf was gone. The bartender said, "She left two minutes ago—right after a phone call."

"Damn. Agnes and her phone call. I *knew* that was a bad idea," said Bill, gritting his teeth. We drove up Main Street and looked in at the grocery store and coffee shop. No Susie. We drove back to Agnes's house, and circled back.

"She's probably hiding someplace and watching us right now," said Bill. "Let's grab a bite and smoke her out."

We ate a sandwich, then looked at the church and school. The chapel was cast concrete in the shape of a giant tepee, some fifty feet high. To me, it was not successful architecture, but perhaps it worked for the Indian worshipers.

When we drove back to the Buffet Bar we found Susie Tall Wolf sitting on a bar stool. She was in her thirties, with long black hair and a slim figure, but her closed, blank face was without prettiness. Bill sidled up casually. "So where you been, Susie?"

She barely turned to look at him and pushed back a strand of her long black hair. "Oh, just around, visiting some friends."

"Good. Are you ready to go now?" he asked gently.

Susie took a slow drag on her cigarette and flicked off the ash. She exhaled and spoke softly. "I'm not going."

"Why not?" asked Bill.

"I can't. I'm drunk."

"You don't look that drunk to me."

"Don't want to go. I'll be sick in the car."

"You can sleep in the car."

"Just not going."

"Aw, c'mon, Susie."

She shook her head, avoiding his eyes. Bill smiled grimly. "Okay, if that's the way you want it." As we left the bar, I looked back and saw a bearded white man in a cap and cut-off sweatshirt put his arm around her.

Montana's 1989 Centennial Cattle Drive.

Chapter 22

The Great Montana Cattle Drive: The Cowboy's Woodstock

This is the last cowboy song
The end of a hundred year waltz
The voices sound sad as they're singing along
Another piece of America is lost.

      Ed Bruce, "The Last Cowboy Song," 1988

Just after dawn, I crawled out of my canvas tent to witness a scene that uncannily resembled Charlie Russell's painting *Bronc to Breakfast*. Among the circled wagons a wild-eyed gray gelding crow-hopped around tents and over sleeping bags, narrowly missed a pan of bacon sizzling over a campfire, then dumped his rider in a heap near a team of jumpy Percherons. Next to me, Mike Cowan, a cowboy out of Big Timber, laughed heartily. "Hell, I haven't had so much fun since the hogs ate my baby brother!" The great Montana Centennial Cattle Drive had begun.

For six dusty days and one cold, rainy night in early September, Montana celebrated its statehood centennial with a giant cattle drive that was flirting with legend even before it hit the road. Two years before, the cartoonist Stan Lynde, fellow cartoonist Barry McWilliams, and Billings rancher Jim Wempner were talking over the hood of a dented pickup when an idea struck: Why not stage the largest cattle drive in recent history? The original plan, which called for ten thousand cattle and up to five thousand riders, was so preposterous that it wouldn't go away. When the three cofounders turned the idea over to the nonprofit Latigo Corporation to handle legal and financial details, it degenerated into doomsaying, political infighting, and talk of cancellation. As recently as two weeks before the drive, the Latigo Corporation was short of major corporate support, the city of Billings still didn't know the exact route, and the Humane Society went to court claiming that it was cruel to drive cattle ten miles a day.

By Labor Day, however, a smaller drive of 2,812 head of cattle (many of them longhorns), 208 wagons, and over 2,400 horsemen had rolled into the town of Roundup ready to ride sixty miles south to the Billings stockyards. I arrived at the encampment on Sunday with a horse named Step Easy from the Van Cleve ranch in Big Timber (the guest ranch I'd always visited with my family). For two days, over fifteen thousand visitors made Roundup into one of Montana's larger communities.

In the fields and stockyards east of town, horse trailers with license plates from all over the West disgorged thousands of spotted Appaloosas, strawberry roans, and white-socked sorrels; big-footed Clydesdales were hitched to authentic Conestoga wagons; buckaroos in woollies rode herd on thousands of longhorn cattle. Hundreds of tents—mostly heavy white canvas, for authenticity—dotted the fields. The centerpiece was a two-hundred-foot-long, red and white striped beer tent provided by Anheuser-Busch.

Though the cattle drive had done virtually no national advertising, the saddle-leather grapevine drew greenhorns from as far away as New York, Canada, Sweden, and Switzerland. In spite of these pilgrims, the majority of the participants were real horse people, old-time ranchers marked by a patina of hard winters and hot summers. We all filed through green canvas tents to be processed like military recruits: computer-printed registration cards, hospital-style plastic ID wristbands, ID numbers for our horses, feed cards for our horses, meal cards for ourselves, legal releases, vet inspections of horses and cattle. Clint Eastwood never had to do this on *Rawhide,* nor did John Conrad in the great days of the open-range roundups. Yet in sheer numbers of horses and cattle, the Centennial Cattle Drive could equal those far-off days.

After feeding and watering my horse, I spent the evening in the giant beer tent listening to the music of Billy Waldo and the Flying Grizzlies, then fell asleep in my old-fashioned pyramid-shaped canvas tent.

At dawn, we struck camp and I walked a half mile to the corrals to find my horse. The cacophony of rattling wagons and rearing horses hit Step Easy like Methedrine. His panicked eyes roamed the swirling panorama of strange horseflesh, desperately searching for a familiar muzzle or rump. Between prancing fits, I saddled and mounted him. He had just finished a series of petulant bucks when I heard a familiar voice: "What kind of drugs you feeding your nag?"

It was Scott McMillion, over from Livingston to cover the drive for the *Bozeman Daily Chronicle*. Scott was six feet four inches, and his horse, really a pony meant for a kid, was too small. His legs hung down on either side like training wheels on a bicycle. Scott wasn't even wearing cowboy boots, and his hat would have looked better on Mickey Spillane. If he hadn't been press, some cattle-drive official who was a stickler for authenticity might have busted him on dress code.

"Where'd you get that donkey?" I asked.

"It's a horse, and I rented it," said Scott.

"What's his name?"

"Two-Ninety."

"Two-Ninety? That's not a horse's name."

"Asked the outfitter and he couldn't remember it. So I call him by his registration number. Horse wouldn't know the difference anyway."

With a shout from the wagon boss, the wagons rolled out at 11 A.M. Parading through the cheering crowd in Roundup, Step Easy was bug-eyed, lathered, and prancing. Scott rode up beside me on Two-Ninety, and said laconically, "I think your horse is going to blow a fuse." He dropped back in the crowd just as Step Easy bent his neck in a bow and began a dance medley on the asphalt. My arms were already sore from reining him back, and I began to dread a week on this horse.

We rode ten miles toward low dry hills called the Bull Mountains. The wagon train stretched four miles long. Step Easy slowed to an agitated but steady trot. I ate lunch as I rode, chewing my ham sandwich to the rhythm of his hooves. In midafternoon we were "attacked" by seven Indians in full war paint and regalia, which didn't do much for Step Easy's serenity. Peace signs were exchanged with the warriors, and they joined the wagon train for several miles. Gwen Petersen, a sixty-year-old humorist-poet from Big Timber, said, "I offered myself as a hostage but they turned me down." Only a handful of Indian ranchers were participating in the cattle drive itself; most local Indians hadn't forgotten that cowboys and cattle brought the red man's doom.

It was four o'clock when we turned into a dusty valley and circled the wagons. Fifty huge water troughs awaited our thirsty horses, and they were empty in minutes. The water tub Step Easy chose held rusty-looking pond water garnished with algae, water skeeters, and even one small frightened minnow, but he slurped eagerly. We tied up to hitching racks made of steel cable stretched at the lower end of the valley. I was thirsty and tired, but a cowboy always takes care of his horse first. I unsaddled Step Easy, whipped out my feed card, and got him fifteen pounds of hay and five pounds of "cake"—shotgun-shell-sized green pellets made of grain. Step Easy was so undone by the day's ordeal that he seemed despondent as he nibbled. He was a long way from the Van Cleves' Lazy K Bar Ranch, and I felt sorry for him.

The wagons formed ten large circles and the tents went up. I was associated with the Big Timber cowboys in the Pink Circle—a color that got a few laughs from sissy bashers. Being a light sleeper, I camped away from the wagons in the pine trees. "I guess you ain't afraid of the rattlers," chuckled one old cowhand. "Lost this finger to one when I was working out Glendive way in '51. Heh-heh." He held up a gnarled hand missing a pinkie finger. You never can tell with a story like that; more likely a whiskey-laced afternoon in the garage with a Skilsaw.

Two food services provided the above-average trail food—heavy on the beef, naturally. My feed card said: "Hand this ticket in for punching when collecting your grub. If you lose this ticket you starve." The harsh code of the West.

As dusk came, campfires were lit, and guitars and accordions came out of the wagons. I fell asleep to the strains of "Red River Valley" and awakened at dawn to mules braying. Breakfast was melon, scrambled eggs, bacon, and gravy over biscuits. A row of Port-a-Potties took care of bladder and bowel.

By ten we were saddled, hitched, and on the trail again. We wound our way through the Bull Mountains, a low scrubby range on the southern end of Musselshell County. It was a hot, dusty ride, and we reached camp just as the sky turned a resentful gray. As we unsaddled, the wind blew tumbleweeds and loose hats across the fields, spooking the horses. A Port-a-Pottie blew over with a man inside; he rolled out festooned in wet toilet paper, shouting, "What's so funny?"

That evening in the big Anheuser-Busch tent a preacher married a couple from Eureka, Montana, and the beer flowed on into the night. I met people from all over the world. There was a Swiss named Hans who could barely speak English. There was Ingemar from Sweden. The only black cowboy on the drive, Paras Reddy, was a handsome fellow with a neatly trimmed mustache and a big gray Stetson. He was not an African-American, but a dark Hindu, a Chicago banker who'd been born in Madras, India. While we were talking, a tall, rough-looking cowboy with a beer-moistened mustache came up to Paras. He looked like he'd had a few, and he didn't look friendly.

"You know," he said, "you just cost me a hundred bucks."

"How did I do that?" answered Paras politely.

"'Cause I just bet a guy that there wouldn't be any blacks on this cattle drive." His stern face suddenly broke into a grin. "I lost—so let me buy you a beer." That's Montana cowboy logic for you.

The cattle drive was really three separate entities: the main cattle herd of three thousand; followed by a hundred longhorns owned by cattle breeder Jim Leachman; and finally the social herd—that is, the thousands of riders and wagons bringing up the rear. I'd barely glimpsed the big cattle herd, so on the third morning I buttonholed Jim Wempner, one of the drive's cofounders. In his early sixties, Jim had grown a full white beard for the drive. "We'll look at Leachman's longhorns first," he said. "Then cut cross-country and follow the main herd."

We were joined by cartoonist Stan Lynde, another cofounder. Lynde was a dapper dresser, wearing a custom-made twenty-beaver hat, a silk scarf around his neck, and a long linen duster. Born in Montana and raised on a sheep ranch on the Crow Indian Reservation, he created the syndicated cartoon strip "Rick O'Shay." Looking over the wagons, Stan prophesied, "People who missed this drive will be kicking themselves years from now. It's the cowboys' Woodstock."

A fast trot over a ridge and the noise of the wagons faded. We loped across open grassland that ran for miles, turning our horses toward a plume of dust in the distance. A half hour later we came across Jim Leachman trailing his herd of longhorns. Some of the bigger cows had horns that spanned five feet from tip to tip. These were the descendants of the original breed driven up from Texas in the 1860s. Hardy enough to stand the heat and cold, the longhorns were also fierce enough to run off marauding wolves and coyotes with their horns.

Clean-shaven, with graying hair and steel gray eyes, Jim Leachman wore a flat-brimmed hat, long brown overcoat, and knee-high boots, looking every inch a cattle baron. Leachman wasn't really in the meat business. He's a breeder of fine bulls, and his family have been among the most influential Angus breeders in the country for almost thirty years. Last year, in one sale, he auctioned off a thousand bulls to breeders. He keeps longhorns only for pleasure.

One of Leachman's drovers was a young, blond-bearded rancher named Mike Story. In 1866, Mike's great-great-grandfather Nelson Story became the first man to drive longhorn cattle from Texas to Montana, a journey of two thousand miles. Story was attacked by Indians, his cattle were stampeded by rustlers, and his men were shot at by outlaws and jayhawkers, but he knew that if he could just make it to Virginia City there were ten thousand hungry miners waiting for him. Indians killed two of his men and wounded several others, but he forged on. Mike Story is humbly proud of his ancestor. "This drive's a bit easier," he said with a smile, "don't you think?"

We caught up with the main cattle herd an hour later. The longhorns, shorthorns, Angus, and Herefords were strung out in a river of hoof-driven dust almost three miles long. A hundred drovers, hand picked from each of Montana's fifty counties, kept them plodding southward at an easy pace. As they bawled and wagged their horns, Wempner murmured, "Isn't that a beautiful sight?"

That evening, during the festivities under the great tent, the press and about a hundred special guests gathered at the Charter ranch. A whole beef was roasted underground, and our plates were heaped with homemade muffins and five different kinds of beans. It was more than just a friendly get-together over good chow. Steve and Jeanne Charter were promoting the Northern Plains Defense Council, an organization committed to balancing environmentalism and farming. The group started in the seventies to stand up to the coal interests who were strip-mining the rangelands.

As Steve pointed out, the small family ranch was in dire straits. "In 1975 a rancher would have to sell fifteen calves to buy a pickup truck. Today it costs him forty-five calves to buy the same truck." Small ranchers also face competition from agribusinesses, which are building up a monopoly on supplies, grain, and beef processing. In a populist speech, Steve implored us to recognize the dead end this kind of approach spells for the West. "In recent times family-based ranching has restored the grasses of the rangeland. It's also improved the quality of the beef. When the decisions on running this rangeland are taken out of the family kitchen and made exclusively in the boardrooms of big corporations, we're all in trouble." The applause, of course, was enthusiastic.

Riding on the drive were about sixty doctors, nurses, and EMTs, all equipped with walkie-talkies. Statisticians and doomsaying "experts" had predicted as many as five deaths and scores of injuries to humans and beasts. By midweek, two horses had died of colic and several cattle had fallen off a cliff, but only a handful of humans were injured. An ex–marine commando broke his arm while chasing his horse around the corrals on the first day, but he returned to the drive the next day with a cast. A guy from Georgia sat on a prickly pear cactus and had to have the spines yanked from his gluteus by one of the nurses. Another man had a rope burn on his hand that became infected and spread to his lymph glands. A woman sustained a broken shoulder when her horse reared and dropped her on the road. A wagon tipped over, injuring a photographer.

Ten-year-old Stevie Williams of Columbus, riding the drive with his uncle, understood how dangerous a horse can be. Five years ago his father died when his horse threw him off a cliff. Stevie, who is deaf but can read lips, felt it was important to be on the cattle drive, and to ride the same horse that had killed his father.

The drive had its share of celebrities. U.S. Senator Max Baucus, scion of an old-time Montana sheep-ranching family, canceled all his appointments in Washington to ride the whole drive, while Senator Conrad Burns came just for the day. Jim Adamson, Montana's only astronaut, rode the whole trip and was even thrown from his horse. One evening he told the crowd, "Going for a three-million-mile ride through outer space is exciting, but nothing compared to this cattle drive!"

In spite of the many unpaid volunteers, the drive cost almost a million dollars, sponsored in part by Anheuser-Busch, Coca-Cola West, and Motorola. (All profits made by the Latigo Corporation were destined to endow a scholarship fund for rural students.) Still, the enterprise was hardly elitist or glitzy. It was a long, dusty parade to celebrate pride in the Montana way of life—even if everybody got a little too self-congratulatory over the myth of the cowboy. Cofounder Barry McWilliams took the microphone one night to tell a beer-guzzling crowd, "This is the greatest gathering of horses and horsemen in America since the Battle of Gettysburg!" That may be hyperbole, but it was certainly the greatest in Montana since Custer's demise at the Battle of the Little Bighorn.

On our last morning, I awakened at 4 A.M. to the sound of men harnessing a team. It was dark and raining lightly, but I could see the lights of Billings in the valley below. I stowed my tent in a mule-drawn wagon, wolfed a quick breakfast, and in the wet dawn I saddled Step Easy for the last time. By six the wagons were rolling down the rimrock and through the outskirts of Billings.

Almost fifty thousand Montanans had risen at dawn to greet us. Kids, heavy women in pantsuits, and old men in caps stared, smiled, and waved. As we clomped by service stations, fast-food stands, and a shopping mall, the asphalt rang with hoofbeats and wagon wheels. Beyond the riders and wagons rose the modern skyscrapers of Billings—a peculiar collage of the West's past and present.

What did two thousand grubby, unshaven horsemen riding down from the rimrock in the drizzling rain mean? An old man in a battered Stetson waved and wiped his eyes with his bandanna. We were not just part of a Marlboro ad. As the ritual horsemen of manifest destiny, we were a dynamic if self-conscious emblem of the western ability to challenge, conquer, prosper, and endure—not so much as individuals, but as a team.

An hour later we trotted down First Avenue and turned near the stockyards. The wagons and horses halted in a field overlooking Interstate 90 and an oil refinery. The trail-drive euphoria faded as I unsaddled Step Easy and found torn flesh and blood on his left flank. I'd protected him on the tie line all week, putting him between quiet geldings instead of mares (generally the kickers and biters), but last night a horse's teeth had ripped a three-inch gash in his neck. As Barbie Van Cleve and I loaded Step Easy into the trailer bound for Big Timber, I looked in his eyes for some recognition in our parting. I'd grown attached to him, but he wanted no part of me.

Billings was whooping it up at the Spur and at the Northern Hotel bar. No doubt there was already whiskey-enhanced mirth and myth making in progress. I could have joined in, but the highway called.

My great-great-uncle,
Richard Harlow, founder of
Harlowtown and the Montana
Railroad. (Courtesy Montana
Historical Society)

Above: My grand-
father, Barnaby
Conrad, at age
nineteen in
Harlowtown,
1906.

Left: My father,
Barnaby Conrad,
at age six in
1928.

My grandmother, Helen Hunt
Conrad, at the Lazy K Bar
Ranch in 1929.

Chapter 23

Uncle Dick Harlow and the Jawbone Railroad

Trouble was the normal condition. The owners of
the ranches held us up with shotguns and hesitated
to sell us supplies, fearing that they wouldn't
get paid.

Richard Harlow on his railroad, circa 1900

In 1895 my great-great-uncle Richard Harlow began construction on the Montana Railroad, better known as the Jawbone Railroad. The original Jawbone went 157 miles: it started from Lombard on the Missouri River (south of Helena), followed Sixteenmile Creek to the town of Ringling, from there turned up the Musselshell Valley to Two Dot, then to Harlowton and north over Judith Gap to Lewistown. I wanted to follow the old rail bed from its start, but local ranchers (including Ted Turner) had locked the gates at Lombard. So from Bozeman I drove north on Route 411. In minutes the blacktop gave way to gravel road and I flipped *Red Cloud* into four-wheel drive.

Born near Springfield, Illinois, Harlow went to law school before moving to Helena in 1886 and entering the real-estate business. Nine years later, he married Josephine Maud Barnaby, John Conrad's sister-in-law. Obsessed with a vision of Helena as a transportation hub, Harlow vowed he would build a railroad to the flourishing silver-mining town of Castle, but the financial panic of 1893 shut down the project. Undeterred, Harlow reorganized and raised more capital in the East, and his engineer, A. G. Lombard, told him they would finish the railway "before the snow flies." Instead, it took three hard years. Working in the fall when the creek was low, they built fifty-four bridges as the railroad looped back and forth across Sixteenmile Creek. In spring it became a raging torrent that washed out the canyon wall. It was dangerous work for little pay. A worker made two dollars a day and then paid the company five dollars a week for room and board. The engineer's teenage son was partially blinded and had most of his fingers blown off by dynamite caps. Years later Harlow recalled, "We had trouble with labor, with our engineering parties, and it seemed with everything with which we came in contact." It was Harlow's smooth talk or "jawboning" that kept skeptical financiers from pulling out—hence the name.

Richard Harlow liked to make up names for his rail towns. Maudlow was a contraction of his wife's name, Maud Harlow. Another train stop, Josephine, was named for Maud's mother, the murdered Mrs. Barnaby. Dorsey was named for Harlow's grandmother. The town of Fannalulu was named for two pretty young girls, Fanny and Lulu, who came to Harlow's house for tea. It was a ghost town even at its inception, and no one ever lived there; Harlow just put it on a map to impress railroad officials before he sold them the line. "There were few towns and less provocation for them, but I put in plenty," he said.

I braked as three deer bounded across the road. This was beautiful country, still wild, and after twenty miles I began to wonder if I had passed Maudlow by accident. Then, coming around a sharp bend, I saw the town. Maudlow was nothing more than a few old houses in need of a paint job. The general store was boarded up, and the old hotel still stood but didn't function. I knocked on one door, but getting no answer, I moved on.

The road to Ringling wove through sagebrush gullies, then through pastures dotted with cattle. A coyote slunk through a cut field looking for mice or gophers. Coming around the corner, I skidded to a halt; in the center of the road was a two-foot boulder that had tumbled out of the hillside. I was just able to squeeze around it. Over the next hill I nearly ran head-on into a rancher's truck. Neither one of us expected another vehicle to break the stillness.

Named for the circus family, Ringling was nearly dead, with just the post office and JT's Bar remaining active, so I did not linger. Near Summit the dirt road left the old rail bed. The original plans called for the railroad to go only to the mining town of Castle (now a ghost town), but Harlow used his magic tongue to extend the Jawbone's route to the town of Merino—now Harlowton—a center for Montana's swiftly growing sheep industry. The hills were patched with sagebrush; the scattered railroad ties stuck out of the earth like blackened bones. Just past Lennep once stood the town of Grove-land—Harlow's contraction of Grover Cleveland—but it too was gone. There wasn't much to Martinsdale except the Mint Bar, so I kept rolling. A mile later I hit blacktop and headed east to Twodot—named for cattleman "Two Dot" Wilson—which consisted of Montana's two most common en-terprises: a dead bank building and a lively bar.

Harlowton lay just north of the Musselshell River. The Jawbone railroad arrived here with fanfare in 1900, and the town grew to nearly three thou-sand citizens and neighbors. Harlow's line played an important role in the settlement of the central plains of Montana, serving homesteaders and the enormous wool industry. Harlow sold the Jawbone to the Chicago, Milwau-kee, and Puget Sound Railroad in 1908 for $3.5 million and retired to the East but kept his ranch in Montana for summer visits. His daughter Katharine married first an admiral (who drowned saving her life), then an English lord. His granddaughter married a psychiatrist in Marin County, California.

With the Great Depression and a number of other disasters, the railroad became an anachronism, and when the Milwaukee Railroad collapsed in 1974, the rails were ripped up and the right of way was sold to local ranch-ers. Today, with barely a thousand residents, Harlowton is a tired hamlet.

On Central Street I passed the Stockman's Bar, the Oasis Bar, and Biegel's Bar before parking *Red Cloud* in front of Harlowton's landmark, the Graves Hotel. Built in 1906, the six-story hotel is made of rough-quarried stone with wooden trim painted white and green. If it stood by a lake or seashore, the Graves would be a charming inn and business would be booming; but it's in a dying railroad town in the middle of the prairie where most people don't stay unless they have to.

Housed in an old storefront, the Musselshell Museum displayed the pre-dictable collections of arrowheads, buffalo skulls, handmade quilts, di-nosaur bones, and cookstoves from the homesteading era. My favorite was a photograph of a trained buffalo jumping on cue from a thirty-foot tower into a pond surrounded by bleachers. Oddly, there were no photographs of the town's founder.

I knew what Harlow looked like—a patrician with a high forehead, wire-rim glasses, and brushlike mustache—because my grandfather Barnaby kept a photograph of him on his desk all his life, and looked to his beloved Uncle Dick as a father figure. My grandfather was an even-natured man, but his early childhood had been so painful after his parents' divorce in Helena that he never discussed it. Born in 1887, he was schooled in England, then at the Hill School in Pennsylvania, and finally at Yale, but he spent his summers in Montana working on Uncle Dick's railroad and the Harlow ranch. The cowboys got a kick out of his slight English accent, but he was happy here. My grandfather was an excellent rider, and in a family album is a photograph of him at eighteen wearing woollies, the sheepskin chaps favored by Montana cowboys at the time, and a six-shooter. Now few cowboys wear woollies, and fewer carry pistols.

In 1969, my father received a letter from eighty-two-year-old Henry Johnston, a boyhood friend of my grandfather's, who recounted an incident that shows how rough Harlowton was at the turn of the century:

> In the spring of 1905 Ike Gravelle terrorized Montana and Wyoming. He was a throwback from Jesse James and a prototype of Dillinger. His favorite method of operation was to demand $25,000 from the Northern Pacific, in default of which he threatened to blow up a bridge or a station. Of course the railroad refused to pay tribute and he did considerable damage before he was caught.
>
> The courthouse was only a couple of blocks away from your great-uncle Dick Harlow's house and your dad and I attended every session. It was a sensational trial and we two impressionable teenagers got a big charge out of our proximity to one of the most dangerous desperadoes of the decade. The trial ended on the fifth day, the judge adjourned for lunch and announced that he would charge the jury on reconvening. Barney and I went home and after luncheon returned to the courthouse.
>
> Just as we rounded the corner a fusillade of shots rang out. I can still hear them as they flew around our heads. We threw ourselves to the ground as we saw Ike, revolver in hand, running full speed across the square. It seemed a confederate had managed to put a gun in his hand as he was being brought into court. Ike shot and killed one of the deputies guarding him and wounded the other.
>
> When he ran out of the courthouse a horse was supposed to have been tethered for him nearby but something went wrong and there was no horse so he was forced to flee on foot. As he ran across the square every armed citizen, and there were many who carried guns in those days, took a pot shot at him. He was run to ground in the base-

ment; the police rushed in and shortly emerged carrying Ike's body. He had shot himself through the head.

At this time John Conrad was obsessed with his Yukon mining project, but he was still in touch with his son. He encouraged Barnaby to drop out of Yale to attend the Colorado School of Mines. Forget Shakespeare; there was a fortune to be made in the Yukon, where the poet Robert Service and Jack London were spinning legends. In one of my grandfather's notebooks, I found a 1911 notation indicating that he possessed the number of John's safe-deposit box in a New York City bank. He also shipped some of John's cattle to Skagway, Alaska, to feed his miners at Conrad City. Barnaby also managed the sale of various parcels of Canadian land when John desperately needed cash. But at some point, for reasons unknown, he broke off all relations with his father. Whether he ever visited the Yukon project I'll never know.

During his time in Harlowton, my grandfather had an Indian girlfriend named Fern, a photograph of whom I found in a photo album. She was very pretty, but he never truly loved anyone except Judge Hunt's daughter, Helen. Barnaby was eighteen and a boxer at Yale when he met my grandmother; he was a charming but shy young man, and it took him ten years to win her. He courted her on horseback in Helena, and by buggy in Washington. Once in New York he hired a car and took her out to the country for a picnic, to show her how to fire his Colt .45, the gun that had won the West. Being from Montana, she already knew how.

After they married in 1915, Barnaby started a successful investment banking firm in San Francisco with branches in Los Angeles, Portland, and Seattle. During the Great War he enlisted in an airborne squadron at the Great Lakes Naval Training Station, where his best friend was Donald MacMillan, the famed arctic explorer. He had his uniforms tailored at Brooks Brothers, but he never saw action. For the most part, his life was a quiet one with annual fishing and hunting trips to Alaska with his pal, author Stewart Edward White.

The hot blood in that generation went to his older sister, Florence, who eloped to Paris with an American who gave her a child, left her, and was later shot for philandering; she then married a French general Lannusse. She was a famed horsewoman and acclaimed photographer. During both world wars she ran an ambulance corps. As the Germans advanced in 1940, she had her orderlies drive sixty trucks to the Louvre, where they removed the Winged Victory of Samothrace and other treasures. These were hidden in the countryside through the entire war. After the Liberation, Florence received the Croix de Guerre. Her French descendants are aristocrats and like to chase stags on horseback, but they are quite proud of their frontier roots in Montana.

My grandfather had little interest in Europe and spent nearly every summer in Montana at the Lazy K Bar Ranch. When he rode the range he wore English boots, a tweed jacket, and a pith helmet, but he let my uncle and father go buckaroo style. In contrast to his own father, he was a caring parent and took home movies of his boys catching grasshoppers with their hats, fishing in Big Timber Creek, and riding in horse races with real cowboys. He began the morning with boxing lessons for the boys (my father went on to be captain of his college boxing team) and ended it reading them Kipling and Stevenson. He never spoke of John Conrad and changed the subject if he was brought up.

Sometime after World War II, he was riding in California and hit his head hard on a low-hanging tree branch and went to the hospital. He never fully recovered. There is a 1954 photograph of him, an old man in a hospital bed looking at his namesake, me at age two, with tragic puzzlement in his eyes. He died a few months later, and a large part of our family heritage, good and bad, died with him.

The author and guide Sandy Pew canoeing
the Yellowstone in 1989.

Chapter 24

Canoeing the Yellowstone with Captain Clark

I deturmined to have two canoes made out of the
largest of those trees and lash them together
which will cause them to be Sturdy and fully
sufficient to take my small party & Self with
what little baggage we have.
                Captain William Clark, journal entry for
                                    July 20, 1806

On a sunny afternoon in mid-September, Sandy Pew and I lowered ourselves into a heavily laden, seventeen-foot canoe and shoved off into the Yellowstone River. We were near the Tom Minor Basin, a few miles north of Yellowstone Park. If all went well, we would descend over five hundred miles of the longest undammed river in the United States, crossing all of Montana, and pull out at Fort Buford, North Dakota. If things went badly, we might end up on a sandbar as the green canoe got sucked all the way down to the Gulf of Mexico.

Sandy's wife, Tesie, her blond hair glinting in the sunlight, took photographs as we moved out into the river's current. Suddenly she gasped. "The car keys!"

"I've got 'em," I said, pulling them from the pocket of my shorts. The swift current gripped us, and Tesie ran along the bank to keep up. I chucked the glittering ball of keys forty feet across the water to the grassy bank. Tesie ducked into the brush, and held the keys aloft with a triumphant smile. She waved good-bye, and the river took us around the bend.

This trip was adventure based on historical precedent, going back to Montana's first white intrusion. From the time we hit the town of Livingston, we would follow part of the same route Captain William Clark took in 1806. After the Corps of Discovery reached the Pacific Ocean, the explorers separated. Clark's party turned southeastward to the Yellowstone, while Lewis followed the Missouri, and they were reunited at the confluence of the two rivers.

Well planted in our minds was the fact that Clark made his trip in July, when the water was higher and faster. Traveling later in the year, we suspected that the current would be slow, and an early fall might dump snow on us. However, we had three major advantages over Clark: we wouldn't be attacked by Indians; we didn't have to paddle unwieldy rafts made of cottonwood trees; and we had repellent for the swarms of mosquitoes that nearly drove Clark's men crazy. We also had several bottles of good whiskey and a map.

As we skirted the first whitewater, neither Sandy nor I was convinced of my abilities as a canoeist, but within an hour we'd settled into a fine rhythm and made twenty miles through Paradise Valley that day. At the Loch Leven fishing access we pitched tents in a strong warm wind out of the south that made a fire unnecessary. The hot winds continued all night and I slept fitfully, waking at seven to see a dark storm scudding out of the southwest. It took two hours to eat, break camp, and pack the canoe. I didn't like the heavy clouds building behind us over the Yellowstone Park area, but Sandy hoped to outrun them.

After lunch near Wineglass Narrows, we entered a series of rapids. The cottonwoods and willows on the banks rushed by, and I began to feel confident in my paddling as we approached Livingston. Near the Brand S lumber yard, Sandy said, "I wonder how the bridge will be."

Around the next bend we faced our first man-made danger. The cement pilings of the bridge were set about fifteen feet apart, and with the water low, the bones and sinews of the river showed. There was a nasty crosscurrent under the right-hand span where a small tree lay pinioned. "We're in *big* trouble," said Sandy. "Get over the side, quick."

We wrestled the canoe to a gravel shoal and reconnoitered. The right span with the crushed tree was out. The center span was a tricky mix of currents that could broadside the canoe into the cement pilings. The far left span was a tight squeeze, but the current was manageable. "Paddle hard left!" shouted Sandy. "Now paddle right!" We shot through the foamy flume and coasted though the eddies.

Through the afternoon, dozens of blue herons appeared on the river-banks, and two sandhill cranes, distinguished by their heavy bodies and croaking call, flew over in broad-winged strokes. A male osprey carried a trout in his talons, the fish's head pointed straight ahead for aerodynamic stability.

We passed new log cabins on the north shore with high price tags, part of a trend toward twenty-acre ranchettes that catered to out-of-staters but threatened the river's wild aspect. "Fifteen years ago we had a chance to really protect this river," said Sandy. "The local ranchers voted it down as a violation of property rights and freedom. I believe it was short-sighted. Because what the ranchers really treasure is the same thing the so-called environmentalists want—unspoiled, undeveloped land. 'Don't fence me in' could be the same thing in two different languages if they'd talk sensibly to each other."

The hot tail wind kept us moving along, and by five o'clock dark storm clouds from Yellowstone Park had swooped in. "Better pull over before she hits," said Sandy.

The canoe bow ground into the gravel bar and we got out on the beach. As we zipped our foul-weather gear over rubber waders, a sheet of cold rain slammed us hard. The wind rose to forty-five miles an hour, and I clung to the canoe for balance. Thunder cracked, and lightning illuminated a nearby hill. I looked around for cover but Sandy shouted, "Just get wet and cold if we stay here. Let's make a run for it!"

We shoved off. The wind caught us, beating against our backs. "We must be doing eighteen miles an hour!" Sandy shouted above the gale's roar. "Fastest I've ever been in a canoe!" We flew down the river, using our paddles for balance and direction only. As the Yellowstone veered near the interstate, a passing trucker saw us and blew his horn.

The storm faded to a drizzle, the wind dropped, and at dusk we reached the outskirts of Big Timber. We unpacked the gear, dragged the canoe under the cottonwoods, and camouflaged it with dead branches. Shouldering our small backpacks, we walked a half mile into town.

In its heyday during the twenties, the Grand was a good little hotel, but it then became a crash pad for drunk sheepherders and worse. Five years ago, a couple of easterners completely renovated it. Now each bedroom had its own retro-Victorian character and the hallways were cozily lined with nineteenth-century naive paintings of crimson forest fires and moose standing in lakes. Today the hotel serves as a social center for Big Timber's residents, hosting weddings, anniversaries, and funerals. Brooke Shields, who recently bought a ranch nearby, comes in and isn't bothered by autograph hounds.

The next morning we paddled past fields of grain and Angus cattle, hearing the buzz of a combine reaper, invisible behind trees, and smelling the scent of freshly cut hay. "That's the second and last cutting of the year," said Sandy, looking up at the sky. We glided by a two fishermen in a McKenzie boat working the far bank.

"What flies are you using?" I asked the guide.

"Hoppers."

I immediately snipped the Woolly Worm off my leader and attached a Joe's Hopper. The very first cast brought a fifteen-inch brown out from the bank. Five minutes later a rainbow followed, enough for breakfast, so I put the rod away.

Camping under cottonwoods that evening, we watched the sun set on the river. The old stone-fly nymph carcasses stuck to the rocks were a reminder that summer was long past. On the opposite bank, two raccoons came down to drink. A doe mule deer wandered into camp, flip-flopped her ears when she saw Sandy tending the fire, and backtracked into the woods. When three sandhill cranes flew over, Sandy said, "I love those birds. They always make me happy." A seven-eighths moon rose, and the geese flew over us all night honking.

I crawled out of my tent at 6 A.M. to find frost on the ground and rivets of ice poxing my tent fly; fog cloaked the river. We put coffee on the Coleman propane stove. Three hours later, the heat of the midday sun made it hard to remember the frosty dawn. When we stopped for lunch on an island, I stripped off my jeans and traded long underwear for shorts. "Catch three more trout. That's your assignment," said Sandy.

We shoved off and headed into a tight bit of river that ran along deep-cut grassy banks. Working the banks with a Joe's Hopper, I took a pair of twelve-inch rainbows. An hour later we hit a mile-long stretch where the railroad had dumped boulders to hold the riverbank. I cast the fly six inches from the bank, and it disappeared in a swirl. This fish took line off my reel. Two minutes later, a sixteen-inch brown came to net. With dinner aboard, I put my rod aside and we made time with the paddles. The valley narrowed to pine forest, and the water sped up as we entered and exited rocky gorges. By six we still hadn't reached Columbus, and a decision had to be made: camp now in fading daylight, or risk going all the way to town.

"There's a good campsite in a park near the bridge," said Sandy. "I just don't know if we can make it before dark."

By seven we still hadn't made Columbus. The sun dropped lower by the minute. The dark river was hard to gauge for rapids. I felt we'd made a mistake, that we were doing something foolhardy. It was evening now, and the river was dangerous if you couldn't see it.

Then, around the bend, car lights crossed the river. "That's the bridge to Absarokee," said Sandy. The dark graveled shore welcomed our canoe's bow. We set up our tents on the edge of the campground, cooked the trout, and walked into town.

The New Atlas Bar was an old saloon, filled with hundreds of stuffed animals: cougars, elk, wolves, bobcats, coyotes, and eight-foot rattlesnake skins. The glass eyes in the elk were a little crazed, the tails on the coyotes drooped, and the fur on all had been varnished with nicotine. Some regulars at the bar wore that same glazed patina.

Columbus had the distinction of being one of the last towns in Montana to hang a man for murder, according to the bartender. "Around World War II. He murdered a family. They caught him and brought him in on horseback at dawn. He was whimperin' and cryin'. So they gave him a bottle of whiskey and he drank most of it. Then they hanged him in a warehouse. You had to know someone to get in to watch."

"Hang 'em high is what I say," added a bleary-eyed barfly in a Stetson caked with sweat. "Somebody'll learn somethin' from the experience."

"What was his name?" I asked.

"I don't know, what was it?" said the bartender.

"You really care?" said the barfly. "'Cause nobody here does."

In the morning, we entered the flow of the river, passing sheep farms along the bank—one belonging to Mel Gibson, the actor, who moved here recently. Sandhill cranes, herons, golden eagles, kingfishers, and grebes were abundant. Huge numbers of blackbirds infested the trees, and ospreys plied the air. "This is where western and eastern Montana divide, including plants and animals," said Sandy.

The river current suddenly slowed and the pines gave way to barren hills and mesas in the distance, yet along the riverbanks the dense fetid vegetation resembled Louisiana more than Montana. As evening came, the whitefish grew giddy feeding on a massive hatch of ephemera fluttering off the river. I was pretty sure we'd left trout country, but when we stopped at five and camped between felled cottonwoods, I couldn't resist casting over the dimpled river. The second cast brought a strike. Unfortunately, it was a seventeen-inch whitefish. Four more succumbed in ten minutes. A whitefish puts up a sporty fight, but it just doesn't measure up to a trout.

About ten o'clock I had just finished cleaning the dishes when we saw car lights roaming the dark field behind us. Civilization was never far from the banks of the Yellowstone, the life source of this valley.

"Uh-oh," said Sandy. "Here comes Rancher Jones."

The last thing we needed was to have an irate rancher barging in with a shotgun and telling us to get off his property in the middle of the night. The headlights filtered through the cottonwoods, but veered to the right, then were extinguished. "Could just be kids out drinking beer," Sandy reckoned. We waited, but hearing no one stalking us, we extinguished the fire and got into our tents to read. An hour later, the car started up and went out the way it came.

In the morning we reached the town of Laurel and hid the canoe in bushes near the bridge. Changing our waders for running shoes, we walked a mile into town to buy supplies. As we passed a belching Cenex refinery, Sandy said, "That's a converter to refine oil to gasoline. My father invented it. He was an engineer at Sun Oil, the family business. Originally out of Pennsylvania. Not for me, though."

There was a mildly confessional tone in Sandy's voice. It was the first time he'd talked about his late father, and I sensed he was sharing the confidences of a black sheep. "My brother's on the board of Sun, the company my great-grandfather founded a century ago. It made my father furious that I wanted to be a cowboy and rancher. He nearly disowned me. I had to put myself through Arizona State by breaking horses. In the long run, I don't regret it."

After college, Sandy moved to Buffalo, Wyoming, where he took out a loan and started a registered Hereford ranch. "Looking back, I can't believe the banker gave me the loan. But the ranch did well and I paid back every cent of it." In Wyoming, Sandy married Tesie, an attractive eastern woman five years his senior who had two children from a previous marriage, and together they have a son.

When we bought groceries at the supermarket, I asked for lamb chops. "We don't have lamb except when it's on sale," said the assistant butcher.

"That's baloney," rasped Sandy as we walked down the canned-fruit aisle. "It's because the ranchers have a lock on the market to push their beef and keep the lamb out." This was ironic, since turn-of-the-century Montana was one of the largest sheep-raising states.

Back on the river, the current slowed to a crawl and we paddled solidly that afternoon. On the outskirts of Billings, we slid under the overpass of

Interstate 90, and it occurred to me that it had taken us five days to make a trip that would have taken less than two hours by automobile.

Around the bend loomed spires, towers, and white spheroid storage tanks like something from a science-fiction movie. Montana Power ran a huge operation on the Yellowstone, turning coal into electrical energy. "Hear that squeaky sound?" asked Sandy. "It's the conveyor belt lifting the coal up to be processed. I visited the plant once. I don't like them much, not on the river. But I guess they're a necessary eyesore."

The urban bustle of Billings soon passed. Flocks of cormorants passed overhead. We waved to a man gathering firewood on a sandbar and saw two boys chasing insects with a butterfly net. At five o'clock we looked for a campsite, bypassing land with No Trespassing signs or trees marked with Day-Glo red paint. "Property owner's rights," said Sandy. "It's what this country is all about."

An unposted island offered us its small cottonwoods and wind-flattened grass. It was a balmy evening, so after setting up camp I took a bath in the Yellowstone. We ate steaks, beans, and salad washed down with a cabernet sauvignon. For dessert, around eleven o'clock, the dark river served us the loud smack of a beaver slapping his tail.

Up before seven, we gulped cold cereal and a cup of coffee on the propane stove and were soon in the boat. At ten-thirty we paddled under a sign hanging from a wire stretched across the river: "Danger Ahead, Diversion, Portage Necessary." We'd heard about this: the Huntley Project, built in 1968. A few hundred yards ahead, the river forked around an island capped with a cement breakwater. We heard a dull roar to the right—the main branch of the river.

"That's where the five-foot cement diversion wall should be," said Sandy. "About ten people, most of them teenagers, have been killed here over the years."

The left channel looked safe enough, and we floated slowly on the millpond-still water. "Stand up and tell me what you see," said Sandy.

Rising unsteadily, I stood up in the bow of the canoe, and what I saw was not good. Fifty feet in front of us was a second diversion wall. The water dropped two feet onto jagged rocks.

"Okay," said Sandy. "This left channel is out. We're going to have to head for the island and portage until we hit the main channel again."

An hour later, we launched in the roar below the five-foot falls and were back in the flow. A Burlington Northern coal train snaked along the river, and I could smell the chugging industrial skunk full of burning oils, coal dust, and grinding metal parts. "If Captain Clark were reincarnated today, I wonder what he'd think of a Burlington Northern engine bearing down on him. He'd never seen a train before, much less a power plant," said Sandy.

A warm head wind rose out of the east, bearing two white pelicans with black wing markings. My left shoulder joint felt as though the tendons were wearing out. Bald eagles and golden eagles flew overhead. A mink scampered along the bank, unaware of our presence. Enormous carp fed in scores, gulping foam off the water with rubbery lips. I had developed a deep loathing for them and, to relieve the tedium of paddling, enlisted Sandy in an attempt to stalk and kill one with my paddle, but with no success.

The beauty of the river was sometimes spoiled by stretches of rusting riprap with an eerie sense of planned obsolescence. You could make out old Chevys, De Sotos, and Buicks from the forties to the sixties—a graveyard of American mobility embedded in the muddy banks. Ranchers also used broken slabs of cement curbs, sidewalks, and street sections with the yellow crosswalk paint still visible. The detritus of the automobile age was pressed into the earth, a wall of modern junk holding back yesteryear's buffalo skulls, old campfire stones, and broken arrowheads.

The river widened, and frost-yellowed leaves of the cottonwoods flashed in the late afternoon sun. Etched with wind and water, the sandstone cliffs looked like ancient temples. A huge rock in the middle of the river had been worn into the shape of a mushroom the size of a truck. Eddies behind the rock sucked hungrily at our bow.

The silhouette of a rusting iron bridge rose through the cottonwoods, and just beyond was the grassy top of Pompey's Pillar. I let out a war whoop and Sandy grinned. "You're a *real* tenderfoot, Conrad, but I'll forgive you this time."

This large sandstone mesa marked the most important moment of our pilgrimage in search of Captain Clark. The expedition had gone ashore here on July 25, 1806, at about four in the afternoon. "This rock I ascended and from its top had a most extensive view in every direction," wrote Clark. He named the site for Pompey, son of their seventeen-year-old translator, Sacajawea, not for the Roman general.

A recent book claimed that all the wild grapes Clark had observed are gone from the Yellowstone Valley. But when we pulled our canoe up to a muddy bank below Pompey's Pillar, I found several healthy vines. Judging from the tracks in the mud, raccoons also had found the grapes, and I thought Clark would be pleased.

Pompey's Pillar is Montana's first historical monument and bears the only physical record—anywhere in America—of Lewis and Clark's extraordinary journey across the then-uncharted West. The pillar is privately owned by a man named John Foote, who lives in Billings and is trying to sell it to the state. Mr. Foote's father bought the 356-acre site in 1955 and developed it as an attraction. Near the closed-up ticket office lay a replica of Clark's vessel made of two cottonwood dugouts lashed together. A splinter group of Clark's men had followed the Yellowstone on horseback, but Indians stole their mounts, and when they reached Pompey's Pillar, they made two bull boats out of buffalo hide stretched over a wooden frame.

The small grassy park, closed for the season, was neat and well kept. "The Footes have done a better job than the state would. The state would have blacktopped the whole thing and ruined it," commented Sandy.

Just before sunset we climbed a path cut in the rock on the sloping side of the pillar. We found a wall of signatures and graffiti, some already a century old, including the one I'd hoped for. Carved into the sandstone, in an almost adolescent script, was:

Wm. Clark

1806

That was it—the only human record that Lewis and Clark left in their four-thousand-mile round-trip reconnaissance of the Louisiana Purchase.

Standing in the dry grass on top of the two-hundred-foot-high bluff, we could see for forty miles in either direction, up and down the Yellowstone River. Clark had his last view of the Rocky Mountains from this point. A mile from us, looking like a Lionel toy train, trundled three locomotive engines towing fifty cars of coal. Trains had run by this site for a century after the Northern Pacific laid its track. It occurred to me that John Conrad would've seen Pompey's Pillar many times as he traveled by train between Billings and Butte. I had no way of knowing whether the pillar or history had interested my great-grandfather, but I doubted it: he was too busy trying to make history himself. Entrepreneurs look to the future, not the past.

That night, we ate roast chicken and broke out a bottle of red wine to toast Lewis and Clark. Much has been written about the two men's personalities, but the historian Paul Russell Cutright perhaps limned them best: "Lewis was a dreamer, intent, fine-drawn, reserved, unwavering, generally humorless. Clark was warm, companionable, a good judge of men, an easy conversationalist . . . highly successful in meeting the demands of actual living." Lewis and Clark were both Virginians and had fought Indians together under General "Mad Anthony" Wayne. Clark was the superior officer, and when Jefferson later appointed Lewis as the leader of the Corps of Discovery, Lewis unhesitatingly invited his old friend along.

The two men differed in training. Lewis was relatively well read and had been tutored by Jefferson when he served as the president's secretary, learning how to prepare specimens and preserve skins and plants. Before the expedition, Lewis completed a two-month cram course in Philadelphia, studying astronomy, natural history, and paleontology with the leading scientific minds of the time.

The more sanguine, redheaded Clark was largely unschooled, as the spelling in his diary indicates. But he was a practical man, an excellent mapmaker, with a talent for sizing up Indians. Above all he was an expert at wilderness survival. In the absence of Lewis on the Yellowstone, Clark's journals took on new zoological value. He described vegetation and plant species used in medicine by the Indians. He recorded the massive herds of buffalo, the many wolves, and the even more numerous grasshoppers: "It may be proper to observe that the emence Sworms of Grasshoppers have destroyed every sprig of Grass for maney miles . . . ." But the most often mentioned critter in the journal was the mosquito: "Musquetors excessively tormenting."

Sandy speculated that the seventeen-year-old Sacajawea and Clark had a romance (in spite of the fact that her French-Canadian husband was also on the trip). "When all of Clark's journals fell into the river after a canoe tipped over, Sacajawea jumped into the river and saved them," said Sandy. "There's more to that kind of effort than duty, if you ask me." Both of us found it curious that no history has been able to pin down whether Sacajawea died as a young woman or (according to one reliable source) as a ninety-five-year-old on the Shoshone reservation in Wyoming.

Sandy identified more with Clark; I with Lewis. And for a while, with the red wine percolating through our brains, we imagined ourselves as those intrepid explorers. After washing the dishes, I went into my tent, hung my flashlight overhead, and read about the aftermath of the expedition. After enjoying the initial accolades, Meriwether Lewis died mysteriously from a gunshot wound at a Tennessee roadside inn in 1809. It was up to his companion, now known as General Clark and serving as governor of Missouri Territory, to get the historic journals published.

Clark enlisted the aid of Nicholas Biddle, a well-known Philadelphia attorney, who edited the journals and then approached publishers. The manuscript underwent difficulties in finding a willing publisher, but in 1814, a total of 1,417 copies were put on the market. They sold briskly, but neither Lewis's heirs nor Clark made any profits from the book that tells our country's greatest story of exploration.

On our eighth morning on the river there was no wind, and the temperature was a bracing forty degrees. I buried the fire under sod so that no trace of our overnight visit remained. We each made a solitary pilgrimage of farewell to the pillar. In the canoe, we didn't talk about Clark anymore. The river slowed and the yellow stone cliffs rose in curious geometric patterns, like etched microchip circuits magnified a thousand times in stone. We began to question the topographical maps. "The riverbed changes constantly," said Sandy. "These maps are ten years old, and a good flood can wipe out any island." The only thing we knew was that with the current and our paddling, we could make about five miles an hour and about thirty-five miles a day.

Reaching the bridge near Custer, we made camp and bathed in the river, slapping at our backs to keep the mosquitoes at bay. Refreshed, we walked a mile into town as darkness fell, and I felt a fall chill. The cold air was spiked with skunk, a smell I have always liked. My flashlight's beam revealed a Franz Kline–ish collage of black and white fur smashed flat to the asphalt. Only the pads of the skunk's feet had remained three-dimensional. Then came the sickly sweet odor of silage from a farm. "It's fermented hay," explained Sandy. "Farmers feed it to dairy cows in the winter to stimulate their milk production. Think it gets them drunk, too."

We walked under the interstate ramp and headed into Custer, a dull little town. At the D&L Café we had miserable vegetable soup and a passable hamburger, then went over to the Junction City Saloon.

The owner was Gary, a big man with a heavy belly and gap teeth. He ran a good bar, constantly swabbing the woodwork with a striped rag. "I lived in Bozeman but got tired of the college kids. So I bought this place. I like it here. People are friendly." He pointed to a mounted fish on the wall. "Caught that one near Craig on a number-twelve Joe's Hopper. Five-pound brown."

"Nice piece of taxidermy."

"Yup. It sure is."

Another scotch helped me more deeply appreciate the beauty of Gary's mounted trout. I telephoned my father in California to tell him I was okay; then we walked back to the river. Even with the flashlight, we had difficulty negotiating the embankment and finding the trail. Emboldened by the whiskey, I ended up in a bramble patch, cursing the thorns ripping across my hands. Inside my tent, I smelled the field outside, pungent with pigweed, and heard one last car rumble across the bridge to Musselshell.

The days were hot, and paddling in shorts, both of us were becoming brown as Indians. Passing the outflow of the Bighorn River, I remembered Crow Fair and my day of fishing with Bill Yellowtail far upstream; it seemed a long time ago. Another unmarked diversion dam halted us at midafternoon, but we avoided a portage by using ropes along the north shore. We camped on a pebbly shoal east of Froze to Death Creek. Sandy stayed up until midnight calculating how many river miles we had made: so far, some 275 miles total, with an average of thirty-four miles a day.

The next day took us to the Forsyth Dam, and five miles downstream to a sandy shoal. Walking away from camp to make a latrine, I saw what looked like a gray and white striped throw rug scurrying along the ground in my general direction—a badger. He veered away and quickly disappeared.

Local badgers had fascinated John James Audubon, who ventured to Fort Union, on the eastern border of Montana, in 1843. Shortly after his arrival at the fur-trading fort, Audubon purchased a live badger from an Indian squaw. He tried to keep it in his room but found it "so mischievous, pulling about and tearing to pieces every article within its reach and trying to dig up the hearth stones," that he had to move it to an adjacent room. There it burrowed under the hearthstones, and Audubon had to reach in and drag it out whenever he wanted to draw it. "It was provoked at the near approach of anyone and growled continuously at all intruders. It was not, however, very vicious and would suffer one or two of our companions to handle and play with it at times." Audubon brought this remarkable pet back to New York, along with a mule deer and a Swift fox, which is now largely extinct in Montana.

We didn't trust the warm weather to hold. To make time, we got on the river an hour earlier and stayed a half hour longer. Our arm muscles and shoulders now bulged from the paddling. The ligaments in my left shoulder were strained, but we had to keep up the pace, especially with the head winds. Near a rail stop called Jopa six wild turkeys clucked along the bank, all hens except one young gobbler. Deer were everywhere. We passed the mouth of the Tongue River at 6 P.M., sailed under the first bridge at Miles City, and reached the boat ramp a half hour later. I was dead tired but excited. We'd been on the river for ten days.

Up on the riverbank, a middle-aged couple stood by a Chevy camper truck and waved to us. We waved back. The next thing we knew, Albert Lahn and his wife, Joyce, were loading our gear into the back of their camper. We chained the canoe to a tree, rode into Miles City, and checked into the old Olive Hotel, the place I'd stayed during my previous visit. The Lahns joined us for a drink at the bar.

Albert was born in this town and had worked for the old Milwaukee Railroad and in road construction. His grandfather came up from Paris, Texas, in the 1880s at age seventeen and rode for the LU Ranch. His grandmother came out from Kansas in a covered wagon. Joyce worked down at the *Miles City Star*. Her father was a German immigrant; her mother was one-quarter Cheyenne.

Albert had done just about every kind of job there is in Montana. "Worked for a while at the N Bar N. Biggest sheep outfit around—a hundred and fifty-six sections. They'd give you hard work and three glorious meals a day during lambing. We'd be out all night with the ewes, and when they'd throw a lamb we'd put a small canvas tepee over 'em both to keep 'em together. Next morning we'd mark 'em. That way you knew which lamb belonged to which ewe."

What Albert knew best about Miles City was its houses of prostitution. "There were three cathouses, each with about six girls. It cost five dollars a poke up until the fifties, and I'm telling you they had some good-lookin' women. Started going when I was fifteen. Not for me some high school girl who would want flowers, a movie, and a Coke and then not give you more than a kiss on the cheek. No, sir! I knew what to do with my hard-earned dollars on a Saturday night.

"Those working girls knew how to treat a man right. Medically inspected every thirty days. Judy Jones was the best working girl I ever knew. I was seventeen, and that was the first piece of tail I ever got. When the preachers ganged up on the cathouses and drove 'em out, Judy went back to Minnesota. I was sorry to see her go." Then, as an afterthought: "Course, that was long before I met Joyce."

Joyce smiled and patted his hand.

Albert also remembered the early days of the Bucking Horse Sale. "We were paid five dollars a ride bareback and ten for saddle broncs. We'd line up behind the corrals. There were always too many cowboys. You'd put your rigging on a horse and some guy who was bigger would pull your rigging off and say, 'That's my horse.' If he was too big, you might step aside. Otherwise you'd fight."

Albert and Joyce had been married thirty-five years, but it wasn't always placid. "She can be a vicious beast. Can't you?"

I couldn't tell if Albert was pulling my lanyard or not. Joyce smiled indulgently.

"She's acting real sweet for you boys right now, but she once threw a cup of hot coffee at me. There are marks on the woodwork from her throwing pots and pans. When she gets mad she screams dirty words in Cheyenne. She talks nice to you guys, but get her mad and she becomes *a savage vicious beast!* You don't believe me? There are *scars* on my ankles from where she's bitten me. There are *scars* on my arms, too. When she gets that way, I have to *slam* her head against the wall. Then I have to—"

"Albert," said Joyce calmly, "let these hungry boys get something to eat. It's almost eight o'clock."

"Anything you say, dear." He gave her a kiss and winked at me. The gold in his teeth showed. "See you boys tomorrow."

After breakfast, Albert and Joyce took us down to the riverside in their truck. We had almost finished lashing our gear into the canoe when a car drove up. "That's our daughter, Mosie," said Albert. "Surprised she made it up so early. Saw her last night and she was into her eighth beer."

Mosie came down the path with a free-swinging gait. In her twenties, she had a puffy look to her face but a bright smile. In her hand was a cold six-pack of beer.

"How about letting your old man have one of those?" said Albert.

Mosie gave us a friendly, hungry look. "Saw you guys yesterday walking near the Olive. Boy, you're in good shape," she said. "You bachelors?"

Albert began to fuss. "Now, don't be telling all the other girls in Miles City, Mosie, or they'll all jump in the canoe with these fellers and sink 'em before they reach Fort Buford!"

"Boy, I'd like to go on a trip like that," said Joyce quietly.

"Me, too," said Mosie. "Let me get a picture," she added, fiddling with her Instamatic. "Not every day we see two guys like you come floating down the river. It's not for me, of course. For my girlfriends."

"*Sure* it is," said Albert, winking at me.

Sandy and I shook hands all around and shoved off into the current. One last wave at the bend in the river, and Albert, Joyce, and Mosie were out of sight.

An hour south of Miles City we hit the rapids Albert had warned about. Strung across the river were suitcase-sized hunks of rock. They were treacherous, and we just managed to zigzag through.

The country broadened into miles of sagebrush and desert known as the Big Open. It was late afternoon when to the south a birdlike silhouette appeared in the air and grew enormous by the second. The humming became a volcanic roar as an air force bomber passed just a hundred feet over the treetops and flew directly at us. I felt like a sardine in the shadow of a manta ray. Two more followed in the next five minutes. We had paddled into the flight pattern of the Strategic Air Command.

Sandy and I had shared the canoe for twelve days now. Though we got along well, a certain tedium had set in. Sandy explained this rationally. "It's an expedition, not a vacation."

The confluence of the Powder River was hard to miss. No more than ten feet wide and a foot deep, it spewed a coffee-colored silt into the Yellowstone that discolored the river for miles. The high banks, carved by centuries of water, revealed two dark layers of coal running fifty feet above us. Then the black stripe dipped down to the waterline and the river was filled with huge boulders of coal that broke off into the current. Sandy wondered aloud, "What do you think this river will be like fifty years from now?"

"Unchanged," I replied, with more hope than certainty.

The sandy point we chose for camp was infested with wolf spiders, enormous gray and brown speckled beasts over an inch long that clustered under our tents. We had become used to them, sort of, but only because they hadn't gotten into our sleeping bags yet. Coyotes howled at the stars as we drank our whiskey in the warm dry night. It never got below fifty degrees.

All the next day autumn held us in her grasp. Honking flocks of wild geese took off from the islands, and the river was dappled with yellow cottonwood leaves and goose feathers. We reached Glendive at noon and pulled the canoe up under the shadows of the main bridge. Clambering up the steep banks, we found ourselves on Bell Street.

This town had begun as a rotgut saloon—"Glen's Dive"—and prospered in the cattle and homestead eras. Now, like most of eastern Montana, it showed the effects of a dwindling population and a major depression. Plenty of Space Available signs were posted on Main Street. We filled four water jugs from a faucet poking from the wall of a drugstore, then bought a bottle of scotch at the state liquor store.

We ate lunch drifting downriver from Glendive's last bridge, gratified that this was the last town for fifty miles. I had come to trust the river for wonder more than these worn-out settlements.

"Look," said Sandy. On the bank sat the fattest beaver I'd ever seen, the size of a small Labrador retriever. The beaver slipped into the water and slapped his tail. He surfaced ten feet away, slapped his tail harder, and disappeared. "His ancestors were the whole reason the white man even came to this region," said Sandy. "And this was one of the two main routes for furs out of the Rockies."

In 1829 the American Fur Company, owned by John Jacob Astor, opened a trading post called Fort Union on the Missouri River just above where it meets the Yellowstone. It became a headquarters for the fur trade. (Thanks to the gentlemanly craving for beaver felt hats, Astor became one of America's first millionaires.) Trade remained brisk until 1837, when smallpox wreaked havoc on the Plains Indians.

The first Sioux appeared in the vicinity of Fort Union in 1847, pushed upstream by white encroachment. By the 1860s they were openly hostile to both whites and other Indian tribes, disrupting trade at the fort and killing travelers. In 1867 the U.S. Army dismantled Fort Union and used the wood to create Fort Buford. It was to this fort that survivors of the Seventh Cavalry were taken after the Custer massacre, and it was here that Sitting Bull eventually surrendered.

Downstream, we passed the first canoe we'd seen on the whole river. It was pulled up on a shoal. A bearded hunter in camouflage lay resting in the stern with a beer propped on his chest. "My buddies are out tracking a deer they hit," he said. "Where you headed?"

"Fort Buford, North Dakota."

"Where'd you come from?"

"Livingston."

"*Livingston?* No shit! That's what—three hundred miles?"

"Four hundred and fifty," said Sandy.

The hunter raised his beer in a salute, then warned, "When you get down to the Intake, get over to the right side for your portage. Trouble's on the left."

Four hours later we heard the roar of falling water, big water. The Intake was the largest diversion dam on the Yellowstone and had a reputation for eating unwary boaters. On our left was the intake apparatus to divert water for irrigation, so we quickly maneuvered to the right, pulling into a muddy backwater near a wall of boulders ten feet high. I stepped out of the canoe and my foot sank into mud up to my knee. It was nearly quicksand. The only place to portage was right over this wall of boulders.

It took us an hour to haul the canoe. On the shore below the six-foot falls were trailers and people fishing from lawn chairs. Two bait fishermen were handily hauling in bright orange channel catfish. Kids ran around barefoot chasing a manic spaniel. It seemed like the last day of something, and I felt the seasons changing. We repacked the canoe and floated a quarter mile to an isolated campsite near a huge fallen tree.

The reason people other than resident farmers know of Intake is due to an ichthyological phenomenon. In 1962, a local man was fishing for northern pike near the irrigation diversion when he hooked something big. When he dragged it ashore, it was a twenty-eight pound paddlefish, a species that has appeared in fossils over 70 million years old. The last time one had been caught in the Yellowstone was in 1912. The paddlefish looks like a shark with a cricket bat for a nose and is so primitive that it has a three-chambered heart, a notochord instead of a spine, and cartilage instead of bone (a shark-like characteristic of no other freshwater fish except the sturgeon). By all rules of evolution, the paddlefish should have gone the way of the saber-toothed tiger and the woolly mammoth. They had been in the Yellowstone for eons, and been known on the Missouri, but when the Garrison Dam in North Dakota flooded their spawning grounds, they started coming farther up the Yellowstone.

Paddlefish in the Yellowstone usually run twenty to seventy pounds, but one was caught in the Missouri that weighed one hundred forty-two pounds. Because paddlefish eat only plankton and microscopic organisms, they can't be caught with bait, so anglers attach big treble hooks to their line, cast into the riffles below the intake, and snag the paddlefish. This brutal summer ritual has become so popular that strict limits and licensing are enforced to make sure the paddlefish won't disappear.

Though the fish's white, lobstery meat has long been considered a delicacy, a new industry is in the offing—paddlefish caviar. A mature paddlefish holds about five pounds of rich gray eggs that are nearly indistinguishable from sturgeon caviar. The Glendive Chamber of Commerce, which has exclusive rights to the caviar, collects about ten thousand pounds of caviar annually from fishermen—and sells it for thirty dollars a pound to a Florida middleman. Then the eggs are sold in New York stores for twenty-five dollars per *ounce.*

It was dark and we were sitting by the fire drinking coffee after dinner when lightning flashes stitched the skyline. In five minutes, the wind gusted in at forty miles an hour, blowing sparks from our fire high into the air and whipping sand into our eyes. "Better check the tents," said Sandy.

It was too late. At my campsite sat a lonely pair of wet Reeboks. Off in the windy darkness a strange blob rolled across the prairie like a tumbleweed. My tent was running away with all my gear inside. I tackled it, wrestling the tent into the lee of a cottonwood grove, where I tied rocks to the stake loops. All night long the wind raged and rain splattered the flimsy shelter. I didn't sleep well, dreaming that a huge cottonwood limb would break off and crash through my tent.

The wind made breakfast chaotic. Powdered milk blew out of our cereal before we could anchor it with water. Fire ashes and sand swirled around us, sending grit into our eyes and teeth. We loaded the canoe and shoved off. The only good news was a chilly wind pushing us eastward to the North Dakota border. "We've done over 480 river miles," said Sandy proudly.

Shifting to the north, the wind brought an hour of heavy rain, which numbed our hands and faces. We got out and towed the canoe for a mile, slogging through the shallows in our waders. It turned out we could paddle faster, so we clambered back in. Heavy waves battered us, swamping the canoe. It was more like crossing a long lake than paddling downriver. The wind abated, but the temperature dropped further. Our breath grew frosty.

Sandy, who has a mild diabetic condition, became low on blood sugar and his eyes took on a dopey cast. I forced him to eat two honey-covered granola bars and he perked up. Our campsite that evening was in a sheltered gully below a thicket of cottonwoods. Sandy's blood-sugar level fell again, and his speech was slurred until cheese and crackers brought him around.

By morning the air temperature was down to thirty-five degrees, our coldest day yet. The cloudy skies and northwest wind didn't promise much warmth. Today was October 2, and fall had come with a rush to the eastern plains of Montana; it could snow any minute. Two weeks of paddling had invested our muscles with power, and we began to push ourselves like runners on the last leg of a marathon. We steadily stabbed our paddles into the river. The Sidney bridge appeared twenty minutes early and we kept going for another hour. On a sandy treeless island, we had to eat our sandwiches while walking to keep the circulation going in our legs.

The river had widened, and there were fewer geese and more deer. We had dropped nearly three thousand feet in elevation from our start near Livingston, and it no longer felt like Montana; we might as well have been traveling through a wintery Missouri. For the next three hours we put in the best paddling of our lives, reaching the Fairview bridge just before five. We didn't break stroke. The sun was setting on our left, turning the cottonwood banks to a warm glowing orange. Deer in pairs watched as we approached, then darted into the bushes with their white tails whipping like flags of surrender.

I was ready to surrender myself. Cold and tired, I knew it would snow that night.

"If we don't make it to Fort Buford in twenty minutes, we'll have to camp in the dark," said Sandy.

Each time we went around a bend I thought it would be the last, yet the confluence with the Missouri still lay ahead. By six-thirty the sun had set, so the river was lit only from the sun's reflection in the sky.

"The Yellowstone's never going to let us go," said Sandy, not seeming to mind that prospect. He was completely happy here on the river, happier than he would have been in a warm house. His hay was baled for the winter, and he could take time off. But after five months on the road, I was feeling the weight of the calendar.

A silvery channel of water entered on the left, the Missouri itself. "We're here," said Sandy quietly.

We rested our paddles on the gunwales, gliding into the mixing currents of the two greatest rivers of Montana. We had paddled 550 miles in seventeen days to experience this moment, and I felt a mixture of exhilaration and sadness. This was where Clark stuck a note on a pole on August 4, 1806, to tell Lewis that, due to the heavy concentration of mosquitoes, he would meet him downstream. Eight days later they were reunited, and the rest is the history of the West.

In the dark we could just make out a cement boat ramp on the far bank and pulled for it. As we stepped onto land, our knees were so cramped by the cold that we hobbled like cripples. My hands and ears were numb. It was exactly thirty degrees on the thermometer, with the mercury steadily falling. It began to snow. We didn't really know where we were—somewhere near Fort Buford—but by following a road for half a mile, we finally saw the lights of the superintendent's house. A dog barked and the door opened, sending a welcoming bar of light across the frozen ground. The journey was over.

Looking south by Ingomar.
(Photo copyright © John Smart)

Chapter 25

Pronghorns and Train Robbers

What is life? It is a flash of firefly in the night. It is
a breath of a buffalo in the winter time. It is as
the little shadow that runs across the grass and
loses itself in the sunset.

Chief Crowfoot (Isapwo Muksika), Blackfoot,
circa 1900

Round about us the army of buffalo-hunters—red men and
white—were waging the final war of extermination upon
the last great herds of American bison seen upon this
continent. Then came the cattleman, the "trail boss"
with his army of cowboys, and the great roundups. Then
the army of railroad builders. That—the railway—was
the fatal coming. One looked about and said, "This is
the last West." It was not so. There was no more West
after that. It was a dream and a forgetting, a chapter
forever closed.

L. A. Huffman, pioneer photographer, from
unpublished notes circa 1900

The early snow had melted back into Indian summer. I drove to Rock
Springs on a gravel road that ran through dry prairie. I passed a pond that
looked like it was covered with snow, but it was alkaline deposit. No other
car or human appeared for an hour. This was antelope country, and I slowed
to watch a herd just fifty feet from the road: tan and white bodies, slender

running legs, black shiny horns. The biggest buck, his horns pronged like boat hooks, fixed me with his wide-set dark eyes, gauging my threat. Then he bolted, flying across the prairie with his harem in pursuit.

I was driving through Garfield County, nearly the size of Connecticut, which has less than 0.3 people per square mile. This was the Big Open, where John Conrad and the other early cattle barons had once ranged vast herds. Few ranchers maintained big herds now, and many of the towns that once served dirt-poor homesteaders had died out a half century ago.

There was an endlessness to the land. Nothing here but sky and grass. All it lacked in its emptiness was what it once possessed—buffalo. Near here in 1886 the Smithsonian's William Hornaday found the last wild buffalo herd in the United States and killed twenty-five of them, sending the hides and horns to honor the National Museum of Natural History in Washington. Later the Plains Indians began doing the ghost dance, an appeal to God to bring back the buffalo and a lost way of life.

Recently there had been serious talk about turning the parched prairie and badlands into something called the Buffalo Commons. Environmentalists argued that the fifteen-thousand-square-mile Big Open is a national treasure and should be made into a wildlife preserve where hundreds of thousands of antelope, deer, elk, and buffalo (along with wolves and grizzlies) could roam free across a vast plain, similar to the great game parks of Africa. It would stretch from the Missouri River to the Yellowstone—part of a greater Buffalo Commons that might one day include arid sections of the western Dakotas, western Nebraska, and areas of Texas, Colorado, New Mexico, and Wyoming.

The main proponents of this idea were Frank Popper, head of Rutgers University's urban studies department, and his wife, Deborah, who had studied the plains for two decades. Carefully noting the declining population, lack of business growth, and cyclical drought conditions, the Poppers called the settling of the Great Plains "the largest, longest running agricultural and environmental miscalculation in American history." They suggested that the Buffalo Commons could be created through a consortium of public and private owners and institutions.

Montana's Big Open—twice the size of Massachusetts—is currently home to fewer than three thousand people. As a wildlife preserve, it would be one of the greatest in the world, a place of aboriginal glory in the heartland of America. It would attract amateur naturalists and fee-paying hunters alike. The Poppers suggested that the area's dwindling human population might do better economically by catering to hunters and tourists than by ranching and farming in an inhospitable climate. Though it would cost millions of dollars to gradually wean these people away, in the long run it would be cheaper than paying the agricultural subsidies they received from the government. And the commons would be a magnificent natural treasure.

Many of the hearty, aging natives, some descended from homesteaders, were offended by the Buffalo Commons idea. Their romance of the West remains one of self-reliance and confrontation with nature; repopulating the area with the American bison is not high on their list of dreams. Dayton Duncan, the author of *Miles from Nowhere,* said that for outsiders to remove these people from their land would be as heartless as what the cattlemen and homesteaders did when they displaced the Indian inhabitants a century ago. But blizzards and heat still devastate cattle herds, which are less hardy than the buffalo, and in the end nature itself may make the decision.

I was reminded of Charlie Russell's warm feelings for the buffalo:

> I remember one day we were looking at a buffalo carcass and you said Russ I wish I was a Sioux Injun a hundred years ago and I said me to Ted thairs a par of us.
> I have often made that wish since an if the buffalo would come back tomorrow I wouldent be slow shedding to a brich clout and youd trade that three duce ranch for a buffalo hoss and a pair of ear rings like many I know, your all Injun under the hide and its a sinch you wouldent get home sick in a skin lodge.

At a forlorn crossroads with no dwelling in sight for twenty miles, I drove north by Purgatory Hill State Monument. The country rose up in badlands, wind-carved temples of doom striated with black, red, and gray sediment. Trees were rare in this land, and it was hard to imagine human beings wanting to live out here; but desolation had a subtle seductive beauty. Dusk came as I followed a dirt road out of Glasgow to the Billingsley ranch. The white aluminum-sided ranch house was attached to the original homestead. As I pulled up to the house, the screen door opened and snapped shut.

Jack Billingsley was a short trim rancher in his late forties, with friendly blue eyes framed in wire-rim glasses. The Billingsleys arrived here in 1910 and managed to cling to the heat-cracked gumbo as other homesteaders were beaten away by harsh winters and drought. Today Jack Billingsley ran a small ranch and supplemented his income by outfitting for hunters. Over the phone he had virtually guaranteed me an antelope.

Jack's wife, Andy, a blond woman with some Indian blood in her, guided me through the boot-filled mudroom to a dinner table laden with fried chicken, mashed potatoes, and salad. Their son, Jay, a stringy high school junior with a thin mustache, stopped gnawing on a drumstick to shake my hand. Two hunting guests at the table, a father and son from Connecticut, had shot their limits of antelope. Exhausted from the long drive, I retired early to the Billingsleys' guest quarters, a three-bedroom trailer parked behind the house. At about five I heard the men from Connecticut slam doors and drive off in their van. They were heading home without bothering to see the rest of Montana, and I was glad they had taken their meat and left their money. As dawn broke I walked across the dew-wet grass to the house, where I smelled bacon frying.

When the buffalo were plentiful on the plains, so were the antelope. But when the big herds were wiped out, the Indians, whites, and predators like wolf and coyote reduced the antelope numbers drastically. Thanks to game regulation, in the last twenty years antelope have made a remarkable comeback. In western Montana, antelope licenses are limited and awarded by lottery; but in eastern Montana and throughout the Great Plains, antelope abound. There had been such a bumper crop this year that out-of-staters like myself could easily apply for a buck and even a doe license. If the antelope weren't killed, the excess population would starve on the plains this winter.

I grew up shooting ducks and pheasant, but when I lived in a city, killing something as big as a deer or antelope seemed an unnatural ambition. I'd been in Montana for five months now, a land where killing big animals—whether an Angus steer or a bull elk—was entirely normal. On his visit to Montana, John Steinbeck noted, "The calm of the mountains and the rolling grasslands had got into the inhabitants. It was hunting season when I drove through the state. The men I talked to seemed to me not moved to a riot of seasonal slaughter but simply to be going out to kill edible meat." One in five Montanans hunt; in California it is one in two hundred.

You hunt antelope by driving a pickup slowly through hot country, scanning sagebrush hills for small white dots dancing in the heat waves. A high-powered spotting scope enlarges these dots into the white fur bottoms of antelope. Then you search out the black face and curving horns of a buck. A big buck has a horn that measures over sixteen inches from base to tip, following the curve. The animals are skittish and will take off if the pickup gets too close. Too close can be a mile away. The antelope explode with the speed of shattered mercury, their thin sinewy shanks launching them away at forty miles an hour. Unlike deer, which bound, antelope gallop like racehorses. They don't jump over fences, but slither under them. Sometimes they get hung up in the wire and die, but here there were few fences to stop them.

Jack braked the pickup and fixed his binoculars on a distant hill. "There's a big group. Should be a couple of bucks." We took out the rifle and went into a stalk down a dry creek bed. A small rattlesnake slithered away from us. A hawk passed overhead, its shadow running along the contour of the creek bed until it swooped away. We were within two hundred yards when three white-tailed deer jumped from the brush, alerting the herd, which melted into the heat mirage like white and tan ghosts.

I wiped perspiration from my face as Jack scanned the horizon with his glasses. "There's another herd farther on." We kept moving quietly down the gully. Twenty minutes passed. As the sun rose, the heat increased. Jack eased his head up over the edge of the creek bed, ducked back down, and motioned me to come up beside him. He chambered a shell and passed the rifle to me. I thumbed off the safety and crawled into position among the prickly pear.

A huge buck stood just seventy-five yards away. Sweat dripped into my eyes, blood pounded through my eardrums, and I hyperventilated with excitement. The scope's cross hairs flickered across the antelope's shoulder as my hands quivered. I couldn't catch my breath. The buck stood at an angle. His black-masked face looked directly at me as I pulled the trigger. The whole herd took off, led by the unblemished buck.

"You shot over him," said Jack. "Don't worry. We'll get another chance."

That night at dinner, Jack said that nearby Glasgow, a town of thirty-five hundred people, was barely surviving. There were three hundred empty houses, and they'd lost sixty businesses in the last year. Jack's son, Jay, retired to the living-room couch to read *Huckleberry Finn* for school. When I said it was a good book, he replied, "Yeah, but it would be a lot easier to take in if it was on television." A champion wrestler in the 121-pound class, Jay spent his spare time selling magazine subscriptions to earn money to buy a bow for hunting deer and antelope. I obliged him with a year's subscription to the *Atlantic*.

Up at six the next morning, Jack and I took the pickup and headed across the creek to the south. We scouted a herd of antelope, but they took off immediately at high speed. We stalked a smaller group up a coulee for a quarter of an hour, and I passed up a three-hundred-yard shot at a magnificent buck. Another bunch came into position and moved away, but I didn't mind; I liked being out in this country with a purpose. When this hunt ended, other things in my life would end.

We walked by an old homestead, a bleached wooden shack with the roof caving in, the interior still covered with newspaper for insulation. We ate lunch in silence. Jack wasn't much of a talker, and I saw no reason to fill air time. A dozen antelope emerged from the lee of a distant ridge. The naked eye saw just spots moving in the heat waves, but Jack had the spotting scope. "Now we're talking. Two good bucks."

We drove the truck over one hill and they didn't spook, so we parked and got out quietly. We moved in a crouch over a ridge, then duck-walked behind another. I pulled cactus spines from my kneecap.

A dozen black Angus cows were spread across the field below, bedded down in the heat. The antelope herd moved behind them. The two bucks glanced at our hill occasionally. The geography of the land was deceptive. We duck-walked to the knob of the hill, where Jack took off his hat and peeked around. He drew back quickly. "There he is—your buck." He loaded the rifle and handed it to me.

Hidden by the hump of grass-covered gumbo, I propped my elbow against the embankment and sighted. The buck was 150 yards away now, still a long shot for my unpracticed eye. His black pronged horns were thick at the base and perfectly formed. His shoulders were heavy. After two days of hunting, there was a rightness in the moment. I slid the wavering cross hairs over his body until they rested on his shoulder. I let out my breath, the rifle cracked, and the herd exploded. The buck ran ten yards before somersaulting heavily into the sagebrush. I chambered another shell. The buck didn't even twitch as we walked up to it.

"He's stone dead," said Jack. "Congratulations on your first antelope." Jack smiled and shook my hand. Then he took my permit tag and tied it to a hind leg above the sharp black hoof. The curved horns were thick and gnarled at their bases, and the tips turned inward to yellow ivory points. "He's an old one. Look at this," said Jack, pulling back the lips to show worn broken teeth. "He's at least seven, and they don't live past eight."

With a sharp knife Jack cut the metatarsal scent glands out of the buck's hind legs and put them aside so as not to contaminate the meat. Then he left to get the truck. The silence of the country filled in, and for a quarter of an hour I was alone with the dead antelope. It was the most beautiful animal I'd ever seen, and I watched the glistening dark eyes grow dull. I admired the buckskin and white markings on the throat and the forked black horns. There are no mistakes in nature. I watched a fly land on the sheet of fresh blood from the exit wound. Stroking the fur, I felt the stiffness of each bristle and smelled the pungent odor from the sagebrush he had eaten all his life. The hunt was a privilege, not a right, and my soul somersaulted between joy and sorrow. I would not forget this day. As I ate antelope that winter, I would remember the herds running through the badlands, and smell the sage, and wonder at the great good luck of it all.

I drove west along the northern plains, following Highway 2 through Saco, Malta, and Wagner, running along the tracks of the Burlington Northern. The towns were nothing to remember except for an occasional café and truck stop. They were dying and might not exist in twenty years. These were railroad towns, created by capitalists like my ancestors and populated through somewhat bogus promotional schemes that brought settlers from the East Coast and Europe. Now their descendants, young people who saw a better life in Arizona or California, were leaving the Great Plains. The western theme of riding into town, then riding out again, still played.

It was near the town of Wagner that Robert LeRoy Parker, alias Butch Cassidy, and Harry Longabaugh, alias the Sundance Kid, and their pal Kid Curry Logan robbed a Great Northern train on July 3, 1901. They had robbed banks and trains for twelve years, from Colorado and Utah to North Dakota and New Mexico, but the Wild Bunch's last haul was the best. Their last American caper started when Kid Curry boarded the westbound Great Northern Coast Flyer as it pulled into Malta for a water stop. The bandit climbed onto the blind baggage and, as the train pulled out of the station, crawled to the coal tender and dropped down onto the engine platform. He pointed his gun at the train engineer and the fireman, and they understood he meant business.

A few miles down the track at the Exeter switch near Wagner, Kid Curry ordered the train to halt near a bridge over the Milk River, where the rest of the outlaws were hidden. Two bandits covered the passengers. To keep the curious from coming forward, they fired random shots into the coaches. Three of these warning shots ricocheted, wounding the brakeman and two passengers. Kid Curry and another outlaw ordered the train disconnected— from the express car back. The rest of the train was pulled a short distance up the track, where its safe was blown open with dynamite. The bandits found forty thousand dollars in unsigned bank notes shipped from the U.S. Treasury in Washington for delivery to banks in Helena. They politely bade the trainmen good-bye, crossed the Milk River, and headed south.

Butch traveled to the East Coast and eventually caught a ship to Argentina, where he met up with Harry Longabaugh and his girlfriend, Etta Place. The trio went down to the mountainous region of Patagonia, bought a ranch, and became well liked by the locals, who admired their horsemanship. Perhaps out of financial need, perhaps out of boredom, Butch and Sundance began robbing Argentine banks.

It is fairly certain that the Sundance Kid died in a shoot-out in Bolivia in either 1908 or 1911. The irrefutable evidence, however, is that Butch Cassidy returned from South America and lived out a quiet life in Spokane as a machinist under the name William Phillips, finally dying of rectal cancer in 1937. Three decades later, Butch's eighty-six-year-old sister swore that in 1925 her brother had dropped by to eat blueberry pie with her family. Dozens of other old-timers reported seeing Cassidy years later, from Utah to Wyoming. For western romance, it is still better to die young in a shoot-out than unknown in a county hospital.

As I approached the edge of the Fort Belknap Indian Reservation, near Dodson, an Amtrak train sped past me, westbound for Glacier Park and Seattle. It still followed the route created to open the Northwest, but now it was the only passenger train operating in Montana—maybe the only train worth robbing in the whole state. After five months on the road, I was weary. I would have liked to be on that train now, ordering lunch—even if it was a microwaved burger—and watching the prairie fly by. Then I wished I were on another older train, the Great Northern Coast Flyer, at the turn of the century, helping Butch Cassidy stuff crisp bank notes into a gunnysack as my getaway horse snorted impatiently. And I thought: *We must seize what adventure we can from life, for the rest is of little consequence.*

The miles of prairie flew by; the shadow of my car remained constant on the asphalt. The prairie was dry as a bone until I came down off a ridge and spied a stream flanked with alders and a strip of green grass. There were acre-wide fields of yellow daisies with brown button centers. Beyond lay purple carpets of lupine. Old homestead shacks stood abandoned, time-blistered shells of white men's dreams, built atop ancient buffalo bones. A red-tailed hawk on a fence post leaned into the wind. Grain silos rose from the plains like cathedrals of aluminum. Then I saw hay bales rolled up in disks five feet in diameter. A herd of three hundred glistening black Angus cattle appeared, their tails smudged with green manure. Power lines swept across the country, strung with yellow plastic balls to warn low-flying pilots.

Driving between wheat field, cattle range, and prairie, I thought how a barbed-wire fence always led to a house, a road always led to a town, a railroad track always led to a depot—and on across the nation that had once been a vast hostile wilderness. I lifted my eyes above the fences and imagined what this land had been without barbed wire, without cattle and sheep, without gold and coal mines, without wheat fields and alfalfa, without telephone poles and roads. Just the wild, unscarred prairie rolling for hundreds of miles, earth covered with tall native grass holding lark and badger, and even the grizzly, and in the distance a cloud of dust would rise from a herd of buffalo—to celebrate a wildness gone. You did not have to be Indian to do the ghost dance. On a beautiful day in Montana, it was hard to believe God didn't exist in a sky so blue and so vast, where the clouds seemed like perfect countries unto themselves. And for a moment, just a moment, I wished the pioneers, the buffalo hunters, and cattlemen like my ancestors had never dreamed of the West.

Bibliography

Most of my research was conducted in the Helena Historical Society, whose library has a copy of the unpublished memoirs of William H. Hunt, as well as correspondence between William G., Charles E., and John H. Conrad and their colleagues Marcus Daly, Thomas Power, and Samuel Hauser. The society publishes *Montana, The Magazine of Western History*, which proved useful to me, especially Will Roscoe's excellent article on Crow berdaches in the winter 1990 issue. Periodicals consulted include the *Great Falls Tribune, Billings Gazette, Helena Herald, Livingston Enterprise, Red Lodge Picket, Fort Benton River Press*, and *Benton Record*. The personal papers of Charles E. Conrad and his family are in a special collection at the Mansfield Library at the University of Montana, Missoula.

A Selected Bibliography

Baker, Don. *The Montana Railroad, Alias: The Jawbone*. Boulder, CO: Fred Pruett, 1990.

Bell, William Gardner. *Will James: The Life and Works of a Lone Cowboy*. Flagstaff, AZ: Northland Press, 1987.

Brown, Mark H., and Felton, W. R. *The Frontier Years: L. A. Huffman, Photographer of the Plains*. New York: Henry Holt and Company, 1955.

Connolly, Christopher P. *The Devil Learns to Vote*. New York: Covici, Friede, 1938.

Diettart, Gerald A. *Grinnell's Glacier: George Bird Grinnell and Glacier National Park*. Missoula, MT: Mountain Press Publishing Company, 1992.

Doig, Ivan. *Ride with Me: Mariah Montana*. New York: Atheneum, 1990.

Duncan, Dayton. *Miles from Nowhere: Tales from America's Contemporary Frontier.* New York: Viking Penguin, 1993.

Duncan, Dayton. *Out West: An American Journey.* New York: Viking Penquin, 1987.

Farr, William E. *The Reservation Blackfeet, 1882–1945: A Photographic History of Cultural Survival.* Seattle: University of Washington Press, 1984.

Grinnell, George Bird. *The Passing of the Great West: Selected Papers of George Bird Grinnell.* Edited, with an introduction and commentary, by John F. Reiger. Norman: University of Oklahoma Press, 1972.

Guthrie, A. B., Jr. *The Big Sky.* Boston: Houghton Mifflin Company, 1947.

Hanna, Warren L. *The Life and Times of James Willard Schultz (Apikuni).* Norman: University of Oklahoma Press, 1986.

History of Montana, 1739–1885. Chicago: Warner, Beers & Company, 1885.

Hugo, Richard. *Selected Poems.* New York: W. W. Norton & Company, 1979.

James, Will. *Cow Country.* New York: Charles Scribner's Sons, 1931.

James, Will. *Lone Cowboy: My Life Story.* New York: Charles Scribner's Sons, 1930.

Jordan, Teresa. *Cowgirls: Women of the American West.* Garden City, New York: Anchor Books, Doubleday & Company, 1984.

Lewis, Meriwether, and Clark, William. *A History of the Lewis and Clark Expedition.* Edited by Elliot Coues. 4 vols. New York: Francis P. Harper, 1893.

Malone, Michael P. *The Battle For Butte: Mining and Politics on the Northern Frontier, 1864–1906.* Seattle: University of Washington Press, 1981.

Malone, Michael P., and Roeder, Richard B. *Montana: A History of Two Centuries.* Seattle: University of Washington Press, 1976.

Mather, R. E., and Boswell, F. E. *Hanging the Sheriff: A Biography of Henry Plummer.* Salt Lake City: University of Utah Press, 1987.

Matthews, Anne. *Where the Buffalo Roam.* New York: Grove-Atlantic, 1992.

Miller, Joaquin. *An Illustrated History of the State of Montana.* Chicago: The Lewis Publishing Co., 1894.

Murphy, James E. *Half Interest in a Silver Dollar: The Saga of Charles E. Conrad.* Missoula, MT: Mountain Press Publishing Company, 1983.

Murphy, Jere C. *The Comical History of Montana: A Serious Story for Free*

People. San Diego, CA: E. L. Scofield, Publisher, 1912.

Murray, John A., ed. *The Great Bear: Contemporary Writings on the Grizzly.* Anchorage: Alaska Northwest Books, 1992.

Olmsted, Gerald W. *Fielding's Lewis and Clark Trail.* New York: Fielding Travel Books, William Morrow & Company, 1986.

Overholser, Joel. *Fort Benton: World's Innermost Port.* Helena, MT: Falcon Press Publishing Co., 1987.

Paladin, Vivian, and Baucus, Jean. *Helena, an Illustrated History.* Helena, MT: Bar-Wineglass Publishing Co. with Falcon Press Publishing Co., 1983.

Pointer, Larry. *In Search of Butch Cassidy.* Norman: University of Oklahoma Press, 1977.

Roscoe, Will. "The Life and Times of a Crow Berdache," *Montana: The Magazine of Western History.* Winter 1990: 47–55.

Russell, Charles M. *Trails Plowed Under.* New York: Doubleday, Doran & Company, 1927.

Schultz, James Willard (Apikuni). *Blackfeet and Buffalo: Memories of Life among the Indians.* Edited and with an introduction by Keith C. Seele. Norman: University of Oklahoma Press, 1962.

Sharp, Paul F. *Whoop-Up Country: The Canadian-American West, 1865–1885.* Norman: University of Oklahoma Press, 1978.

Spence, Clark C. *Montana: A History.* New York: W. W. Norton & Company, 1978.

Spence, Clark C. *Territorial Politics and Government in Montana, 1864–89.* Urbana: University of Illinois Press, 1975.

Tirrell, Norma. *Montana.* Photography by John Reddy. Oakland, CA: Compass American Guides, 1991

Toole, K. Ross. *Montana: An Uncommon Land.* Norman: University of Oklahoma Press, 1959.

Toole, K. Ross. *Twentieth Century Montana: A State of Extremes.* Norman: Univesity of Oklahoma Press, 1972.

Tucker, Patrick T. *Riding the High Country.* Edited by Grace Stone Coates. Seattle, WA: Fjord Press, 1987.

Yellowtail, Thomas. *Yellowtail: Crow Medicine Man and Sun Dance Chief.* An autobiography as told to Michael Oren Fitzgerald; introduction by Fred Voget. Norman: University of Oklahoma Press, 1991.

If you'd like to help preserve Montana's natural beauty, contact the following organizations for information on land preservation programs:

The Greater Yellowstone Coalition
Box 1874
Bozeman, MT 59771
(406) 588-1593

Montana Wildlife Federation
P.O. Box 1175
Helena, MT 59624
(406) 449-7604

The Nature Conservancy
32 South Ewing
Helena, MT 59601
(406) 443-0303